History in the Age of Vikings
Volume 1

Introduction by Mark Bussler
Editing and Layouts by Ephraim Durnst
Based on the works of Paul B. Du Chaillu
Cover design by Mark Bussler

www.CGRpublishing.com

Best of Gustave Doré Volume 1:
Illustrations from History's Most
Versatile Artist

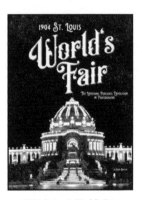

1904 St. Louis World's Fair:
The Louisiana Purchase Exposition
in Photographs

How to Draw Womens' Eyes:
Inspired by Classic Illustrations
Volume 1

The Viking Ship.

Introduction

HISTORY IN THE AGE OF VIKINGS: VOLUME 1

by Mark Bussler

Everyone who travels down the rabbit hole of history finds themselves fascinated by the allure and mystique of the Vikings. Who were these people who conquered the North, invaded and settled Britain, and discovered America years before Columbus?

Any information about the Vikings is fascinating and informative, particularly 19th-century discoveries, which add a level of contemporary enthusiasm and intrigue.

I discovered Paul B. Du Chaillu's 1889 series of *Viking Age* books while researching other projects. Immediately, I found myself immersed in the beautiful illustrations depicting the Viking artwork, weapons, and unearthed relics.

Like the Viking artifacts they cover, these priceless tomes of knowledge sat on a shelf covered in dust, unloved, waiting to be discovered by future archaeologists in a bog one thousand years from now.

We launched a rescue operation to restore these fabulous tomes of priceless information for modern readers and historians. Our intent was to restore the print quality to its original form and improve it if possible. In some cases, we separated the artwork and enlarged it for modern readers to absorb the detail.

I hope that you enjoy the detailed images and enhanced layout that we could achieve with modern tools. Durnst repaired the text and enlarged it for presentation. In total, across three volumes, we restored more than 1360 images for people in times yet to come to learn about people in times that once were.

Pictured on the previous page is "The Viking Ship" from the 1893 World's Fair in Chicago. Known as the World's Columbian Exposition, the Fair was held in honor of the 400th anniversary of Columbus' discovery of the New World. To celebrate their heritage, Norway brought a stunning reproduction of a Viking ship.

The colorful ship was a popular exhibit on the shore of Lake Michigan. It served as a not-so-subtle reminder to all who attended that the Fair should have been called "The World's Viking Exposition."

Mark Bussler

- Bussler is the writer of T*he World's Fair of 1893 Ultra Massive Photographic Adventure* series, *The White City of Color, 1915 San Francisco World's Fair in Color, 1904 St. Louis World's Fair: The Louisiana Purchase Exposition in Photographs*, and more. He is also president of CGR Publishing, cover designer, and lead restoration engineer.

Table of Contents

VOLUME 1

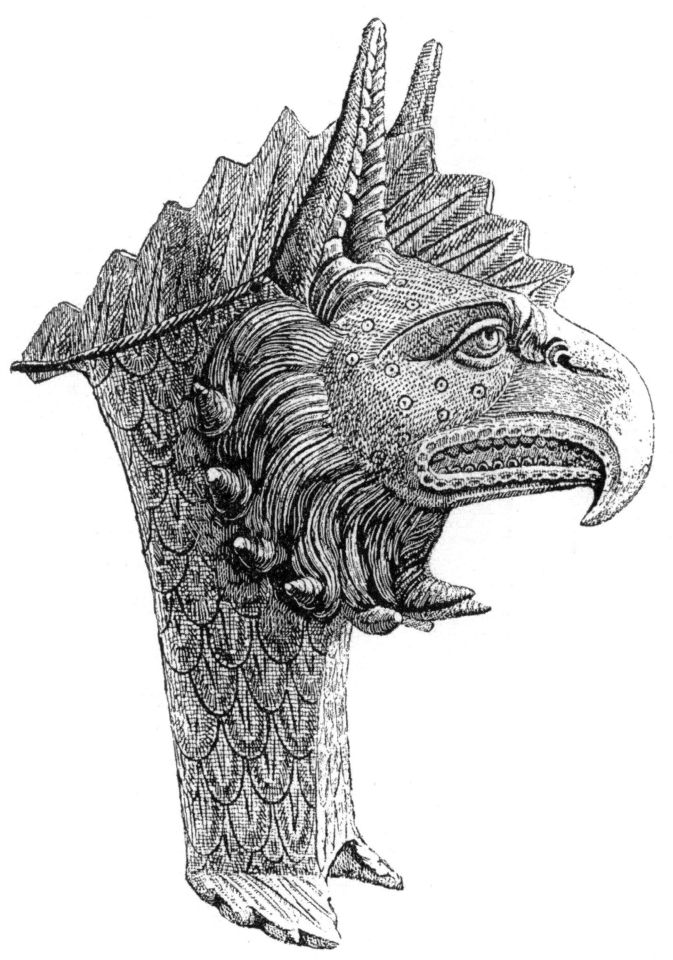

VIKING SHIP, USED FOR BURIAL (GOKSTAD, NORWAY).

(Length of keel, 60 feet; total length, 75 feet; broadest part, 15½ feet; depth from the upper part of bulwark to bottom of keel, 3½ feet.)

Judging from the number of holes seen, which were about 18 inches below the gunwale, it carried sixteen oars, and was consequently a sixteen-seater. Its preservation is due to the blue clay in which it was partly embedded, the upper part being eaten away owing to the clay being mixed with sand, thus allowing the rain and air to penetrate. It is entirely of oak, clinker built, calked with cows' hair spun in a sort of cord.

PREFACE.

WHILE studying the progress made in the colonisation of different parts of the world by European nations, I have often asked myself the following questions :—

How is it that over every region of the globe the spread of the English-speaking people and of their language far exceeds that of all the other European nations combined ?

Why is it that, wherever the English-speaking people have settled, or are at this day found, even in small numbers, they are far more energetic, daring, adventurous, and prosperous, and understand the art of self-government and of ruling alien peoples far better than other colonising nations ?

Whence do the English-speaking communities derive the remarkable energy they possess ; for the people of Britain when invaded by the Romans did not show any such quality ?

What are the causes which have made the English such a pre-eminently seafaring people ? for without such a characteristic they could not have been the founders of so many states and colonies speaking the English tongue !

In studying the history of the world we find that all the nations which have risen to high power and widespread dominion have been founded by men endowed with great, I may say terrible, energy ; extreme bravery and the love of conquest being the most prominent traits of their character. The mighty sword with all its evils has thus far always proved a great engine of civilisation.

To get a satisfactory answer to the above questions we must go far back, and study the history of the race who settled in Britain during and after the Roman occupation. We shall thus find why their descendants are to-day so brave, successful, energetic and prosperous in the lands which they have colonised; and why they are so pre-eminently skilled in the art of self-government.

We find that a long stretch of coast is not sufficient, though necessary, to make the population of a country a seafaring nation. When the Romans invaded Britain, the Brits had no fleet to oppose them. We do not until a later period meet with that love of the sea which is so characteristically English:—not before the gradual absorption of the earlier inhabitants by a blue-eyed and yellow-haired seafaring people who succeeded in planting themselves and their language in the country.

To the numerous warlike and ocean-loving tribes of the North, the ancestors of the English-speaking people, we must look for the transformation that took place in Britain. In their descendants we recognise to this day many of the very same traits of character which these old Northmen possessed, as will be seen on the perusal of this work.

Britain, after a continuous immigration which lasted several hundred years, became the most powerful colony of the Northern tribes, several of the chiefs of the latter claiming to own a great part of England in the seventh and eighth centuries. At last the time came when the land of the emigrants waxed more powerful, more populous than the mother-country, and asserted her independence; and to-day the people of England, as they look over the broad Atlantic, may discern a similar process which is taking place in the New World.

The impartial mind which rises above the prejudice of nationality must acknowledge that no country will leave a more glorious impress upon the history of the world than England. Her work cannot be undone; should she to-day sink beneath the seas which bathe her shores, her record will for ever stand brilliantly illuminated on the page of history. The great states which she has founded, which have inherited her tongue, and which are destined to play a most important part in the future of civilisation, will be witnesses of the mighty work she has accomplished. They will look back with pride to the progenitors of their race who lived in the glorious and never-to-be-forgotten countries of the North, the birth-place of a new epoch in the history of mankind.

As ages roll on, England, the mother of nations, cannot escape the fate that awaits all; for on the scroll of time this everlasting truth is written—birth, growth, maturity, decay;—and how difficult for us to realise the fact when in the fulness of power, strength, and pride! Where is or where has been the nation that can or could exclaim, "This saying does not apply to me; I was born great from the beginning; I am so now, and will continue to be powerful to the end of time." The ruined and deserted cities; the scanty records of history, which tell us of dead civilisations, the fragmentary traditions of religious beliefs, the wrecks of empires, and the forgotten graves, are the pathetic and silent witnesses of the great past, and a sad suggestion of the inevitable fate in store for all.

The materials used in these volumes, in describing the cosmogony and mythology, the life, religion, laws and customs of the ancestors of the English-speaking nations of to-day, are mainly derived from records found in Iceland. These parchments, upon which the history of the North is written, and which are begrimed by the smoke of the Icelandic cabin, and worn by the centuries which have passed over them, recount to us the history and the glorious deeds of the race.

No land has bequeathed to us a literature, giving so minute and comprehensive an account of the life of a people. These *Sagas* (or " say ") record the leading events of a man's life, or family history, and date from a period even anterior to the first settlement of Iceland (about 870 A.D.).

Some Sagas bear evident traces of having been derived, or even copied, from earlier documents now lost: in some cases definite quotations are given; others are evidently of a fabulous character, and have to be treated with great caution; but even these may be used as illustrating the customs of the times at which they were written. Occasionally great confusion is caused by the blending of the similar names of persons living at different periods.

My method of putting together the series of descriptions which will be found in the 'Viking Age' has been as follows :—

By reading carefully every Saga—and there are hundreds of them—dealing with the events of a man's life from his birth to his death, I was able to select the passages bearing on the various customs. When in one Saga the bare fact of a birth, or a marriage, or a burial, or a feast, etc., etc., was mentioned, in others full details of the ceremonies connected with them were found. After thus collecting my material, which was of the most superabundant character, I went over it and selected what seemed to me to be the best accounts of the various customs with which I deal in these volumes. I have not been content with the translations of other persons, but have in every case gone to the original documents and adopted my own rendering of them.

Some extracts from the Frankish Chronicles are given in the Appendix, as showing the power of the Northmen, and bearing strong testimony to the truthfulness of the Sagas. If I had not been afraid of being tedious, I could also have given extracts from Arabic, Russian, and other annals to the same effect.

The testimony of archæology as corroborating the Sagas forms one of the most important links in the chain of my argument; parchments and written records form but a portion of the material from which I have derived my account of the 'Viking Age.' During the last fifty years the History of the Northmen has been unearthed as it were—like that of the Egyptians, Assyrians, and Romans—by the discovery of almost every kind of implement, weapon, and ornament produced by that accomplished race.

The Museums of Denmark, Sweden, Norway, England, France, Germany, Russia, are as richly stored with such objects as are the British Museum, the Louvre, the Museums of Naples and Boulak with the treasures of Egypt and Pompeii.

I have myself seen nearly all the objects or graves illustrated in this book, with the exception of a few Runic stones which have now disappeared, but are given in an old work of Jorgensen.

As my materials expanded themselves before me I felt like one of those mariners of old on a voyage of discovery. To them new lands were continuously coming into view; to me new materials, new fields of literary and archæological wealth unfolded themselves incessantly. Thus carried away by enthusiasm and the love of the task I had undertaken, I have been able to labour for eight years and a half on the present work, with some interruptions from exhaustion and impaired health. May I, then, ask the indulgence of a public, which has always been kind to me, for all the shortcomings of my work ?

I have received valuable assistance from many friends, but I desire especially to express my thanks to Mr. Bruun, the Chief Librarian of the Royal Library of Denmark, for his great kindness in allowing me so many privileges during the years I have worked in Copenhagen ; to Mr. Birket Smith, of the University Library of Copenhagen ; and Mr. Kaalund, Keeper of the Arna Magnæan Collection of Manuscripts, for the uniform courtesy they have shown me ; among antiquarians, to my friend Professor George Stephens, author of the magnificent work, 'Northern Runic Monuments,' for his readiness in giving me all the information and help I needed, which sometimes occupied much of his valuable time (several illustrations of the runic stones, etc., in these volumes are taken from his work) ; to Mr. Vedel, Vice-President of the Royal Society of Antiquarians ; to Messrs. Herbst, Sophus Muller, and Petersen, of the Royal Museum of Northern Antiquities, for their great courtesy ; I am also indebted to the works of the following distinguished antiquarians which have been invaluable to me in my researches and which have furnished me with many of the illustrations for my book : Ole Rygh, Bugge, Engelhart, Nicolaysen, Sehested, Steenstrup, Madsen, Sàve, Montelius, Holmberg, Jorgensen, Baltzer, and Lorange ; also to the works of the historians, Keyser, Geijer, Munch, Rafn, Vigfusson. My sincere thanks are also due to my young friend Jon Stefánsson, an Icelandic student, for his constant help in rendering the translations of the Sagas as accurate and literal as possible ; and to my old friend Mr. Rasmus B. Anderson, late American Minister to Denmark, and translator of the 'Later Edda,' etc. ; in England, to Messrs. A. S. Murray, Franks, and Read, of the British Museum ; to Dr. Warre, the head master of Eton, and to General Pitt Rivers, author of a valuable work on the excavations in Cranborne Chase, which contains objects strikingly similar to those of Scandinavia; also to my friends Mr. J. S. Keltie and Mr. Arthur L. Roberts; to my old friends Messrs. Clowes, who have taken great pains in carrying out what has proved to be a very difficult task for the printer, and who have had the work over two-and-a-half years in type.

I must thank, above all, my esteemed and venerable publisher, John Murray, for the great interest he has taken in the present work, which has tried his patience and liberality many a time, and also for the many years of uninterrupted friendship and the pleasant business relations (unhampered by any written agreement whatever), which have existed between us from the time when I came to him almost a lad, and he first undertook the publication of 'Explorations in Equatorial Africa,' in 1861, not forgetting my dear friends, his sons, John and Hallam, the former of whom has assisted me materially in seeing the work through the press, and my old companion Robert Cooke.

I cannot close this preface without thanking my old and ever true friend Robert Winthrop, of New York, descendant of the celebrated Colonial Governor of Massachusetts, to whom I dedicated "The Land of the Midnight Sun," for his unfailing kindness and sympathy during the years I have been engaged in the present work.

PAUL B. DU CHAILLU.

NEW YORK, *September*, 1889.

A LIST OF THE PRINCIPAL SAGAS

QUOTED IN

THE VIKING AGE,

INCLUDING THE PERIODS WITH WHICH THEY DEAL.

Name of Saga.	Century with which they deal.
The Earlier Edda	These are Mythical, and no accurate date can be affixed to them.
The Later Edda	
Fórnaldarsögur contains :—	
Völsunga	
Hervara	
Thorstein Vikingsson's (father of Fridthjof) ..	Partly Mythical.
Ketil Hæng's sons	
Grim Lodinkinnis'	
Fridthjof's	
Hrolf Kraki's	VI. (?)
Half's	VI. (?)
Sögubrot	VI.–VII. (?)
Ragnar Lodbrok's	VIII. (?)
Ragnar Lodbrok's Sons'	VIII. (?)
Norna Gest's	
Gautrek's	
Orvar Odd's	
Herraud and Bosi's	No date can be assigned to these.
Egil and Asmund's	
Hjalmter and Ölver's	
Göngu Hrolf's	
An Bosveigi's	

 ✱✱ The above dates are all more or less conjectural, and the Sagas are chiefly valuable as illustrating manners and customs.

Egil's	Middle of IX. to end of X.
Njala's	End of X. to beginning of XI.
Laxdæla	IX.–XI. (886–1030).
Eyrbyggia	IX.–XI. (890–1031).
Islandinga Sögur contains :—	
I. Hord's Saga	X. (950–990).
II. Hœnsa Thoris' Saga	X.–XI. (990–1010).
III. Gunnlaug Ormstunga's Saga	X.–XI.
IV. Viga Styr's Saga	X.–XI.
V. Kjalnesinga Saga	IX.–XI.
VI. Gisli Súrsson	X.

Name of Saga.	Century with which they deal.
Droplaugarsona Saga	X.
Hrafnkel Freysgodi	X.
Bjorn Hitdæla Kappi	First half of XI.
Kormak's	X.
Fornsögur contains :—	
I. Vatnsdæla Saga	IX.–XI. (c. 870–1000).
II. Floamanna Saga	X. (c. 985–990).
III. Hallfred's Saga	End of X.
Gretti's Saga	X.–XI. (Grettir died 1031).
Viga Glum	X.
Vallaljots	Beginning of XI.
Vapnfirdinga	IX.–X.
Thorskfirdinga, or Gullthóri's	X. (c. 900–930).
Heidar Viga (continuation of Viga Styr's)	First half of XI.
Fœreyinga	X.–XI. (c. 960–1040).
Finnbogi Rami's	X.
Eirek the Red	X.
Thátt of Styrbjörn (nephew of Eirek the Victorious, who fell at the battle of Fyrisvellir, 983)	X.
Landnama	IX.–X. (the colonisation of Iceland).
Islendinga bok	IX.–XI. (c. 874–1118).
Ljosvetninga	990–1050.
Vemund's Saga	End of X. century.
Svarfdœla	First half of X. century.
Biskupa Sögur contains :—	
Kristni Saga	X.–XII. (c. 980–1120).
Sturlunga	XII.–XIII.(c.1120-1284).
Fornmanna Sögur contains :—	
I. Sagas of Kings of Norway	
II. Jomsvikinga Saga	X.
III. Knytlinga Saga	XI.–XII.
IV. Fagrskinna (short history of Kings of Norway from Halfdan the Black to Sverrir)	IX.–XII.
Heimskringla Saga contains the Ynglinga Saga, the great work of Snorri Sturluson	Written in first half of XIII. cent., giving history of the Kings of Norway and Sweden from Odin down to 1177.
Flateyjarbok contains lives of Kings of Norway, etc.	
Fostbrædra Saga	XI. (c. 1015–30).
Konung's Skuggsja	XIII.
Rimbegla	XIV.
Orkneyinga	IX.–XIII. (c. 870–1.06).

A LIST OF THE PRINCIPAL KINGS OF DENMARK, NORWAY, AND SWEDEN,

SOME OF WHOM HAVE SAGAS OF THEIR OWN.

KINGS OF DENMARK.

	A.D.		A.D.
Gorm	900–940	Hörda Knut	1035–1042
Harald Bluetooth	945–985	Magnus the Good, ruled	
Svein Tjuguskegg.. ..	985–1014	over Denmark and	
Harald	1014–1018	Norway	1042–1047
Knut the Great	1018–1035	Svein Ulfsson	1047–1075

KINGS OF NORWAY.

(Mostly petty Kings.)

	A.D.		A.D.
Halfdan the Black, died	860	Knut the Great reigned	1028–1035
Harald Fairhair, reigned	860–930	Magnus the Good ,,	1035–1047
Eirik Bloodaxe ,,	930–934	Harald Hardradi ,,	1047–1066
Hakon the Good ,,	934–960	Olaf the Quiet ,,	1066–1093
Harald Grafeld (greyskin)		Magnus Barefoot ,,	1093–1103
reigned	960–965	Three sons :—Eystein,	
Hakon Jarl the Great, the		Olaf, Sigurd Jórsalafari	1103–1130
hero of the battle of		Civil war —Harald Gilli,	
Gomsviking, reigned	965–995	Magnus the Blind, and	
Olaf Tryggvason ,,	995–1000	others..	1130–1162
Eirik Jarl .. ,,	1000–1015	Magnus Erlingsson .	1162–1184
St Olaf. .. .. ,,	1015–1028	Sverrir (Sigurdson) ..	1184–1202

KINGS OF SWEDEN.

(Not mentioned in the Odinic Genealogies, vol. i. p. 67.)

			A.D.
Ivar Vidfadmi	Kings of Swe- den and Den- mark.	Eymund and Björn ..	800–830
Harald Hilditönn		Olaf and Eymund ..	c. 850
Sigurd Hring		Eyrik Eymundsson died	c. 882
Ragnar Lodbrók		Björn Eiriksson and Hring	900–950
Björn Ironside.		Eirik the Victorious ..	c. 950–994
Eirik and Refil.		Olaf Skaut-konung ..	c. 994–1022
		Önund Jakob	c. 1022–1050
		Eymund the Old ..	c. 1050–1060
		Steinkel Rögnvaldson	c. 1060–1066

Vinland

Ísland

Fœreyjar

Finnmör

Hálogaland

Bjarmaland

Gond
Vik

Dwina

Noreg &
Svithjód

Thrandheim

Finnland

Aldeigia
(í Aoga)

Nougrad
Nyni Novgorod

Hjaltland

Kyrjalaland

II

Volga

Suðreyjar

Orkneyar

Eistland

Jarislei

II

Uppsalir

Holmgard

Skotland

Gautland

Viking

II Volga

Norðun
byrland

Jötland
Danmörk

Kurland
Palteskja
(Pplotsk)

Gardarik

Jotunheim

Irland

Mön
Dyflin

England

Egan

Thomaborg

Ríz

Vedrofjord

Humra

Frisland

Vindland

Kœnugard
(Kief)

Asgard?

Don II

Flæmings
land

Dnepr

Kertch

Valland

Leira (Loire)

Garisa

Luna

Bolgaraland

Spánn

Rómaborg

Mikligard (Constantinople)

Tyrkland

Lissibon

Grikkland

Njörva-sund

Sikiley

Kipr

Bláland
(Serkland)

Krit

Jórsalir
(Jerusalem)

I. *Trade route of Væ, rings (by Dnieper)*
II *Trade route of Værings (by Volga and Don)*

Walker & Boutall sc.

GEOGRAPHY AND NOMENCLATURE OF THE VIKING AGE

THE VIKING AGE.

CHAPTER I.

CIVILISATION AND ANTIQUITIES OF THE NORTH.

Early antiquities of the North—Literature: English and Frankish chronicles
—Early civilisation—Beauty of ornaments, weapons, &c.

A STUDY of the ancient literature and abundant archæology of
the North gives us a true picture of the character and life of
the Norse ancestors of the English-speaking peoples.

We can form a satisfactory idea of their religious, social,
political, and warlike life. We can follow them from their
birth to their grave. We see the infant exposed to die, or
water sprinkled,[1] and a name bestowed upon it; follow the
child in his education, in his sports; the young man in his
practice of arms; the maiden in her domestic duties and
embroidery; the adult in his warlike expeditions; hear the clash
of swords and the songs of the *Scald,* looking on and inciting
the warriors to greater deeds of daring, or it may be recounting
afterwards the glorious death of the hero. We listen to the
old man giving his advice at the *Thing.*[2] We learn about
their dress, ornaments, implements, weapons; their expressive
names and complicated relationships; their dwellings and
convivial halls, with their primitive or magnificent furniture;
their temples, sacrifices, gods, and sacred ceremonies; their
personal appearance, even to the hair, eyes, face and limbs.
Their festivals, betrothal and marriage feasts are open to us.
We are present at their athletic games preparatory to the stern
realities of the life of that period, where honour and renown
were won on the battle-field; at the revel and drunken bout;

---

[1] A kind of baptism.

[2] The assembly of the people.

behold the dead warrior on his burning ship or on the pyre, and surrounded by his weapons, horses, slaves, or fallen companions who are to enter with him into *Valhalla*;[1] look into the death chamber, see the mounding and the *Arvel*, or inheritance feast.

These Norsemen had carriages or chariots, as well as horses, and the numerous skeletons of this animal in graves or bogs prove it to have been in common use at a very early period. Their dress, and the splendour of their riding equipment for war, the richness of the ornamentation of their weapons of offence and defence are often carefully described. Everywhere we see that gold was in the greatest abundance. The descriptions of such wealth might seem to be very much exaggerated; but, as will be seen in the course of this work, the antiquities treasured in the museums of the North bear witness to the truthfulness of the records. The spade has developed the history of Scandinavia, as it has done that of Assyria and Etruria, but in addition the Northmen had the Saga and Edda literature to perpetuate their deeds.

We are the more astonished as we peruse the Eddas and Sagas giving the history of the North, and examine the antiquities found in the country, for we hear hardly anything about the customs of the people from the Roman writers, and our ideas regarding them have been thoroughly vitiated by the earlier Frankish and English chronicles and other monkish writings, or by the historians who have taken these records as a trustworthy authority.

Some writers, in order to give more weight to these chronicles, and to show the great difference that existed between the invaders and invaded, and how superior the latter were to the former, paint in a graphic manner, without a shadow of authority, the contrast between the two peoples. England is described as being at that time a most beautiful country, a panegyric which does not apply to fifteen or twenty centuries ago; while the country of the aggressor is depicted as one of swamp and forest inhabited by wild and savage men. It is forgotten that after a while the people of the country attacked were the same people as those of the North or their

---

[1] The hall and abode of the slain.

descendants, who in intelligence, civilisation, and manly virtues were far superior to the original and effete inhabitants of the shores they invaded.

The men of the North who settled and conquered part of Gaul and Britain, whose might the power of Rome could not destroy, and whose depredations it could not prevent, were not savages; the Romans did not dare attack these men at home with their fleet or with their armies. Nay, they even had allowed these Northmen to settle peacefully in their provinces of Gaul and Britain.

No, the people who were then spread over a great part of the present Russia, who overran Germania, who knew the art of writing, who led their conquering hosts to Spain, into the Mediterranean, to Italy, Sicily. Greece, the Black Sea, Palestine, Africa, and even crossed the broad Atlantic to America, who were undisputed masters of the sea for more than twelve centuries, were not barbarians. Let those who uphold the contrary view produce evidence from archæology of an indigenous British or Gallic civilisation which surpasses that of the North.

The antiquities of the North even without its literature would throw an indirect but valuable light on the history of the earlier Norse tribes, the so-called barbarians, fiends, devils, sons of Pluto, &c., of the Frankish and English chronicles. To the latter we can refer for stories of terrible acts of cruelty committed by the countrymen of the writers who recount them with complacency; maiming prisoners or antagonists and sending multitudes into slavery far away from their homes. But the greatest of all outrages in the eyes of these monkish scribes was that the Northmen burned a church or used it for sheltering their men or stabling their horses.

The writers of the English and Frankish chronicles were the worst enemies of the Northmen, ignorant and bigoted men when judged by the standard of our time; through their writings we hardly know anything of the customs of their own people. They could see nothing good in a man who had not a religion identical with their own.

Still allowance must be made for the chroniclers; they wrote the history of their own period with the bigotry, passions, and hatreds, of their times.

B 2

The striking fact brought vividly before our mind is that the people of the North, even before the time when they carried their warfare into Gaul and Britain, possessed a degree of civilisation which would be difficult for us to realise were it not that the antiquities help us in a most remarkable manner. and in many essential points, to corroborate the truthfulness of the Eddas and Sagas.

The indisputable fact remains that both the Gauls and the Britons were conquered by the Romans and afterwards by the Northern tribes.

This Northern civilisation was peculiar to itself, having nothing in common with the Roman world. Rome knew nothing of these people till they began to frequent the coasts of her North Sea provinces, in the days of Tacitus, and after his time the Mediterranean. The North was separated from Rome by the swamps and forests of Germania—a vague term given to a country north and north-east of Italy, a land without boundaries, and inhabited by a great number of warlike, wild, uncivilised tribes. According to the accounts of Roman writers, these people were very unlike those of the North, and we must take the description given of them to be correct, as there is no archæological discovery to prove the contrary. They were distinct; one was comparatively civilised, the other was not.

The manly civilisation the Northmen possessed was their own; from their records, corroborated by finds in Southern Russia, it seems to have advanced north from about the shores of the Black Sea, and we shall be able to see in the perusal of these pages how many Northern customs were like those of the ancient Greeks.

A view of the past history of the world will show us that the growth of nations which have become powerful has been remarkably steady, and has depended upon the superior intelligence of the conquering people over their neighbours; just as to-day the nations who have taken possession of far-off lands and extended their domain, are superior to the conquered.

The museums of Copenhagen, Stockholm, Christiania, Bergen, Lünd, Göteborg, and many smaller ones in the provincial towns of the three Scandinavian kingdoms, show a most wonderful collection of antiquities which stand unrivalled in Central and Northern Europe for their wealth of weapons and costly objects of gold and silver, belonging to the bronze and iron age, and every year additions are made.

The weapons found with their peculiar northern ornamentation, and the superb ring coats-of-mail, show the skill of the people in working iron. A great number of their early swords and other weapons are damascened even so far back as the beginning of the Christian era, and show either that this art was practised in the North long before its introduction into the rest of Europe from Damascus by the Crusaders, or that the Norsemen were so far advanced as to be able to appreciate the artistic manufactures of Southern nations.

The remnants of articles of clothing with graceful patterns, interwoven with threads of gold and silver, which have fortunately escaped entire destruction, show the existence of great skill in weaving. Entire suits of wearing apparel remain to tell us how some of the people dressed in the beginning of our era.

Beautiful vessels of silver and gold also testify to the taste and luxury of those early times. The knowledge of the art of writing and of gilding is clearly demonstrated. In some cases, nearly twenty centuries have not been able to tarnish or obliterate the splendour of the gilt jewels of the Northmen. We find among their remains—either of their own manufacture or imported, perhaps as spoils of war—*repoussé* work of gold or silver, bronze, silver, and wood work covered with the thinnest sheets of gold ; the filigree work displays great skill, and some of it could not be surpassed now. Many objects are ornamented with *niello,* and of so thorough a northern pattern, that they are incontestably of home manufacture. The art of enamelling seems also to have been known to the artificers of the period.

Objects, many of which show much refined taste, such as superb specimens of glass vessels with exquisite painted subjects—unrivalled for their beauty of pattern, even in the museums of Italy and Russia—objects of bronze, &c., make us pause with astonishment, and musingly ask ourselves from what country these came. The names of Etruria, of ancient Greece, and of Rome, naturally occur to our minds.

Other objects of unquestionable Roman and Greek manufacture, and hundreds and thousands of coins, of the first, second, third and fourth centuries of the Christian era, show the early intercourse the people of the North had with the western and eastern Roman empire, and with Frisia, Gaul, and Britain.

A careful perusal of the Eddas and Sagas will enable us, with the help of the ancient Greek and Latin writers, and without any serious break in the chain of events, to make out a fairly continuous history which throws considerable light on the progenitors of the English-speaking people, their migrations northward from their old home on the shores of the Black Sea, their religion, and the settlement of Scandinavia, of England, and other countries.

CHAPTER II.

ROMAN AND GREEK ACCOUNTS OF THE NORTHMEN.

The three maritime tribes of the North—The fleets of the Sueones—Expeditions of Saxons and Franks—Home of these tribes—The tribes of Germania not seafaring—Probable origin of the names Saxons and Franks.

ROMAN writers give us the names of three maritime tribes of the North, which were called by them *Sueones, Saxones,* and *Franci.* The first of these, which is the earliest mentioned, is thus described by Tacitus (circ. 57–117 A.D.) :—

"Hence the States of the Sueones, situated in the ocean itself, are not only powerful on land, but also have mighty fleets. The shape of their ships is different, in that, having a prow at each end, they are always ready for running on to the beach. They are not worked by sails, nor are the oars fastened to the sides in regular order, but left loose as in some rivers, so that they can be shifted here or there as circumstances may require."[1]

The word *Sviar,* which is constantly met with in the Sagas to denote the inhabitants of Svithjod (Sweden), or the country of which Upsala was the capital, corresponds somewhat to the name Sueones, and it is highly probable that in *Sueones* we have the root of *Sviar* and of *Svithjod.* The ships described by Tacitus are exactly like those which are described in this work as having been found in the North.

It stands to reason that the maritime power of the Sueones must have been the growth of centuries before the time of Tacitus, and from analogy of historical records we know that the fleets of powerful nations do not remain idle. Hence we must come to the conclusion that the Sueones navigated the sea long

---

[1] "Sueonum hinc civitates, ipso in oceano, præter viros armaque classibus valent. Forma navium eo differt quod utrinque prora paratam semper appulsui frontem agit. Nec velis ministrantur, nec remos in ordinem lateribus adjungunt: solutum, ut in quibusdam fluminum, et mutabile, ut res poscit, hinc et illinc remigium" (Germ. xliv.).

before the time of Tacitus, an hypothesis which is implied by the Eddas and Sagas as well as by the antiquities discovered.

That the Sueones, with such fleets, did not navigate westward further than Frisia is not credible, the more so that it was only necessary for them to follow the coast in order to come to the shores of Gaul, from which they could see Britain, and such maritime people must have had intercourse with the inhabitants of that island at that period; indeed, the objects of the earlier iron age discovered in Britain, which were until lately classed as Anglo-Roman, are identical with those of the country from which these people came, i.e., Scandinavia.

The Veneti, a tribe who inhabited Brittany, and whose power on the sea is described by Cæsar, were in all probability the advance-guard of the tribes of the North; their ships were built of oak, with iron nails, just as those of the Northmen; and the people of the country in which they settled were not seafaring.[1] Moreover, the similarity of the name to that of the Venedi, who are conjecturally placed by Tacitus on the shores of the Baltic, and to the Vends, so frequently mentioned in the Sagas, can scarcely be regarded as a mere accident.

" The Veneti have a very great number of ships, with which they have been accustomed to sail to Britain, and excel the rest of the people in their knowledge and experience of nautical affairs; and as only a few ports lie scattered along

---

[1] " Hujus est civitatis longe amplissima auctoritas omnis oræ maritimæ regionum earum, quod et naves habent Veneti plurimas, quibus in Britanniam navigare consuerunt, et scientia atque usu nauticarum rerum reliquos antecedunt, et in magno impetu maris atque aperto, paucis portibus interjectis, quos tenent ipsi, omnes fere qui eo mari uti consuerunt, habent vectigales " (Gallic War, iii. c. 8).

" Namque ipsorum naves ad hunc modum factæ armatæque erant; carinæ aliquanto planiores, quam nostrarum navium, quo facilius vada ac decessum æstus excipere possent; proræ admodum erectæ, atque item puppes ad magnitudinem fluctuum tempestatumque accommodatæ; naves totæ factæ ex robore ad quamvis vim et contumeliam perferendam; transtra pedalibus in latitudinem trabibus confixa clavis ferreis digiti pollicis crassitudine; ancoræ pro funibus ferreis catenis revinctæ; pelles pro velis alutæ-que tenuiter confectæ, hæ sive propter lini inopiam atque ejus usus inscientiam, sive eo, quod est magis verisimile, quod tantas tempestates Oceani tantosque impetus ventorum sustineri, ac tanta onera navium regi velis non satis commode posse arbitrabantur. Cum his navibus nostræ classi ejusmodi congressus erat, ut una celeritate et pulsu remorum præstaret; reliqua, pro loci natura, pro vi tempestatum, illis essent aptiora et accommodatiora. Neque enim his nostræ rostro nocere poterant (tanta in his erat firmitudo), neque propter altitudinem facile telum adjiciebatur, et eadem de causa minus commode copulis continebantur. Accedebat, ut, cum sævire ventus cœpisset et se vento dedissent, et tempestatem ferrent facilius, et in vadis consisterent tutius, et ab æstu relictæ nihil saxa et cautes timerent; quarum rerum omnium nostris navibus casus erat extimescendus " (c. 13).

that stormy and open sea, of which they are in possession, they hold as tributaries almost all those who have been accustomed to traffic in that sea. . . ."

"For their own ships were built and equipped in the following manner: Their ships were more flat-bottomed than our vessels, in order that they might be able more easily to guard against shallows and the ebbing of the tide; the prows were very much elevated, as also the sterns, so as to encounter heavy waves and storms. The vessels were built wholly of oak, so as to bear any violence or shock; the cross-benches, a foot in breadth, were fastened by iron spikes of the thickness of the thumb; the anchors were secured to iron chains, instead of to ropes; raw hides and thinly-dressed skins were used for sails, either on account of their want of canvas and ignorance of its use, or for this reason, which is the more likely, that they considered that such violent ocean storms and such strong winds could not be resisted, and such heavy vessels could not be conveniently managed by sails. The attack of our fleet on these vessels was of such a nature that the only advantage was in its swiftness and the power of its oars; in everything else, considering the situation and the fury of the storm, they had the advantage. For neither could our ships damage them by ramming (so strongly were they built), nor was a weapon easily made to reach them, owing to their height, and for the same reason they were not so easily held by grappling-irons. To this was added, that when the wind had begun to get strong, and they had driven before the gale, they could better weather the storm, and also more safely anchor among shallows, and, when left by the tide, need in no respect fear rocks and reefs, the dangers from all which things were greatly to be dreaded by our vessels."

Roman writers after the time of Tacitus mention warlike and maritime expeditions by the Saxons and Franks. Their names do not occur in Tacitus, but it is not altogether improbable that these people, whom later writers mention as ravaging every country which they could enter by sea or land, are the people whom Tacitus knew as the Sueones.

The maritime power of the Sueones could not have totally disappeared in a century, a hypothesis which is borne out by the fact that after a lapse of seven centuries they are again mentioned in the time of Charlemagne; nor could the supremacy of the so-called Saxons and Franks on the sea have arisen in a day; it must have been the growth of even generations before the time of Tacitus.

Ptolemy (circ. A.D. 140) is the first writer who mentions the Saxons as inhabiting a territory north of the Elbe, on the neck of the Cimbric Chersonesus.[1] They occupied but a small space, for between them and the Cimbri, at the northern extremity of the peninsula, he places ten other tribes, among them the Angli.

About a century after the time of Ptolemy, Franks and Saxons had already widely extended their expeditions at sea. Some of the former made an expedition from the Euxine, through the Mediterranean, plundered Syracuse, and returned without mishap across the great sea (A.D. circ. 280).[2]

"He (Probus) permitted the Bastarnæ, a Scythian race, who had submitted themselves to him, to settle in certain districts of Thrace which he allotted to them, and from thenceforth these people always lived under the laws and institutions of Rome. And there were certain Franks who had come to the Emperor, and had asked for land on which to settle. A part of them, however, revolted, and having obtained a large number of ships, caused disturbances throughout the whole of Greece, and having landed in Sicily and made an assault on Syracuse, they caused much slaughter there. They also landed in Libya, but were repulsed at the approach of the Carthaginian forces. Nevertheless, they managed to get back to their home unscathed."

"Why should I tell again of the most remote nations of the Franks (of Francia), which were carried away not from those regions which the Romans had on a former occasion invaded, but from their own native territory, and the farthest shores of the land of the barbarians, and transported to the deserted parts of Gaul that they might promote the peace of the Roman Empire by their cultivation and its armies by their recruits?"[3]

---

[1] Ἐπὶ τὸν αὐχένα τῆς Κιμβρικῆς χερσονήσου Σάξονες (Geog. lib. ii. c. 2).

[2] Βασιάρνος δε, Σκύθικον ἔθνος, ὑποπεσόντας αὐτῷ προσέμενος κατῴκισε Θρακίοις χωρίοις· καὶ διετέλεσαν τοῖς Ῥωμαίων βιοτεύοντες νόμοις. καὶ Φράγκων τῷ βασιλεῖ προσελθόντων καὶ τυχόντων οἰκήσεως μοῖρά τις ἀποστᾶσα, πλοίων εὐπορήσασα, τὴν Ἑλλάδα συνετάραξεν ἅπασαν καὶ Σικελίᾳ προσσχοῦσα καὶ τῇ Συρακουσίων προσμίξασα πολὺν κατὰ ταύτην εἰργάσατο φόνον. ἤδη δὲ καὶ Λιβύῃ προσορμισθεῖσα, καὶ ἀποκρουσθεῖσα δυνάμεως ἐκ Καρχηδόνος ἐπενεχθείσης, οἷά τε γέγονεν ἀπαθὴς ἐπανελθεῖν οἴκαδε. (Zosimus. de Probo, i. 71).

[3] "Quid loquar rursus intimas Franciæ nationes jam non ab iis locis quæ olim Romani invaserant, sed a propriis ex origine sui sedibus, atque ab ultimis barbariæ littoribus avulsas, ut, in desertis Galliæ regionibus collocatæ et pacem Romani imperii cultu juvarent et arma delectu?" (Eumenius. Constantin. Aug. c. vi.)

"There came to mind the incredible daring and undeserved success of a handful of the captive Franks under the Emperor Probus For they, having seized some ships, so far away as Pontus, having laid waste Greece and Asia, having landed and done some damage on several parts of the coast of Africa, actually took Syracuse, which was at one time so renowned for her naval ascendancy. Thereupon they accomplished a very long voyage and entered the Ocean at the point where it breaks through the land (the Straits of Gibraltar), and so by the result of their daring exploit showed that wherever ships can sail, nothing is closed to pirates in desperation." [1]

In the time of Diocletian and Maximian these maritime tribes so harassed the coasts of Gaul and Britain that Maximian, in 286, was obliged to make Gesoriacum or Bononia (the present Boulogne) into a port for the Roman fleet, in order as far as possible to prevent their incursions.

" About this time (A.D. 287) Carausius, who, though of very humble origin, had, in the exercise of vigorous warfare, obtained a distinguished reputation, was appointed at Bononia to reduce to quiet the coast regions of Belgica and Armorica, which were overrun by the Franks and Saxons. But though many of the barbarians were captured, the whole of the booty was not handed over to the inhabitants of the province, nor sent to the commander-in-chief, and the barbarians were, moreover, deliberately allowed by him to come in, that he might capture them with their spoils as they passed through, and by this means enrich himself. On being condemned to death by Maximian, he seized on the sovereign command, and took possession of Britain." [2]

Eutropius also records that the Saxons and others dwelt on the coasts of and among the marshes of the great sea, which

---

[1] " Recursabat quippe in animos illa sub Divo Probo et paucorum ex Francis captivorum incredibilis audacia et indigna felicitas, qui a Ponto usque correptis navibus Græciam Asiamque populati nec impune plerisque Libyæ littoribus appulsi ipsas postremo, navalibus quondam victoriis nobiles ceperant Syracusas, et immenso itinere pervecti Oceanum, qua terras irrupit intraverant atque ita eventu temeritatis ostenderant nihil esse clausum piraticæ desperationi quo navigiis pateret accessus" (Eumenius Panegyr. Const. Cæs. xviii. circ. A D. 300)

[2] " Per hæc tempora (i.e. 287) etiam Carausius, qui vilissime natus in strenuæ militiæ ordine famam egregiam fuerat consecutus, cum apud Bononiam per tractum Belgicæ et Armoricæ pacandum mare accepisset, quod Franci et Saxones infestabant, multis barbaris sæpe captis, nec præda integra aut provincialibus reddita aut imperatoribus missa consulto ab eo admitti barbaros ut transeuntes cum præda exciperet atque hac se occasione ditaret ; a Maximiano jussus occidi purpuram sumpsit et Britannias occupavit" (Eutropius, Breviarium Historiæ, ix. ch. 21).

no one could traverse, but the Emperor Valentinian (320-375) nevertheless conquered them.

The Emperor Julian calls the

"Franks and Saxons the most warlike of the tribes above the Rhine and the Western Sea."[1]

Ammianus Marcellinus (d. circ. 400 A D.) writes:—

"At this time (middle of the 4th century), just as though the trumpets were sounding a challenge throughout all the Roman world, fierce nations were stirred up and began to burst forth from their territories. The Alamanni began to devastate Gallia and Rhætia; the Sarmatæ and Quadi Pannonia, the Picts and Saxons, Scots, and Attacotti constantly harassed the Britons."[2]

"The Franks and the Saxons, who are coterminous with them, were ravaging the districts of Gallia wherever they could effect an entrance by sea or land, plundering and burning, and murdering all the prisoners they could take."[3]

Claudianus asserts that the Saxons appeared even in the Orkneys:—

"The Orcades were moist from the slain Saxon."

These are but a few of many allusions to the same effect which might be quoted.

That the swarms of Sueones and so-called Saxons and Franks, seen on every sea of Europe, could have poured forth from a small country is not possible. Such fleets as they possessed could only have come from a country densely covered with oak forests. We must come to the conclusion that Sueones, Franks, and Saxons were seafaring tribes belonging to one people. The Roman writers did not seem to know the precise locality inhabited by these people.

---

[1] Orat. 1. Φράγκοι καὶ Σάξονες τῶν ὑπὲρ τὸν Ῥῆνον καὶ τὴν ἑσπερίαν θάλατταν ἐθνῶν τὰ μαχιμώτατα.

[2] "Hoc tempore velut per universum orbem Romanum bellicum canentibus buccinis, excitæ gentes sævissimæ limites sibi proximos persultabant. Gallias Rhætiasque simul Alamanni populabantur; Sarmatæ, Pannonias et Quadi; Picti, Saxonesque, et Scoti, et Attacotti Britannos ærumnis vexavere continuis" (Rerum Gestarum, lib. xxvi. s. 4).

[3] "Gallicanos vero tractus *Franci*, et *Saxones* iisdem confines, quo quisque erumpere potuit terra vel mari, prædis acerbis incendiisque et captivorum funeribus hominum violabant" (Ammianus Marcellinus, d. circ. 400, lib. xxvii. c. 8, § 5).

[4] "Maduerunt Saxone fuso Orcades; incaluit Pictorum sanguine Thule; Scotorum cumulos flevit glacialis Ierne." (De Cons. Hon. iv. 31.)

It would appear that these tribes must have come from a country further eastward than the Roman provinces, and that as they came with ships, their home must have been on the shores of the Baltic, the Cattegat, and Norway; in fact, precisely the country which the numerous antiquities point to as inhabited by an extremely warlike and maritime race, which had great intercourse with the Greek and Roman world.

The dates given by the Greek and Roman writers of the maritime expeditions, invasions, and settlements of the so-called Saxons and Franks agree perfectly with the date of the objects found in the North, among which are numerous Roman coins, and remarkable objects of Roman and Greek art, which must have been procured either by the peaceful intercourse of trade or by war. To this very day thousands upon thousands of graves have been preserved in the North, belonging to the time of the invasions of these Northmen, and to an earlier period. From them no other inference can be drawn than that the country and islands of the Baltic were far more densely populated than any part of central and western Europe and Great Britain, since the number of these earlier graves in those countries is much smaller.

Every tumulus described by antiquaries as a Saxon or Frankish grave is the counterpart of a Northern grave, thus showing conclusively the common origin of the people.

Wherever graves of the same type are found in other countries we have the invariable testimony, either of the Roman or Greek writers of the Frankish and English Chronicles or of the Sagas, to show that the people of the North had been in the country at one time or another.

The conclusion is forced upon us that in time the North became over-populated, and an outlet was necessary for the spread of its people.

The story of the North is that of all countries whose inhabitants have spread and conquered, in order to find new fields for their energy and over-population; in fact, the very course the progenitors of the English-speaking peoples adopted in those days is precisely the one which has been followed by their descendants in England and other countries for the last three hundred years.

It is certain that the Franks could not have lived on the coast of Frisia, as they did later on, for we know that the country of the Rhine was held by the Romans, and, besides, as we have already seen, Julian refers to the Franks and Saxons as dwelling above the Rhine. Moreover, till they had to give up their conquests, no mention is made by the Romans of native seafaring tribes inhabiting the shores of their northern province, except the Veneti, and they would have certainly tried to subjugate the roving seamen that caused them so much trouble in their newly-acquired provinces if they had been within their reach.

From the Roman writers, who have been partially confirmed by archæology, we know that the tribes which inhabited the country to which they give the vague name of Germania were not seafaring people nor possessed of any civilisation. The invaders of Britain, of the Gallic and of the Mediterranean coasts could therefore not have been the German tribes referred to by the Roman writers, who, as we see from Julius Cæsar and other Roman historians, were very far from possessing the civilisation which we know, from the antiquities, to have existed in the North.

" Their whole life is devoted to hunting and warlike pursuits. From childhood they pay great attention to toil and hardiness ; they bathe all together in the rivers, and wear skins or small reindeer garments, leaving the greater part of their bodies naked." [1]

Tacitus, in recording the speech of Germanicus to his troops before the battle at Idistavisus, bears witness to the uncivilised character of the inhabitants of the country.

" The huge targets, the enormous spears of the barbarians could never be wielded against trunks of trees and thickets of underwood shooting up from the ground, like Roman swords and javelins, and armour fitting the body . . . . the Germans had neither helmet nor coat of mail ; their bucklers were not even strengthened with leather, but mere contextures of twigs

---

[1] " Vita omnis in venationibus atque in studiis rei militaris consistit. Ab parvulis labori ac duritiæ student . . . in fluminibus promiscue perluuntur et pelli- bus aut parvis rhenonum tegimentis utuntur magna corporis parte nuda " (Cæsar De Bello Gallico, vi. 21).

and boards of no substance daubed over with paint. Their first rank was to a certain extent armed with pikes, the rest had only stakes burnt at the ends or short darts."[1]

Now compare these descriptions with the magnificent archæology of the North of that period—as seen in these volumes—from which we learn that the tribes who inhabited the shores of the Baltic and the present Scandinavia had at the time the above was written reached a high degree of civilisation. We find in their graves and hoards, coins of the early Roman Empire not in isolated instances, but constantly and in large numbers, and deposited side by side with such objects as coats of mail, damascened swords and other examples of articles of highly artistic workmanship.

Three kinds of swords are often mentioned by the Northmen —the *mœkir*, the *sverd*, and the *sax*, while among the spears there is one called *frakki*, or *frakka*.

The double-edged sword was the one that was in use among the Romans, and they, seeing bodies of men carrying a weapon unlike theirs—single-edged, and called Sax— may have named them after it, and the Franks, in like manner, may have been called after their favourite weapon, the Frakki ; but we see that neither the *sax* nor the *frakki* was confined to one tribe in the North. There is a Saxland in the Sagas—a small country situated east of the peninsula of Jutland, about the present Holstein—a land tributary to the Danish or Swedish Kings from the earliest times, but far from possessing the warlike archæology of the North, it appears to have held an insignificant place among the neighbouring tribes.

In the Bayeux tapestry the followers of William the Conqueror were called Franci, and they always have been recognised as coming from the North.

The very early finds prove that the Sax was not rare, for it occurs in different parts of the North and islands of the Baltic. The different swords and spears used were so common and so

---

[1] " Nec enim immensa barbarorum scuta, enormes hastas, inter truncos arborum et enata humo virgulta perinde haberi quam pila et gladios et hærentia corpori tegmina . . . . non loricam Germano, non galeam, ne scuta quidem ferro nervo ve firmata, sed viminum textus vel tenues fucatas colore tabulas, primatu utcunque aciem hastatam, cæteris proœnata aut brevia tela " (Tacitus Annals, ii. 14).

well known to everybody, that we have no special description of them in the Sagas, except of their ornamentation; but in the Saga of Grettir there is a passage which shows that the Sax was single-edged.

Gretti went to a farm in Iceland to slay the Bondi Thorbjorn and his son Arnor. We read—

"When Gretti saw that the young man was within reach he lifted his *sax* high into the air, and struck Arnor's head with *its back,* so that his head was broken and he died. Thereupon he killed the father with his *sax.*"

Whatever may be the origin of local names employed by the Roman writers we must look to the North for the maritime tribes described by them; there we shall find the home of the earlier English people, to whose numerous warlike and ocean-loving instincts we owe the transformation which took place in Britain, and the glorious inheritance which they have left to their descendants, scattered over many parts of the world, in whom we recognise to this day many of the very same traits of character which their ancestors possessed.

CHAPTER III.

THE SETTLEMENT OF BRITAIN BY NORTHMEN.

The Notitia—Probable origin of the name England—Jutland—The language of the North and of England—Early Northern kings in England—Danes and Sueones—Mythical accounts of the settlements of England.

BRITAIN being an island could only be settled or conquered by seafaring tribes, just in the same way as to-day distant lands can only be conquered by nations possessing ships. From the Roman writers we have the only knowledge we possess in regard to the tribes inhabiting the country to which they gave the vague name of Germania. From the Roman records we find that these tribes were not civilised and that they were not a seafaring people.

Unfortunately the Roman accounts we have of their conquest and occupation of Britain, of its population and inhabitants, are very meagre and unsatisfactory, and do not help us much to ascertain how the settlement in Britain by the people of the North began. Our lack of information is most probably due to the simple reason that the settlement, like all settlements of a new country, was a very gradual one, a few men coming over in the first instance for the purpose of trade either with Britons or Romans, or coming from the over-populated Northto settle in a country which the paucity of archæological remains shows to have been thinly occupied. The Romans made no objection to these new settlers, who did not prove dangerous to their power on the island, but brought them commodities, such as furs, &c., from the North.

We find from the Roman records that the so-called Saxons had founded colonies or had settlements in Belgium and Gaul.

Another important fact we know from the records relating

VOL. I.

to Britain is that during the Roman occupation of the island the Saxons had settlements in the country; but how they came hither we are not told.

In the *Notitia Dignitatum utriusque imperii*, a sort of catalogue or "Army List," compiled towards the latter end of the fourth century, occurs the expression, "Comes litoris Saxonici per Britannias"—Count of the Saxon Shore in Britain. Within this litus Saxonicum the following places are mentioned:— Othona, said to be "close by Hastings"; Dubris, said to be Dover; Rutupiæ, Richborough; Branodunum, Brancaster; Regulbium, Reculvers; Lemannis, West Hythe; Garianno, Yarmouth; Anderida, Pevensey; Portus Adurni, Shoreham or Brighton.

This shows that the so-called Saxons were settled in Britain before the Notitia was drawn up, and at a date very much earlier than has been assigned by some modern historians.

The hypothesis that the expression "litus Saxonicum" is derived from the enemy to whose ravages it was exposed seems improbable. Is it not much more probable that the "litus Saxonicum per Britannias" must mean the shore of the country settled, not attacked, by Saxons? The mere fact of their attacking the shore would not have given rise to the name applied to it had they not settled there, for I maintain that there is no instance in the whole of Roman literature of a country being named after the people who attacked it. If, on the other hand, the Saxons had landed and formed settlements on the British coasts, the origin of the name "Litus Saxonicum" is easily understood.

Some time after the Romans relinquished Britain we find that part of the island becomes known as England; and, to make the subject still more confusing, the people composing its chief population are called Saxons by the chroniclers and later historians, the name given to them by the Romans.

That the history of the people called Saxons was by no means certain is seen in the fact that Witikind, a monk of the tenth century, gives the following account of what was then considered to be their origin [1]:—

---

[1] "Nam super hac re varia opinio est, aliis arbitrantibus de Danis Northman- | nisque originem duxisse Saxones, aliis autem aestimantibus, ut ipse adoles-

"On this there are various opinions, some thinking that the Saxons had their origin from the Danes and Northmen; others, as I heard some one maintain when a young man, that they are derived from the Greeks, because they themselves used to say the Saxons were the remnant of the Macedonian army, which, having followed Alexander the Great, were by his premature death dispersed all over the world."

As to how Britain came to be called England the different legends given by the monkish writers are contradictory.

The *Skjoldunga Saga*, which is often mentioned in other Sagas, and which contains a record down to the early kings of Denmark, is unfortunately lost: it would, no doubt, have thrown great light on the lives of early chiefs who settled in Britain; but from some fragments which are given in this work, and which are supposed to belong to it, we see that several Danish and Swedish kings claimed to have possessions in England long before the supposed coming of the Danes.

Some writers assert that the new settlers gave to their new home in Britain the name of the country which they had left, called *Angeln*, and which they claim to be situated in the southern part of Jutland; but besides the Angeln in Jutland there is in the Cattegat an Engelholm, which is geographically far more important, situated in the land known as the Vikin of the Sagas, a great Viking and warlike land, from which the name Viking may have been derived, filled with graves and antiquities of the iron age. There are also other Engeln in the present Sweden.

In the whole literature of the North such a name as Engeln is unknown; it may have been, perhaps, a local name.

In the Sagas the term *England* was applied to a portion only of Britain. the inhabitants of which were called *Englar, Enskirmenn.* Britain itself is called *Bretland*, and the people *Bretar.*

"Öngulsey (Angelsey) is one third of Bretland (Wales)" (Magnus Barefoot's Saga, c. 11).

---

ceutulus audivi quendam praedicantem de Graecis. quia ipsi dicerent, Saxone reliquias fuisse Macedonici exercitus qui secutus magnum Alexandrum inmatura morte ipsius per totum orbem sit dispersus" (Ann. lib. 1).

c 2

Another part of the country was called *Nordimbraland.*

It is an important fact that throughout the Saga literature describing the expeditions of the Northmen to England not a single instance is mentioned of their coming in contact with a people called *Saxons,* which shows that such a name in Britain was unknown to the people of the North. Nor is any part of England called Saxland.

To make the confusion greater than it is, some modern historians make the so-called Saxons, who were supposed to have come over with the mythical Hengist and others, a distinct race from the Northmen, who afterwards continued to land in the country.

In the Sagas we constantly find that the people of England are not only included among the Northern lands, but that the warriors of one country are helping the other. In several places we find, and from others we infer, that the language in both countries was very similar.

" All sayings in the Northern (norræn) tongue in which there is truth begin when the Tyrkir and the Asia-men settled in the North. For it is truly told that the tongue which we call Norræn came with them to the North, and it went through Saxland, Denmark, Sweden, Norway, and part of England " (Rimbegla, iii. c. i.).

" We are of one tongue, though one of the two, or in some respects both, are now much changed " (Prose Edda, ii.)

" Then ruled over England King Ethelred, son of Edgar (979). He was a good chief; he sat this winter in London. The tongue in England, as well as in Norway and Denmark, was then one, but it changed in England when William the Bastard won England. Thenceforth the tongue of Valland (France) was used in England, for he (William) was born there " (Gunnlaug Ormstunga's Saga, c. 7).

That the language of the North should have taken a footing in a great part of England is due, no doubt, to the continuous flow of immigration, from the northern mother country, which entirely swamped the former native or British element.

The story given in the English or Irish chronicles of the appearance of the Danes, in A.D. 785, when their name is first mentioned, is as little trustworthy as that of the settlement of

England, and bears the appearance of contradiction and confusion in regard to names of people and facts.

We must remember that the Sueones are not mentioned from the time of Tacitus to that of Charlemagne (772–814), and certainly they had not disappeared in the meantime.

What were the Danes doing with their mighty fleets before this? Had their ships been lying in port for centuries? Had they been built for simple recreation and the pleasure of looking at them, or did their maritime power arise at once as if by magic? Such an hypothesis cannot stand the test of reasoning. The turning of a population into a seafaring nation is the work of time. Where in the history of the world can we find a parallel to this story of a people *suddenly* appearing with immense navies? Let us compare by analogy the statement of the chronicles with what might happen to the history of England in the course of time.

Suppose that for some reason the previous history of England were lost, with the exception of a fragment which spoke of her enormous fleet of to-day. Could it be reasonably supposed that this great maritime power was the creation of a few years?

A few years after the time fixed as that of their first supposed appearance we find these very Danes swarming everywhere with their fleets and warriors, not only in England, but in Gaul, in Brittany, up the Seine, the Garonne, the Rhine, the Elbe, on the coasts of Spain, and further eastward in the Mediterranean.

The Sueones, or Swedes, reappear at the close of the eighth and commencement of the ninth centuries by the side of the Danes, and both called themselves Northmen. Surely the maritime power of the Sueones, described by Tacitus, could not have been destroyed immediately after his death, only to reappear in the time of Charlemagne, when it again becomes prominent in the Frankish annals.

A remarkable fact not to be overlooked is that, in the time of Charlemagne, the Franks and Saxons were not a seafaring people, though their countries had an extensive coast with deep rivers. The Frankish annals never mention a Frank or Saxon fleet attacking the fleets of the Northmen, or preventing them from ascending their streams, though Charlemagne ordered ships to be built in order to resist their incursions.

While the country of the Saxons was being conquered by this Emperor, we find that the Saxons themselves had no vessels on the Elbe or Weser in which, if defeated, they could retire in safety, or by help of which they could prevent the army of their enemies from crossing their streams. Such tactics were constantly used by the Northmen in their invasions of ancient Gaul, Britain, Germania, Spain, &c.

Thus we see. that, though hardly more than three hundred years had elapsed since the time when, according to the Roman writers, the fleets of the Franks and Saxons swarmed over every sea of Europe, not a vestige of their former maritime power remained in the time of Charlemagne, and the Saxons were still occupying the same country as in the days of Ptolemy.

Pondering over the above important facts, the question arises, Were not the Romans mistaken in giving the names of Saxons and Franks to the maritime tribes of whose origin, country, and homes they knew nothing, but who came to attack their shores? Were not these so-called Saxons and Franks in reality tribes of Sueones, Swedes, Danes, Norwegians? The Romans knew none of the countries of these people. It seems strange, if not incredible, to find two peoples, whose country had a vast sea-coast and deep rivers, totally abandoning the seafaring habits possessed by their forefathers.

It cannot be doubted that Ivar Vidfadmi, after him Harald Hilditonn, then Sigurd Hring and Ragnar Lodbrok and his sons, and probably some of the Danish and Swedish kings before them, made expeditions to England, and gained and held possessions there. Several distinct records, having no connection with each other, being parts of different Sagas and histories, with the archæology, form the evidence.

"Ivar Vidfadmi (wide-fathomer) subdued the whole of Sviaveldi (the Swedish realm); he also got Danaveldi (Danish realm) and a large part of Saxland, and the whole of Austrriki (Eastern realm, including Russia, &c.) and the fifth part of England. From his kin have come the kings of Denmark and the kings of Sweden who have had sole power in these lands" (Ynglinga Saga, c. 45).

The above is corroborated by another quite independent source.

"Ivar Vidfadmi ruled England till his death-day. As he lay on his death-bed he said he wanted to be carried to where the land was exposed to attacks, and that he hoped those who landed there would not be victorious. When he died it happened as he said, and he was *mound-laid*. It is said by many men that when King Harald Sigurdsson came to England he landed where Ivar's mound was, and he was slain there. When Vilhjálm Bastard came to the land he broke open the mound of Ivar and saw that the corpse was not rotten; he made a large pyre, and had Ivar burned on it; then he went up on land and got the victory" (Ragnar Lodbrók's Saga, c. 19).

We find that not only did the Norwegians call themselves Northmen, but that both Danes and Sueones were called Northmen in the Frankish Chronicles.[1]

"The Danes and Sueones, whom we call Northmen, occupy both the northern shore and all its islands."

So also Nigellus (in the reign of Louis Le Debonnaire).[2]

"The Danes also after the manner of the Franks are called by the name of Manni."

The time came when the people of the North, continuing their expeditions to Britain, attacked their own kinsmen. After the departure of the Romans the power of the new comers increased, and as they became more numerous, they became more and more domineering: the subsequent struggles were between a sturdy race that had settled in the country and people of their own kin, and not with Britons, who had been so easily conquered by the Romans, had appealed to them afterwards for protection, and had for a long period been a subject race. It is not easy to believe that the inhabitants of a servile Roman province could suddenly become stubborn and fierce warriors, nor are there any antiquities belonging to the Britain of yore which bear

---

[1] "Dani et Sueones, quos Northmannos vocamus, et Septentrionale litus et omnes in eo insulas tenent" (Vita Caroli Magni, c. 12; Eginhard, historian and friend of Charlemagne).

[2] "Dani more quoque Francisco dicuntur nomine Manni."

witness to a fierce and warlike character displayed by the aboriginal inhabitants.

From the preceding pages we see that Franks and Saxons are continually mentioned together, and it is only in the North we can find antiquities of a most warlike and seafaring people, who must have formed the great and preponderating bulk of the invading host who conquered Britain.

Britain after a continuous immigration from the North, which lasted several hundred years, became the most powerful colony of the Northern tribes, several of whose chiefs claimed a great part of England even in the seventh century. Afterwards she asserted her independence, though she did not get it until after a long and tedious struggle with the North, the inhabitants and kings of which continued to try to assert the ancient rights their forefathers once possessed. Then the time came when the land upon which the people of these numerous tribes had settled became more powerful and more populous than the mother country; a case which has found several parallels in the history of the world. To-day the people of England as they look over the broad Atlantic may perhaps discern the same process gradually taking place. In the people of the United States of North America, the grandest and most colossal state founded by England or any other country of which we have any historical record, we may recognise the indomitable courage, the energy and spirit which was one of the characteristics of the Northern race to whom a great part of the people belong. The first settlement of the country, territory by territory, State by State—the frontier life with its bold adventures, innumerable dangers, fights, struggles, privations and heroism—is the grandest drama that has ever been enacted in the history of the world. The time is not far distant, if the population of the United States and Canada increases in the same ratio as it has done for more than a hundred years, when over three or four hundred millions of its people will speak the English tongue; and I think it is no exaggeration to say that in the course of time one hundred millions more will be added, from Australia, New Zealand and other colonies which to-day form part of the British Empire, but which are destined to become independent nations.

In fact we hesitate to look still further into the future of the English race, for fear of being accused of exaggeration.

There is a mythical version of the settlement of Britain contradictory of the Roman records. This version is that of Gildas whose 'De Excidio Britanniæ' is supposed to have been composed in the sixth century (560 A.D.), and whose statements have unfortunately been taken by one historian after the other as a true history of Britain. His narrative, which gives an account of the first arrival of the Saxons in Britain and the numerous wars which followed their invasion, has been more or less copied by Nennius, Bede and subsequent chroniclers, whose writings are a mass of glaring contradictions, diffuse and intricate, for they contain names which appear to have been invented by the writers and which cannot be traced in the language of those times, while the dates assigned for the landing of the so-called Saxons do not agree with one another.

The historians who use Gildas as an authority and try to believe his account of the settlement of Britain by Hengist and Horsa (the stallion and the mare) are obliged, in order to explain away the Roman records, to give a most extraordinary interpretation to the Notitia.

We are all aware that the people of every country like to trace their origin or history as far back as possible, and that legends often form part of the fabric of those histories. The early chroniclers, who were credulous and profoundly ignorant of the world, took these fables for facts, or they may have possibly been incorporated in the text of their supposed works after their time. The description of the settlement of a country must be founded on facts which can bear the test of searching criticism if they are to be believed and adopted ; Gildas and his copyists cannot stand that test, and the Roman records, as corroborated by the archæology and literature of the North and the archæology of England, must be taken as the correct ones.

The mythological literature of the North bears evidence of a belief prevalent among the people, that their ancestors migrated at a remote period from the shores of the Black Sea, through south-western Russia, to the shores of the Baltic.

This belief seems to be supported by a variety of evidence. Herodotus describes a people on the Tanais, the Budini, as being blue-eyed and yellow-haired, with houses built of wood, his description of the walls reminding one of the characteristics of the Danavirki (Herodotus, IV. 21, 108, 109). One of his tribes, the *Thysagetæ*, may possibly be indicated in the *Thursar* of the Voluspa, &c.

When we appeal to Archæology, we find in the neighbourhood of the Black Sea, near to the old Greek settlement, graves similar to those of the North, containing ornaments and other relics also remarkably like those found in the ancient graves of Scandinavia. The Runes of the North remind us strikingly of the characters of Archaic Greek. If we follow the river Dnieper upwards from its mouth in the Black Sea, we see in the museums of Kief and Smolensk many objects of types exactly similar to those found in the graves of the North. When we reach the Baltic we find on its eastern shores the Gardariki of the Sagas, where, we are told, the Odin of the North placed one of his sons, and on the southern shores many specimens have been discovered similar to those obtained in Scandinavia.

In the following chapters the reader will be struck by the similarity of the customs of the Norsemen with those of the ancient Greeks as recorded by Homer and Herodotus; for example, the horse was very much sacrificed in the North, and Herodotus, describing the Massagetæ, says:

"They (the Massagetæ) worship the sun only of all the gods, and sacrifice horses to him" (I. 216).

In regard to the Jutes, Jutland = Jòts, Jötnar; Jötland, Jótunheim, we find them from the Sagas to be a very ancient land and people, and meet several countries bearing kindred names—even to this day we have Gòteborg, in which the *G* is pronounced as English *Y*.

From the Roman, Greek, Frankish, Russian, English, and Arabic records, we must come to the conclusion that the "Viking Age" lasted from about the second century of our era to about the middle of the twelfth without interruption, hence the title given to the work which deals with the history and customs of our English forefathers during that period.

CHAPTER IV.

THE MYTHOLOGY AND COSMOGONY OF THE NORSEMEN.

The three poems giving the mythology and cosmogony of the North—The Vóluspa, Vafthrudnismal, Grimnismal, the Asar, Jótnar, and Thursar—Odin and Vafthrudnir—The nine worlds—Before the creation—The origin of the Hrim Thursar—Birth of Ymir—Birth of Odin—Vili and Ve—The ash Yggdrasil—The well of wisdom—Hel, one of the nine worlds—The bridge Bifrost — Heimdall — Bergelmir born before the creation—The Jötun—Ymir slain by Odin—The deluge of blood—Creation of the world—Divisions of time—End of the world—A new world.

In the three poems called *Voluspa, Vafthrudnismal,* and *Grimnismal,* we have the earliest accounts of the cosmogony and of the mythology of the people of the North. The grand central figure in the mythology is Odin. He and his kin formed the people known as Asar in the lore and literature of the North, and were treated as gods. These poems are too long to be given here in full, but in the following pages we have endeavoured, by means of extracts, to give a more or less consecutive account of the subjects with which they deal.

The Vóluspa was an inspired poem of a Vólva or Sibyl,[1] and embodies the records of the creation of the present world, and of the time prior to it; of the various races, their origin and history, and of the chaos and destruction which finally will overtake mankind.

It is in some places so obscure, that if it had not been partly explained by the later Edda, and had light thrown upon it by the sagas and ancient laws, it would be impossible to understand its meaning; and even now it is most difficult, and in some places impossible to fully comprehend several of its mythical parts, some of which will always remain enigmatical.

Vafthrudnismal is especially interesting as compared with

---

[1] Vóluspa is derived from *vólva, sybil* and *spá,* foretelling. The name *volva* seems to be derived from *volr* (staff, stick). as we see that the sibyls or prophetesses used to walk from place to place with a stick

the Voluspa, with much of which it corresponds, and some part of which it amplifies.

The mythical and the real are so intermingled that it is often impossible to distinguish the one from the other.

In the beginning we are confronted by a chief named Odin, the son of Bor, who lived near the Tanais (the river Don) not far from the Palus Mæotis (the Sea of Azof), and there we find one Asgard, which in all probability had its original in some real locality.

Besides Asar and Jótnar, many other tribes are mentioned which can hardly be regarded as altogether mythical, some of which may have inhabited the far north of the ancient Sweden, or part of the present Russia and Scandinavia; the Thursar, who were also called Hrimthursar (hoar frost), and the Risar, also Bergrisar (mountain Risar), appear from these names to have lived in a cold mountainous country, possibly the region of the Ural Mountains.

Jótunheim, the chief burgh of which was *Utgard*, would appear to be a general, vague name given to a very wide extent of country not embraced in Asaheim (the home of the Asar). Jótunheim, as the name indicates, was the home or country of the Jótnar and Thursar, between whom and the Asar there was fierce enmity.

Some of the Jótnar were considered very wise, and Odin, as the chief of the Asar, determined to go in disguise to Jótunheim, the home of the Jótnar, in order to seek out the Jótun Vafthrudnir[1] (the mighty or wise in riddles), who was renowned for his knowledge. The song begins by representing Odin as consulting his wife, Frigg, as to the advisability of undertaking the journey. The stanzas which follow represent Odin questioning Vafthrudnir in his search for knowledge :—

Then went Odin
To try word-wisdom
Of the all-wise Jótun.
To a hall he came,
Owned by Ymir's father;
In went Ygg at once.[2]

(*As Odin enters he sings—*)
Hail, Vafthrudnir,
I have come into thy hall
To look at thyself;
First I want to know,
If thou art a wise
Or an all-wise Jótun.

---

[1] Vafthrudnir. *Vaf* = weave, or entangle; *thrudnir* = strong. or mighty; hence Vafthrudnir = mighty in riddles which cannot be disentangled.

[2] The awful = Odin.

Vafthrudnir.

Who is the man
That in my hall
Speaks to me?
Thou shalt not
Get out of it
Unless thou art the wiser.

Odin.

I am called *Gagnrad*,[1]
I have now come from my walking
Thirsty to thy hall;
Needing thy bidding
And thy welcome, Jötun;
Long time have I travelled.

Vafthrudnir.

Why standing on the floor
Dost thou speak to me?
Take a seat in the hall.
Then we shall try
Who knows more,
The guest or the old wise one.

Odin.

When a poor man
Comes to a rich one
Let him speak useful things or be
    silent;
Great babbling
I think turns to ill
For one who meets a cold-ribbed[2]
man.

We are told in the Völuspa that Odin, in the quest of information, went to visit the Volva, or Sybil, Heid, who was possessed of supernatural powers of knowledge and foresight. She asks for a hearing from the sons of Heimdal, or mankind, and then proceeds to tell what she recollects:—

I remember Jötnar
Early born,
Who of yore
Raised me;[3]

I remember nine worlds,
Nine *ividi*[4]
The famous world-tree (Yggdrasil)
Beneath the earth.

The nine worlds were—1, Muspel; 2, Asgard; 3, Vanaheim (home of the Vanir); 4, Midgard; 5, Alfheim (world of the Alfar); 6, Mannheim (home of men); 7, Jotunheim (the home of the Jötnar); 8, Hel; 9, Niflheim.

The first beginnings of all things were apparently as obscure to the Volva as to others; nothing existed before the Creation. The world was then a gaping void (Ginnungagap), and there the Jötun Ymir, or the Hrim Thursar, lived. On each side of

---

[1] The one who gives useful advice.

[2] When the heart, which is near the ribs, is cold, the ribs are also cold; therefore this means *cold-hearted*.

[3] Fœda means both to give birth to, to raise, and to feed.

[4] *Ividi*, a very obscure word (only found here in the whole Northern literature), which has been translated differently without any particle of authority in any case, and in each case only as a mere guess. The word *vid* means tree, perhaps the world-tree, *Yggdrasil*, which extended its roots under the world.

Ginnungagap there were two worlds, Niflheim, the world of cold, and Muspelheim, the world of heat.

When Ymir lived .	No earth was there
In early ages .	Nor heaven above,
Was neither sand nor sea,	There was gaping void
Nor cool waves,	And grass nowhere.

" First there was a home (a world) in the southern half of the world called Muspel ; it is hot and bright, so that it is burning and in flames ; it is also inaccessible for those who have no *odals* (or family estates) ; there the one that sits at the land's end to defend it is called a Surt. He has a flaming sword, and at the end of the world he will go and make warfare and get victory over all the gods, and burn the whole world with fire " (Later Edda, c. 4).[1]

The origin of the Hrim Thursar and the Birth of Ymir, who lived in Ginnungagap. and of Odin, Vili, and Ve, is as follows :

" Gangleri asked, ' How was it before the kindreds existed and mankind increased ? ' Hár answered, ' When the rivers called Elivagar had run so far from their sources that the quick venom which flowed into them, like the dross which runs out of the fire, got hard, and changed into ice ; when this ice stood still and flowed no longer, the exhalation of the poison came over it and froze into rime ; the rime rose up all the way into the Ginnungagap.' Jafnhár said, ' The part of Ginnungagap turning to the north was filled with the heaviness and weight of ice and rime, and the opposite side with drizzle and gusts of wind ; but the southern part of Ginnungagap became less heavy, from the sparks and glowing substances which came flying from Muspelheim.' Thridi said, ' Just as the cold and all things come from Niflheim, the things near Muspel were hot and shining ; Ginnungagap was as warm as windless air. When the rime and the breath of the heat met so that the rime melted into drops, a human form came from these flowing drops with the power of the one who had sent the heat ; he was called Ymir, but the Hrimthursar call him Örgelmir. and the kin of the Hrimthursar have sprung from him.' Gangleri asked, ' How did the kin grow from this, or how came it that there were more men : or dost thou believe in the god of whom thou didst tell now ? ' Hár answered, ' By no means do we think him a god ; he was

---

[1] It is well known that the later Edda bears strong marks of the influence of Christianity, and we quote it with caution and only when it essentially agrees with Voluspa and other parts of the earlier Edda.

bad, and all his kinsmen; we call them Hrimthursar. It is told that when asleep he sweated, and then there grew a man and a woman from under his left arm, and one of his feet begot a son with the other; thence have sprung the kin of Hrimthursar. We call Ymir the Old Hrimthurs."

"Gangleri asked, 'Where did Ymir live, or by what?' 'It happened next when the hoar-frost fell in drops that the cow Audhumla grew out of it; four rivers of milk ran from her teats, and she fed Ymir.'

"Gangleri asked, 'On what did the cow feed?' Hár answered, 'She licked the rime-stones covered with salt and rime, and the first day when she licked them a man's hair came out of them in the evening; the second day a man's head; the third day a whole man was there; he is called Buri; he was handsome in looks, large, and mighty; he had Bor for son, who got Besla, daughter of Bolthorn jötun, for wife, and she had three sons, Odin, Vili,[1] Ve; and it is my belief that this Odin and his brothers are the rulers of heaven and earth. We think he is called so. Thus the man whom we know to be the greatest and most famous is called, and they may well give him this name'" ('Gylfaginning,' c. 5).

The ash tree Yggdrasil is one of the strangest conceptions found in any mythology.

An ash I know standing	Three roots stand
Called *Yggdrasil*,	In three directions
A high tree besprinkled	Under the ash Yggdrasil;
With white loam;	Hel dwels under one,
Thence come the dews	The Hrim-thursar under the second,
That drop in the dales;	Under the third " mortal " men.
It stands evergreen	(Grimnismal).
Spreading over the well of Urd.	

Under it stands the well of wisdom for a drink from which Odin pledges his one eye.

"Gangleri said: 'Where is the head-place or holy place of the Asar?' Hár answered: 'At the ash of Yggdrasil, where the gods give their judgments every day.' Gangleri asked: 'What can be told of that place?' Jafnhár said: 'The ash is the largest and best of trees; its branches spread all over the world and reach up over the heaven; three roots of the tree hold it up and spread very widely. One (of the roots) is with the Asar, another with the Hrimthursar where of yore

---

[1] *Vili*, will; *Ve*, sanctuary, holy place. Cf. also 'Lokasenna,' 26; 'Ynglinga,' c. 3.

Ginnungagap was; the third is over Niflheim, and beneath it is Hvergelmin, but Nidhog gnaws its lower part. Under the root turning towards the Hrimthursar is Mimir's well, in which wisdom and intellect are hidden. Its owner is called Mimir; he is full of wisdom, for he drinks from the well of the horn Gjallar-horn. Odin came and asked for a drink of the well, and did not get it till he pawned his eye."

"What more wonders," asked Gangleri, "may be told of the ash?" Hár answered, "Many wonders. An eagle sits in the limbs of the ash and knows many things; between its eyes sits the hawk Vedrfolnir. The squirrel Ratatösk runs up and down the ash and carries words of envy between the eagle and Nidhòg. Four harts run on the limbs of the ash and eat the buds; they are called Dain, Dvalin, Duneyr, and Durathror. So many serpents are in Hvergelmir with Nidhög that no tongue can number them" (Gylfaginning, c. 16).

Heid in the Voluspa tells about the holy tree, and that the horn of Heimdall is hidden under it till the last fight of the gods. Yggdrasil is watered from the water of the well.

She knows that the blast	She sees it poured over
Of Heimdal is hidden	By a muddy stream
Under the bright	From the pledge of Valfödr;
Holy tree,	Know ye all up to this and onward?

Under the tree lived the three Nornir (Genii), who shape the destinies of men.

Thence come three maidens,	The third Skuld;
Knowing many things,	They carved on wood tablets,
Out of the hall	They chose lives,
Which stands under the tree;	They laid down laws
One was called Urd,	For the children of men,
Another Verdandi,	They chose the fates of men.

Hel was one of the nine worlds, and stood under the ash Yggdrasil, where the dead, who did not die on the battle-field, went. Hence, when a man had died, Hel-shoes were put on his feet for the journey.

Odin goes to the world of Hel, in which was the Gnipa cave, in order to inquire about the fate of his son Baldr who had died.

"Odin threw Hel (daughter of Loki) down into Niflheim, and gave her power over nine worlds; she was to lodge all those who were sent to her, namely, those who died of sickness and old age. She has a large homestead there, and her house-walls are wonderfully high, and her doors are large. Her hall is called Eljúdnir, her plate famine, her knife hunger; ganglati (lazy-goer, idler) her thrall; ganglöt (idler) her bondswoman; her threshhold is called stumbling-block; her bed the couch of one who is bed-ridden; her bed-hangings (ársal) the glittering evil. One half of her body is livid, and the other half skin-colour; therefore she is easily known, and her look is frowning and fierce" (Later Edda, c. 34, Gylfaginning).

"It is the beginning of this Saga that Baldr the Good dreamt great and dangerous dreams about his life. When he told them to the Asar they consulted and resolved to ask for safety for Baldr from every kind of danger; Frigg (Odin's wife) took oaths from fire, water, iron, and every kind of metal, stones, earth, trees, sicknesses, beasts, birds, poison, serpents, that they would spare Baldr's life. When this was done and known, Baldr and the Asar entertained themselves thus: he stood up at the Things and some gods shot at him, or others struck at him or threw stones at him. Whatever they did he was not hurt, and all thought this a great wonder. When Loki Lanfeyjarson saw this he was angry that Baldr was not hurt. He changed himself into a woman's shape and went to Frigg in Fensalir. Frigg asked this woman if she knew what the Asar were doing at the Thing. She said that they all shot at Baldr, and that he was not hurt. Frigg said, 'Weapons or trees will not hurt Baldr; I have taken oaths from them all.' The woman asked, 'Have all things taken oaths to spare Baldr's life?' Frigg answered, 'A bush grows east of Valholl called Mistiltein (mistle-toe); I thought it was too young to take an oath.' The woman went away; but Loki took the mistletoe and tore it up and went to the Thing. Hód (Baldr's brother) stood in the outmost part of the ring of people. Loki said to him, 'Why doest thou not shoot at Baldr?' He answered, 'Because I do not see where he is, and also I am weaponless.' Loki said, 'Do like other men and show honour to Baldr; I will show thee where he stands; shoot this stick at him.' Hod took the mistletoe and shot at Baldr as Loki showed him; it pierced Baldr, who fell dead to the ground. This was the most unfortunate deed that has been done among the gods and men. When Baldr was fallen none of the Asar could say a word or touch him with their hands, and they looked at each other with the same mind towards the one who had done this deed, but no one could take revenge; it was such a place of peace. When they tried to speak the tears came first, so that no one could tell to the other his sorrow in words. Odin suffered most from this loss, because he knew best what a loss and damage to the Asar the death of Baldr was. . . ." (Gylfaginning, c. 49).

"It is to be told of Hermód that he rode nine nights through dark and deep valleys and saw nothing before he came to the river Gjoll[1] and rode on the Gjallar bridge,[2] which is covered with shining gold[3] Modgud is the name of the maiden who guards the bridge; she asked him his name and kin, and said that the day before five arrays of dead men rode over the bridge, 'but the bridge sounds not less under thee alone, and thou hast not the colour of dead men; why ridest thou here on the way of Hel?' He answered, 'I am riding to Hel to seek Baldr, or hast thou seen Baldr on the way of Hel?' She answered that Baldr had ridden over the Gjallar bridge, 'but the way of Hel lies downward and northward.' Hermód rode till he came to the gates of Hel; then he alighted and girthed his horse strongly, mounted and pricked it with the spurs; the horse leaped so high over the gate that it touched nowhere. Then Hermód rode home to the hall, alighted, went in and saw his brother Baldr sitting in a high-seat; he stayed there the night. In the morning Hermód asked Hel to allow Baldr to ride home with him, and told how great weeping there was among the Asar. Hel said she would see if Baldr was as beloved as was told; if all things, living and dead, in the world weep over him, he shall go back to the Asar, but remain with Hel (me) if any refuse or will not weep. Then Hermód rose, and Baldr let him out of the hall and took the ring Draupnir and sent it to Odin as a remembrance, and Nanna[4] sent to Frigg a linen veil and more gifts, and to Fulla a gold ring. Then Hermód rode back to Asgard and told all the tidings he had seen or heard. Thereupon the Asar sent messengers all over the world to ask that Baldr might be wept out of Hel, and all did it, men and beasts, earth and stones, trees, and all metals, as thou must have seen that these things weep when they come from frost into heat. When the messengers went home and had performed their errands well, they found a jötun woman sitting in a cave, called Thökk; they asked her to weep Baldr (out of) Hel; she answered—

Thökk will weep	I never enjoyed
With dry tears	A living or a dead man's son;
The burning voyage of Baldr;	May Hel keep what she has.

---

[1] Gjöll (the sounding one).
[2] Gjallar bridge (the bridge of Gjöll).
[3] Modgud (the valkyrja of anger).

[4] Nanna is told of in Baldr's burning, as she, his wife, was burnt with him.

It is guessed that this was Loki Laufeyjarson, who had caused most evils among the Asar."

" Then also the dog Garm, which is tied in front of Gnipa cave, got loose; he is the greatest terror, he fights Tyr and they kill each other " (Gylfaginning, c. 5).

The wicked seem to have died twice: first they die and get into Hel, then they die again and get into *Niflhel* = *Foggy Hel.* The following is one of the answers of Vafthrudnir to Odin :—

Of the runes[1] of Jötnar	In every world;
And those of all the gods	I have gone to nine
I can tell thee true,	Worlds beneath *Nifl-hel* ;
For I have been	There die the men from *Hel.*

The sides of the rim of heaven communicate with each other by a bridge called Bifröst, or the bridge of the Asar, on which Heimdall, the watchman of the gods, stood.

" Heimdall is the watchman of the gods standing on Bifröst Bridge (the rainbow) " (Later Edda, 27).

" Heimdall is named the White As : he is great and holy ; nine maidens bore him as son, and they were all sisters. He is also called Hallinskidi and Gullintanni (gold tooth). His teeth were of gold, his horse is called gold maned. He lived at a place called Himinbjorg (heaven mountains) by Bifröst. He is the warden of the gods, and sits there at the end of heaven to guard the bridge against the Berg Risar (mountain Jotnar) ; he needs less sleep than a bird, he can see equally by night and by day a hundred leagues away, and he hears when the grass grows, or the wool on the sheep, and all that is louder than these. He has the horn called Gjallarhorn, and his blowing is heard through all worlds. The sword of Heimdall is called Höfud " (Gylfaginning, 27).

We find that the Jotnar and Asar were separated from each other by a large river whose waters never freeze.

Vafthrudnir.	Which divides the land
Tell me, Gagnrad, &c.,	Between the sons of Jötnar and the
How the river is called	gods.

---

[1] In Sigurdrifumal it is said the runes were in the holy mead, sent to Asar, Alfar, and Vanir.

D 2

Odin.

Ifing is the river called
That parts the land
Between the sons of Jotnar and the
    gods;

Open shall it flow
All the days of the world;
No ice will come on it.

From Vafthrudnismal we learn of the origin of Bergelmir who was born before the Creation.

It is an important question which are the most ancient people—the Asar, or the ancient kinsmen of Ymir?

Odin.

Tell me . . .
Who of the Asar,
Or of the sons of Ymir,
Was the oldest in early days?

Vafthrudnir.

Numberless winters
Before the earth was shaped
Was Bergelmir born.
Thrudgelmir
Was his father
And Orgelmir his grandfather.

Odin.

Tell me . . .
Whence first Orgelmir came
Among the sons of Jötnar,
Thou wise Jötun.

Vafthrudnir.

From *Elivagar* [1]
Spurted drops of poison
Which grew into a Jötun;
Thence are our kin
All sprung;
Hence they are always too hideous.

Odin.

Tell me . . .
How that strong Jötun
Begat children
As he had not beheld a *gyg* ? [2]

Vafthrudnir.

In the armpit
Of the Hrim-thursar, it is said,
Grew a maiden and a son;
Foot begat with foot
Of that wise Jotun
A six-headed son.

Odin.

Tell me . . .
What thou earliest rememberest,
Or knowest farthest back;
Thou art an all-wise Jotun.

Vafthrudnir.

Numberless winters
Ere the earth was shaped
Was Bergelmir born;
The first I remember
Is when that wise Jötun
Was laid in the flour-bin [3]

In due course Ymir was slain by Odin. Vili, and Ve, the three sons of Bör, who was himself a Jotun, and therefore of the same kin as Ymir. Having slain Ymir, the sons of Bor

---

[1] Elivagar, the streams flowing from the well Hvergelmir in Niflheim froze into a Jotun.

[2] *i.e.*, a Jotun woman.

[3] A kind of trough used for flour; so the boat is called in which he saved his life as is seen by what follows. In the lay of Hyndla we read:—

    " All Jötnar came from Ymir."

proceeded to make the earth out of his body, and to give the sun, moon, and stars their places in heaven. The flow of his blood was so great as to cause a deluge. Bergelmir was the only one of the Hrim-Thursar who escaped in a boat with his wife, and from him came a new race of Hrim-Thursar.

"The sons of Bör slew the Jötun Ymir, but when he fell there flowed so much blood from his wounds that it drowned the whole race of the Hrim-Thursar, except one who escaped with his household. Him the Jötnar called Bergelmir; he and his wife went on board his ark, and thus saved themselves; from them are descended a new race of Hrim-Thursar" (Later Edda).

After the destruction of the earlier Hrim-Thursar we hear how the sons of Bör created the world, and we are told how the earth and the heavens were made from Ymir.

From Ymir's flesh
The earth was shaped,
And from his blood the sea;
The mountains from his bones;
From his hair the trees,
And the heaven from his skull.

But from his brows
The mild gods made
Midgard for the sons of men;
And from his brain
Were all the gloomy
Clouds created.

(Grimnismal.)

We are also told of the creation of the planets and stars, of our world, of the sea, of the moon, and of day and night. The year was reckoned by winters (vetr), and the days by nights (nott).

The year was divided into months (mánud or mánad).

"*Haustmánud* (harvest-month) is the last before winter; *Gormánud* (gore-month, called thus from the slaughter of cattle then taking place) the first month of winter; *Frermánud* (frost-month); *Hrútmánud* (the ram's month); *Thorri* (the month of waning or declining winter); *Gói, Einmánud* . . . . then *Gaukmánud* or *Sádtíd* (cuckoo-month or sowing-tide); *Eggtíd* or *Stekktíd* (egg-tide or weaning-tide); *Sólmánud* or *Selmánud* (sun-month or sæter-month in which the cattle are removed to the sel or sæter); *Heyjannir* (haymaking-month); *Kornskurdarmánud* (grain-reaping month)" (Skaldskaparmal, c. 63).

The month was subdivided into six weeks; each week contained five days. The days were called—Týsdag = Tuesday; Ódinsdag = Wednesday; Thórsdag = Thursday; Frjádag = Friday; Laugardag (bath-day) or Thváttdag (washing-day) = Saturday.

Odin.

Tell me . . .
Whence the moon came
That walks above men,
And the sun also?

Vafthrudnir.

Mundilfori[1] is called
The father of the moon,
And of the sun also;
Wheel round the heaven
They shall every day,
And tell men of the years.

Odin.

Tell me . . .
Whence the day came
That passes over mankind,
Or the night with her new moons?

Vafthrudnir.

Delling (the bright) is called
The father of *Dag* (the day)
But *Nott* (night) was Norvi's[2]
 daughter;
The full moons and the new ones
The good gods made
To tell men the years.
(Vafthrudnismal.)

The following is the origin of Midgard :—

Ere the sons of Bör
Raised the lands,
They who shaped
The famous *Midgard*;
The sun shone from the south
On the stones of the hall;
Then the ground grew
With green grass.

The sun from the south,[3]
The companion of the moon,
With her right hand took hold
Of the rim of heaven;[4]
The sun knew not
Where she[5] owned halls,
The moon knew not

What power he[6] had;
The stars knew not
Where they owned places.

Then all the powers went
To their judgment seats,[7]
The most holy gods
Counselled about this;
To night and the quarters of the
 moon
Gave they names;
They gave names to
Morning and midday,
To afternoon and eve,
That the years might be reckoned.
(Völuspa.)

Then we have the origin of the wind and of winter. Hræsvelg means the swallower of corpses.

---

[1] Mundilfori, from *mondul* = a handle, and *fara* = to go; the one veering or turning round.

[2] A Jotun.

 Sun, in the north, is of feminine gender, and the moon masculine.

[4] The rim of heaven = the line of the sky from the horizon.

[5] The sun.

[6] The moon.

[7] Rokstól—*stol*, seat or stool; *rok*, judgment.

Odin.

Tell me . . .
Whence the wind comes
Who goes over the waves;
Men do not see him.

Vafthrudnir.

Hræsvelg is called
He who sits at heaven's end,
A Jòtun in an eagle's shape;
From his wings
It is said the wind comes
Over all mankind.

Odin.

Tell me. . .
Whence the winter came,
Or the warm summer,
First with the wise gods.

Vafthrudnir.

Vindsval[1] is called
The father of winter,
And *Svasud*[2] the father of summer.

Another amplification of the Creation is given in Gylfaginning.

Thridi said :

"They took Ymir's skull, and made thereof the sky, and raised it over the earth with four sides. Under each corner they set four Dvergar, which were called Austri, East; Vestri, West; Nordri, North; Sudri, South. Then they took glowing sparks that were loose and had been cast out from Muspelheim, and placed them in the midst of the boundless heaven, both above and below, to light up heaven and earth; they gave resting-places to all fires, and set some in heaven; some were made free to go under heaven, but they gave them a place and shaped their course. In old songs it is said that from that time days and years were reckoned."

The creation of the world, and of the heavens and planets, is followed by that of the Dvergar and of man and woman, who were helpless and fateless (their destinies not having been spun by the Nornir); from these two mankind are descended.

Then all the gods went
To their judgment-seats,
The most holy gods,
And counselled about
Who should create
The host of Dvergar

From the bloody surf[3]
And from the bones of Blain.

There did Modsognir[4]
The mightiest become
Of all Dvergar,

---

[1] Wind-chilly.

[2] Sweet mood.

[3] Bloody surf means poetically the sea, and the expression, the bones of Blain, a name nowhere else mentioned in the earlier Edda, seems to refer to a fight, the record of which is lost to us.

[4] Modsognir and Durin, only mentioned here, refer to some lost myth. There seem to have been three kinds of tribes of Dvergar, having for chiefs, respectively, Modsognir, Durin, Dvalin. "Many *man-likenesses* in the earth," namely Dvergar, who are often described as living under the earth.

And Durin next to him;
They two shaped
Many *man-likenesses*
In the ground,
As Durin has told.[1]

*   *   *

It is time to reckon
Down to Lofar,
For mankind (Gónar),
The Dvergar in Dvalin's host,[2]
Those who went
From the stone-halls,
The host of Aurvangar,
To Jöruvellir (battle-plains).

*   *   *

Until out of that host [3]
To the house [4]
Came three Asar
Mighty and mild;
They found on the ground
Ask and Embla,
Helpless and fateless

They had no breath,
They had no mind,
Neither blood nor motion
Nor proper complexion.
Odin gave the breath,[5]
Hœnir gave the mind,
Lodur gave the blood
And befitting hues.

(Völuspa.)

Finally the Völva describes the end of the world.

Eastward sat the old one
In Jarnvid,[6]
And there bred
The brood of Fenrir;
Of them all
One becomes
The destroyer of the sun
In the shape of a Troll.

He [7] is fed with the lives
Of death-fated men;
He reddens the seat of the gods
With red blood;

The sunshine becomes black
After the summers,
And all weather woe-begone.
Know ye all up to this and onward?

The herdsman of the Jötun woman,
The glad Egdir,
Sat there on a mound
And struck a harp,
A bright-red cock,
Called Fjalar,
Crowed near him
In the bird-wood.

---

[1] The five stanzas (Nos. 11, 12, 13, 15, 16) omitted give a long list of names of Dvergar, among them those of Nyi, the growing moon; Nidi, the waning moon; Nordri, the north, &c.; Althjof, all-thief; Dvalin, the delayer, &c., &c.

[2] The Dvergar clan of Dvalin, who is not mentioned before, seems to have been the highest among all the Dvergar.

From Alvismal we may infer that the Dvergar were related to the Thursar.

[3] There seems to be something missing between the stanzas 16 and 17, unless the poet means the host of the Dvergar, who were under the three above-named chiefs.

[4] It seems that the house in which Ask and Embla were to live was in existence already. *Ask* means ash-tree, like *Yggdrasil; Embla* only occurs here in the Völuspa, and it is most difficult consequently to give a meaning to it; the elm-tree is called *alm*, and perhaps is here meant to be in contrast to the ash.

[5] Odin, Hœnir, and Lodur gave them life. Hœnir is mentioned in the later Edda. Lodur is only mentioned in the beginning of Heimskringla.

[6] Jarnvid, or iron forest; the word is only found here and in the Later Edda. The old one means a Jotun woman, Angrboda, by whom Loki begat the Fenrir wolf ('Later Edda,' c. 34).

[7] The son of Fenrir. According to the prose Edda *Mánagarm* is the name of the son of the Fenrir wolf who swallowed the moon. See Gylfaginning, c. 12.

Crowed for the Asar
Gullinkambi (golden-comb),
He rouses the warriors
At Herjaföðr's (host-father);
But another crows
Under the ground,
A dark red cock,[1]
In the halls of Hel.

Garm barks violently
Before the Gnipa cave;
The fetters will break
And the wolf will run;
She (the Völva) knows many tales.
I see further forward
To the doom of the powers
The dark doom of the gods.

Brothers will fight
And become each other's slayers;
The sons of sisters will
Break blood ties.
It goes hard in the world,
There is much whoredom,

An age of axes, an age of swords;
Shields are cleft;
An age of winds, an age of wolves,
Ere the world sinks;
No man will spare
Another man.

The sons of Mimir are moving
But the end draws near,
By the sound of the ancient
Gjallarhorn.
Heimdall blows loud,
The horn is aloft;
Odin talks with
The head of Mimir.

Shakes the standing
Ash Yggdrasil;
The old tree groans,
And the Jötun (Loki) breaks loose;
All are terrified[2]
In the roads of Hel
Before the kinsman of Surt
Swallows it.

---

[1] A third bird not named lives in the halls of Hel. They represent the Jotnar, the Asar, and the third Hel (the home of the dead), and seem to be the wakers of these three different realms.

[2] The Asar, after taking Loki, bound him to a rock with fetters made of the entrails of his son, Vali (who must not be confused with his namesake, Baldr's brother).

"Now Loki was without any truce taken to a cave. They took three slabs, set them on edge, and made a hole in each. They took the sons of Loki, Vali and Nari or Narfi, and changed Vali into a wolf which tore Narfi asunder. Then they took his entrails and with them tied Loki over the three slabs; one was under his shoulders, another under his loins, the third under his knees, and these bands changed into iron. Then Skadi (a goddess) took a poisonous serpent and fastened it above him, so that the poison should drip into his face; but his wife Sigyn stands at his side, and holds a vessel under the poison-drops. When it is full she goes out to pour it down, but in the meanwhile the poison drips into his face; then he shudders so hard that the whole earth trembles; that you call earthquake. There he lies in bands till the doom of the gods" (Gylfaginning, c. 50).

"Loki begat the wolf
With Angrboda,
And Sleipnir
With Svadilfori;
One monster was thought
Most terrible of all;
It was sprung from
The brother of Býleist (= Loki)."
[Hyndluljóð, 40]

The Asar were afraid of Fenrir wolf, Loki's son, and twice tried to chain it, but could not.

"Thereupon they were afraid that they could not chain the wolf; then Allföðr (Odin) sent the servant Skírnir, the messenger of *Frey*, down to Svartálfaheim (world of the black Álfar) to some Dvergar, and had a chain made, called Gleipnir. It was made of six things: Of the noise of the cat, of the beard of women, of the roots of the mountain, of the sinews of the bear, of the breath of the fish, of the spittle of the bird."

At last they succeeded in chaining it with the chain, but Týr lost his right hand, which he was obliged to put into the mouth of the wolf as a pledge.

"When the Asar saw that the wolf

How is it with the Asar?
How is it with the Alfar?
All Jótunheim rumbles,
The Asar are at the Thing;
The Dvergar moan
Before the stone doors,
The wise ones of the rock wall [1]
Know ye all up to this and onward?

Now Garm barks loud
Before Gnipa cave;
The fetters will break,
And the wolf will run.

Hrym[2] drives from the east,
Holds his shield before him.
The Jormungand[3] writhes
In Jotun wrath;
The serpent lashes the waves,
And the eagle screams;
The pale beak tears the corpses;
Naglfar[4] is loosened.

A keel (a ship) comes from the east,
The men of Muspell   .
Will come across the sea,
But Loki is the steerer,[5]

All the monsters
Go with the wolf,
The brother of Býleist (Loki)
Is in the train.

Surt comes from the south
With the *switch-harm* (fire);
The sun of the gods
Flashes from his sword;
Rocks clash,
The Jotun women stagger;
Men walk the road of Hel;
Heaven is rent asunder.

Then comes the second [6]
Sorrow of Hlin,
When Odin goes
To fight the wolf;
And the bright slayer
Of Beli[7] against Surt;
There will fall
The love of Frigg (Odin).

Now Garm barks loud
Before Gnipa-cave;
The fetters will break,
And the wolf will run.

---

was fully tied they took the band which hung on the chain and was called Gelgja, and drew it through a large slab, called Gjoll, and fastened the slab deep down in the ground. They took a large stone and put it still deeper into the ground; it was called Thviti, and they used it as a fastening pin. The wolf gaped terribly and shook itself violently, and wanted to bite them. They put into its mouth a sword; the guards touch the lower palate and the point the upper palate; that is its gag. It groans fiercely and saliva flows from its mouth and makes the river Von; there it lies till the last fight of the gods" (Later Edda, c. 34).

[1] Dvergar.

[2] Hrym. This name occurs nowhere else.

[3] Jormungand is the world serpent, Midgard's serpent, the son of Loki.

"Angrboda was a Jotun woman in Jotunheimar. Loki begat three children by her: Fenrir wolf, Jormungand, or Midgardsorm, the serpent, and Hel. When the gods knew that these three children

were brought up in Jótunheimar, they had foretellings that great misfortune and loss would be caused by them, and all thought much evil must be expected from them, first on account of their mother, and still more of their father. Allfodr (Odin) sent the gods to take and bring them to him. When they came to him he threw the serpent (Midgardsorm) into the deep sea that lies round all lands, and it grew so much that it lies in the middle of the sea round all lands and bites its tail" (Later Edda, c. 34).

[4] "Naglfar." The ship, said in the Later Edda, Gylfaginning 51, to be made of nails of dead men; when it is finished the end of the world comes.

[5] Loki being the chief enemy of the gods.

[6] The first sorrow is not mentioned. Hlin, a maid of Frigg (see Gylfaginning, 35). Her second sorrow is the death of Odin.

[7] Slayer of Beli = Frey.

Then comes the great
Son of Sigfödr (father of victory)
Vidar to slay,
The beast of carrion.[1]
With his hand he lets
His sword pierce
The heart of the Jötun's son,[2]
Then his father (Odin) is avenged.[3]

Then comes the famous
Son of Hlodyn (Thor);
Odin's son
Goes to fight the serpent;
Midgard's defender (Thor)
Slays him in wrath;
All men will
Leave their homesteads;

The son of Fjorgyn (Thor)
Walks nine paces
Reeling from the serpent
That shuns not heinous deeds.

The sun blackens,[4]
The earth sinks into the sea;
The bright stars
Vanish from heaven;
The life-feeder (fire)
And the vapour rage;
The high heat rises
Towards heaven itself.
Now Garm barks loud[5]
Before Gnipa-cave;
The fetters will break,
And the wolf will run.

(Völuspa.)

After the destruction of the world, a new one will arise.

She[6] beholds rising up
Another time
An earth out of the sea,
An evergreen one.

The waterfalls rush;
Above an eagle flies
Which on the mountains
Catches fish.

The Asar meet
On the Idavöll (plain)
And talk about
The mighty earth-serpent
And there speak of
The great events
And of the old runes
Of Fimbultyr.

---

[1] The wolf Fenrir.

[2] Loki is the father of Fenrir-wolf, who is called the Jotun's son, as Loki was a Jötun.

[3] Odin's son, Vidar, avenges his father by slaying the Fenrir-wolf.

[4] Here the Volva again sees how everything is destroyed. Ragnarok, "the doom of the powers and the end of the world," is mentioned in Lokasenna where Loki is taunting the gods; when he comes to Tyr, the latter answers him——

I have no hand
And thou hast no praise;

We are both badly off;
Nor is the wolf well
That in bands shall
Wait for Ragnarok.

In Atlamal Ragnarok is also mentioned in the dreams of Glaumvor (see p. 462). In the later Edda the word is corrupted by having an "r" added, which gives the meaning of *twilight* instead of *doom* of the gods, as it really meant.

[5] The Volva seems never to tire reminding her hearers that the dog Garm barks loud, &c.

[6] The Volva.

CHAPTER V.

MYTHOLOGY AND COSMOGONY—*continued*.

Norse Cosmogony—Midgard, Asgard, and Mannheim—The Asar and Vanir
—Thor and Tyr—The Goddesses—The Apples of Youth.

WHERE the mythical Odin ends in the Völuspa, if there is any
ending to him, is impossible to tell; it appears that he came
and built an earthly *Midgard*,[1] according to the writer of the
Later Edda who gives the tradition and belief of the people
in his day.

Odin himself was originally a Jötun, and it would appear
from the mythological literature of the North that, for some
reason, he wished to found a new religion, and desired to
proclaim himself chief and spiritual ruler over several, if not
all the tribes before mentioned; this claim, from the account
of the fights which took place, must have been hotly con-
tested. In the history of the birth of every nation, something
similar has taken place, and these struggles are always
described with wonderful and often supernatural accompani-
ments. We are led to believe that a devoted band of followers
attached themselves to Odin's cause, and gradually others
joined him; thus forming a community over which he was the
leader. To protect themselves from their enemies, among
whom, according to the Eddas, were included Jötnar and
Thursar, &c., the Asar erected a wall round their country, and
called the whole enclosed land Midgard.

In the centre of Midgard, Odin built for himself, his family,
chiefs, and councillors, *Asgard*,[2] called also Asaheim (home of
the Asar), and Godheim (home of the gods). *As*, in the
Northern language, afterwards denoted one of the gods, who

---

[1] Midgard—*midi*, middle; *gardr*, yard,
enclosed space; also, courtyard and pre-
mises; a house in a village or town; a
stronghold; a fence or wall; a collection
of houses, a farm

[2] Asgard in olden times meant a place
surrounded by walls, and also a collection of houses enclosed by a fence, hence
the modern name in Scandinavia of gård
for farm. The residence of the gods is
also called by this name in the Edda.

in course of time were also deified, and to whom, as well as to Odin, sacrifices were offered.

Within the walls of Midgard, which encircled Asgard, was *Mannheim*,[1] where Odin's adherents dwelt, and hence the name of their country.

"They gave them clothes and names; the men they called Ash, and the women Embla. From them all mankind is descended, and a dwelling-place was given them under Midgard. In the next place the sons of Bör made for themselves, in the middle of the world, a burgh which is called Asgard, and which we call Troja (there dwelt the gods of their race), and thence resulted many tidings and adventures, both on earth and in the sky. In Asgard is a place called Hlidskjalf, and when Odin seats himself there in the high seat he sees all over the whole world, and what every man is doing, and he knew all things that he saw. His wife was Frigg, and she was the daughter of Fjorgvin, and from their offspring are descended the race which we call *Asar*, who inhabited Asgard the ancient, the realm that surrounds it, and all that race are known to be gods, and for that reason Odin is called Allfather" (Later Edda).

After Midgard had been built for the sons of men, there is a golden age on the *Ida-voll* (plain of movement). Altars and hearths were raised by the Asar, showing that work is conducive to happiness.

The Asar met,	They played chess on the grass-plot;
Who raised on the Idavoll	They were cheerful;
Altars and high temples;	They did not lack
They laid hearths,	Anything of gold
They wrought wealth,	Until three
They shaped tongs,	Very mighty
And made tools.	Thurs maidens came (Nornir)
	From Jotunheim.

Then followed a great battle between the Asar and their neighbours, the Vanir. The Asar seem to have been at first defeated, but afterwards made peace. This fight is the most obscure part of the whole of Voluspa.

That fight remembers she	When they pierced
First in the world,	Gullveig[2] with spears,

---

[1] *Mannheimar* (always in plural *mannheimar*, the singular is *mannheim*) means homes of men

[2] The word *Gullveig* is only found as a compound word this once in the literature of the North. *Gull* = gold; *veig*

And burnt her	Or if all the gods
In the hall of Hár;[1]	Should have a feast.
Thrice they burnt	
The thrice-born one,	
Yet still she lives.	Odin had hurled the spear
	And shot at the host;
Then all the gods went	That was moreover the first
To their judgment seats,	Fight in the world.
The most holy gods,	Broken was the timber wall[3]
And counselled about	Of the Asa-burgh;
Whether the Asar should	The war-exposed plains
Tribute pay,[2]	The Vanir trampled on.

A fight is also mentioned in the Ynglinga Saga which seems to be the same as the one referred to in Völuspa.

"Odin went with a host against the Vanir, but they withstood him well and defended their land. Asar and Vanir got the victory by turns; each waged war in the other's land and plundered. When they became tired of this they appointed a meeting for agreement between themselves, and made peace and gave each other hostages. The Vanir gave their foremost men, Njord the wealthy and his son Frey, and the Asar gave a man called Hœnir, and said he was well fitted to be a chief. He was a tall and very handsome man. The Asar sent with him a man called Mimir, who was very wise; in exchange for him the Vanir gave one, who was the wisest among them, called Kvasir. When Hœnir came to Vanaheim he was at once made chief; Mimir taught him everything. And when Hœnir was at the Things or meetings, and Mimir was not near, and some difficult cases were taken to him, he always gave the same answer, 'Let others say what is to be done.' Then the Vanir suspected that the Asar had deceived them in the exchange of men. They took Mimir and beheaded him, and sent his head to the Asar. Odin took the head and besmeared it with the juice of plants, so that it could not rot. He sang charms over it, and by spells made it so powerful that it spoke with him, and told him many unknown things" (Ynglinga, c. 4).

= draught, also strength. It may be a metaphor for the thirst of gold being the root of evil, and the cause of the first fight and manslaying in the world, as the thirst is never dying.

[1] Hár = Odin.

[2] Here evidently the reference is to the war between the Vanir and the Asar.

This shows that they had been defeated. Feast means sacrifice, which was always followed by the feast; this would imply that they wanted to make a sacrifice for peace or victory.

[3] A stockade made like Danavirki or other strongholds in the north.

Thór was one of the greatest of the Norse gods after Odin ; indeed, these with Frey formed a sort of triad.

"Thór is the foremost of them (the gods) ; he is called Asa-Thór or Öku-Thór. He is the strongest of all gods and men. His realm is Thrúdvángar (= plains of strength), and his hall is called Bilskirnir ; in it there are 540 rooms. It is the largest house built by men. (See Grimnismal.) Thór owns two he-goats, which are called Tanngnjóst (tooth-gnasher) and Tanngrísnir (tooth-gnasher), and a chariot (reid), on which he drives and the he-goats draw it. Therefore he is called Oku-Thór (= the driving Thór). He also owns three costly things. One of them is the hammer Mjolnir which the Hrim Thursar and Berg Risar know when it is aloft, and that is not strange, for he has broken many a head of their fathers or kinsmen. The next best of his costly things is the belt of strength. When he girds himself with it his Asa-strength doubles. He owns a third thing. which is worth much, iron-gloves, without which he cannot hold the handle of the hammer. No man is so wise that he may reckon up all his great feats, but I can tell thee so many tales of him that the hours will be whiled away before I have told all that I know."

" Hár said : ' Furthermore there is an As called Týr. He is the boldest and most daring and has much power over victory in battles. It is useful for valiant men to make vows to him. It is a saying that the one surpassing others in valour and fearing nothing is Tý-brave. He is so wise that the wisest man is called Tý-wise. One of the proofs of his daring is this. When the Asar persuaded the Fenriswolf to allow them to tie it with the chain Gleipnir, it did not believe that they would untie it till they laid Týr's hand into its mouth as a pledge. When they would not untie it then it bit off his hand at the place now called Wolf-joint (wrist). He is therefore onehanded and said not to be the reconciler of men ' " 'Later Edda, Gylfaginning, 21).

The Later Edda differs from the Grimnismal in giving the number of gods or Asar which it mentions. When Gylfi asks how many Asar there are he is told twelve, and the names of Odin, Höd, and Baldr are omitted from the list. Only a few of these gods seem to have been of sufficient prominence to have had sacrifices offered to them, as is seen in the chapter on Religion, and we cannot depend on the Later Edda for reliable information concerning them.

"The Asar went to their feast, and the twelve Asar who were to be judges sat down in the highseats: their names were—Thór, Njörd, Frey, Týr, Heimdall, Bragi, Vidar, Vali, Ull, Hœnir, Forseti, Loki" (Later Edda).

The following extract from the Later Edda gives us the names of the principal goddesses, with their leading characteristics.

"Gangleri said: 'Who are the Asynjar?' Har answered: 'Frigg is the highest; she has a very splendid house called *Fensalir*. The second is Sága, who lives at Sökkvabekk, a large place. The third is Eir; she is the most skilled healer (=physician). The fourth is Gefjon, who is a maiden, and those who die as maidens wait upon her. The fifth is Fulla; she is also a maiden with loose hair, and wears a golden band round her head; she carries the ashen box of Frigg and takes care of her shoe-clothes (=shoes and stockings), and partakes in her secret counsels. Freyja is next in rank to Frigg; she is married to a man called Ód, their daughter is Hnoss; she is so beautiful that fine and costly things are called after her—hnoss. Ód went far off and left Freyja weeping, and her tears are red gold. She has many names; that is because she called herself by different names when she went among foreign nations in search of Ód; she is called Mardoll, Horn, Gefn, and Sýr. She owns the *Brisinga* necklace. She is called *Vanadis* (dis (goddess) of the Vanir). The seventh is Sjofn; she applies herself much to turning the minds of men to love, both males and females; from her name a loving mind is called *sjafni*. Lofn is so mild and good to invoke that she gets Allfodr (Ódin) or Frigg to allow the marriages of men, male and female, though they have been forbidden or flatly refused; from her name is lof (leave), and that which is lofat (= praised) by men. Vár listens to the oaths of men and the private agreements which men and women make between themselves; these are called *várar*, and she punishes those who break them. Vor is wise and asks many questions, so that nothing can be hidden from her; when a woman knows a thing she is *vor* (= aware) of it. Syn guards the door of the hall (Valhalla) and shuts it to those who are not to enter; therefore when some one denies a thing he is said to put down *syn* (= negation, refuse). Hlin has to guard the men whom Frigg wishes to save from danger. Snotra is wise and of good manners; a wise man or woman is called *snotr* from her name. Gna, Frigg sends into various worlds on her errands; she has a horse which runs on air and water, called *Hófhvarfnir* (= hoof-turner)" ('Later Edda,' Gylfaginning, 35).

The gods, it would seem, had it in their power, if not to secure everlasting life, at least to retain perpetual youth, unlike poor Tithonus of the well-known Greek myth. It may not be inappropriate to continue here the legend relating to this. Idun, the wife of Bragi, who was celebrated for his wisdom and eloquence, kept in a box the apples which when the gods felt old age approaching they ate in order that they might keep their youth till Ragnarök.

"Odin, Loki and Hœnir went from home over mountains and uninhabited land, and it was not easy for them to get food. When they came down into a valley they saw a herd of oxen, took one of them and prepared it for the fire. When they thought it was cooked they took it off, but it was not cooked. A second time, after waiting a little, they took it off, and it was not cooked. They considered what might be the cause of this. Then they heard a voice in the tree above them which said that he who sat there caused this. They looked up, and a large eagle sat there. The eagle said: 'If you will give me my fill of the ox, it shall be cooked.' They assented, and the bird came slowly down from the tree, sat down on the hearth, and at once gobbled up the four shoulder-pieces of the ox. Loki got angry, took a large pole, raised it, and with all his strength struck the eagle. At the blow the eagle flew into the air. The pole adhered to its body, and the hands of Loki to one end of it. The eagle flew so that Loki's feet touched the rocks, the stone-heaps and the trees. He thought his hands would be torn from his shoulders. He shouted, eagerly asking the eagle to spare him, but it answered that Loki would never get loose unless he swore to make Idun leave Asgard with her apples. Loki promised this, got loose and went to his companions, and no more tidings are told about their journey till they reached home. At the appointed time Loki enticed Idun to go to a wood out of Asgard by saying he had found apples which she would prefer to her own, and asked her to take her own apples with her to compare them. Thjassi Jótun then came in an eagle's shape and took Idun and flew away to his abode in Thrymheim. The Asar were much grieved at the disappearance of Idun, and soon became grey-haired and old. They held a *Thing* and asked each other for news of Idun. The last seen of her was when she walked out of Asgard with Loki. He was brought to the *Thing* and threatened with death or torture. He got afraid and said he would fetch Idun from Jötunheim, if Freyja would lend him the hawk-skin which she owned. When he got it he flew north to Jötunheim, and one day came to Thjassi Jötun, who was sea-fishing. Idun was alone at home. Loki changed her into a nut, held her in his claws and flew as fast as he could. When the Asar saw the hawk flying with the nut and the eagle pursuing they went to the Asgard-wall and carried thither bundles of plane-shavings. When the hawk flew into the burgh it came down at the wall. The Asar set fire to the plane-shavings, but the eagle could not stop when it lost the hawk, and the fire caught its feathers and stopped it. The Asar were near, and slew Thjassi inside the Asgard-wall, which is a very famous deed. Skadi, his daughter, took helmet and brynja and a complete war-dress, and went to Asgard to avenge her father. The Asar offered her reconciliation and *wergild*,[1] and first that she might choose a husband from among them, not seeing more than their feet. She saw a pair of very beautiful feet, and said : 'This one I choose ; few things can be ugly in Baldr.' But it was Njörd of Nóatún." (Later Edda, Bragarœdur, c. 56.)

---

[1] Wergild, indemnity.

CHAPTER VI.

ODIN OF THE NORTH.

The Odin of the North—The forefathers of the English—Their migration from the shores of the Black sea—The geographical knowledge of the Norsemen—Tyrkland the home of Odin—Sigrlami, one of the sons of Odin—Odin establishes his family in the North—Death of Odin in the North—Attributes of Odin—Poetical names of Odin—Sleipnir, the horse of Odin—Odin as a one-eyed man.

In the Norse literature we find Odin referred to not only as a god, but as a hero and leader of men. It is not necessary to believe that any real person of the name of Odin ever existed, but from the frequency with which a migration northwards is mentioned, and from the details with which it is described, it is legitimate to infer that the predecessor of the Norsemen came from the south or south-east of Europe—probably, to judge from literature and archæology combined, from the shores of the Black Sea.

At the time of Odin's arrival in the North we find not only a country called Gardariki, which is often mentioned in the Sagas, and seems to have adjoined the south-eastern shores of the Baltic, but also the large Scandinavian peninsula and that of Jutland, and the islands and shores of the Baltic, populated by a seafaring people whose tribes had constant intercourse with each other, and, to judge by the finds, seem to have had an identical religion. These people intermarried with the Asar who came north with Odin, and hence arose tribes called half-Risar and half-Troll.

"It is written in old books that Alfheimar[1] were north in Gandvik and Ymisland, between it and Hálogaland. And before the Tyrkjar and Asiamen came to the Northern lands, Risar and half-Risar lived there; then the nations (peoples)

---

[1] Alfheimar. In one text, Jötunheimar. In later times Risar, Troll, and Dvergar became synonymous with giants, dwarfs, and wizards.

were much mixed together; the Risar got wives from Mannheimar, and some of them married their daughters there" (Hervarar Saga, ch. i.).

The account given in the Hervarar Saga agrees with that in the Ynglinga Saga, which is important not only as giving an idea of the conception the people of the North had of our world, but as describing the names of the lands and countries mentioned in the earlier Eddas and Sagas.

"The round of the world on which men dwell is much cut by the sea; large seas stretch from the outer sea round the earth into the land. It is known that a sea runs from Njörva-sund (Straits of Gibraltar) all·the way up to Jorsalaland (the land of Jerusalem). From it a long bay runs north-east, called the Black Sea, which separates the three parts of the world; the part east of it is called Asia, but the one west of it is called Europa by some, and Enea by others. North of the Black Sea is the great or the cold Sweden; some say that Sweden is no smaller than Serkland (the land of Saracens) the great; some say she is as large as Blaland (the land of the blue (black) men) the great. The northern part of Sweden is uninhabited, on account of frost and cold, as the southern part of Blaland is on account of the sun's burning heat. In Sweden there are many large herads (districts).

There are also many kinds of people and many tongues; there are Asar, Dvergar, and Blamenn (blue (black) men), and many kinds of strange people; there are beasts and dragons wonderfully large. From the north, in mountains which are beyond all settlements, a river springs that flows through Sweden; its right name is Tanais; it was in old times called Tanakvísl,[1] or Vana-kvísl; it flows into the Black Sea. The land round Vanakvísl was then called Vanaland or Vanaheim (home or world of the Vanir). This river[2] separates the two-thirds of the world; east of it is Asia, and West of it is Europa" (Ynglinga Saga, 1).

"A large mountain ridge runs from north-east to south-west; it separates Sweden the Great[3] from other lands. South of the mountain, not far off, is Tyrkland; there Odin owned a great deal of land. At that time the chiefs

---

[1] Kvisl—a forked river, one of the forks where they unite—it also means a branch of a tree.

Vana-kvisl means the river of the Vanir; it is supposed now that it was the river Don which flows into the Sea of Azow, but it is doubtful.

[2] This was probably the river Don, which is near the Ural Mountains.

[3] Svíthjód the Great seems to be Russia—Norway, Sweden, perhaps Denmark and the shores of the Baltic.

of the Rómverjar (Romans) went widely about the world and underlaid (conquered) all nations; and many chiefs on that account left their lands. As Odin was foreknowing and skilled in witchcraft he knew that his descendants would live in the northern part of the world. Then he set his brothers Vili and Vé to rule Asgard; he left, and all the Díar with him, and many folk. First he went westwards to Gardaríki, then southwards to Saxland. He had many sons; he became owner of land at many places in Saxland, and left his sons to defend Saxland. Then he went northwards to the sea and settled on an island; that place is now called Odinsey (Odin's island) in Fjón (Fýen). Then he sent Gefjon [1] northwards across the Sound to discover lands; she came to Gylfi, and he gave her one plough-land. Then she went to Jotunheim and there got four sons by a Jötun; she changed them into oxen, and harnessed them to the plough, and drew the land out to sea, and westwards, opposite to Odinsey, and the land is called Selund (Zealand); she afterwards lived there. Skjold, a son of Odin, married her; they lived at Hleidra (Leire). There is a lake or sea called Lög (Màlaren). The fjords in the Log lie as the nesses in Selund. When Odin heard that Gylfi's land was good he went there, and he and Gylfi made an agreement, for Gylfi thought he had not strength enough to withstand the Asar. Many devices and spells did Odin and Gylfi use against each other, and the Asar always got the better of them. Odin took up his abode at the Log (Malaren), which is now called the old Sigtúnir; there he made a great temple and sacrificed according to the custom of the Asar. He gave abodes to the temple-priests; Njörd lived at Nóatún, Frey at Uppsalir, Heimdall at Himinbjörg, Thor at Thrúdvang, Baldr at Breidablik; he gave good abodes to them all" (Ynglinga, c. 5).

While Odin, according to the sages, was in Sweden [2] his son Sigrlami ruled over Gardaríki; during the life of his father or after his death he had to fight against the Jotnar, and, like Skjold his brother, he married a daughter of King Gylfi, who ruled over the present Sweden, whose authority is made to extend to the principal islands which form part of the present Denmark.

"At this time the Asia-men and Tyrkjar came from the east and settled in the northern lands; their leader was

[1] Gefjon was one of the Asynjur.
[2] Svithjód=Sweden, but it can hardly be taken in these early Sagas as exactly corresponding to modern Sweden.

called Odin; he had many sons, and they all became great and strong men. One of his sons was called Sigrlami; to him Odin gave the realm now called Gardaríki; he became a great chief over that land; he was handsomer than any man. He was married to Heid, the daughter of King Gylfi; they had a son called Svafrlami." (Hervarar, c. 2).

Sigrlami fell in a fight against Thjassi the Jòtun. When Svafrlami heard of his father's death he took for himself all his realm, and became a powerful man. It is said that on one occasion when riding in a forest he chased a stag for a long time, and did not kill it until sunset, when he had ridden so far into the forest that he lost his way. He saw a large stone and two Dvergar beside it, whom he was going to sacrifice to the gods, but on their begging to be allowed to give a ransom for their lives Svafrlami asked their names. One was called Dyrin, the other Dvalin. Svafrlami at once recognised them to be the most skilful of Dvergar, and insisted upon their making a sword for him, the hilt to be of gold, and the scabbard to be ornamented and inlaid with gold. The sword was never to fail, and never to rust; to cut iron and stone as well as cloth: and it was to bring victory in all battles and duels (einvigi) to every one who carried it.

On the appointed day Svafrlami came to the rock; the Dvergar gave him the sword; but Dvalin, standing in the door of the stone, said: "Thy sword, Svafrlami, shall be a man's bane (death) every time it is drawn; and with it shall be performed the greatest nithing's deed; it also will be thy death." Svafrlami then struck at the Dvergar so that both edges of the sword entered into the rock, but the Dvergar ran into the rock. Svafrlami, we are told, called the sword Tyrfing, and carried it in battles and single fights; with it he killed in a duel Thjassi the Jotun, his father's slayer, whose daughter Frid he married" (Hervarar Saga, c. 3).

We not only have accounts of how this Odin established his family in the North, but also how he died there. Feeling that his days were coming to an end, he prepared to die on a pyre, as was the custom of those times; and we find the belief existed that after his death he returned to the old Asgard.

"Odin fell sick and died in Sweden. When he was at death's door he let himself be marked (wounded) with a spear-point, and said he was the owner of all the men slain by weapons, and would go into Godheim (the world of the gods), and there welcome his friends. Now the Swedes thought he had gone to the old Asgard, and would live there for ever. Then there again arose worship of Odin, and vows were made to him. The Swedes often thought he appeared to them in dreams on the eve of great battles; to some he gave victory, others he invited home; either of these alternatives was considered good. After death he was burnt with great splendour.[1] It was their belief that the higher the smoke rose in the air the more glorious would the burnt man be in heaven,[2] and the more property that was burnt with him the wealthier would he be " (Ynglinga Saga, c. 10).

Whether a hero and leader of the name of Odin ever lived or not we cannot tell, but that we know from the records the people believed that he and the Asar had existed, and the creed they had established was their religion; and this belief lasted with many to the end of the pagan era, which did not entirely disappear till the twelfth century. Odin and some of the Asar were deified and worshipped in all the countries of the North, and with the lapse of time their fame increased.

"Odin was a mighty warrior and travelled far and wide, and became owner of many realms (countries). He was so successful that in every battle he gained the victory, and at last his men believed that in every battle victory was in his power. It was his custom, when he sent his men into fight or on other errands, first to lay his hands on their heads and give them bjanak;[3] they believed that luck would then be with them. Also it happened that whenever his men were in need on land or at sea they called on his name, and always felt relieved by it; for every kind of help they looked to him. He often went so far away that he was on a journey many seasons" (Ynglinga, c. 2).

"It is said with truth that when Asa-Odin, and with him the Díar,[4] came into the northern lands, they began and taught those ídróttir[5] which men afterwards long practised. Odin was the foremost of them all, and from him they learned the *idróttir*, for he first knew them all, and more than any other. He was highly honoured on account of the following things. He looked so fair and noble when he sat with his friends that

---

[1] People were buried with their wealth.

[2] The one who owned the burning in the text. Heaven means space, not a blessed abode.

[3] This word is not found elsewhere in Scandinavian literature.

[4] See priest.

[5] Idróttir, a name for all kinds of athletic and intellectual games.

every mind was delighted; but when he was in a host, then he looked fierce to his foes. This was because he knew the ídróttir of changing looks and shapes in any way he liked. Another of his ídróttir was that he spoke with such skill and so glibly that all who listened thought it the only truth; he always spoke in poetry (hendingar) like that which now is called skáldskap (skaldship, poetry). He and his temple-priests are called Ljódasmidir (lay-smiths, song-smiths), for that ídrótt came from them into the northern lands. Odin had power to cause his foes to grow blind or deaf or full of fear, and to make their weapons bite no more than wands (sticks of wood). His own men fought without armour madly, like dogs or wolves, bit their shields, and had the strength of a bear or bull; they cut down the foe, and neither fire nor iron hurt them. That is called berserksgang (rage or fury of Berserks)" (Ynglinga, c. 6-7).

In the poetical language of the Sagas and Eddas a very great number of figurative names are given to Odin, which show how numerous his attributes were believed to be, and many of which recall the language of Homer; among them we may mention :—

The thunderer.[1]	The feared one.	The god of hosts.
Father of ages.	The rover.	The father of all.
The wise walker.	The serpent (from his being able to assume its shape).	The wish-god.
The lord		The wind-whispering.
The helmet bearer.		The burner.
The cheerful.	The soother.	The wide-ruling.
The loving one.	God of the hanged.[2]	The work-skilled.
The high one.	God of the ravens.	The swift-riding.
The fickle.	God of victory.	The god of battle.
The true-guessing one.	God of the Gautar.	The almighty god.
The evil-eyed.	The shouting god.	The host blinder.
The manifold.	The one-eyed one.	The true one.
The wise in beguiling.	The fierce one.	The long-bearded.
The much knowing.	God of the earth.	The god of cargoes.
The father of victory.	Friend of Mimir.	The father of hosts.
The father of the slain.	The foe of the Fenrir-wolf.	The useful adviser.
The conqueror in fights.		The shaper of battle.
The entangler.	The lord of the spears.	The swift rider.

"Then Thridi said: Odin is the highest and oldest of the Asar; he rules over everything, and, however mighty the

---

[1] We must here remark that nowhere is Thor called the God of Thunder.

[2] See Havamal, the lord of the gallows; see Havamal where he is said to have hung on a tree.

other gods are, they all serve him as children a father. Frigg, his wife, knows the fates of men though she cannot prophesy. Odin is called Allfödr, because he is the father of all the gods; he is also called Valfödr, because all those who fall in battle (valr = the slain) are his chosen sons. These he places in Valhöll and Vingólf (a hall owned by the goddesses), and then they are called Einherjar. He is also called Hanga-gud (god of the hanged), Hapta-gud (god of the chained), and Farma-gud (god of cargoes), and he gave himself still more names when he was at King Geirrod's Gangleri said: 'Wonderfully many names have you given to him, and surely it needs great wisdom to know the events which are the reasons of every one of these names.' Hár answered: 'Great wits are needed to explain this carefully, but, to tell it shortly, most of the names have been given because, as there are many different tongues in the world, every nation thinks it necessary to change his name according to their language, that they may invoke and pray to him for themselves. His journeys have given rise to some of these names, and they are told among people'" (Later Edda, c. 20).

"Two ravens[1] sit on his shoulders and tell into his ears all the tidings, which they see or hear; these are Hugin and Munin. At the dawn of day he sends them out to fly all over the world, and they come back at day-meal time (the biggest meal of the day); hence he knows many tidings; therefore he is called Hrafnagud (Raven-god)" (Gylfaginning, c. 38).

Among the earlier myths connected with Odin may be mentioned the following account of the origin of his horse Sleipnir.

"Gangleri asked: 'Who owns Sleipnir the horse, or what hast thou to tell of him?' Hár answered: 'Thou knowest nothing about Sleipnir nor whence he sprang, but it will seem

---

[1] Grimnismál, 19-20, also mentions these ravens.

19.

The battle-tamer (Odin) feeds
Geri and Freki,
The famous father of hosts (Herjafödr)
And by wine alone
The weapon-famous
Odin always lives.

20

Hugin and Munin
Fly every day
Over the wide earth;
I am afraid Hugin
Will not come back,
But still more of Munin.

Poetical names were given to these ravens by Eyvind Skalda-spillir; they are called the Swans of Farmatýr (the god of cargoes), i.e., the Swans of Odin.

to thee worth a hearing. In early times when the gods had built up Midgard and made Valhalla there came a smith who offered to make a burgh for them in three seasons (half-years) so good that it would be strong and safe against

Fig. 1.—Earlier runic stone at Tjängvide, Gotland, with the eight-footed horse of Odin. —Height about 5 feet ; width, 4 feet 4 inches ; thickness, 1 foot. Another similar stone with representation (in relief) of an eight-footed horse has been found also in Laivide in Gotland.

Bergrisar (mountain-jötnar) and Hrimthursar, though they entered Midgard. In the place of wages he wanted to marry Freyja and get the sun and moon. The Asar came together to counsel among themselves, and it was agreed with the smith that he should get what he wanted if he could make the burgh in one winter, but if any part of it was unfinished on the first day of summer he was to lose his pay; he would not be allowed to use the help of any man in the work. When they told him these conditions he asked leave to make use of his horse Svadilföri; on the advice of Loki this was conceded to him. The first day of winter he began to build the burgh, and during night he carried stones on his horse to it; the Asar wondered much how the horse could drag such large rocks, and it did much more work than the smith. Strong witnesses were brought and many oaths were taken at their agreement, because the jötun thought it unsafe to stay with the Asar if Thor, who had gone to Austrveg (eastern countries) to kill Jötnar, should come home. As the winter passed the building of the burgh proceeded, and it was so high and strong that it could not be taken. When three days of the winter were left it was almost all finished except the gate. Then the gods sat down on their judgment-seats and tried to find an expedient; one asked the other on whose advice Freyja was to be married in Jötunheimar and air and heaven defiled by taking sun and moon away and giving them to the Jötnar; they all agreed that the causer of most evils, Loki Lanfeyjarson, had caused this, and that he deserved an evil death if he did not find a way to cause the smith to lose his pay. They rushed at Loki, who got afraid, and took oaths that he would manage, whatever it might cost him, that the smith should lose his pay. The same evening when the smith drove out with his horse Svadilföri, to fetch stones, a mare ran out of the wood towards it and neighed to it. When the stallion saw what kind of horse this was he got wild, tore his ropes and ran towards it; the mare ran into the wood, and the smith followed and wanted to get hold of it, but the horses continued running all night, and no work was done that night; next day, as before, the work did not proceed. When the smith saw that the work could not be finished he got into Jötun-fury. When the Asar knew for certain that he was a Bergrisar (mountain jötun), they could not keep their oaths and called Thor; he came at once, and then the hammer Mjollnir went aloft; he paid him for the work, not by giving him the sun and moon, but by preventing him from living in Jötunheimar; at his first blow the jötun's skull was broken into small bits, and he was sent down to Nifl-hel. But Loki had had such dealings with Svadilföri that he gave birth to a foal; it was grey, and with eight feet, and it is the best horse among gods and men " (Gylfaginning, 41–42).

Odin was believed not only to give victory to his favourites, but other gifts, and is represented as coming to the aid of his followers, in the guise of an one-eyed old man—

Ride shall we	Eloquence to manv,
To Valhalla,	And wisdom to men ;
To the holy place.	Fair winds to warriors,
Let us ask the father of hosts	And song to poets,
To be kind (to us) ;	And luck in love
He pays and gives	To many a man.
Gold to his host ;	
He gave to Hermód	She (Freyja) will worship Thór,
A helmet and brynja,	And ask him
And to Sigmund	That he always
He gave a sword.	Be at peace with thee ;
	Though he is no friend
He gives victory to his sons,	To the jótun-brides.[1]
And wealth to some ;	

[Hyndluljód.]

" King Siggeir ruled Gautland ; he was powerful and had many men ; he went to King Volsung and asked him to give Signy to him in marriage. The king and his sons received this offer well ; she herself was willing, but asked her father to have his way in this as in other things referring to herself. Her father made up his mind that she should be married, and she was betrothed to Siggeir. The wedding-feast was to be at King Volsung's, and Siggeir was to come to him. The king prepared as good a feast as he could. When it was ready the guests and Siggeir's men came on the appointed day ; Siggeir had many men of rank with him. It is said that great fires were made along the hall,[2] and the large tree before mentioned stood in the middle of the hall, and that when men were sitting before the fires in the evening a man walked into the hall whom they did not know. He wore a spotted hekla (frock) ; he was barefooted, and had linen breeches fastened to his legs ; he had a sword in his hand, and wore a hood low down over his face ; he was very grey-haired, and looked old, and was one-eyed.[3] He went to the tree, and drew the sword, and stuck it into the trunk so that it sank up to the hilt. No man dared to speak to him. He said : ' He who pulls this sword out of the trunk shall get it as a gift from me, and will find that he never had a better sword in his hand than this one.' The old man then went out, and no one knew who he was, or where he went. Then all the foremost men tried to

---

Because he was always fighting against the Jotnar.

[2] The fires were always in the centre, lengthwise.

[3] This man was Odin, who is always represented as having only one eye.

pull out the sword, and could not. Sigmund, the son of King Völsung, pulled it out as easily as if it had been quite loose. No man had seen so good a sword, and Siggeir offered three times its weight in gold for it. Sigmund answered that he should have pulled it out; now he should never get it, though he offered all the gold he owned " (Volsunga, c. 3).[1]

Of Odin it is said

" Odin changed shapes; then his body lay as if sleeping or dead, and he was in the shape of a bird or a beast, a fish or a serpent, and in the twinkling of an eye went into far-off lands on his own errands or on those of other men. Besides, he could, with words only, extinguish fire, calm the sea, and turn the winds into whatever direction he wished. He had a ship called Skídbladnir, on which he crossed large seas; it could be folded together like cloth.[2] He had with him Mimir's head, which told him many tidings (news) from other worlds. Sometimes he raised (awaked) dead men out of the earth (ground), or sat down beneath hanged men (hanging in gallows);[3] therefore he was called the lord (dróttin) of the ghosts or of the hanged[3] He had two ravens, which he taught to speak, and they flew far and wide over lands (countries) and told him many tidings. Therefore be became very wise. So much lewdness followed this witchcraft when it was practised that it was thought a disgrace for men to practise it; and the priestesses (gydjur) were taught the idrótt. Odin knew where property was hidden in the ground, and he knew songs by which he unlocked (opened) the earth, the rocks, and the stones, and the mounds, and bound (held fast) with mere words those who dwelt in them, and went in and took what he wished. On account of these powers he became very famous; his foes feared him, but his friends trusted in him and believed in him and his power. He taught most of his idróttir to the sacrificing-priests; they were next to him in all wisdom and witchcraft. Many others, however, learned a great deal of them, and from them witchcraft has spread widely and been kept up long. But men worshipped Odin and the twelve chiefs (hofdingï) and called them their gods, and believed in them long afterwards " (Ynglinga Saga, ch. 7.)

---

[1] Cfr. also Volsunga Saga, c. 11.

[2] The story of Odin's ship reminds one of the tent mentioned in the ' Arabian Nights,' which could cover an army, and yet could be folded and carried in a small pocket.

[3] Odin himself hung in Yggdrasil to learn wisdom, and this is a like custom (Havamal, 139); it seems that Odin learned wisdom from the one hanging in the gallows by sitting under it.

CHAPTER VII.

THE SUCCESSORS OF ODIN OF THE NORTH.

Njörd the successor of Odin—Frey succeeds Njörd—A great temple built at
Uppsalir by Frey—The ship of Frey—Death of Frey—Frey's death kept
secret from the people—Freyja, the priestess—Fjolnir, the son of Yngvi
Frey—Svegdir—Genealogies of the Norse chiefs from Odin Skjöld, the
founder of the Danish branch of chiefs.

ACCORDING to the sagas, after the death of Odin, Njörd of
Nóatún became the ruler of the Swedes.

"Thereupon Njörd of Nóatún became ruler over the Swedes,
and continued the sacrifices; the Swedes called him their
dróttin (lord); he gathered taxes from them. In his days
there was very good peace, and seasons were so good in every
respect that the Swedes believed that Njörd ruled over good
seasons and the wealth and welfare of men. In his days most
of the Díar died, and all of them were afterwards burnt and
sacrificed to. Njörd fell sick and died; he also let himself be
marked (with a spear) before he died, as a token that he
belonged to Odin The Swedes burnt him, and wept very much
over his mound " (Ynglinga, c. 11).

"Njörd of Nóatún then begat two children. His son was
Frey and his daughter Freyja. They were beautiful in looks
and mighty. Frey is best of the Ásar. He rules the rain
and the sunshine, and also has power over the growth of the
ground. It is good to make vows to him for good seasons
and peace. He also rules over men's fortune in property."
(Gylfaginning, c. 24.)

In Vafthrudnismal Odin asks Vafthrudnir the origin of
Njörd.

Odin.	*Vafthrudnir.*
Tell me . . .	In Vanaheim
Whence Njörd came	The wise powers shaped him,
Among the sons of Asar;	And gave him to the gods as a
He rules hundred-fold	hostage;
Temples and altars	At the doom of the world
And he was not born among	He will come back again,
Asar.	Home to the wise Vanir.

The Njórd who is related to have been punished by uncontrollable sadness for falling in love with Gerd and sitting on Odin's high-seat is a mythical Njord.

"A man was called Gýmir whose wife Orboda was of Berg (mountain) Risar kin. Their daughter Gerd was the most beautiful of all women. One day Frey had gone to *Hlidskjalf* [1] and could see over all worlds. When he looked to the North he saw on a farm a large and fine house towards which a woman was walking. When she lifted her arms, opening the door, a light shone from them on the sea, and the air and all worlds were brightened from her. His great boldness in sitting down in the holy seat thus was revenged upon him, for he went away, full of sorrow. When he came home he did not speak or sleep or drink and no one dared question him. Then Njörd called to him Skirnir, the shoe-boy of Frey, and told him to go to Frey, address him and ask with whom he was so angry that he would not speak to men. Skirnir said he would go, though not willingly, as unfavourable answers might be expected from him. When he came to Frey he asked why he was so sad and did not speak to men. Frey answered that he had seen a beautiful woman and for her sake he was so full of grief that he would not live long if he should not get her. 'Now thou shalt go and ask her in marriage for me and take her home hither whether her father is willing or not; I will reward it well.' Skirnir answered that he would undertake this message if Frey gave him his sword. This sword was so good that it fought of itself. Frey did not fail to do this and gave it to him. Skirnir then went and asked the woman in marriage for him and got her promise that she would come after nine nights and keep her wedding with Frey. When Skirnir had told Frey of his journey Frey sang :

Long is one night,	Often a month to me
Long is another,	Shorter seemed
How can I endure three ?	Than one half of this wedding-night.

(Later Edda, Gylfaginning, 37)

After the death of Njórd, Frey, one of his sons, succeeded him as high priest of the sacrifices, and, according to tradition, built the great temple at Upsala, which became of great repute as a most holy place among the people of the North, who came

---

[1] A high seat from which Odin could see over all worlds. (Gylfaginning, 17) In the older Edda there is a long poem, Skirnismál or Skirnisfor, on the story of Njörd falling in love with Gerd.

from all parts of the country to assist at the sacrifices. The Sagas say that great Things were held there, all important quarrels settled, friendship sealed, and peace concluded between chieftains and countries.

"Frey took the realm after Njörd; he was called the dróttin of the Swedes, and took taxes of them. He was as well liked as his father, and in his days also were good seasons. Frey raised a large temple at Uppsalir, and had his head burgh (höfud stad) there; all his taxes, lands, and loose property he gave thereto. That was the beginning of the Uppsalir wealth, which has been kept up ever since.

"In his days the peace of Fródi[1] (King in Denmark) began; then there were good seasons in every land. The Swedes attributed that to Frey. He was worshipped more than other gods, because in his days the people of the land became wealthier than before, on account of the peace and the good seasons. His wife was called Gerd, daughter of Gýmir;[2] their son was Fjölnir. Another name of Frey was Yngvi; this name was long afterwards used among his kin as a name of honour, and his kinsmen were afterwards called Ynglingar. Frey fell sick; when he was near death they took counsel and allowed few men to see him; they made a large mound ready for him with a door and three holes. When Frey was dead they carried him secretly into the mound and told the Swedes that he was alive, and kept him there for three winters. They poured all the taxes into the mound, the gold through one hole, the silver through another, and the brass pennings through the third. Then peace and good seasons continued" (Ynglinga, c. 12).

"When all the Svíar knew that Frey was dead, and peace and good seasons continued, they believed it would last while Frey was in Svithjód, and would not burn him, and called him the god of the world (veraldar god), and sacrificed ever since chiefly to him for good seasons and peace" (Ynglinga, c. 13).

After the death of Frey, Freyja, the daughter of Njörd, became the priestess, and offered the sacrifices.

"Freyja upheld the sacrifices, for she alone of the godar was then living, and she became so renowned that all high-born

---

[1] The peace of Frodi, so called from the chief who ruled Denmark at the time, and who must have become very celebrated.

[2] Gymir, a jotun of whom nothing is known.

women are called *fruvor*.[1] Thus every woman is the freyja of her property, and she who has a household is hús-freyja[2] (house-wife). Freyja was rather many-minded (fickle); her husband was Ód; her daughters were Hnoss (costly thing) and Gersemi (precious thing); they were very beautiful, and the costliest things are called by their names" (Ynglinga, c. 13).

According to the Ynglinga, Yngvi Frey was the son of Njord, and Fjölnir the son of Yngvi Frey. Fjölnir ruled over the Swedish and Upsala domain, and died in Zeeland. A strong friendship existed between him and Fródi the grandson of Skjold, the son of Odin, and it was the custom of these two chiefs to visit each other.

"Fjölnir the son of Yngvi Frey then ruled over the Swedes and the Upsala-wealth; he was a powerful king, and peace-happy and season-happy. At that time Peace-Fródi was at Hleidra (Leire); they were friends and invited each other. When Fjölnir came to Fródi in Zeeland there was a great feast prepared for him, and people were invited to it from far and wide. Fródi had a large house; in it there had been a large vat, many feet high, held together by large timbers; it stood in the lower story, and there was a loft above in which there was an opening through which the drink could be poured in; the vat was full of mixed mead,[3] a very strong drink. In the evening Fjölnir and his men were shown to their room on the next loft. In the night he went out on the svalir (a kind of balcony) to look for something; he was overcome with sleep and dead-drunk. When he returned to his room he walked along the balcony to the door leading into the next room, and there he missed his footing and fell into the mead-vat and perished" (Ynglinga, c. 14).

Svegdir succeeded his father, Fjölnir, and though several generations had passed away since the death of the last Odin, the veneration towards Asgard, the old home of the earlier Odin, was strong in the heart of the people.

"This Sweden they called Mannheimar (the world of men), but the large Sweden they called Godheimar (the world of gods); from Godheimar many tidings and wonders were told" (Ynglinga, c. 10).

"Svegdir took the realm after his father; he made a vow

---

[1] A lady is still called *fru* all over Scandinavia.

[2] In Icelandic Sagas house-wife is *hús-freyja*; but in modern Icelandic, *hús-frú*.

[3] *i.e.*, mixed with water.

to search for Godheim and Odin the old. He went with twelve men far and wide about the world; he came to Tyrkland and to Sweden the great, and met there many of his friends and kinsmen, and was five winters on that journey.[1] Then he came back to Sweden, and stayed at home for some time. He had married a woman called Vana in Vanaheim; their son was Vanlandi. Svegdir went again in search of Godheim. In the eastern part of Sweden there is a large bœr called Stein (stone); there stands a rock as large as a big house. One evening after sunset, when Svegdir ceased drinking and went to his sleeping-house, he saw a Dverg sitting outside the rock. Svegdir and his men were very drunk, and ran to the rock. The Dverg stood in the door and shouted to Svegdir to come in if he wanted to meet Odin. Svegdir rushed into the rock, which at once closed upon him, and he came not back" (Ynglinga, c. 15).

A description of the leading events in the life of each of the remaining mythical or semi-mythical rulers named in the genealogies is given in the Ynglinga, but we have only thought it necessary to place before the reader these few typical examples, as the scope of the work will not admit of a fuller treatment of the subject; though some extracts have been incorporated in the Chapter on Customs, &c.

The Northern chiefs traced their ancestry from this Odin of the North, whose influence had become so great with King Gylfi that two of his sons, as we have seen, married the latter's daughters.

When reading the Saga literature we are particularly struck by the frequent references made to pedigrees in which the people of the North took great pride. There are three great genealogical branches through which the Northern chiefs traced their descent from Odin.

"All who are truly wise in events know that the Tyrkjar and Asia-men settled in the northern lands. Then began the tongue which has since spread over all lands. The leader of these people was called Odin, and to him men trace their families"[2] (Sturlaug's Saga (Fornaldarsögur, 111), c. 1).

These genealogical branches are:—1. The *Ynglinga*; or that of Hálfdán the black, the nephew of Rognvald Jarl. 2. The

---

[1] This would imply that Sweden was east of Vanaheim.

[2] Cf. also Herraud and Bosi's Saga, c 1

Háleygja; or that of Hakon Jarl the great. 3. The *Skjöldunga;* or that of Harald Hilditonn or the Danish branch.

If we could admit that these genealogies are more or less correct, and if we struck an average by generations (of thirty years) the result would make Odin live about the beginning of the Christian era; if a longer average of life is allotted, he would have lived some centuries before that date. But of course the genealogies must be treated as in the main mythical.

The *Ynglingatal,*[1] a genealogical poem,[2] composed for Rögnvald Heidumhœri (the uncle of Harald Fairhair), traces the family of Rögnvald through thirty generations up to Odin, and being probably composed a little after 900, it would make Odin live *about* 100 *before Christ.*

Ari in ch. 12 of Islendingabók traces his family through thirty-seven degrees up to Yngvi Tyrkja King.

These are the names of the forefathers of the Ynglingar and Breidfirdingar (Men of Breidifjord):—

1. Yngvi Tyrkjaking.
2. Njörd Sviaking.
3. Frey.
4. Fjölnir, who died at Frid-Fródi's.
5. Svegdir.
6. Vanlandi.
7. Vísbur.
8. Dómaldi.
9. Dómar.
10. Dyggvi.
11. Dag.
12. Alrek.
13. Agni.
14. Yngvi.
15. Jörund.
16. Aun the old.
17. Egil Vendikráka.
18. Ottar.
19. Adils at Uppsalir.
20. Eystein.
21. Yngvar.
22. Braut-önund.
23. Injgald the evil.
24. Ólaf, wood-chopper (tretelgja).
25. Hálfdán Whiteleg Upplendinga-king.
26. Godrod.
27. Ólaf.
28. Helgi.
29. Ingjald, the son of the daughter of Sigurd, son of Ragnar Lodbrok.
30. Oleif the white (king in Dublin).
31. Thorstein the red.
32. Glei Feilan, the first of them who settled in Iceland.
33. Thórd gellir.
34. Eyjólf, who was baptized in his old age when Christianity came to Iceland.
35. Thorkel.
36. Gellir, the father of Thorkel and Brand and Thorgils, Ari's father.

As another example of these genealogies we give that of

---

[1] Cf. also Ynglinga Saga, and *Prologue to Heimskringla.*

[2] The *Ynglingatal* is not given, as it is tedious, and would be uninteresting to the general reader.

The Skjoldunga Branch.

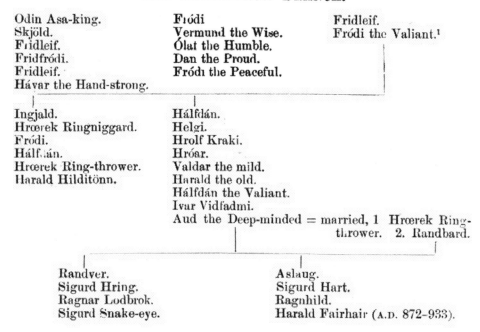

Odin Asa-king.	Fiódi	Fridleif.
Skjöld.	Vermund the Wise.	Fródi the Valiant.[1]
Fridleif.	Ólaf the Humble.	
Fridfródi.	Dan the Proud.	
Fridleif.	Fródi the Peaceful.	
Hávar the Hand-strong.		

Ingjald.	Hálfdán.
Hrœrek Ringniggard.	Helgi.
Fródi.	Hrolf Kraki.
Hálfdán.	Hróar.
Hrœrek Ring-thrower.	Valdar the mild.
Harald Hilditönn.	Harald the old.
	Hálfdán the Valiant.
	Ivar Vidfadmi.
	Aud the Deep-minded = married, 1 Hrœrek Ring-thrower. 2. Randbard.

Randver.	Aslaug.
Sigurd Hring.	Sigurd Hart.
Ragnar Lodbrok.	Ragnhild.
Sigurd Snake-eye.	Harald Fairhair (A.D. 872–933).

The following passage from the 'Later Edda,' which refers to this branch, may help the curious to fix the dates of these chiefs. According to it Odin the hero lived some years before the beginning of the Christian era.

"Skjold (Shield) was the son of Odin, from whom the Skjoldungar are descended. He dwelt in and ruled over the lands now called Danmork, which were then called Gotland Skjold had a son, Fridleif, who ruled the lands after him.

Fridleif's son Fródi got the kingship after his father, about the time when the Emperor Augustus made peace all over the world; then Christ was born. As Fródi was the most powerful of all kings in the Northern lands, all who spoke the Danish (Dansk) tongue[2] attributed the peace to him, and the Northmen called it the Peace of Fródi. No man did harm to another, even if he met the slayer of his father or his brother bound or loose; no thieves or robbers were then found, so that a gold ring lay for a long time in Jalangr-heath (*i.e.*, was not taken by any one)" ('Later Edda.' Skáldskaparmal, c. 43).

---

[1] Fródi had two sons, Ingjald and Hálfdán. From the first was descended the great Harald Hilditönn, who was defeated by his kinsman Sigurd Hring at the Bravalla-battle, see p. . From the second was descended Harald Fairhair, the ancestor of the Dukes of Normandy, and so indirectly of Queen Victoria.

[2] This was written after all the petty kingdoms of Denmark had been consolidated into one; the term Danish tongue at earlier periods did not exist, but *Norrœna*, or Northern tongue, was used instead.

CHAPTER VIII.

THE STONE AGE.

Prehistoric ages of man—Use of metal unknown—First traces of man—Weapons of flint, bone, &c—Graves of the Stone Age—Introduction of domestic animals—The cromlech or dolmen always near the sea—Gallery or passage graves—The passage grave of Karleby—Stone coffin graves—Sepulchral chambers—Objects of the Stone Age.

WE have now given accounts of the literature which contains the earliest records of the people of the North. Let us pause and study for a while its archæology, which will throw considerable light also on its inhabitants and their customs.

It is now generally recognised by archæologists that all people who have advanced to a certain degree of civilisation have passed through three periods of development, which according to the material of which their implements, weapons, and utensils were made, have been named the *stone*, the *bronze*, and the *iron* age. We have very abundant evidence that the people of the North passed through these three stages, and indeed had reached the iron age before they came within the ken of history. Beginning with the stone age, let us see what we can learn of the civilisation of the North from the various articles which were in use during the three stages.

The finds in the North have been classified under the name " *grave,*" " *bog,*" and " *earth* " *finds;* that is, objects found in graves, bogs, or in the ground. In the latter case they are often hidden under stones, in obedience to the injunctions of Odin. Those of the iron age are found as far as 69° North latitude

The custom of burying different objects with the dead, and also that of throwing objects and weapons into springs or bogs, or of hiding them in the ground, has helped in a most remarkable manner to give us an idea of the industries and daily life of the people there at a remote period.

In the earliest age the use of metal was unknown, the weapons were made of stone, horn, and bone,[1] and towards the close of this age pottery was made.

The first traces of man in some parts of the present Scandinavia are the *kjokkenmoddinger* (kitchen refuse heaps), consisting of oyster and mussel shells, bones of fish, birds, and mammals, such as the deer, bear, boar, beaver, seal, ure-ox, wolf, fox, &c., &c., with remains of clay vessels. Among and near these heaps of refuse are found a great number of rude implements and weapons made of flint, bone, horn, and broken flint chips, also fireplaces made of a few stones roughly put together, thus showing that the inhabitants lived in a very primitive state.

No graves of the earliest period of the stone age have thus far been found in the North. Towards the latter part of this age we see a great improvement in the making of weapons and tools; the latter were beautifully polished, and graceful in form. Domestic animals had also been introduced, as shown by the bones of cattle, horses, sheep, pigs, and dogs, that have been found in the graves. Beads of amber and bone were worn as ornaments. The graves of the stone age discovered in the present Scandinavia and on the islands and shores of the Baltic may be classified in four groups: the *cromlech* or *dolmen*; the *passage* or *gallery graves*; the *free-standing stone coffins*; and the *stone coffins covered by a mound*[2]

The cromlechs consist of from three to five large stones standing upright, and so placed as to form a ring, with a large block or boulder on the top. These were intended for a single body, buried in a sitting position, with flint implements and weapons. The walls of the chamber were made by large stones, smooth inside, and the floor consisted of sand or gravel. Certain marks on the tops of stones seem to indicate that

---

[1] Antiquities of the stone age have been found in bogs at Hæbelstrup; Sandbjerg, near Horsholm, Læsten, near Randers; Kjœi, Ringkjobing Amt, Jutland, Samso, &c, and in mounds Among them are numerous amber beads; flint tools from 4½ to 10 ins long, many having teeth like a saw; axe-blades, chisels, spear-points, and ornaments.

[2] The following contents of a *Dolmen* at Luthia, Vestergotland, are typical — 5 spear-heads, 1 arrow-head, 19 rough flint axes, 4 bone pins, 18 bone beads, 4 amber beads, 11 pierced teeth of bears dogs, and pigs, several bones of cows and a great number of skeletons.

sacrifices to the dead were prevalent; holes about 2 inches in width are found on the roofs of some cromlechs and passage graves. These cromlechs always occur near the sea, seldom

Fig. 2.—Cromlech near Haga, Bohuslän.

more than seven miles from the coast. The other graves of the stone age are often found far inland, but they are almost always near a lake or river having connection with the sea.

Fig. 3.—Cromlech (stendös) with concave recesses on the roof-stone, near Fasmorup, in Skåne.

The cromlechs which appear to be the latest graves of this age have a much wider distribution than the other forms; they are found in nearly all the provinces where the older forms of graves occur. Most of them were in or on the top of a mound, which almost always had the roof, and in most cases

Fig. 4.—One of three oblong cromlechs, distance between each about 120 feet, length 52 feet, and width 20 feet, position north and south, Lille Rorbœk, Zeeland The central one had two stone-built chambers, both with the entrance from the east The southern burial chamber is now destroyed, while the northern is completely preserved. It is 5½ feet long, and 3 feet wide, and has four walls of stone, three of which support a stone roof

part of the wall, uncovered. The mound, which is generally round, sometimes oblong, is surrounded at its base by stones

Fig. 5.—Sepulchral chamber covered with a mound, Kallundborg, Zeeland; height about 16 feet. In levelling the mound the earth was found to contain articles which tend to show the existence of a "kjökkenmödding."

often very large; when this was oblong, the grave was nearer the one end than the other.

Gallery or passage graves consisted of a chamber and a

Fig. 6.—Passage grave on Axvalla heath, near Lake Venern, Vestergötland, Sweden, situated on a hill overlooking a flat country. Numerous graves belonging to that period are found in the neighbourhood.

The walls are made by large slabs, those in the passage being lower than the slabs of the quadrangle. The roof is of flat slabs of granite, 5 to 6 feet above the floor, a similar one serving as a door, closing the outer end of the passage, which is 20 feet long, and $2\frac{1}{2}$ to 3 feet broad, and 3 feet high. The mortuary itself (the quadrangle) is 32 feet long by 9 feet broad.

The dead sit along the walls, young and old, men and women, the chin resting in both hands, with their legs drawn up. Thin slabs form the cells round each skeleton, and are about 3 feet high, consequently do not reach the roof. Arrow points, knives, etc., of flintstone, are found with the men, pieces of amber with the women.

Numbers of similar graves are found in Sweden and Denmark, a single grave sometimes containing nearly one hundred bodies.

Fig. 7.—Plan of above grave.

narrow gallery leading into it, the whole being covered by a mound, the base of which was generally surrounded by a circle of larger or smaller stones.

The chamber in a passage grave is either oblong, square, oval, or nearly round; the walls are formed by large upright blocks, not quite smooth, though even on the inside; the interstices are generally carefully filled up with gravel or fragments of stone, and birch bark is sometimes found between the blocks. The roof was formed by immense flat slabs or blocks, smooth on the under side, but rough on the top, the

Fig. 8.—Passage grave near Karleby—front view; length of the main gallery, covered by nine large stones, 52 feet; width, 7 feet; length of passage, 40 feet; height, 6 feet.

interstices being closed in the same manner as those in the walls. The floor is sometimes covered with small flat stones, but usually with earth. On the long side of the chamber there is an opening, from which a passage was built in the same manner as the chamber, only longer and narrower. This passage, or more precisely its inner part, was covered with blocks resembling the roof blocks of the chamber, but smaller; near the inner opening of the passage, and the outer end of its covered part a kind of door setting has been often found, consisting of a stone threshold and two narrow door-posts.

Fig. 9.—Side view of passage grave near Karleby.

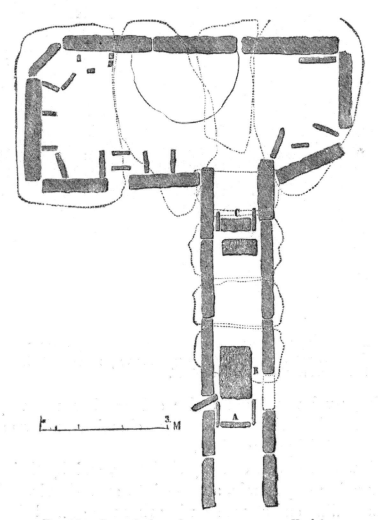

Fig. 10.—Ground-plan of passage grave near Karleby.
The irregular lines show the position of the slabs covering the grave.

The passage graves vary much in size. The length of the chamber is generally from 11½ to 23 feet, its width from 5 to 10 feet; height from 3½ to 4½ feet. The passage is often as long as the chamber, or even longer, and its width is from 2 to 4 feet, and height from 3 to 5 feet. But some are much larger, and are called giants' graves. One of the largest of these graves is that of Karleby, near Falkoping, Vestergotland, in Sweden, where a great number of the graves of the stone age have been found.

Fig. 11.—Stone coffin (hällkista) near Skattened, in Södra Ryrs parish, Vestergötland, 21¼ feet in length. Graves of this type are very numerous in Bohuslan also, and in Dal and south-western Vermland.

This grave[1] was found under a large but not very deep mound, and is divided into a large chamber and two smaller ones, separated by stone slabs.

In it were remains of sixty skeletons, and by their side a large number of poniards, spear-points, arrow-heads, and other objects of flint and stone, showing that the grave belonged to

---

[1] Of the 140 passage graves at present known in Sweden, more than 110 have been found in Skaraborglan, and most of these near Falköping.

Fig. 12.

Mound, Broholm. Sepulchral chamber made of boulders, with short passage leading to it. Stones from 4 feet 15 inches to 4 feet high, and 2½ to 4 feet wide; inside of the chamber 9 feet wide. Only four stones remain of the passage leading to the chamber, which is about 2 feet wide, and turns south-west. The space between the

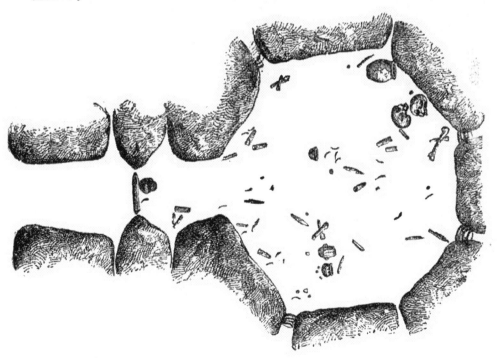

boulders is filled with small stones. In the chamber were charcoal and different things. To the left of the entrance lay remains of two skulls close to each other; and spread in every direction were daggers, blades, and points of spears, points of arrows, numerous amber beads, a necklace of amber, four clay vessels, and fragments of others, &c

Fig. 13.—Plan of above Mound.

the period when stone implements were still in use; but among the skeletons in the lower part of the grave a couple of bronze beads and a bronze spear-point were found.

Fig. 14.—Entrance to passage grave at Uby, Holbæk amt, Denmark. Diameter 100 feet, height 14 feet. The length of the chamber is 13½ feet, width 7½ feet, height 7½ feet. Entrance towards the south passage is 18 feet long, 2½ feet wide, and 5½ feet high. There were found in the passage many human bones and several flint implements and three small clay urns.

The isolated stone coffins were formed of flat upright stones, and were four-sided, though the two longer sides were not parallel, thus making the coffin narrower at one end than at the other. Most of them were probably covered with one or more stones; and although these have in many places long ago been destroyed or removed, they are sometimes still found in their place. The direction of these coffins is almost always from north to south, and they are generally surrounded by a mound of stones of more or less stone-mixed earth. This form of grave was probably the outcome of the omission of

Fig. 15.—Interior of the passage grave at Uby. The spaces between the large stones filled with pebbles. The roof is formed by two large stones which have been cut from a large block.

the passage. Several intermediate forms have been found, showing how the passage was gradually lessened until it can only be traced in the opening which narrows at the south end of the coffin.

The length of the stone coffin was generally from 8 to 13½ feet, width from 3 to 5 feet, height from 2½ to 5 feet. A few, especially in Vestergötland, are from 19½ to 31 feet in length, one of the longest graves of this kind in Sweden being one on Stora Lundskulla, in Vestergotland, with a length of 34 feet, and width of 8 feet. Nearly all other stone coffins found are, like the gallery graves, without a stone at the southern end. This cannot be accidental.

Besides the stone coffin above described, several have been

Fig. 16.—Clay urn—Stone age—⅓ real size. In passage grave, Stege, island of Möen, Baltic, found with remains of some skeletons. Two stone axes, a flint saw, 2 arrow-points, 3 spear-heads, fragments of clay vessels with covers, pieces of a wooden tub, 2 awls of bone, a chisel of bone, 3 flint wedges, 2 flat scrapers of flint, and 17 amber beads for necklace were also found in the grave. The same mound was afterwards used for burials belonging to the bronze age, with cinerary urns with burned bones, on the top of which was a double-edged bronze knife, &c

found covered with a mound. The chambers are generally formed of upright flat stones, and roofed also with stones. They are generally smaller than the stone coffins, being from 6 to 10 feet long, and closed on all four sides; sometimes, however, there is found in the southern end an opening as previously mentioned.

POTTERY.

Fig. 18.—Clay vessel found near Fredericia, Jutland.
⅓ real size

Fig. 19.—Clay urn, Stone age grave, with flint
weapons and amber-heads. ⅓ real size. Island of
Möen

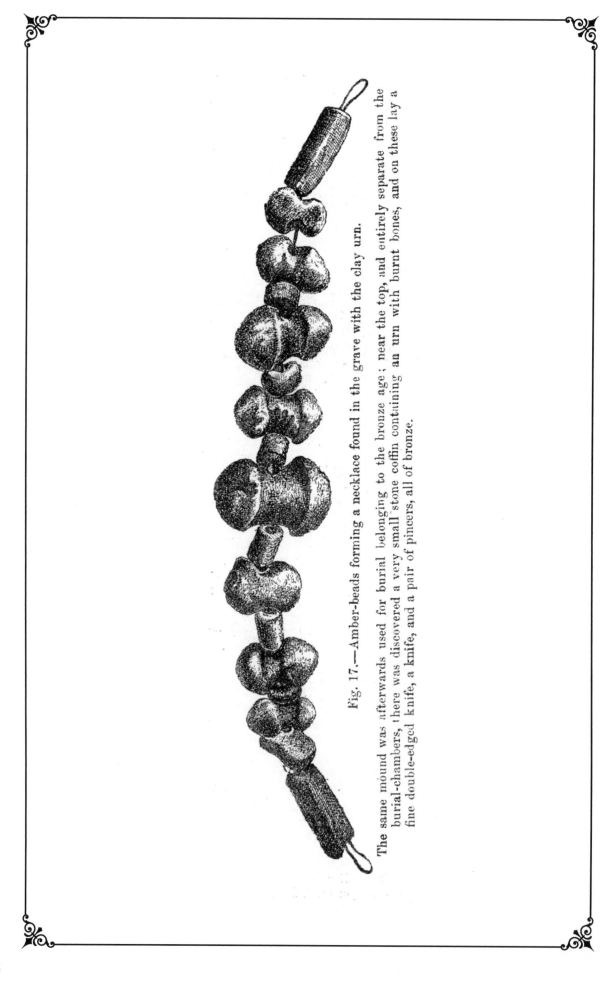

Fig. 17.—Amber-beads forming a necklace found in the grave with the clay urn.

The same mound was afterwards used for burial belonging to the bronze age; near the top, and entirely separate from the burial-chambers, there was discovered a very small stone coffin containing an urn with burnt bones, and on these lay a fine double-edged knife, a knife, and a pair of pincers, all of bronze.

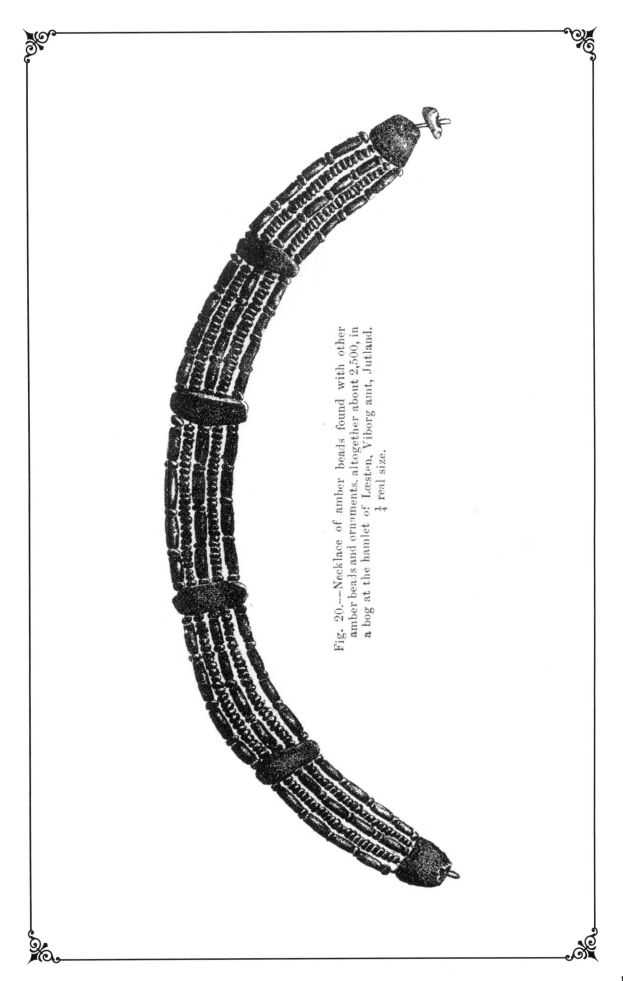

Fig. 20.—Necklace of amber beads found with other amber beads and ornaments, altogether about 2,500, in a bog at the hamlet of Læsten, Viborg amt, Jutland. ½ real size.

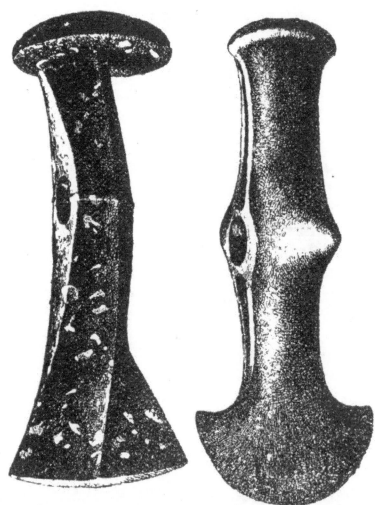

Fig. 22.—Stone axes, of the form of some bronze axes. Several specimens in the Copenhagen Museum. $\frac{1}{3}$ real size.—Fyen.

The two axes in this page are given on account of their peculiar form, similar to that of the bronze age. Many other forms of weapons will be found illustrated in 'The Land of the Midnight Sun.'

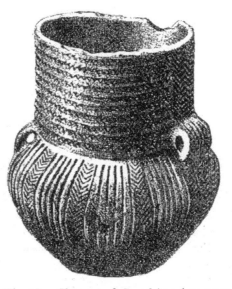

Fig. 23.—Clay vessel found in a burial chamber with flint implements and other objects near Aalborg, Denmark. $\frac{1}{3}$ real size.

Fig. 24.—Clay vessel found in a large passage grave, with flint, and other implements, near Haderslev, Slesvig. $\frac{1}{3}$ real size.

Fig. 21.—Clay vessel which had a top, Stone age. $\frac{1}{3}$ real size.—Möen.

CHAPTER IX.

THE BRONZE AGE.

Abundance of gold—Stone occasionally used for arrow-heads—Pottery—
Graves—Commencement of cremation—Objects of this period—Proficiency in the art of casting—Weapons—Ornaments more varied than in
the stone age—The Kivik grave—Oak coffins—Clothing of the bronze
age—Sewing implements—Burnt and unburnt bodies sometimes found
in the same grave—Gold vessels and ornaments—Bronze vessels—Battle-
horns—Bronze knives.

WHILE the three ages to some extent overlap, while we find
stone articles running into the bronze age, and bronze and
even stone into the iron age, still the distinction between the
three periods is too clearly marked to be overlooked. Thus
in the bronze age, characterised by the use of that metal and
of gold, the weapons were almost entirely of bronze; amber
still continued to be used for ornaments, and towards the close
of this epoch glass, in the shape of beads, and iron appeared,
but silver seems to have been unknown. Sometimes stone
continued to be used for arrow-heads and spear-points.

The pottery shows a distinct improvement on that of the
stone age.

The graves of the bronze age, as in the preceding stone
age, are covered by a mound of earth, or a cairn, and contain
several burial places. During the latter part of the bronze
age the custom of burning the dead was introduced, but
in the earlier part the bodies were unburnt. When the
custom of cremation commenced and how long it lasted
it is utterly impossible to tell, but from the numerous finds
it is evident that it must have been in use long before iron
became known. The graves of this period also generally
lie on the top of some high hill, or the cairns are placed
on the summit of some promontory having an unobstructed
view of the sea or some large sheet of water. These graves

prove that the shores of the Baltic and of the Cattegat were once thickly inhabited by a people having the same customs and religion; and from the situations of the graves, as well as from the objects, etc., in them, we learn that they were a seafaring people North of the great lakes on the large Scandinavian peninsula these antiquities become more rare, thus showing that country not to have been so thickly settled.

From the finds of beautiful and often costly antiquities belonging to the bronze age,[1] and from their great numbers, the fact is brought vividly to our mind, that even before iron was discovered there existed in those regions a remarkable culture

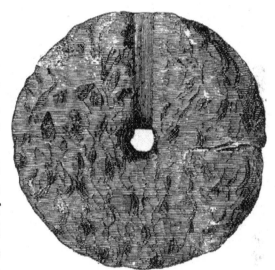

Fig. 25.—Cake of a rosin-like substance made of a paste of birch bark, and containing fragments of amber, used as a kind of putty to fill up the hollows of objects of bronze, &c., found in bogs and urns belonging to the bronze age.

The people had attained very great proficiency in the art of casting, most of the objects are cast, and some of the weapons have still the mark of the clay upon them; the model was sometimes made of wax and clay put round it, the bronze was cast into the mould thus made, and the wax melted into the mould which afterwards was broken in order to take out the sword or object manufactured. Some of the small daggers especially are marvels of casting, which could not be surpassed to-day. The largest swords are cast in one piece. In the collection at Copenhagen nine of these are perfect, the size of the longest being from 35 to 38 inches. The swords, daggers, poniards often have their hilts ornamented or twisted with threads of gold.

The weapons of the bronze epoch are the same as those of

---

[1] Some of the forms of these antiquities are met with in parts of Germany, Hungary, England, and elsewhere in Europe, whilst others, by far the most numerous, are peculiarly Northern

the stone age; poniards, axes, spears, bows and arrows. The sword and the shield seem to have been in common use; one of these now in Copenhagen was found covered with thin gold.

The simple ornaments of the stone age are replaced by more varied and beautiful ones. Gold jewels and vases become common and testify to the wealth of the people. In this age as in the preceding age of stone, the people of the North attained a greater degree of proficiency, and seem to have possessed a higher degree of civilisation than the people of Central and Northern Europe belonging to the same period.

The graves containing unburnt bones which belong to the early period of the bronze age are very similar to those of the preceding period of the stone age, they contain several skeletons then finally decrease in size until they become about 7 feet long, or just large enough to contain one body.

The bodies were often not buried in stone chambers but in coffins made of the trunks of oak trees. It may be that at a later period the customs of burning bodies and burying bodies unburnt co-existed, as will be seen in the account of the iron age. The warrior was buried with his weapons just as in the stone age.

One of the most interesting graves which I have seen, belonging, probably, to the bronze age, is the Kivik cairn (see p. 88), near the sea on a beautiful bay near the town of Cimbrisham. This monument is the only one of its kind known in the North. It shows perfect resemblance to others of the bronze age, and differs only from the cairns found on the hill-tops of Bohuslan in its larger size. We have looked with great care at the tracings, which are not so deep as those of the rock-tracings situated in the neighbourhood. The signs carved on the stones are evidently symbolical, and were so made as to look upon the great chief that had been buried there.

The Kivik grave, like many others belonging to the bronze age situated by the sea, is about 700 feet in circumference. The coffin, of flat upright slabs, was discovered in 1750; its length is fourteen feet; width, three feet. It is formed by

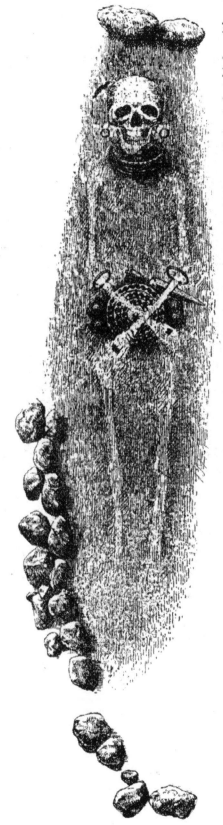

Fig. 26.—Skeleton in a grave, about 8 feet 5 inches long, lying south-west and north-east. The mound, which was about 4 feet high, with a diameter of 50 feet, contained in the centre another grave. Hesselagergaard, Broholm, Fyen. The original position of the head of the warrior was 19 inches from the line of stones. The warrior was buried with his weapons just as in the stone age. The following were some of the objects found in the grave: Fragments of a bronze fibula, a little above the head to the right. Two bronze rings, on each side of the head, 6 inches from it. A bronze necklet; 13 inches below the lower edge of the necklet was a large, flat, bronze titulus (sort of shield boss) ornamented with three rows of spirals. Above the edge of the large titulus was a bronze dagger, in a scabbard, 8½ inches long.

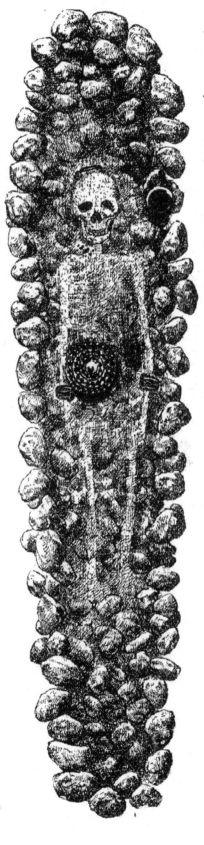

Fig. 27.—Man buried with ornaments. Grave, 9 feet 6 inches long, 2 feet 3 inches wide, in a mound, Hesselagergaard. Among the ornaments were some spiral bracelets and finger rings, amber beads and one light blue glass bead.

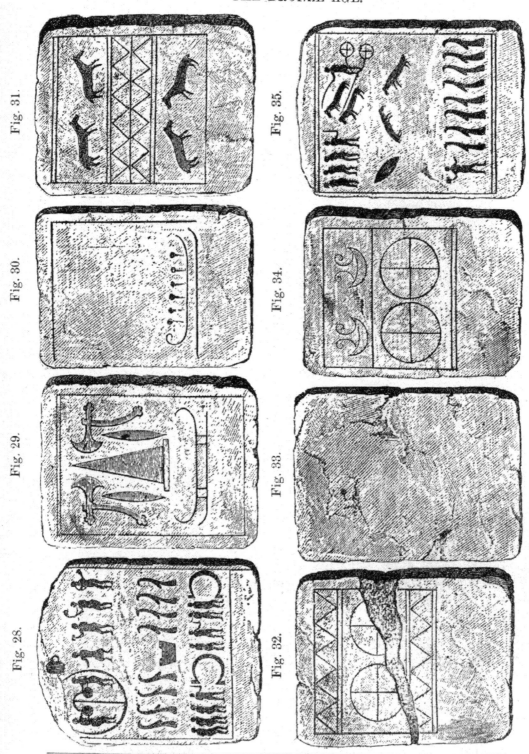

Fig. 31.

Fig. 30.

Fig. 29.

Fig. 28.

Fig. 35.

Fig. 34.

Fig. 33.

Fig. 32.

Slab, from the Kivik grave.[1]

[1] In one of the slabs (Fig. 28) there seems to be a representation of a kind of sacrificing altar, with figures of persons coming towards it, as if they were coming there for some object. There seem to be men blowing horns. In Fig. 29 are a ship and a large cone, on each side of which are an axe and another object or sign the significance of which is unknown.

Fig. 30 has only a ship.

Fig. 31 has four-footed animals, the lower ones coming in opposite directions, and the others going the same way; but the two subjects are separated by peculiar marks.

four slabs on each side, and one at the north end. These were nearly four feet high, three feet wide, and eight to nine inches thick, and placed side by side. The inner surfaces were more or less smooth, though neither cut nor polished, and on these were the tracings. Two of these stones were lost about seventy

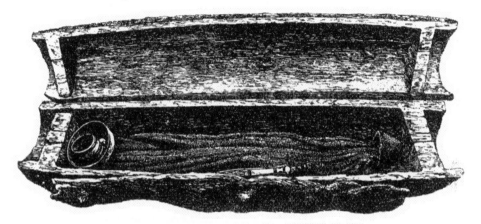

Fig. 36.—Oak coffin. Kongshöi find (Jutland).

years ago. The grave was covered with three slabs, and pointed north and south.

In a mound at Havdrup in Ribe amt, Jutland, there were found in 1861 three well-preserved oak coffins. The contents of two had been taken out before the discovery was notified

Fig. 37.—Oak coffin. with skeleton body covered with a woollen cloak, Treenhöi, Jutland ; one half serving as bed.

to the authorities, but the third was found in the state shown in the illustration. Near this mound was that of Kongshöi. containing four well-preserved oaken coffins. The contents of these were however not as well preserved as those in the coffins of Treenhöi. At the top of this mound there were discovered clay urns with burnt bones.

In some of these oaken coffins are found wooden bowls with handles, and ornamented with inserted pins of tin.

The articles of dress, found in a most extraordinary state of preservation in the oak coffin, kept from decay no doubt by the tannin in the oak, show how the people of the North dressed well before iron had come into use among them. These are the earliest perfect garments known, and even the latest

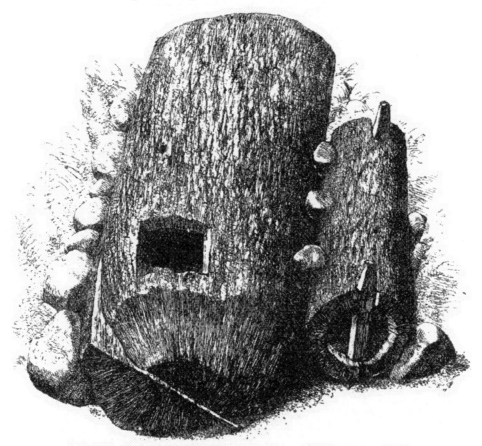

Fig. 38.—Oak coffin, Treenhöi, Jutland ; one half serving as bed.

period to which they belong cannot be far from three thousand years ago, and they may be of a much earlier date.

Among the most interesting graves which have given remarkable results in regard to dress are the mounds of Treenhoi by Vandrup, near Kolding, in Jutland.

In a man's grave was a small cap covering the head of the body, which was wrapped in a deer-skin, composed of several sewn pieces of woven material, and ornamented outside with woollen threads, which had been inserted, and terminating with knots.

On the left side under the cloak lay a bronze sword in a wooden sheath, of lath lined with deer-skin, the hair being inside. The hilt was ornamented by an oval bronze button at

Fig. 39.—Cap.   Fig. 40.—Woollen shawl.   Fig. 41.—Cap.

Fig. 42.—Coarse woollen cloak.   Fig. 43.—Woollen skirt held by a striped band.

Articles of clothing, Treenhöi, Jutland.

its top. There were no traces of leggings or other protection for the legs, but the feet seem to have been protected by strips of wool, and to have had leather shoes or sandals on.

The graves of women contain daggers, which may possibly imply that the women had been warriors; also large spiral rings, various ornaments, finger-rings, bracelets, glass beads, &c.

Women's dress of the bronze age seems to have consisted of the skirt and bodice as at the present time, but the men's clothes were quite different from those of the iron age; in the earlier time trousers were not worn, while we see them in use in the latter.

Many sewing implements of bronze have been found in the graves, the needles like those of the stone age are sometimes made of bone, but many are of bronze; awls were used to pierce the holes in garments that were made of skins, and some peculiar shaped knives have been found which were probably used in the making of skin clothing, or in cutting leather.

Fig. 44.—Woman's skirt and bodice of wool, found with bronze ornaments, and a bronze poniard with horn handle by the side of the body which had been wrapped in a deer-skin.—Aarhus, North Jutland.

In a grave-mound near Aarhus, in North Jutland, a coffin made of two oak logs was found. The bottom of the coffin was covered with an untanned ox or deer-hide. On this lay a large cloak, made of coarse wool and cattle-hair. In the cloak, which was partly destroyed, was wrapped the skeleton of a woman dressed. The hair was long and dark, and a net covered the head, tied under the chin.

Burnt and unburnt bodies are sometimes found in the same

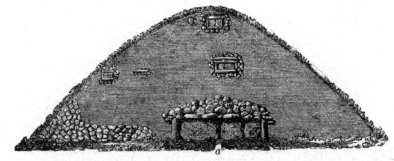

Fig. 45.—Profile of mound of the bronze age, with large coffin and unburnt body, and stone cist with cinerary urn containing burnt bones, also three smaller stone cists filled with burnt bones. Dömmerstorf. S. Halland.

Fig. 46.—Mound and sepulchral cist. The stones in this grave were of size of the fist, and formed a pavement of a diameter of about a yard. The urn contained burnt bones, among which were found a bronze awl, and fragments of a bronze saw.

mound; the latter generally at the bottom of the graves, the former at the top, this shows that the graves with unburnt

Fig. 47.—Mound at Elsehoved. Fyen. At the bottom, in the centre of the mound, was found an irregular grave filled with earth, of about 4 feet 9 inches in length, 1 foot 9 inches in width, 1 foot 10 inches in depth (measured inside). Outside, on the natural soil, was spread a bed of earth, rich in charcoal, which contained remains of burnt bones and pieces of a clay urn, &c.

bodies are considerably the older of the two. A mound with several graves may possibly have been the burial place of one family. The graves of the later bronze age are more numerous on the shores of the Baltic than in other parts of Europe. Sometimes the burnt remains have been found wrapped in clothing, and placed in an ordinary sized coffin, but more generally these burnt bones are preserved in urns of clay enclosed in a small stone cist.

Fig. 48.—Cairn covered with earth, bronze age, Kongstrup, Zealand. Diameter nearly 40 feet; height, 10 feet; covered with about 3 feet of clay, containing over thirty urns, one of which was fastened with a resin-like substance; with burnt bones and cinders, protected by little sepulchral cists made of slabs.

These stone cists of about the length of an average man are interesting as indicating the transition to the small ones containing burnt bones; some of these of a size large enough for an unburnt body have contained only a small heap of burnt bones, and evidently belonged to the period when the cremation of the dead began to prevail. Many of these little

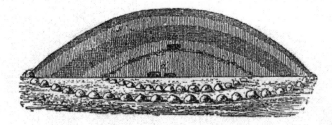

Fig. 49.—Mound of the bronze age, covering a double ring of stones; diameter of outside ring 86 feet; containing several burial-places, with urns and burnt bones.—Near Kallundborg, Zealand.

cists are only large enough to enclose a clay pot, in which the bones were collected; sometimes no coffins were found, but only clay pots containing ashes, a small bronze knife, a bit of bronze saw, or something of that kind. In some cases the bones were put simply into a hole in the mound and the whole covered with a stone slab.

Fig. 50.—Clay vase; ⅛ real size. Found in stone cist in the mound with an urn containing burnt bones, among which lay two bronze knives.—Mound at Gjöttrup, near Lögstör, Denmark

Fig. 51.—Pot of burned clay; ¼ real size. Found in a mound with urns and bronze objects.—Vidstrup, Hjörring amt, Denmark.

Fig. 52.—Cinerary urn, ⅓ real size. Burnt bones.—Holstein.

Fig. 53.—Cinerary urn, ⅓ real size. With burnt bones.—Jutland.

Fig. 54.—Fragment of woollen cloth. Real size. Found at the bottom of a mound at Dömmestorp, in Halland; in a fold of it lay a well-preserved bronze poniard with its leather scabbard. The shawl was 5 feet long and 20 inches wide.

Fig. 55.—Maglehöj mound; height about 14 feet, diameter 40 to 50 feet; with sepulchral chamber, height, 5 feet; width, 5½ feet; length, 7 feet. Inside the chamber the ground was laid with cobble-stones; on top of these flint-stones, 2 to 3 inches in thickness; and then again a layer of cobble-stones, and among these were found: a diadem of bronze, two pieces of shields or breast-armour, the blade of a dagger, &c., &c.—Zeeland.

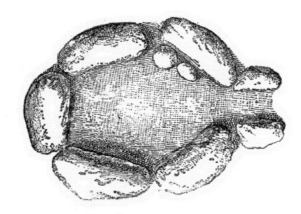

Fig. 56.—Floor of chamber.—Maglehöj.

Fig. 57.—Interior of chamber with cinerary urn.—Maglehöj.

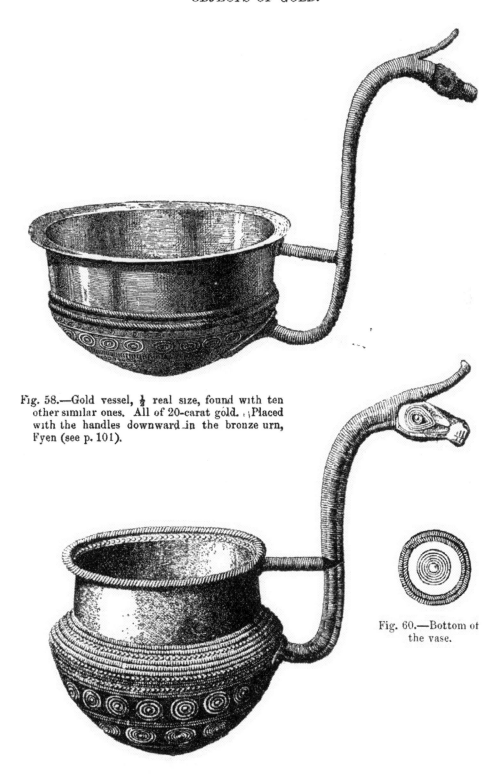

Fig. 58.—Gold vessel, ½ real size, found with ten other similar ones. All of 20-carat gold. Placed with the handles downward in the bronze urn, Fyen (see p. 101).

Fig. 60.—Bottom of the vase.

Fig. 59.—Gold vessel, ⅓ real size, handle surrounded with gold threads. Found with a gold vessel in a mound, Zeeland.

Fig. 61.—Gold vessel, about ½ real size, found under a slab,
Halland.   Weight, 2 oz. 5 dr.

Fig. 62.—Design forming the
bottom part of the vase.
¼ real size.

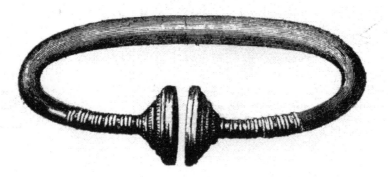

Fig. 63.—Bracelet of solid gold, ¾ real size; weight, 6 oz.—Scania.

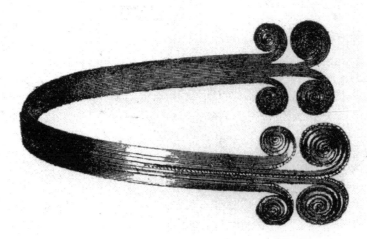

Fig. 64.—Diadem of gold, ⅔ real size, Balsby, Scania; deposited, together with four
massive bronze axes, upon a slab below the surface of the ground.

Fig. 65.—Hollow bracelet of gold, real size, found with four spiral gold bracelets near a large stone.—Skarje, Bohuslan.

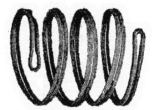

Fig. 66.—Spiral ring of double thread of gold.—Scania.

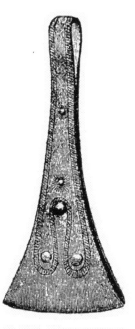

Fig. 67.—Pincers of gold. Real size.—Halland.

Fig. 68.—Bronze pincers. ¾ real size.—Fyen.

Fig. 69.—Bronze pincers. Real size.—Scania.

H 2

Vessels of bronze are uncommon in the graves; some by their form seem to be of Greek origin, while others appear to be of Northern make. Some beautifully cast, and of peculiar shape, seem to have been made to be suspended. Some are

Fig. 70.—Bronze vessel, with representation of sun ship, with prow and stern alike, as in northern ships. ⅓ real size.—Bog near Aaborg, Denmark.

ornamented with the svastica [1] and other symbolic signs, and may have been used to carry offerings to the gods.

---

[1] The Svastika, or Suvastika. is in its essential form a cross with bent arms 卐 卍, but with many modifications. As a symbol, it is found widespread over a large part of the Old World. It is certainly of ancient origin, but autho- rities are disagreed as to its symbolical significance. Other symbols equally diffi- cult to interpret, found in Norse remains, are the three dots, circle of dots, triangles, the triskele ꝏ, &c.

Fig. 71.—Bronze vase, in which were found eleven gold vessels with handles like illustration. Representation of sun ship. ⅓ real size.—Bog find, Rönninge, Fyen, Denmark.

Fig. 72.—A vase of bronze found in a grave-cist in a mound, Fyen. The cist was three feet wide, built of stone slabs, with one on the top. ⅓ real size.

Fig. 73.—Bronze vase, with burnt bones, a gold arm-ring, four double buttons (two of gold and two of bronze), two bronze knives, &c., Denmark

The bogs [1] of Denmark contain large horns or trumpets, made entirely of bronze, with pendant chains (see p. 104).

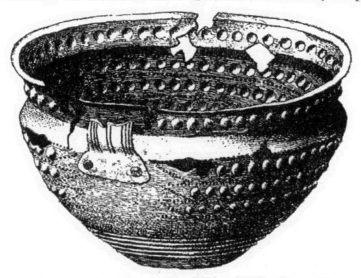

Fig 74.—Bronze vase. ½ real size.—Broby, Denmark.

Fig. 75.—Bronze pail. ¼ real size —Ögemose, Denmark.

---

[1] In a bog by Taarup several pieces of bronze, such as arm rings, spear-points, chisels. &c, were found.

Near Aarup, Jutland, two bronze earrings of a similar pattern, two bracelets made of convex bronze bands with engraved ornaments, a solid gold ring for the hair, three spiral-shaped loops of gold with bowl-shaped buttons at the ends. The engraved ornaments seem to point to the fact that the engraving needle was known in the bronze age.

Somewhat similar objects have been found in other bogs.

Nothing exactly corresponding to them has yet been discovered in other countries. They have been cast in several pieces, and with surprising skill, and are carefully fastened together

Fig. 76.—Hanging vase of bronze. ½ real size.—Bog, Senäte, Vestergötland.

Fig. 77.—¼ real size.
Svastica.

Fig. 78.—⅓ real size.
Scania.

Fig. 79.—¼ real size.

Patterns of the bottom of different vases.

by rivets which interlace each other. Sometimes they have been buried in the bogs in a broken state, but generally have been so well preserved that they can still be blown. They produce a dull and not very loud sound. On one occasion

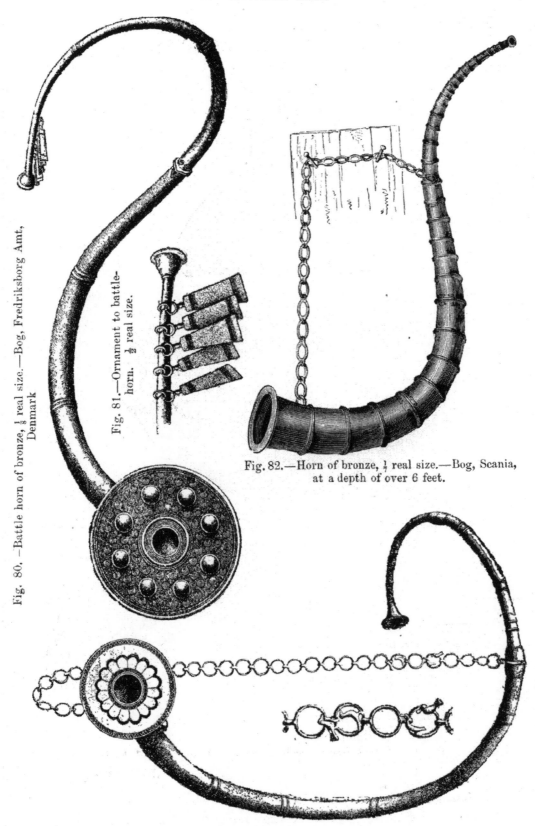

Fig. 80.—Battle horn of bronze, ⅓ real size.—Bog, Fredriksborg Amt, Denmark

Fig. 81.—Ornament to battle-horn. ⅓ real size.

Fig. 82.—Horn of bronze, ¼ real size.—Bog, Scania, at a depth of over 6 feet.

Fig. 83.—Battle horn of bronze, with chain ornamented with birds; ⅛ real size, or 30 inches long.—Bog, Ribe Amt, Denmark

they have been found with a shield of bronze and a few bronze swords, hence their use in battle may be inferred. But generally several of them are found together, rarely less than two, and sometimes as many as six on the same spot.

A perfectly unique find belonging to the bronze age is that

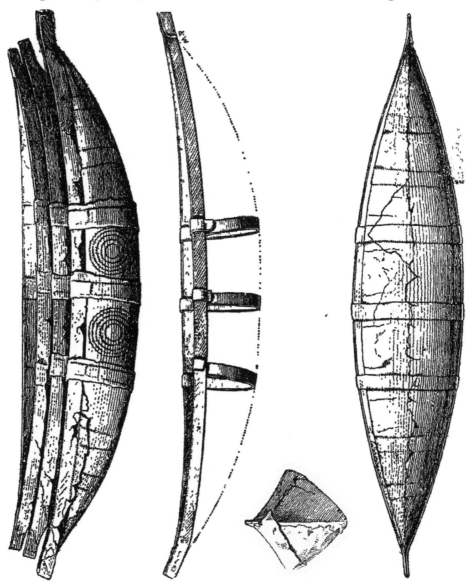

Fig. 84.—Bronze boats covered with gold.—Nors parish, North Jutland.

discovered at Nors parish, Northern Jutland, in 1885. In an urn, greatly damaged, were about 100 small boats of bronze canoe-shaped, about four to five inches in length, placed one into another, all covered inside and outside with a thin sheet of gold; some have been found to be ornamented with concentric rings on the side. What was the meaning of the offering or find will always remain a mystery.

The curiously-shaped knives, which are found in very great numbers, seem to be peculiar to the North, and the North of Germany. What they were used for is hard to tell, possibly as sacrificial knives. It can hardly be doubted that the signs upon them are symbolical; some may be representations of the sun-ship, others are somewhat like minute representations of the rock-tracings, or designs upon Greek coins, while the heads of horses remind us of the gold vases represented in this chapter.

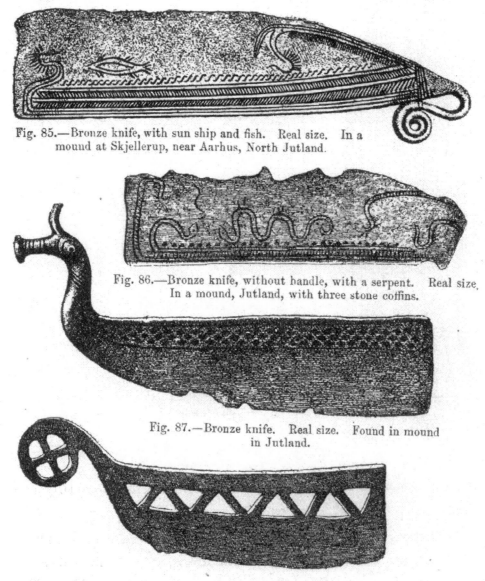

Fig. 85.—Bronze knife, with sun ship and fish. Real size. In a mound at Skjellerup, near Aarhus, North Jutland.

Fig. 86.—Bronze knife, without handle, with a serpent. Real size. In a mound, Jutland, with three stone coffins.

Fig. 87.—Bronze knife. Real size. Found in mound in Jutland.

Fig. 88.—Bronze knife in clay urn, with burnt bones, two other knives, &c. ⅔ real size.—Denmark.

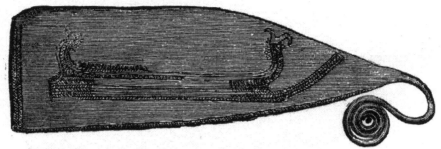

Fig. 89.—Bronze knife, with a vessel. ⅔ real size. In a mound.—Fyen.

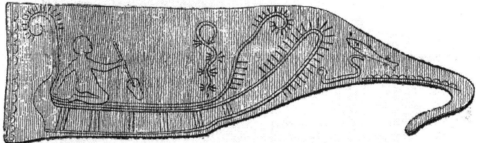

Fig. 90.—Bronze knife.—Jutland.

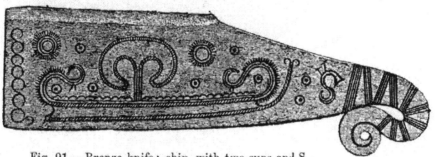

Fig. 91.—Bronze knife; ship, with two suns and S.
Skanderborg Amt, Denmark. ⅔ real size.—Jutland.

Fig. 92.—Bronze knife, with ship, sun, and triskele. ⅔ real size.
—In an urn in Holstein.

Fig. 93.—Bronze knife, mound at Dömmestorp, Halland, in a ruined stone cist. Rea. size.

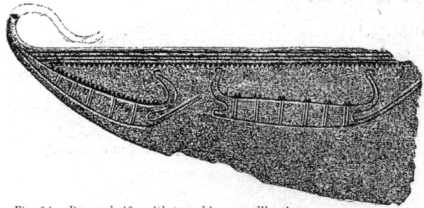

Fig. 94.—Bronze knife, with two ships very like those
on rock-tracings.   Real size.—In a mound near Vimose on Fyen.

Fig. 95.—Bronze knife, Scania.   Real size.—Scania.

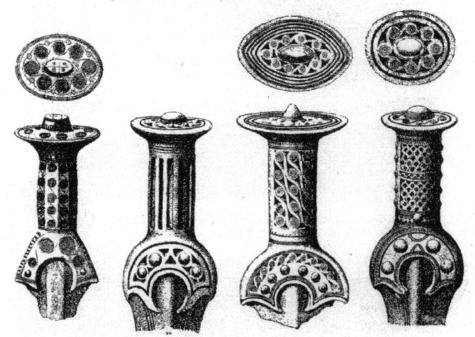

Fig. 96.—In a   Fig. 97.—Found in a field   Fig. 98.   Fig. 99.—Found with
mound.—Zeeland.   in Fyen, near Svendborg.   bones and charcoal in
                  with two other swords.   a mound.—Fyen.

Handles of bronze swords.   ⅓ real size.

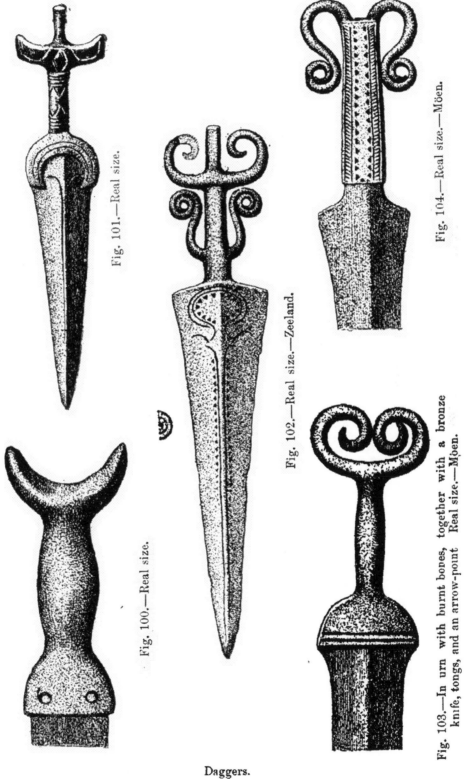

Fig. 101.—Real size.

Fig. 100.—Real size.

Fig. 102.—Real size.—Zeeland.

Fig. 104.—Real size.—Möen.

Fig. 103.—In urn with burnt bones, together with a bronze knife, tongs, and an arrow-point   Real size.—Möen.

Daggers.
" Varying in size from 3 inches to 6½ inches.

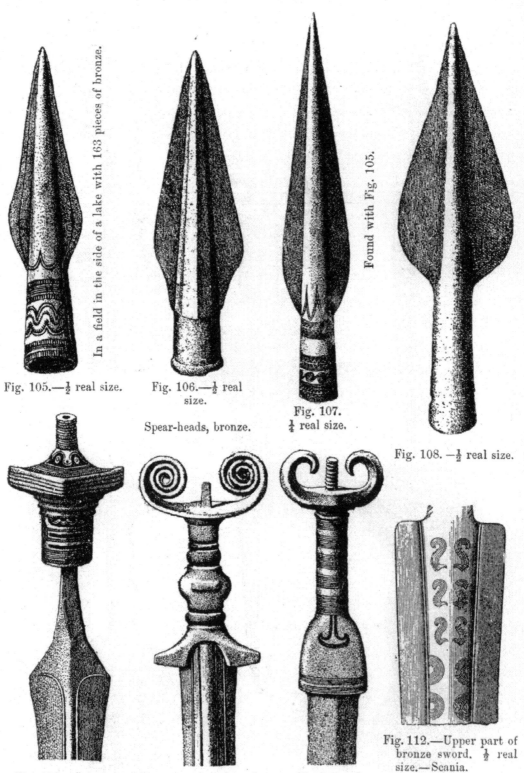

In a field in the side of a lake with 163 pieces of bronze.

Found with Fig. 105.

Fig. 105.—½ real size.

Fig. 106.—½ real size.

Spear-heads, bronze.

Fig. 107. ¼ real size.

Fig. 108. —½ real size.

Fig. 109.—In a bog, Falster. ⅓ real size.

Fig. 110.—In a bog, Jutland. ⅓ real size.

Fig. 111.—In mound, Jutland. ⅓ real size.

Fig. 112.—Upper part of bronze sword. ½ real size.—Scania.

Swords.—These peculiar bronze swords are found in various towns in England and Germany.

Fig. 113.—Spear-point of bronze. ½ real size. In a heap of coals with twenty other spear-points.—Nordre Aurdal, Christiania.

Fig. 114.—Spear-head of bronze. ¼ real size.—Fäl-köping, Vestergötland.

Fig. 115.—Knife of bronze. ⅙ real size. In stone coffin in a mound, Island of Moen, in the Baltic, with a sword and a knife.

Fig. 116.—Knife of bronze. ⅓ real size.

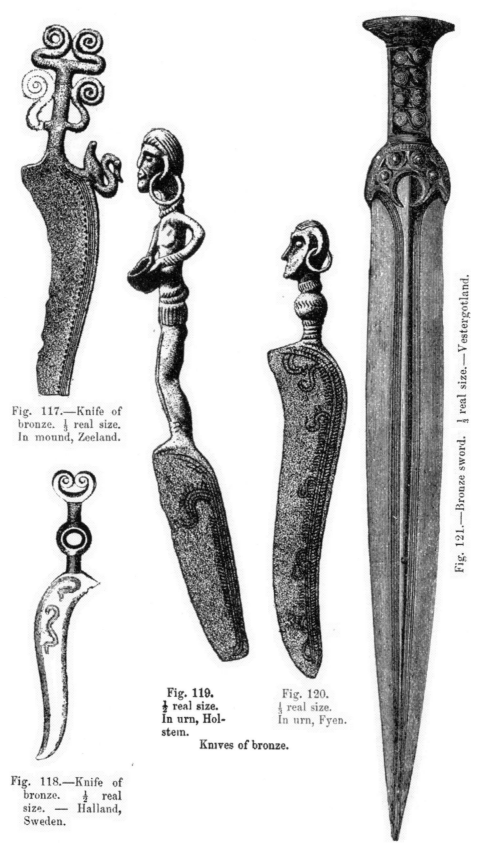

Fig. 117.—Knife of bronze. ⅓ real size. In mound, Zeeland.

Fig. 118.—Knife of bronze. ½ real size. — Halland, Sweden.

Fig. 119. ½ real size. In urn, Holstein.

Fig. 120. ⅓ real size. In urn, Fyen.

Knives of bronze.

Fig. 121.—Bronze sword. ⅓ real size.—Vestergotland.

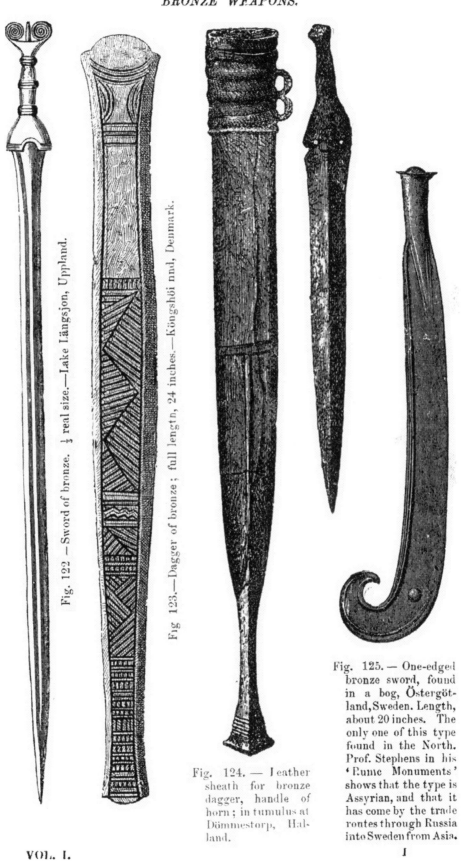

Fig. 122 — Sword of bronze. ⅓ real size.—Lake Längsjon, Uppland.

Fig 123.—Dagger of bronze ; full length, 24 inches.—Kŏngshöi mad, Denmark.

Fig. 124. — Leather sheath for bronze dagger, handle of horn ; in tumulus at Dömmestorp, Halland.

Fig. 125. — One-edged bronze sword, found in a bog, Östergöt-land, Sweden. Length, about 20 inches. The only one of this type found in the North. Prof. Stephens in his 'Rune Monuments' shows that the type is Assyrian, and that it has come by the trade routes through Russia into Sweden from Asia.

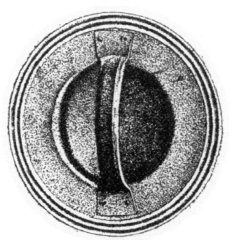

Fig. 26.—Bronze shield with handle. ⅓ real size.—Denmark.

Fig. 127.—Thin shield of bronze, ⅛ real size, found in a bog at a depth of a little more than 3 feet · 66 inches full size diameter; bird like figures round centre.—Halland.

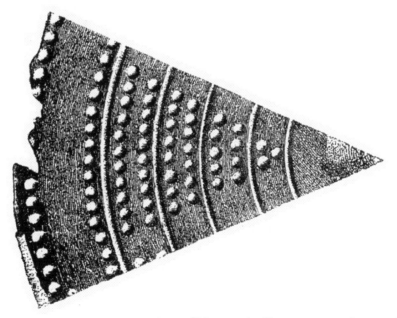

Fig. 128.—One-eighth part of a small bronze shield, measuring only 27 inches in diameter. containing eight triangles; ½ size. In a bog, Falster.

I 2

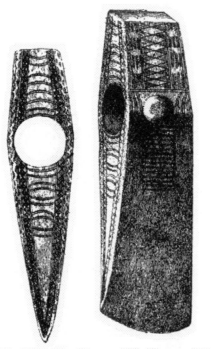

Fig. 130.—⅓ real size.

Fig. 129.—⅓ real size.—Flensborg amt, Denmark.

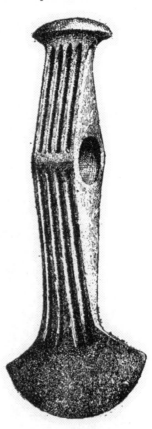

Fig. 131.—Massive bronze axe, ⅓ real size, ornamented on three sides.—Veile amt, Denmark

Bronze axes.

Fig. 132.—In Randersfjord, Jutland. ½ real size.

Fig. 133.—Bronze axe; ½ real size.—Scania.

Fig. 134.—Bronze axe; ⅓ real size.—Bohuslän, Sweden.

Fig. 135.—⅓ real size. Ploughed up in a field, Zeeland.

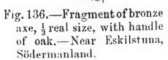

Fig. 136.—Fragment of bronze axe, ½ real size, with handle of oak.—Near Eskilstuna, Södermanland.

Fig. 137.—Axe of thin layer of bronze, ½ real size, cast upon a mould of clay, ornamented with some round plaques of gold, in the midst of which are pieces of amber.—Södermanland, Sweden

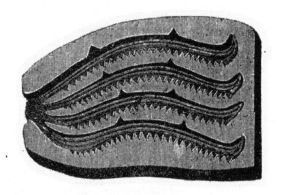

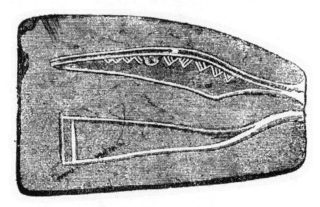

Fig. 138.—Two forms of stone for casting; one for four saws, the other for two knives. ⅓ real size.—Scania.

Fig. 139.—Necklace of bronze. ⅓ real size.—Bog, V.-Götland.

Fig. 140.—Saw of bronze. ½ real size.—Denmark.

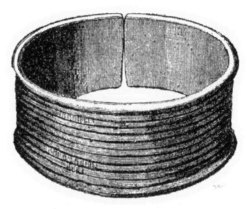

Fig. 141.—Bronze ring. Real size.—Denmark.

Fig. 142.—One of two bronze bracelets round wrist of skeleton in tumulus, Dommestorp, Halland. ⅔ real size.

Fig. 143.—Bronze ring. Real size.—Denmark.

Fig. 144.—Bronze bracelet. ½ real size.—Denmark.

Fig. 145.—Fibula of bronze. ⅔ real size. Found with a bronze ring in bog, Zeeland.

Fig. 146.—Head ornament or hair-ring. Little less than ½ size.

Fig. 147.—Long spiral bracelet, found near a big stone, Scania.

Fig 148.—Tutulus of bronze, with many other objects, in a large mound at Bosgården, near Lund. Sweden.

Fig. 149.—Bracelet. ½ real size.—Denmark.

Fig. 150.—Bracelet of bronze. ⅔ real size.—Scania.

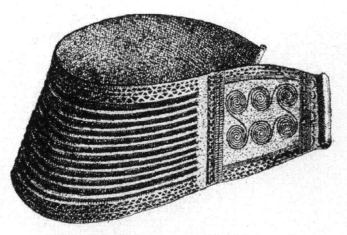

Fig. 151.—Diadem of bronze. ½ real size.—Denmark.

Fig. 152.—Button of bronze. Real size.—Scania.

Fig. 153.—Button found with other objects in a small clay urn, with burnt bones, surrounded by little slabs; real size.—Dömmestorp, Halland.

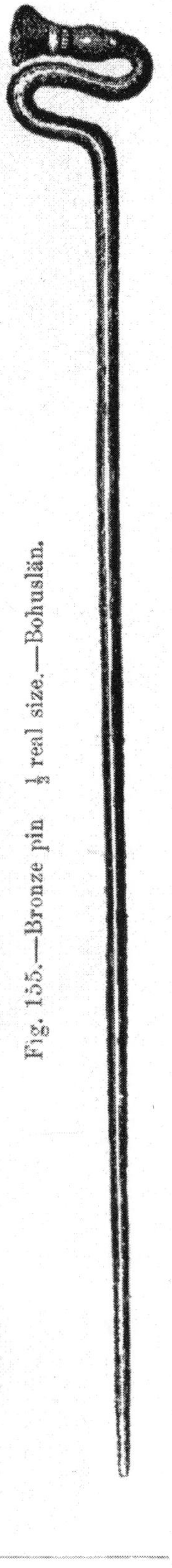

Fig. 155.—Bronze pin ⅓ real size.—Bohuslän.

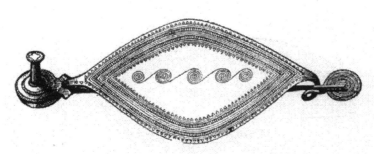

Fig. 154.—Fibula of bronze. ⅔ real size.—Scania.[1]

---

[1] See 'Land of the Midnight Sun' for other ornaments of bronze.

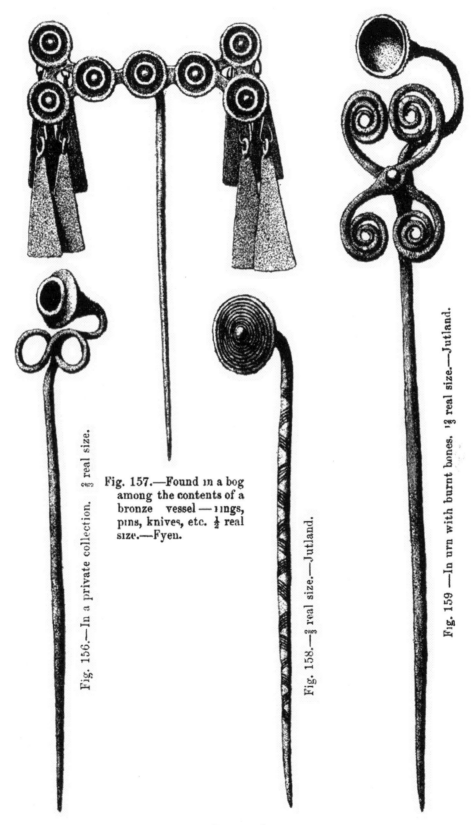

Fig. 156.—In a private collection. ⅔ real size.

Fig. 157.—Found in a bog among the contents of a bronze vessel — rings, pins, knives, etc. ½ real size.—Fyen.

Fig. 158.—⅔ real size.—Jutland.

Fig. 159 —In urn with burnt bones, 1⅓ real size.—Jutland.

Bronze pins.

Fig. 160.—Bracelet of gold.
½ real size.

Fig. 161.—Twisted necklace of bronze, ½ real size, found in a bog at a depth
of 1m. 5c. at Langhö, Södermanland.

Fig. 162.—Ornament of bronze, ⅛ real size, for wooden pail.— Bog of Balkåkra,
near Ystad, Scania.

CHAPTER X.

THE IRON AGE.

The three historic ages overlap each other—Division of the iron age by archæologists—Gradual development in the mode of burial during the three ages—Appearance of silver, lead, and glass—Greek and Roman objects—Cinerary deposits—Cremation—The Kannikegaard cemetery—Primitive kettle-shaped graves—Intentional destruction of weapons and armour in graves—Cinerary urns—Symbolic signs—Ornaments of the iron age.

IN the iron age, when the knowledge of all the metals was known, and weapons were made of iron, bones were still sometimes used for arrow-heads; this age gradually merges into the historic period. It is impossible to assign definite limits of time to the three prehistoric ages; they run by degrees into each other; the classification specifies no division of time, but marks degrees of development in man.

Northern archæologists divide the iron age in the North into the *earlier*, *middle*, and *later* iron age, in the same manner as they have divided the preceding stone and bronze ages; and it may safely be said that in all these ages the North surpasses other countries in the beauty and number of its objects. All the antiquities, as well as the Eddas and Sagas, plainly show that the people who inhabited the eastern and southern shores of the present Scandinavia[1], the islands of the Baltic, and the southern shores of that sea, to a certain distance inland, which now comprise Northern Germany, were of the same origin and belonged to the same race; and the

---

[1] During the stone and bronze ages the population of Norway was not as great as that of Sweden, Denmark, and the islands of the Baltic. It is only during the iron age that that country becomes more thickly settled, and approximates somewhat in its population to the neighbouring countries; bronze finds have occurred in Norway as far north as 66° 10′ N. latitude.

vast number of weapons of various kinds testify equally with the records to the warlike character of the people. The finish of the weapons of the later stone age is something wonderful, many of them are as polished as glass; the weapons of bronze are equally remarkable.

In the beginning of the iron age appear the shears, which are very similar to those now in use. Clothes during this period were generally kept together by pins and buckles, which have been found in great numbers; horns were used as drinking cups, and domestic vessels of glass, bronze, silver, gold, wood, or burnt clay, and objects of Roman manufacture, dice, checkers or draughtsmen, and chessmen, have also been unearthed.

At a very early period of this age remains of brynjas, or coats of ring armour, have been found in graves where burning of the dead has taken place; this shows that they were known in the North even in the beginning of the Christian era, if not before; they are also met with in graves of a later period, and in the bog finds of the third and fourth century

Along with iron the people became also acquainted with silver, lead, glass, &c., and knew the art of soldering and gilding metals. The jewels and ornaments in their design and workmanship show a considerable advance in taste.

At what time the use of iron began to be known among the people and when it superseded bronze is impossible to tell: the change must have taken place a long time before the ships of the Suiones were described by Tacitus, a wonderful example of the accuracy of whose description is found in the Nydam boat of which I will speak hereafter. Iron is very abundant in Sweden and Norway, and bog iron was no doubt plentiful in the islands of the Baltic; the use of the latter is proved by masses of slag, weapons, &c. found in the earliest graves of the iron age. The use of the bronze of the preceding period continued, and many objects of bronze are evidently of home manufacture.

The earliest graves[1] belonging to this iron age in the North

---

[1] Mixed finds precede the advent of each age. Stone implements or weapons are found together with those of bronze, and later bronze implements, which are the forerunners of the approaching iron age, are found with those of iron. Examples of such are—a grave at Stonholt, Viborg Amt, containing pearl of glass mosaic, with bronze poniard; grave at Alstrup, Aalborg Amt, containing iron

are called by Northern archæologists *depôts cineraires* (cinerary deposits). These graves are round bowl-shaped holes, the excavations being from about two to four feet in diameter, and three to four feet deep: into these the remains of the funeral pyre, such as burnt bones of the corpse, ashes, charcoal, fragments of clay, urns, ornaments, jewels, other objects

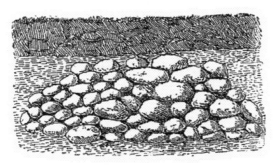

Fig. 163.—Cinerary deposit. Hole, filled with stones, 4½ feet deep, 3 feet in diameter.—Fyen.

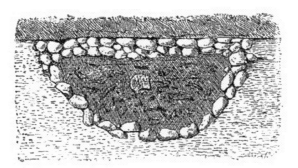

Fig. 164.—Cinerary deposit. Grave, 5 feet in diameter, 4 feet deep, lined with cobble stones, burnt bones, and broken fragments of clay urns.—Fyen.

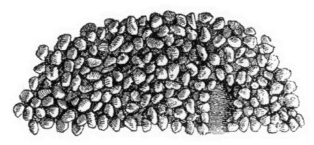

Fig. 165.—Cinerary deposit. Grave, 16 feet long, 6 feet wide, running from north-west to south-west, with hole 2½ feet deep, containing burnt bones and fragments of ornamented clay urns, remains of a large one-edged knife, &c.—Gronneskev field, Fyen.

weapons alongside an urn in which were a knife and ring of bronze; grave at Assens on Fyen, containing early iron age fibula, with bronze knife, saw, and needle; at Helsinge Zealand, grave with iron pin and bronze objects; at Brandtbjerg, near Soro, Zealand, fragments of iron fibula and objects from bronze age, &c

and weapons are thrown in, without order or method. The burnt bones and the charcoal are scattered sometimes over a bed covering a certain space, or sometimes in a heap together.

In other graves the antiquities are found resting on the black mould itself. What were the causes which led to the temporary disuse of the mound-burials we cannot tell.

Then came a period when after the burning of the corpse on the pyre the pieces of the bones were gathered into urns of clay, wooden buckets with metal mountings, vessels of bronze or glass bowls; these latter being very rare. These urns, &c., which are frequently found covered, for protection, by other vessels, were placed in chambers of varying sizes, those of the earliest graves being made of slabs, and just large enough to contain the sepulchral urn.

It should be mentioned that the development of the form of these graves runs in an unbroken chain, beginning with the large grave chamber of the stone age, and culminating in the insignificant receptacles for preserving a mere handful of burnt bones.

These graves are found sometimes singly, and at others in many hundreds, and even thousands, together.

The Kannikegaard cemetery on the island of Bornholm in the Baltic, and that of Mollegaard by Broholm on the island of Fyen, are perhaps the two richest antiquarian fields of the earliest iron grave period. Kannikegaard must have been a very large common graveyard; it is over 1,000 feet long and over 150 feet wide, and formed, no doubt, part of a more extensive burial ground, as there are other graves some 200 feet further on. In nearly all the graves scorched stones have been found, often in such quantities that they nearly fill the grave; a clay urn was also often found standing at the bottom of the burnt spots or lying on its side, sometimes with the bottom up or in broken pieces; many graves contain no antiquities, and hold only burnt bones and charcoal.[1]

[1] Broholm, situated on the S E coast of Fyen, forms the centre of the area of a magnificent archæological field, which extends about four kilometres all around it. In order to give an adequate idea of the richness of the place, I cannot do better than use the language of the late Herr F. Sehested, who in three summers discovered more than 10,000 different pieces belonging to the three ages above mentioned

In no other part of Europe do we see such a vast number of graves of this period, showing that the North must then have been inhabited by a far more dense population than other countries; from the number and contents of these *depôts cineraires,* we gather that the population burned its dead in large burial-grounds.

The practice of burning the dead had already become common in the latter part of the bronze age, and prevailed most extensively, if not entirely, during the iron period immediately following it.

Connected with the burning of the dead was the intentional damage done to objects which were exposed to the heat of the funeral pyre. Special care seems to have been taken to render swords and other weapons thoroughly useless. Swords are cut on the edges, bent and twisted; shield bosses are dented or flattened; and jewels and other objects are entirely ruined, and the illustrations seen in these volumes will show how thorough the destruction was. Bent swords and shield bosses, &c., were sometimes placed over the cinerary urn, at other times they were put at their side.

We find that the same custom also existed during the cremation period of the bronze age,[1] many of the swords of that period being broken in several places.

Among the objects most commonly found are shears, iron knives, silver and bronze fibulæ, glass beads, melted or whole in many of which the colours are unaltered, and as fresh as if made to-day; iron and bone combs, tweezers of iron, amber beads, buckles, dice, draughtsmen, fragments of trappings for horses and waggons, ornaments of gold and silver, fragments of cloth, weapons, iron keys, fragments of bronze and iron vessels, iron clinch nails, spurs of bronze and iron (showing that horses were used at a very early period in the North), clay urns, &c., &c. A remarkable fact is that the earliest

---

[1] In an urn in a mound near Veile, Jutland, was found a bent bronze poniard; and in another mound at Mors, Jutland, an urn containing burnt bones and a bent bronze poniard.

Sehested mentions (1) a bronze sword broken in four pieces, total length about 2 feet 8 inches with point missing; (2) fragments of a bronze sword with hollow handle broken at the top of the handle; (3) handle of sword with fragments of broken blade; (4) fragments of a spearhead broken near its socket. These objects had been intentionally rendered useless.

swords seem to be chiefly single-edged, a departure from the

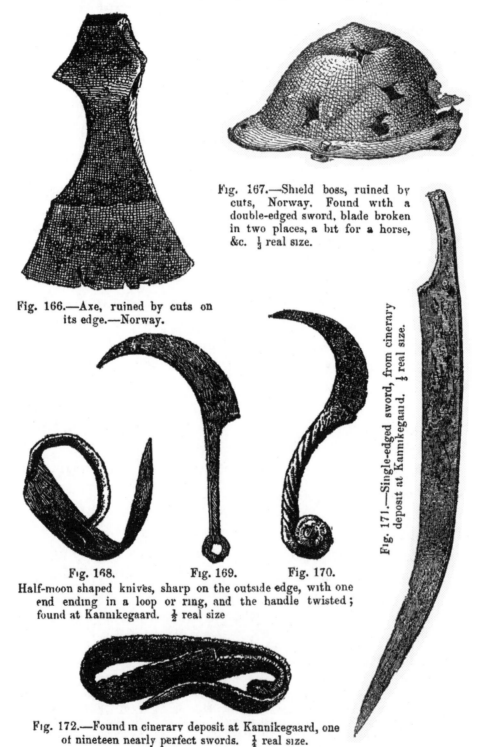

Fig. 166.—Axe, ruined by cuts on its edge.—Norway.

Fig. 167.—Shield boss, ruined by cuts, Norway. Found with a double-edged sword, blade broken in two places, a bit for a horse, &c. ⅓ real size.

Fig. 168.   Fig. 169.   Fig. 170.
Half-moon shaped knives, sharp on the outside edge, with one end ending in a loop or ring, and the handle twisted; found at Kannikegaard. ½ real size

Fig. 171.—Single-edged sword, from cinerary deposit at Kannikegaard. ⅓ real size.

Fig. 172.—Found in cinerary deposit at Kannikegaard, one of nineteen nearly perfect swords. ¼ real size.

shape of the bronze swords: the fragments of the shields are of wood, with heavy iron bosses and handles.

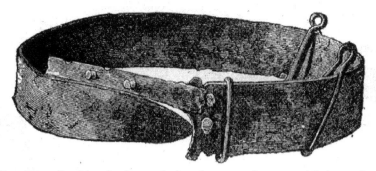

Fig. 173.—Double-edged sword, found over a clay urn with burnt bones. ½ real size.—Öland.

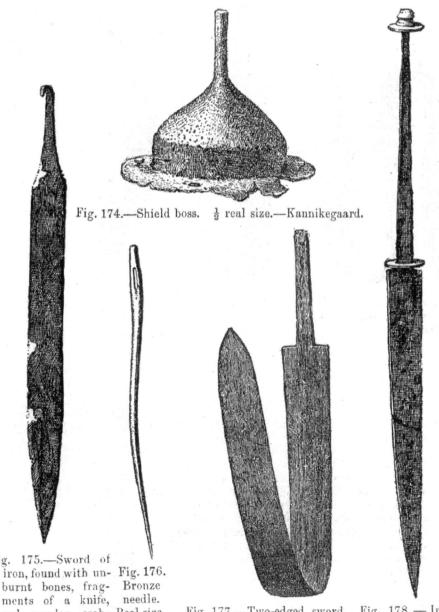

Fig. 174.—Shield boss. ½ real size.—Kannikegaard.

Fig. 175.—Sword of iron, found with unburnt bones, fragments of a knife, and wooden scabbard. Kannikegaard. ¼ real size.

Fig. 176. Bronze needle. Real size. Kannikegaard.

Fig. 177.—Two-edged sword, found in cinerary deposit at Kannikegaard. ¼ real size.

Fig. 178.— Iron knife; ⅓ real size. Kannikegaard.

K 2

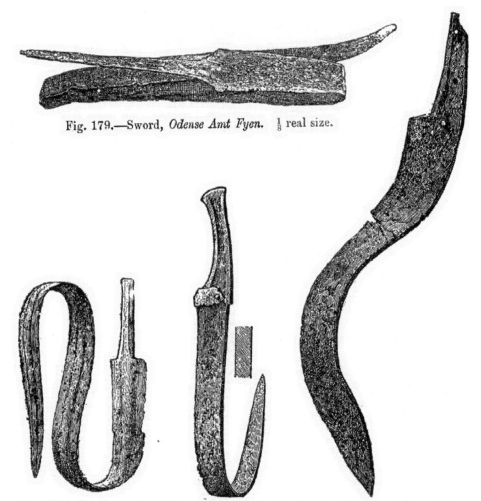

Fig. 179.—Sword, *Odense Amt Fyen.* ⅛ real size.

Fig. 180.—Bent sword. real size.—Kannike-gaard.

Fig. 181.—Single - edged sword, found in cinerary deposit Bornholm.

Fig. 182.—Single - edged sword, from cinerary deposit at Kannikegaard.

Fig. 183.—Sword from the grave-place near Horsens; found with a bronze kettle, containing burnt bones, a heavy finger-ring of gold, a torn shield-boss of bronze, a shield handle of iron with nails of bronze, a spear-head, two iron spurs, one pair of iron shears, two knives, one iron buckle, bronze mountings for a drinking horn, melted glass, fragments of a pan and sieve of bronze, different mountings of silver, numbers of pieces of melted iron and bronze; not far from the grave were found more than thirty urns containing burnt bones, and several skeleton graves.

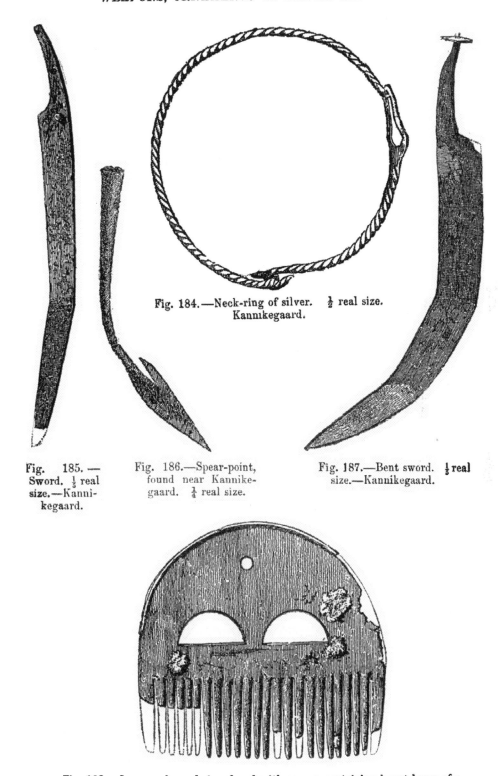

Fig. 184.—Neck-ring of silver. ½ real size. Kannikegaard.

Fig. 185. — Sword. ⅓ real size.—Kanni-kegaard.

Fig. 186.—Spear-point, found near Kannike-gaard. ¼ real size.

Fig. 187.—Bent sword. ⅓ real size.—Kannikegaard.

Fig. 188.—Iron comb, real size, found with an urn containing burnt bones of a child, &c , with other objects.

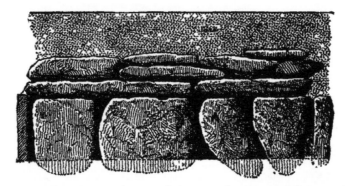

Fig. 189.—Stone cist with three layers of stone on the top, containing unburnt bones —Kannikegaard.

Fig. 190.—Inside of stone cist. Length, 6½ feet; width, 2 feet 10 inches; height, 22 inches. On left shoulder of skeleton, under the right shoulder, on the breast and by the head, were silver fibulæ.—Kannikegaard.

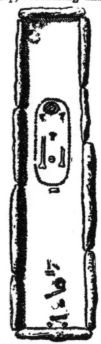

Fig. 191.— Stone coffin, 7½ feet long, 20 inches wide, 18 inches high, showing how the beads were placed.—Kannikegaard.

Fig. 192.—Fibula of bronze, plated with silver. ⅔ real size. Found in a piece of woollen cloth, with numerous beads, &c., in a stone coffin.—Kannikegaard.

Fig. 193. —Bead of gold and silver mixed.
Real size.—Kannikegaard.

Fig. 194.—Mosaic bead, of red colour
Real size.—Kannikegaard.

Fig. 195.—Mosaic bead, real size, found
with a silver ring.—Kannikegaard.

Fig. 196.—Glass bead. Real size.—
Kannikegaard.

Fig. 197.—Fibula of bronze: on its pin
was a piece of linen—found with mosaic
beads in a stone coffin. Real size.—
Kannikegaard.

Fig. 198.—Fibula of silver, with fragments
of bone comb, long knife, with remains
of wooden scabbard, &c. Stone coffin
9 feet long. Real size.—Kannikegaard.

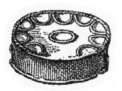

Fig. 199.—Bead of gold and silver mixed,
made of three pieces soldered together.
—Kannikegaard.

Fig. 200.—Axe of iron, found together with human
teeth, horn comb, &c. ½ real size.—Kannikegaard.

157

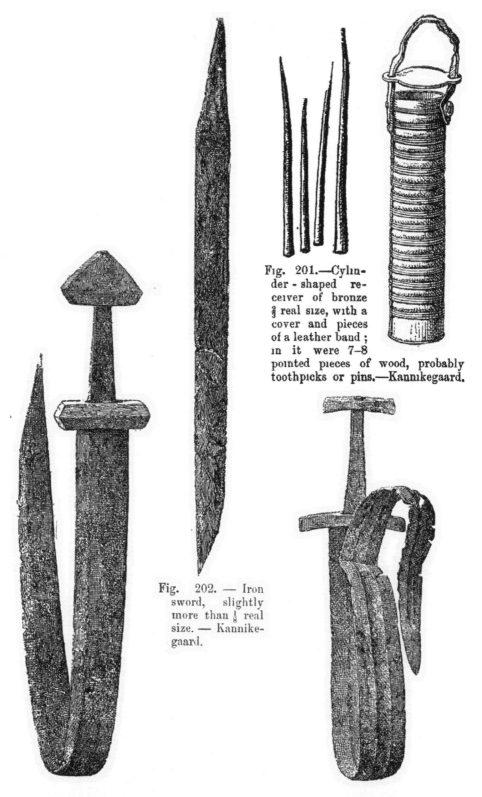

Fig. 201.—Cylin-
der - shaped re-
ceiver of bronze
⅔ real size, with a
cover and pieces
of a leather band;
in it were 7–8
pointed pieces of wood, probably
toothpicks or pins.—Kannikegaard.

Fig. 202. — Iron
sword, slightly
more than ⅛ real
size. — Kannike-
gaard.

Fig. 203.—One-edged sword, from a
grave-mound, Norway. ⅔ real size.

Fig. 204.—Double-edged sword, from a
grave-mound, Norway, found with other
damaged weapons, &c. ⅔ real size.

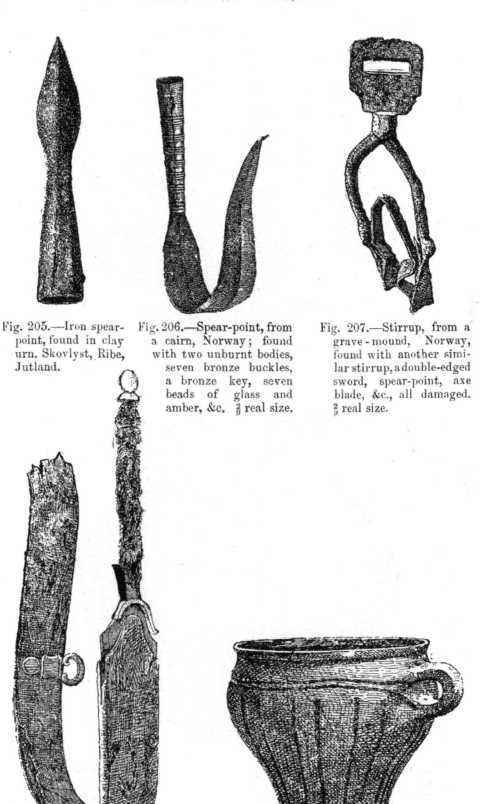

Fig. 205.—Iron spear-point, found in clay urn. Skovlyst, Ribe, Jutland.

Fig. 206.—Spear-point, from a cairn, Norway; found with two unburnt bodies, seven bronze buckles, a bronze key, seven beads of glass and amber, &c. $\frac{2}{3}$ real size.

Fig. 207.—Stirrup, from a grave-mound, Norway, found with another similar stirrup, a double-edged sword, spear-point, axe blade, &c., all damaged. $\frac{2}{3}$ real size.

Fig. 208.—Cinerary urn and bent sword with iron sheath.—Skovlyst, Ribe, Jutland.

The cinerary urns are of different sizes and shapes, many of which are not ungraceful: the clay of which they are made is

Fig. 209.—Black clay urn, with hollow spots, ¼ real size, containing burnt bones —Broholm, Fyen.

Fig. 210.—Clay urn with svastica, ¼ real size, top of which was closed by the bottom of another, containing burnt bones, a pointed iron knife, a needle of bronze, melted lumps of glass from beads of different colours, &c.—Bornholm.

of a black or greyish colour, coarse and rough, porous, and often very tender; the people even at a later period never

seeming to have been skilled in the potter's art. Many of
the designs upon them are peculiar, and were, no doubt,

Fig. 211.—Dark brown clay urn, ⅓ real size.—Mollegaard, Broholm.

Fig. 212.—Urn with fine vertical stripes and punctuation, containing burnt bones,
bone comb with bronze rivets, ornamented with concentric lines along the
back. ¼ real size.—Mollegaard, Broholm.

symbolical. Among these are circles with dots, triangles,
the svastika and triad, &c., &c. Glazed pottery was unknown
in the North.

Fig. 213.—Urn of dark grey colour, containing burnt bones, &c.—Móllegaard, Broholm.

Fig. 214.—Black urn, containing only burnt bones. ¼ real size.—Móllegaard, Broholm.

Fig. 215.—Urn of reddish clay, ⅓ real size, which had another urn on the top like a cover.—Kannikegaard.

Fig. 216.—Small urn real size, containing nothing but earth.—Kannikegaard.

Fig. 217.—Clay urn, ½ real size.—Kannikegaard.

Fig. 218.—Clay urn.—Kannikegaard.

Fig. 219.—Small greyish clay urn found in a burned spot. ⅓ real size.—Möllegaard, Broholm.

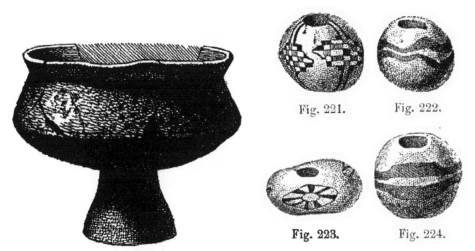

Fig. 221.

Fig. 222.

Fig. 223.

Fig. 224.

Fig. 220.—Urn, ½ real size, and glass mosaic beads, real size; two of the beads found were blue, with bands of red, yellow, and red; two more were blue, with a pattern repeated four times, containing black, yellow, red, and white grounds; one was white, with a wheel-like pattern, repeated three times, having a red centre and black spokes.—Mollegaard, Broholm.

163

225.—Clay urn filled with burnt bones, and numerous objects. ¼ real size
—Möllegaard.

Fig. 226.—Wooden bucket with bronze hoops. ¼ real size. Found in large mound,
with burnt bones, and a piece of gold spiral ring.—Norway.

Fig. 227.—Wooden bucket, with bronze fittings. ¼ real size. Found in a large round
tumulus inside a stone sepulchral chamber, with two pairs of iron scissors, fragments of two double-edged swords, fragments of several arrow-heads, two shield
bosses, &c., &c.—Norway.

164

Fig. 228.—Clay urn, ⅓ real size, found in a tumulus with another clay urn.

Fig. 229.—Clay urn, upside down, to cover a bronze basin, of Roman manufacture, placed on a slab filled with ashes and burnt bones, fragments of bronze ornaments and glass vessels which had been exposed on the pyre; ashes and bones were scattered round, showing the burning to have taken place on the spot ⅓ real size.—Harf Medelpad, Norway.

Fig. 230.—Clay urn in a stone cist containing the remains of a skeleton. &c. ¼ real size.—Sojvide, Gotland.

In Gotland, the graves are made of lime slabs. Some of these stone cists are not deep under the ground, and without apparently any mound.

Fig. 231.—Clay urn, ¼ real size, found in a round mound, inside a sepulchral chamber of the length of 6 feet, width 2 feet, height 1 foot 8 inches.—Norway.

Fig. 232.—Clay urn, ½ real size, found in a mound containing a large stone cist, with fragments of iron objects and another clay urn.—Norway.

Fig. 233.—Clay urn, in a mound. Bohuslan.

Fig. 234.—Clay urn in a stone cist.— Gotland.

Fig. 235.—Clay urn, covering one filled with burnt bones. ¼ real size.—Nafverstad, Bohuslän.

Fig. 236.—Clay urn, with three partitions (on the outside are ten knobs), found, with fragments of a belt hook, under a stone slab. ⅔ real size.—Himmelshöi, Bornholm.

237.—Clay urn, ⅓ real size, found in a round mound, inside a sepulchral chamber.—Stavanger, Norway.

Fig. 238.—Clay urn, ¼ real size, found in a mound.—Norway.

L

Fig. 239.—Clay urn, ¼ real size, containing burnt bones.—Norway. Earlier iron age.

Fig. 240.—Clay urn, ¼ real size, found in a mound placed over burnt bones contained in a clay urn.—Norway. Earlier iron age.

Fig. 241.—Clay urn.—Norway. ½ real size. Skeleton grave, found with five other clay urns, a silver fibula, &c.

Fig. 242.—Clay urn filled with burnt bones and covered with another vase. ¼ real size. Found in a large round tumulus—Bohuslän.

Fig. 243.—Clay urn, containing burnt bones and fragments of a bone comb, glass beads, lever balance of spindle, &c., found, covered with a slab, in an oblong mound. ⅓ real size. Earlier iron age.

Fig. 244.—Iron urn or kettle, 10 inches high, 12¾ inches in diameter, and 6 inches deep. —Norway. Three other kettles of same shape and workmanship have been found: one in a grave-mound.

Fig. 245.—Bronze cinerary urn; ⅓ real size.—Norway.

L 2

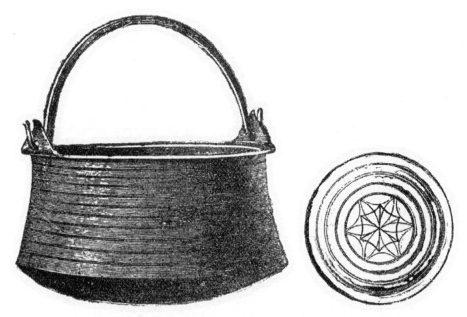

Fig. 246.—Bronze kettle, ½ real size.—Norway. Found under a slab in the border of a round mound. It contained burnt bones, among which was a gold bracelet, and other objects.

Fig. 247.

Fig. 248.

Small clay vessels found in an oblong mound at Greby, Bohuslän, found with a clay urn filled with burnt bones, on which were fragments of a bone comb, glass beads, &c. ½ real size. Earlier iron age.

Fig. 249.—Round clay urn, found in a mound, Greby, Bohuslän, containing burnt bones and two melted glass beads, &c. ¼ real size. Earlier iron age.

Fig. 250.—Clay urn, ¼ real size, contain
ing burnt bones, found inside a sepul
chral chamber of stone, 6 feet long,
nearly 4 feet wide, and 3 feet high,
in a round tumulus.—Norway

Fig. 251.—Cinerary vase of clay, ⅓ real
size, found surrounded by burnt bones
in a mound at Bjorko. Later iron age.

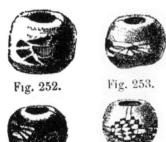

Fig. 252.   Fig. 253.

Fig. 254.   Fig. 255.

Four of seven mosaic glass beads, real
size.—Broholm grave.

Of variegated colours, yellow, white, black,
blue, and red, and of different designs.
Besides those represented were 26 blue
glass beads, one of which had red stripes,
one red, another lilac; there were also
eight amber beads, different shapes, and
a fibula of bronze, to which was attached
a coarse woven cloth, &c.

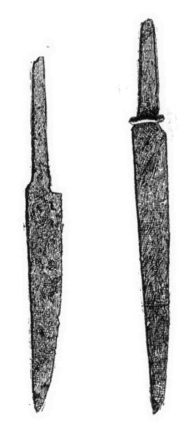

Fig. 256.   Fig. 257.

Iron knives, ½ real size, in an urn on
the top of burnt bones without coal
and ashes.—Mollegaard, Broholm.

171

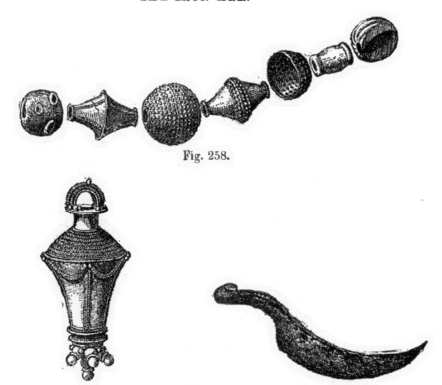

Fig. 258.

Fig. 259.—Porcelain beads, and beads of gold and silver mixed. Real size. —Bornholm. Earlier iron age.

Fig. 260.—Curved iron knife, ½ real size, and with the remains of a large urn containing burnt bones.

Fig. 261.--Iron knife, ⅓ real size; found in a cinerary urn containing burnt bones, two pairs of shears, a buckle, awl, and ring, all of iron; a bronze fibula, &c.— Mollegaard, Broholm

The following objects in one grave in Möllegaard will give a thorough idea of the destruction wrought on the pyre.

Fig. 262.—Handle of iron for kettle.—Möllegaard.

Fig. 263.—Remains of a damaged iron instrument and silver fibula rusted together. Real size.

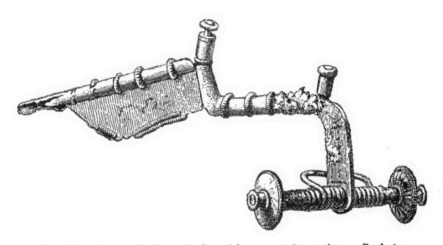

Fig. 264.—Silver fibula and other objects rusted together. Real size.

Fig. 267.—Dark grey, with white eyes.

Fig. 266.—Blue and light green.

Fig. 268. — Red, with red. black, and yellow design

Fig. 265.—Iron comb, ½ real size. Möllegaard.

Melted glass mosaic beads, real size.

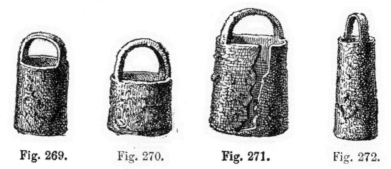

Fig. 269.   **Fig. 270.**   **Fig. 271.**   **Fig. 272.**

Four of eleven iron ornaments, shaped like buckets.   Real size.- -Möllegaard.

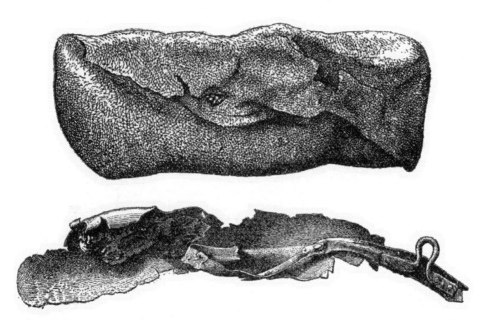

Fig. 273.—Bronze vessel, 9 inches in diameter, with handle fastened with rivets.
It contained numerous articles taken from the pyre, but rust had united them all.

Fig. 274.   Fig. 275.   Fig. 276.—Iron buckle,
Two iron spurs in burnt spot.—Kannikegaard.   ⅔ real size.—Kan-
                                                  nikegaard

Fig. 277.   Fig. 278.

Two prismatic dice, real size, damaged by fire, the sides pointing towards each other always counting seven; found in an urn with burnt bones, remains of a glass cup. &c., one foot under the ground.—Kannikegaard.

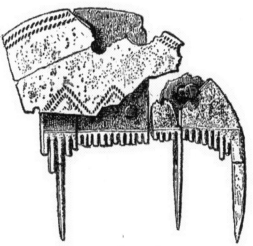

Fig. 279.   Fig. 280.

Fragments of bone comb and iron rivet, real size, found in a cinerary urn.—Broholm.

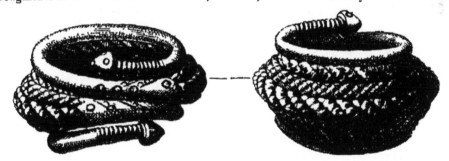

Fig. 281.—Spiral ring of massive gold, showing the two sides, found near a large bronze cauldron, and fragments of the mountings of a carriage, several iron swords, shield bosses, &c. Real size.—Broholm.

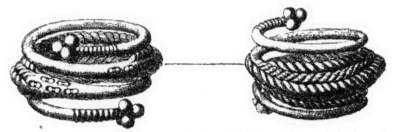

Fig. 282.—Spiral gold ring much alloyed with silver, showing the two sides. Real size.—Broholm.

CHAPTER XI.

RUNES.

Early knowledge of the art of writing—Knowledge of rune writing very remote—Archaic Greek characters—Jewels with earlier runes—Runes on memorial stones—Runic alphabets—The origin of runes—Their mystical meaning—Memorial runic stones—Runic staves—The Runatal—Archaic inscriptions compared with runes.

As the early form of writing known as runes occurs so frequently in connection with these Northern relics, it will be well to devote a chapter to the subject. The written records and finds in the North give numerous examples showing that at a very early period the tribes of the North knew the art of writing. The characters used were called "rúnir" runes.

The knowledge of rune writing was so remote, that it was supposed by the people to have come with Odin, thus showing its great antiquity and possibility of the theory that the runes were brought to the North by the people who had migrated from the south-east, and who may have obtained their knowledge from the Greek colonies situated on the shores of the Black Sea or Palus Mæotis. The numerous runic inscriptions, showing in many cases the archaic form of these characters, bear witness to the truth of the Northern records, though it cannot be denied that they often closely resemble the Etruscan letters. To corroborate these records a considerable number of antiquities, the forms of which are unknown in Italy and are similar to those of the North, have been found in Southern Russia, and may be seen in the museums of that country.

At what early date the art of writing runes became known in the North it is impossible to tell. From the Roman coins found in the Nydam, Vimose, Thorsberg, &c. finds we know that the people knew the art at the period to which the coins belong, but this is far from proving to us that they had just learned the art of writing; people do not learn how to write first on objects of gold and silver; but, at any rate, we can fix a date as early as the second or third century of the Christian era. It must be admitted as surprising, if the Northern peoples were so advanced as to manufacture the beautiful weapons and artistic articles found in the graves and elsewhere, they had not also instituted a coinage of their own.

That the knowledge of runes did not come to the North before that of working iron is almost certain, as no runes have been found there on the objects belonging to the bronze age. A fact we must bear in mind is, that in the earlier graves of the iron age, many of which are of greater antiquity than the bog finds,[1] the objects were so thoroughly destroyed on the pyre, that all traces of runic character upon them would disappear.

Besides the runes found inscribed upon jewels, weapons,

---

[1] I can give an example that has lately come to my knowledge to prove this assertion. Professor Lorange found runes on parts of burnt bones found in a grave which he with Professor Stephens places, judging from the antiquities which belonged to it, as belonging to the sixth century.

"RUNE-INSCRIBED BURNT BONE.

"In a letter dated Feb. 27th, 1886, I received from my friend the gifted Norwegian old-lorist A. Lorange, Keeper of the Bergen Forn-hall, a facsimile drawing of a piece of burnt bone, shortly before found in a grave-urn from the early iron age at Jæderen. Afterwards he kindly sent the original to the Danish Museum, that I might give a faultless engraving. While there, the frail treasure was scientifically treated by Hr. Steffensen, the Conservator, and it is now quite hard and in excellent order. But even when it was taken from the urn, the runes were sharp and quite readable. These Old-Northern letters were elegantly cut, most of them in decorative writing, that is, with two or three strokes instead of one, very much

in the style of the (? 7th century) Old-Danish Bone Amulet found at Lindholm in Scane, Sweden ('Old Northern Run. Mon,' vol. I., p. 219; III., p. 33; 4to Handbook, p. 24); and of the ashen Lance-shaft from the Danish Kragehul Moss, not later than the year 400 ('O. N. Run. Mon,' vol. III., p. 133; 4to Handbook, p. 90).

"This burnt bone is nearly 4 inches long; average width, ½ inch. It bears over forty rune-staves, cut in two lines, in the *Boustrophedon* order.

"From the rune-types and language I judged this piece to date from the 6th century. But as Hr. Lorange was familiar with the build and grave-gear of the tumuli of a similar class, I begged him to say whether—exclusively from his standpoint as archæologist—he agreed with me. He replied, *that he did*.

"If I have read the runes aright, this object also has been a heathen amulet. It is the first burnt bone yet found *risted with runes*. Other such we may have lost, for want of lynx-eyed examination.

"GEORGE STEPHENS,
"Cheapinghaven, Denmark.
"*November* 6, 1886."

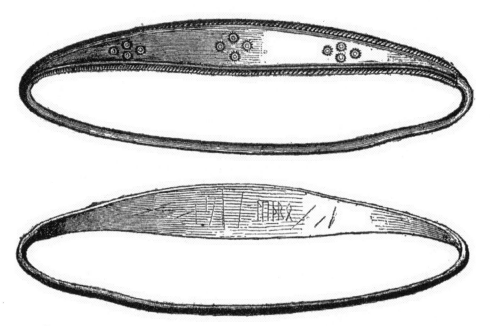

Fig. 283.—Diadem of gold, with earlier runes inside; found in oblong mound of sandy mould with remains of a stone coffin.—Jutland.

Fig. 284.—Silver fibula, with earlier runes,[1] richly gilt, the zigzag and runes filled with blue niello; ⅔ real size; earlier iron age.—Etelhem, Gotland.

[1] Similar runes also occurred on a scabbard found at Varpelev, and on a gold horn.

coins,[1] &c., there are others engraved on rocks and memorial stones, which are of very great antiquity, some of which seem to be earlier than the runes of the bog finds.

There are two alphabets; the earlier one numbered twenty-four, the later sixteen letters.

ᚠ ᚢ ᚦ ᚨ ᚱ ᚲ ᚷ ᚹ : ᚺ ᚾ ᛁ ᛃ ᛇ ᛈ ᛉ ᛊ : ᛏ ᛒ ᛖ ᛗ ᛚ ᛜ ᛟ

f u th o r c g v   h n i y yo p a s   t b e m l ng œ

Earlier Runes from the Vadstena bracteate.

ᚠ ᚢ ᚦ ᚭ ᚱ ᚴ : ᚼ ᚾ ᛁ ᛅ ᛋ : ᛏ ᛒ ᛚ ᛘ ᛆ

f u th o r k h n i a s t b l m œ

Later Runes

The Vadstena alphabet is divided into three sections, each containing eight letters or characters. The earlier runes were written from the right to the left; the later runic inscriptions are read from the left to the right. The later runes differ considerably from the earlier ones, from the gradual changes that took place, some falling out of use, till only sixteen existed in later times. Their signification also changed.

Were it not for the evidence of the finds having runic inscriptions of the fuller runic alphabet, it would have seemed more probable that the less developed one was the earlier; but in the face of the most indisputable proofs of the antiquity of the fuller alphabet, such assertions cannot be made. The only conclusion to which this leads us therefore is, that the runic alphabet must in the course of time have become simplified. There are runic inscriptions which contain both earlier and later runes, but the former at last gradually disappeared.

It seems that the custom of having alphabets on objects

---

[1] Danish coins with runic characters have been obtained from as early a period as that of Svein Úlfsson, or the 12th century. A runic *kefli*, according to its contents, carved soon after 1200, is preserved in the Danish museum. It was found in Vinje church, Upper Telemarken, of Norway. The inscription thereon signifies: *Sigurd Jarlson traced these Runes the Saturday after Botolf's* mass, *when he journeyed hither and would not be reconciled to Sverre, the slayer of his father and brother.* Sigurd was the son of the well-known Erling Skakke; he lost a battle against Sverre in 1200. As the latter died in 1202, it was between these two dates that the unsuccessful attempt at reconciliation occurred. (Stephens, p. 515.)

such as the Vadstena bracteate existed in Greece and Etruria.[1] The earliest graves in the Roman colonies in which there is writing are very few; what writing there is is never in the language of the people, but always in Latin; and nearly all, if not all such graves, are those of Christian people.

The art of writing shows the advanced civilisation of the

Fig. 285.—A fibula of silver, partly gilt, with same runic letters, with slight variations. Real size.—Charnay, Burgundy, France (of Norse origin).

people of the North compared with that of the other

---

[1] Dennis, p. 306. See Signor Gamurrini, who has described and illustrated them (see Ann Inst. 1871, pp. 156–166). Franzius, in his 'Elementa Epigraphices Græcæ,' p. 22, 4to, Berolini, 1840, gives three Greek alphabets found inscribed in the same manner on various objects No. 1, of twenty-four letters, is on the Agyllic vase first engraved by Lepsius ('Annal. Hist. Archæol. Rom.,' vol. viii., p. 186). The second is a fragment, only sixteen letters, found on the wall of an Etruscan sepulchre ('Lanzi Saggio di ling. Etr,' ii, p. 436). The third is incomplete, having only the beginning, or the first fourteen letters.

countries mentioned   The language of Tacitus[1] is plain enough, and any other interpretation is not correct. The assertion made that the knowledge of writing came to the North through the present Germany is not borne out by the facts. Runic monuments do not occur south of the river Eider, either on detached stones or engraved on rocks. The few jewels found scattered here and there, either in France or Germany

Fig. 286.—Neck-ring of gold, with runes; ½ real size; found (1838) in a round mound —Wallachia.

are thoroughly Northern, and show that in these places the people of the North made warfare, as corroborated by the testimony of the Eddas and Sagas, as well as of Frankish and old English and other records.

Great indeed has been, and still is, the harvest of runic monuments or objects in the North. Every year several new objects with these characters are discovered in fields, bogs, and graves, or when old walls or buildings are demolished.

---

[1] Tacitus (Germ. c. 19) says: "*Litterarum secreta viri pariter ac feminæ ignorant*" (Men and women are equally ignorant of the secrets of letter writing)   The earliest Latin inscriptions found in the North have characters unlike the runes.

England, being the earliest and most important of the Northern colonies, possesses many monuments and objects with runes; among them a large knife, now in the British Museum, found in the bed of the Thames, the blade of which is ornamented with gold and silver, and an inscription in runes.[1]

From the sagas we learn that runes were traced on staves, rods, weapons, the stem and rudder of ships, drinking-horns, fish bones, and upon the teeth of *Sleipnir*, &c.

In Runatal (Odin's Rune song), or the last part of Havamal, there is a most interesting account of the use that could be made of runes. It shows plainly that in earlier times they were not used by the people in general for writing; that they were mystic, being employed for conjurations and the like, and therefore regarded with a certain awe and superstition; just as to-day writing is looked upon by certain savage tribes, who cannot be made to understand how speech can be transmitted and kept on paper for an indefinite period.

In this song, Odin is supposed to be teaching some one, and giving advice; he reckons up his arts thus :—

I know that I hung
On the windy tree
Nine[2] whole nights,
Wounded with a spear,
Given to Odin,
Myself to myself,
On the tree
Of which no one knows
From what roots it comes.

They gave me no food
Nor a horn (drink);

I peeled downward,
I caught the runes,
Learned them weeping;[3]
Thence I fell down.

Nine songs of might
I learnt from the famous
Son of Bolthorn, father of Bestla:[4]
And I got a draught
Of the precious mead,
Taken out of Odrerir.[5]

---

[1] In the Royal Library at Copenhagen there exist three most remarkable manuscripts in runic characters, showing the late period at which these still were in use. The first of these manuscripts, bearing the date of 1543, was written as a journal by Mogens Gyldenstjerne (a Danish noble) of Stjernholm, during a voyage into the North Sea undertaken by him in that year. The second bears the date of 1547, and is written as a note on a rough draft of a power of attorney by Bille of Bregentved, another Danish noble. The third is a notice about the last-mentioned estate, also containing a line in runic characters.

The Runic codex containing the Scanian law also contains, in a different hand, a list of Danish kings, and among these one Ambruthe as having been king in Jutland. The time of this codex can be approximately fixed at about the year 1300.

[2] The sacred or mystical number.

[3] We see that Odin had to go through a terrible ordeal to learn the runes.

[4] Bolthorn and Bestla are nowhere else mentioned in the earlier Edda.

[5] Song-rouser, one of the vessels holding the sacred mead.

Then I became fruitful
And wise;
I grew and I throve;
Word followed word
With me;
Act followed act
With me.

Thou wilt find runes
And letters to read,
Very large staves,
Very strong staves,
Which the mighty wise one drew,
And the high powers made,
And the Hropt of the gods (Odin)
  carved.

Odin (carved runes) among the Asar;[1]
Dain with the Alfar;
Dvalin with the Dvergar;
Alsvid (the All-wise)
With the Jötnar;
Some I carved myself.

Better 'tis not to invoke
Than sacrifice too much;
A gift always looks for reward;
Better not to send
Than offer too much;
Thus Thund[2] carved
Before the origin of men;
He rose there;
There he came back.

I know incantations
Which no king's wife knows,
And no man's son.
Help is the first one called,
And it will help thee
Against strife and sorrows,
Against all kinds of grief.

A second I know,
Which the sons of men need,
Who would as leeches live.[3]

The third I know,
If I am in sore need of
Bonds for my foes;
I deaden the edges[4]
Of my foes;
Neither weapons nor wiles hurt for
  them.

The fourth I know,
If men lay
Bonds on my limbs;
I sing (incantations) so
That I can walk;
The fetter flies off my feet,
And the shackles off my hands.

The fifth I know,
If I see an arrow flying,
Shot to harm in the array;
It flies not so fast
That I cannot stay it
If I get sight of it.

The sixth I know,
If a man wounds me
With the roots of a young tree,[5]
Illness shall eat
The man
That lays spells on me,
Rather than me.

The seventh I know,
If I see a hall burning
Round the sitting men;
It burns not so broadly
That I cannot save them;
Such an incantation can I sing.

The eighth I know,
Which for every one is
Useful to learn;
Where hate arises
Among sons of kings
I can allay it soon.

---

[1] From this stanza we learn which tribes or people knew the art of writing runes.

[2] Thund = Odin

[3] Three last lines of stanza are missing

[4] The edges of weapons. Some persons were supposed to have the power to deaden weapons' edges.

[5] Spells on the roots of a young tree or sticks.

M

The ninth I know,
If I am in need
To save my ship afloat,
I hush the wind
On the waves,
And calm all the sea.

The tenth I know,
If I see hedge-riders [1]
Playing in the air,
I cause that
They go astray
Out of their skins,
Out of their minds.

The eleventh I know,
If I shall to battle
Lead my old friends,
I sing under the shields,
And they go with might
Safe to the fray,
Safe out of the fray,
Safe wherever they come from.

The twelfth I know,
If I see on a tree
A halter-corpse swinging;
I carve so
And draw in runes,
That the man shall walk
And talk to me.

The thirteenth I know,
If I do on a young thegn [3]
Water sprinkle;
He will not fall
Though he go into battle;
That man sinks not by swords.

The fourteenth I know,
If I shall reckon up

The gods for the host of men;
Asar and Alfar [4]
I know all well;
Few unwise know so much.

The fifteenth I know,
That which Thjodreyrir [5] sang,
The Dverg, before the door of
Delling; [6]
He sang strength to the Asar
And fame to the Alfar,
Wisdom to Hroptayi. [7]

The sixteenth I know,
If of the comely maiden
I want all the heart and the love,
I change the mind
Of the white-armed woman
And turn all her heart.

The seventeenth I know,
That the youthful maiden
Will late forsake me.
These songs
Wilt thou Loddfafnir [8]
Long have lacked,
Though they are good if thou takest
them,
Useful if thou learnest them,
Profitable if thou takest them.

I know the eighteenth,
Which I will never tell
To maiden or man's wife,
Except to her alone
That holds me in her arms,
Or is my sister;
All is better
That one alone only knows. [9]
This is the end of the song.

---

[1] Witches and ghosts were believed to ride on hedges and tops of houses at night.

[2] Hanged corpse

[3] Man.

[4] Here the Alfar are reckoned among the gods.

[5] The mighty rearer

[6] Delling is the father of Day (Vaf-thrúdnismál, 25; Later Edda).

[7] Odin

[8] Loddfafnir is some one whom Odin is teaching

[9] One must not tell his secret to any one

Now the song of Har is sung,	Hail to him who sang !
In the hall of Har ;	Hail to him who knows !
Very useful to the sons of men,	May he who has learned profit by it !
Useless to the sons of Jotnar.[1]	Hail to those who have listened !

"Atli was a great, powerful, and wise king ; he had many men with him, and took counsel with them how he should get the gold ; he knew that Gunnar and Hogni were owners of so much property[2] that no man had the like of it ; he sent men to the brothers and invited them to a feast in order to give them many gifts ; Vingi was the leader of the messengers. The queen knew of their secret talk, and suspected treachery against her brothers She cut runes, took a gold ring, and tied on it a wolf's hair ; she gave this to the king's messengers. They went as the king had told them, and before they landed Vingi saw the runes and changed them so that they meant that Gudrún wished them to come to Atli. They came to the hall of Gunnar and were well received ; large fires were made before them ; there they drank merrily the best drinks. Vingi said : 'King Atli sent me hither and wanted you to visit him to get honour and large gifts, helmets and shields, swords and coats-of-mail, gold and good clothes, warriors and horses and large estates, and he says he would rather let you than any others have his realm.' Then Gunnar turned his head and said to Hogni : 'What shall we accept of this offer ? He offers us a large realm, but I know no kings owning as much gold as we, for we own all the gold which lay on Gnitaheath, and large skemmas (rooms) filled with gold and the best cutting weapons and all kinds of war-clothes ; I know my horse to be the best, my sword the keenest, my gold the most renowned.' Hógni answered : 'I wonder at his offer, for this he has seldom done, and it is unadvisable to go to him. I am surprised that among the costly things which Atli sent to us I saw a wolf's hair tied on a gold ring, and it may be that Gudrún thinks he has a wolf's mind (mind of a foe) towards us, and that she wants us not to go.' Then Vingi showed him the runes which he said Gudrún had sent. The men now went to sleep, while they continued drinking with some others. Then Hógni's wife, Kostbera, a most handsome woman, went to them and looked at the runes. She and Gunnar's wife, Glaumvör, a very accomplished woman, brought drink. The kings became very drunk. Vingi saw this, and said : 'I will not conceal that King Atli is very heavy in his movements, and too old to defend his realm,

---

[1] We see by this and many other passages that the Jotnar were the enemies of the Asar

[2] Property here means gold

and his sons are young and good for nothing; he wishes to give you power over the realm while they are so young, and he prefers you to enjoy it.' Now Gunnar was very drunk, and a great realm was offered to him, and he could not resist fate; he promised to go, and told it to his brother Högni, who answered: 'Your resolve must be carried out, and I will follow thee, but I am unwilling to go'" (Volsunga, c. 33).

Runes were occasionally used as charms in cases of illness.

Egil went on a journey to Vermaland to collect the tax from the Jarl Arnvid, who was suspected of having slain King Hakon the Good's men when they went thither for this purpose. On the way he came to the house of a bondi named Thorfinn.

"As Egil and Thorfinn sat and took their meal, Egil saw that a woman lay sick on the cross-bench, and asked who she was. Thorfinn answered that she was his daughter Helga. She had been long ill from a very wasting sickness; she could not sleep at night, and was like one *ham-stolen*[1] (crazy) 'Has anything been tried for her illness?' said Egil. Thorfinn said: 'Runes have been traced by the son of a bondi in the neighbourhood, but she is far more ill since than she was before; canst thou do anything for such an illness?' Egil answered: 'It may be that it will not be worse though I take charge of it.' When he had done eating he went to where she lay and spoke to her. He bad that she be taken out of bed and clean clothes put under her, which was done. Then he examined the bed, and there found a piece of whalebone with runes on it. He read them, cut them off, and scraped the chips into the fire; he burned the whalebone and had her clothes carried into the open air. Then Egil sang:—

As man shall not trace runes
Except he can read them well,
It is thus with many a man
That the dark letters bewilder
him.

I saw on the cut whalebone
Ten hidden[2] letters carved,
That have caused to the leek-linden
(woman)
A very long sorrow.

"Egil traced runes, and placed them under the pillow in the bed where she rested. It seemed to her as if she awoke from a sleep, and she said she was then healed, though she

[1] Of witches = shape-stolen. | [2] Undecipherable.

had little strength.   Her father and mother were very glad"
(Egil's Saga, c 75).

When persons were deaf, they communicated with others by
means of runes.

"Thorkel told his sister Orny that the steersman had come
to his house, saying: 'I wish, kinswoman, that thou shouldst
serve[1] him during the winter, for most other men have
enough to do.'   Orny carved runes on a wood-stick, for she
could not speak, and Thorkel took it and read.   The wood-
stick told this: 'I do not like to undertake to serve the
steersman, for my mind tells me that, if I do, much evil
will come of it.'   He became angry because his sister declined,
so that when she saw it she consented to serve Ivar, and continued to do so during the winter" (Thorstein Uxafót, Fornmanna Sogur, 110).

Runes traced on sticks (*kefli*), which were sometimes used.
did not offer proper security against falsification, unless personal runes were used, which however were known only to a
very limited number.

An Icelandic settler named Gris, who had gone on a journey
to Norway, was going back to Iceland from Nidaros (Throndhjem).

"A woman came to him with two children, and asked him
to take them with him.   He asked: 'What have they to do
there?'   She said that their uncle Thorstein Svorf lived in the
district where Gris had a bœr, and that her name was Thorarna.
Gris said: 'I will not do that without some evidence.'   Then
she gave him from under her cloak a stick on which were many
words known to Thorstein.   Gris said: 'Thou wilt think me
greedy for property.'   She asked: 'Ask as much as thou wilt?'
He answered: 'Four hundreds in very good silver, and thou
must follow with the children.'   'It is not possible for me to follow
them,' she said, 'but I will pay what thou askest.'   She told
him the name of the boy Klaufi, and of the girl Sigrid.   Gris
added: 'How hast thou become so wretched, thou who art of
such good kin?'   She replied: 'I was taken in war by Snækoll
Ljotsson, who is the father of these children; after which he
drove me away against my will.'
"Gris had a favourable wind after he had taken these children

---

[1] Take care of his clothes, &c.

on board, and sailed to Iceland into the same river-mouth as usual; and as soon as he had landed he carried away both children, so that no one knew of his coming. That evening he went to Thorstein at Grund, who received him very well, mostly because his son Karl had gone abroad at the time that Gris had been abroad, and Thorstein wanted to ask about his journey. Gris spoke little. Thorstein inquired if he was ill. Gris answered that it was rather that he was not well pleased with his doings; 'for I have brought hither two children of thy sister.' 'How can that be?' said Thorstein. 'And I will not acknowledge their relationship unattested.' Then Gris showed him the stick, and he recognized his words thereon, though it was long since he spoke them. He acknowledged the children, but paid Gris to bring up Klaufi" (Svarfdæla, c. 11).

"Klaufi and Gris sailed from Solskel southward along the Norwegian coast, until they came to an islet, where lay two ships with no men on them. They jumped on board one of the ships, and Klaufi said: 'Tell thou, Gris, who has steered these ships, for here are runes, which tell it.' Gris said he did not know. Klaufi answered: 'Thou knowest, and must tell.' Gris was obliged to do so, against his will, and thus read the runes: 'Karl steered the ship when the runes were carved'" (Svarfdæla, c. 14).

"One summer in the time of King Harald Hardradi it happened, as was often the case, that an Icelandic ship came to Nidaros (Throndhjem). On this ship there was a poor man who kept watch during the night. While all slept he saw two men go secretly up to Gaularas with digging tools and begin to dig; he saw they searched for property, and when he came on them unawares he saw that they had dug up a chest filled with property. He said to the one who seemed to be the leader that he wanted three marks for keeping quiet, and some more if he should wish it. Thorfinn assented to this, and weighed out to him three marks; when they opened the chest a large ring and a thick necklace of gold lay uppermost. The Icelander saw runes carved on the chest; these said that Hakon Jarl had been the owner of this property" (Fornmanna Sogur, vi. 271).

One day Thurid, the old foster-mother of Thorbjörn Öngul, an enemy of Grettir, asked to be taken down to the sea.

"When she came there, she found the stump of a tree with the roots on, as large as a man could carry. She looked at the stump, and had it turned round. On one side it looked as if it had been burred and rubbed. On this side she had a small spot smoothed with a knife. Then she took her knife and carved runes on it, and reddened it with her blood, singing words of witchcraft over it. She walked backwards around the stump, in the opposite direction to the sun's course, and pronounced many powerful incantations thereover. Then she had it pushed out into the sea, and said it should be driven

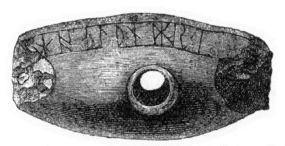

Fig. 287.—Stone axe with earlier runes; ⅔ real size.—Upland.

Fig. 288.—Earlier runic inscription discovered (1872) on a perpendicular bluff 20 feet high and about 200 feet from the shore, at Valsfjord, Fosen, North, Throndhjem. The runes are carved in a perpendicular line from the bottom up. Hardly anything is left of the letters. The Runes; ¹⁄₁₅ real size

out to Drangey, and cause great mischief to Grettir. When Grettir was cutting the stump for firewood with an axe, he wounded himself severely above the knee"[1] (Gretti's Saga, c. 81).

The deeds of warriors were recorded on runic staves:—

Örvar-Odd, when very old, desired to revisit the scenes of his childhood, where a Volva had foretold him that his death would be caused by the head of the horse Faxi, at his birthplace, Hrafnista. When he arrived there he walked around on

---

[1] Cf. also Gretti's Saga, c. 62.

the farm, and his foot struck the skull of a horse, and a viper came out of it and bit him in the leg.

"He suffered so much from this wound that they had to lead him down to the shore. When he got there he said: 'Now you must go and hew a stone coffin for me, while some shall sit at my side and carve that song which I will compose

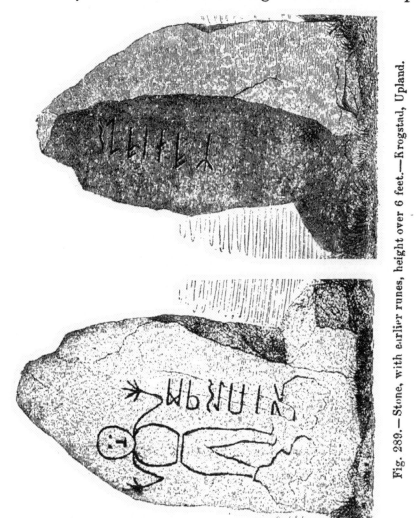

Fig. 289.—Stone, with earlier runes, height over 6 feet.—Krogstad, Upland.

about my deeds and life.' Then he began making the song,[1] and they carved it on a tablet,[2] and the nearer the poem drew to its end, the more the life of Odd ebbed away" (Orvar Odd's Saga; Fornaldar Sógur, p. 558).

---

[1] Kvædi, a poem or song The poem consists of seventy-one stanzas with eight verses each, and the manuscripts are late and corrupted. It is evidently made up from the lives of several warriors, and often exaggerated. e g, that he lived 300 years, and that his height was 16 or 24 feet.

[2] Speldi = tablet, flat piece of wood

"The two brothers Jokul and Thorstein were to meet Finnbogi for a Holmganga.[1] As he did not come, they took a post from the latter's farm; Jokul carved a man's head

Fig 290 —Earlier runes on granite block. About 10 feet high, 4 feet 11 inches at widest part, and 9 inches thick.—Tanum, Bohuslan, Sweden.

at one end, and traced in runes an account of what had occurred that day" (Vatnsdæla, 34) ˙

The inscriptions of the earlier runes, the translation of which must be received with extreme caution, are short. while those of a later period are much longer.

---

[1] A form of duelling.

Fig. 291.—Runic stone. showing transition between earlier and later runes, about 4½ feet above ground; breadth, 2 feet 4 inches.—Stentofte, Blekinge, Sweden.

Fig. 292.—Part of stone block, with earlier runes.—Torvik, Norway. Eight feet 10 inches in length by 2 feet 2 inches wide, with a thickness of from 2⅓ to 3⅛ feet.

Fig. 293.—Red quartz stone, with earlier runes and warrior on horseback. Height, 8 feet 3 inches, but only 6 feet above ground; greatest breadth, 5 feet.—Hagby, Upland.

Fig. 294.—Granite slab of a stone coffin in a grave-mound, forming one of the sides $\frac{1}{13}$ real size.—Torvik, Hardanger, Norway.

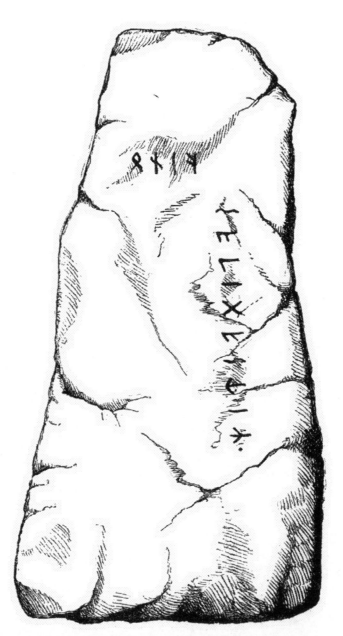

Fig. 295.—Runic stone, earlier runes. Length, 7 feet 2 inches; width, 2 feet 4 inches —Berga, Sodermanland, Sweden [1]

[1] Professor Stephens in 'Handbook of Old Northern Runic Monuments,' says: "The only Northern stone known to me which bears two words, cut far apart and running in different directions. I would therefore suggest that the one name is carved later than the other. Perhaps the husband or wife died first, and shortly after the partner was called away: thus they most likely lay in the same grave, and were remembered on the same block"

Fig. 296.—Runic stone, earlier runes. Height, over 13 feet; greatest width, a little over 3 feet; with letters about 6 inches long; near a dom ring.—Bjorktorp, Blekinge, Sweden. See p. 314 for grave.

Fig. 297.—Earlier runic stone ; about 7 feet 7 inches long, and at its broadest
part 3 feet 6 inches.—Norway.

Fig. 298.—Granite block with earlier and later runes (the earlier runes in the centre). Height, 5 feet 3 inches; greatest breadth, 3 feet; average thickness, 1 foot.— Skå-ang, Södermanland, Sweden.

Fig. 299.—Earlier runic stone,
Sigdal, Norway.

Fig. 300.—Earlier runic stone discovered in
1880, in a ruined grave-mound which
contained a slab stone chest; one of the
side slabs bore runes, and is given here.
It has probably stood on another mound
before it was put to this use.—Bergen
Museum, Torvik, Hardanger, Norway

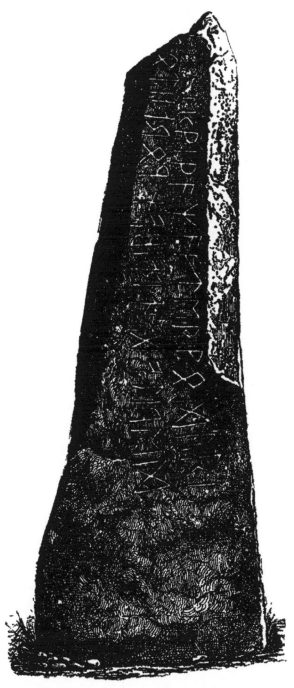

Fig. 301.—Tune stone (with earlier runes) of red granite; found in a graveyard
wall surrounding the church of Tune, near Moss, entrance of Christiania fjord.
Height, 6 feet 7 inches; greatest width, 2 feet 4 inches.

Fig. 302.—Earlier runic inscription on a bluff, 11 feet above high-water mark.—
Væblungsnæs, Romsdal, Norway.

Fig. 303.—Runic stone, having the longest runic inscription known, composed of
over 760 letters. Height, 12 feet; width, 6 feet.—In the Churchyard of Rok,
Ostergotland, Sweden.

Not only do the finds prove to us how extensive were the voyages and journeys of the vikings, but many of the runic stones add their testimony to these and the sagas, often mentioning journeys in distant lands both for peaceful and warlike purposes. There are four runic stones extant on which Knut the Great is mentioned as "Knut who went to England"; the

Fig. 304 —Marble lion, with later runic inscription.   Height, 10 feet.   Now at Venice, whither it was brought from the Piræus in 1687.[1]

Thingamenn or *Thingamannalid* is mentioned on at least two runic stones.

---

[1] Bugge, by comparing the runic inscription on the Piræus marble lion now at Venice, comes to the conclusion that, while the damaged state of the inscription makes it impossible to decipher it as a whole, enough can, however, be read to show its approximate date, and also the home of the tracer. The snake-slings and runes on this lion in all probability are traced by a man from Sweden, who has been among the Værings or Varangians.

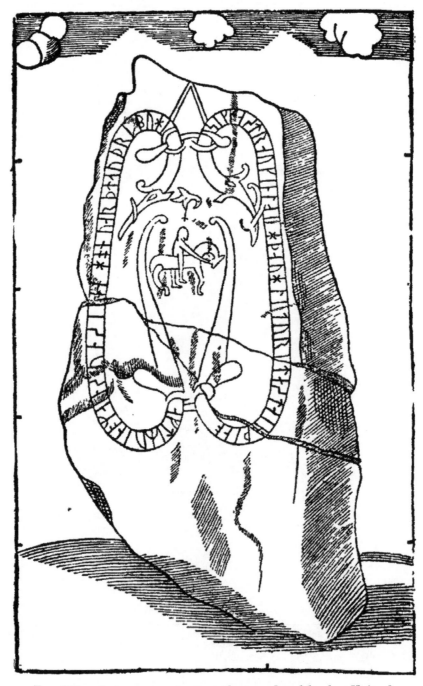

Fig. 305.—Later runic stone, with animal and bird.—Upland.

Fig. 307.—Later runic stone, with birds.—Upland.

Fig. 306.—Later runic stone, with animals, possibly a representation of Fylgja at Svartsjö Castle, Lake Malaren, Sweden.

Fig. 310.—Later runic stone, 7½ feet above the ground. "Sterkar and Hiorvardr erected this stone to their father, Geiri, who dwelt west, in Thikalid (Thingmannalid). God help his soul."—Käistad, Upland.

Fig. 309.—Later runic stone, Edssocken, Upland. "Runa rista lit Rahmualtr huar a Kriklanti uas lisforunki."

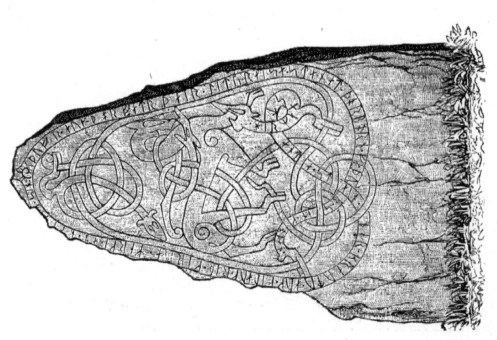

Fig. 308.—Stone with later runes. Height above ground, 10 feet; the width over 5 feet.—Nysätra parish, Upland.

Fig. 311.—King Gorm's stone, with later runes.—Jellinge, Jutland. Front view.

Fig. 312. — Back view of King Gorm's stone.

The inscription on the above stone runs thus, the translation being literal : "*Haraltr kunukr bath kaurua kubl thausi aft kurm (Gorm) fathur sin auk aft thæurui muthur sina, sa haraltr ias sær uan tanmaurk ala auk nruiak auk tana . . . . t kristnæ*" = Harald king bade make mounds these after Gorm, father his and after Thyra, mother his, that Harald who swore, Denmark all and Norway and Dane . . . . to christianize.

The historical mounds of King Gorm and his queen Thyra are respectively 200 and 230 feet in diameter, and about 40 feet high (see p. 183); the burial chamber of King Gorm was of wood, 22 feet long, 4½ feet high, 8 feet wide. In the grave were found a small silver cup, a bronze cross covered with gold, a wooden figure representing a warrior in armour, several metal mountings, &c.

Fig. 313.—Wooden shield with later runes.—Norway

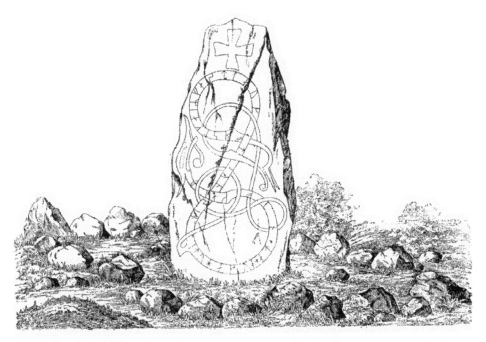

Fig. 314.—Runic stone in shipform grave, Upland. In the grave was found a helmet, apparently made of iron-plate, with ornaments of bronze in imitation of eyebrows; also a helmet-crest. On the helmet were numerous representations of horsemen with spears and carrying shields on their left arms, in front of the horses a snake, and in front of and behind each horseman a bird flying.

Fig. 315.—Baptismal stone font.—Langhem Church, Sweden.

Fig. 316.—Baptismal stone with runes and a representation of Gunnar in the snake-pit, used as font in a church, Bohuslän. No Christian symbol is marked upon it.

Fig. 317.

Fig. 318.

Fig. 319.

Fig. 320.

Baptismal fonts with runic inscriptions, some apparently heathen.

Two rock-tracings found at Ramsund and Gœk, on the southern shores of Lake Mälar, province of Södermanland, Sweden, show how deeply preserved in the memory of the people all over the North is the history of the Volsungar as told in the earlier Edda, and the Saga of that name. To the late Professor Carl Säve we are indebted for the discovery of these two mementoes of the past. I here give the representation of the finer of the two, which is engraved on granite.

The scene is surrounded below by sculpture, and covered with runes above are two serpents twisted together, one without runes. Below the large snake Sigurd on his knee pierces

Fig. 321.—Tracing of later runes illustrating the Eddaic songs and Volsunga saga. Length, 16 feet; width, from 4 to 5 feet.—Ramsund Rock, Södermanland, Sweden.

with his sword the body of the reptile. In the midst between the snake the horse Grani is standing, made fast to a tree where two birds are seen. On the left Sigurd, seated, roasts on the fire, at the end of a stick, the heart of Fafnir. Round the fire are deposited pincers, an anvil, bellows, and hammer; the head of the smith (blacksmith) Regin is seen separated from the trunk. Then above is sculptured an animal, which looks like a fox—no doubt the otter—for the murder of which was given, as ransom, the rich treasure so fatal to Fafnir and to all those who possessed it after him. The runic inscription has not the slightest connection with the scene, not even with Sigurd Fafnisbani. As Mr. Säve remarks, Sigurd or Holmger, and perhaps both, believed that they were descended from Sigurd Fafnisbani, the famous hero of the Volsunga.

The tracing on the stone of Gœk, not far from the city of Strengenæs, is about half the length of that on the Ramsund stone, but of the same width, and is not as fine. The subject is treated in a somewhat similar manner: the hammer is on the ground, while on the Ramsund stone it is in the man's hand. Above the horse Grani is a Christian cross.

The runic inscription, here also upon a snake, surrounds the figures, but has nothing to say about Sigurd Fafnisbani.

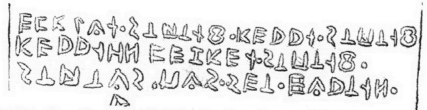

Fig. 322.—Oscan inscription (first three lines) on a bronze tablet in British Museum.

Fig. 323.—Greek inscription on bronze axe from Calabria, in the British Museum.

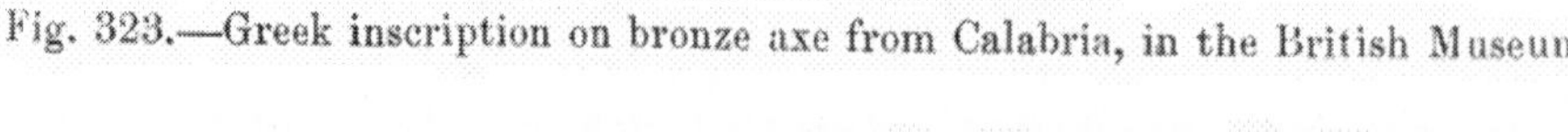

Fig. 324.—Archaic Greek inscription in the British Museum.

From the facsimile illustrations given of Etruscan, Greek and earliest Roman inscriptions chosen at random from the museums, the reader will be able to judge for himself, and probably see how much more closely the earlier runes resemble the Greek archaic and Etruscan inscriptions than the Latin ones.

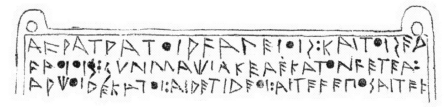

Fig. 325.—Bronze tablet, first three lines. Treaty between the Eleans and Heræans of Arcadia; copied from "Ancient Greek Inscriptions" in the British Museum.

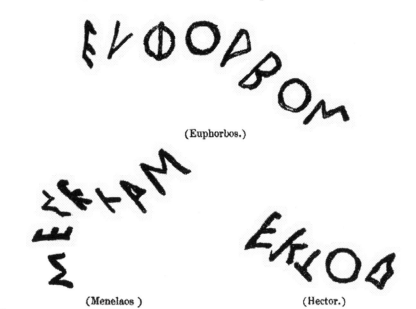

(Euphorbos.)

(Menelaos.) (Hector.)

Fig. 326.—These three archaic inscriptions are found on a vase from Camirus in Rhodes, now in the British Museum.

Fig. 327.—Etruscan inscription on a sepulchral urn in the British Museum.

Fig. 328.—Etruscan inscription on an urn in the British Museum.

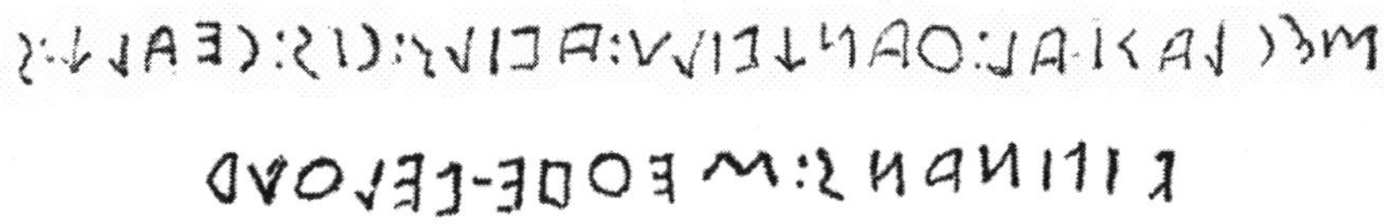

Fig. 329.—Etruscan inscription on a sarcophagus from Toscanella, in the British Museum.

Fig. 330.—Plaque of terra-cotta, representing Poseidon, painted.   **Found near** Corinth.   Now in the Louvre.

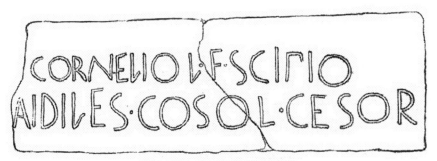

Fig. 331.—Latin inscription.

Fig. 332.—Early Latin inscription: painted on a vase in British Museum.

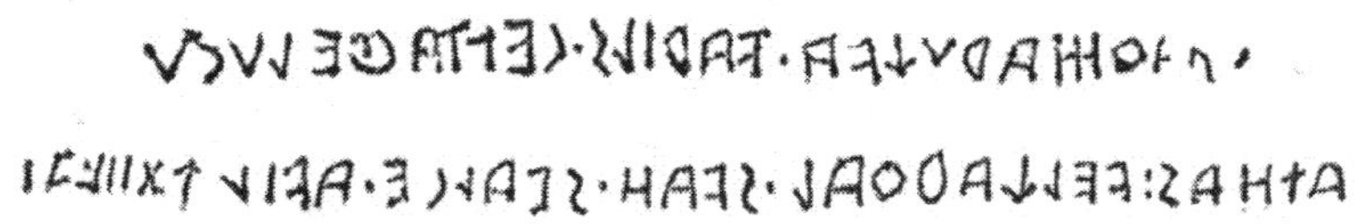

Fig. 333.—Etruscan inscription, on a sarcophagus from Toscanella, in the British Museum.

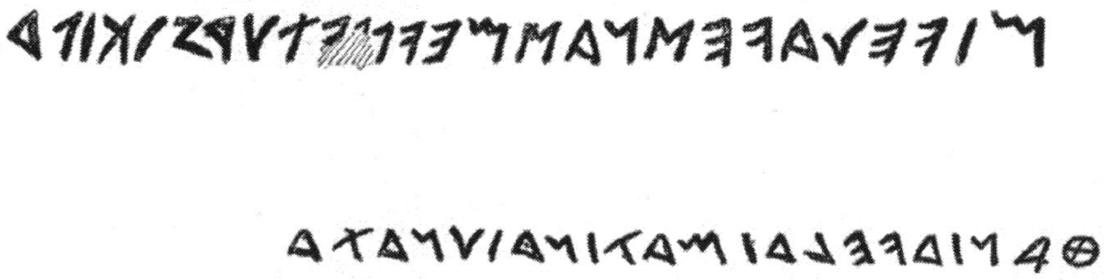

Fig. 334.—On an Etruscan sepulchral monument in terra-cotta, British Museum.

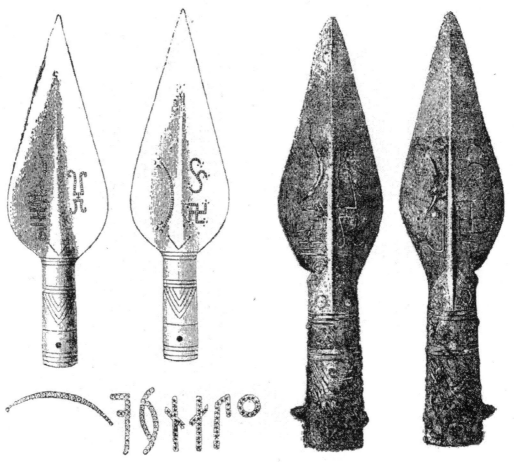

Fig 335.—Bronze spear-point, with earlier runes, and svastica and triskele stamped on it. Length 16½ inches.—Venice, island of Torcello. ½ real size.

Fig. 336.—Iron spear-point, with runes and figures inlaid with silver, discovered in a mound with burnt bones and weapons.—Müncheberg, Mark-Brandenburg. ½ real size.

Fig. 337.—Iron spear-point, with runes and figures inlaid with silver.—Volhynia, Russia. ½ real size.

Fig. 338.—Runic stone found at Collingham, Yorkshire.

CHAPTER XII.

NORTHERN RELICS—BOG FINDS.

Numerous Greek and Roman objects—Intentional destruction of weapons—Thorsberg find—Coats of mail—Garments and harness—Weapons and ornaments—The Vimose find—The sax—Bronze and iron spurs—Carpenter's plane—The Kragehul find—The Nydam find—Discovery of a large oak boat—Its construction—Various weapons, tools, and ornaments—Damascened swords.

BEFORE passing on to other parts of our wide subject, let us examine somewhat more minutely and in detail the various classes of remarkable objects which have been found in the lands of the old Norsemen, belonging to the earlier iron age.

The bog finds[1] are very important, and throw additional light on the earlier history of the people. From them we are able to see how people were dressed, and to learn about their riding equipment, agricultural implements, cooking utensils, household vessels, waggons, tools, and offensive and defensive weapons; from one of these also we were first made acquainted with their sea-vessels. Many of the objects appear to be of Greek or Roman origin, and Roman coins are found, so that we

Fig. 339.—Shield boss of bronze with Latin inscription AELAE-LIANVS. ⅓ real size.—Thorsbjerg find.

can approximate closely the date when the objects were in use, and consequently the taste and manner of living of the period.

---

[1] Bog finds belonging to the bronze age, as well as to the iron age, have been discovered in many places in the North. Those of the bronze age consist chiefly of swords, lance-heads, axes, sickles, &c. Objects of the bronze age are also found deposited under stones or in fields.

We can dress a warrior from head to foot, and wonder at his costly and magnificent equipment, and his superb and well-finished weapons, and can realise how magnificent must have been some of his riding and driving vehicles.

All these antiquarian bog-finds are within very easy access of the sea, varying in depth beneath the surface of the earth—in the Thorsbjerg bog, 10–14 feet; in the Nydam, 5–7 feet;

Fig. 340.—Bronze breast-plate, covered with gold and silver.—Thorsbjerg find.

the Vimose, 4–5 feet. Those of Denmark have proved far richer than those of the present Sweden, Norway, and the countries situated on the eastern and southern shores of the Baltic. In numerous instances the objects are unique, and many present a great similarity to those found in the skeleton graves, such as swords with Roman characters upon them, fragments of wooden buckets, checkers, dice, &c.

Here also, as in the graves where the bodies were burnt, we find objects intentionally damaged. This bending, twisting, and hacking of weapons seems to have been a religious custom. The spear-handles, scabbards, bows, arrow-shafts, and shields are often broken into fragments, or rolled together in inextricable knots. Ringed coats of mail and garments are torn to pieces, which afterwards were wrapped carefully together;

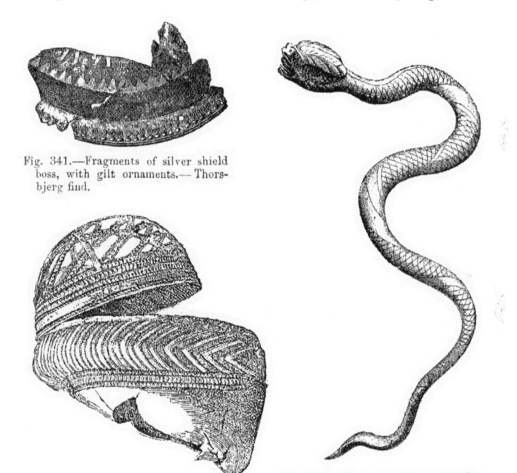

Fig. 341.—Fragments of silver shield boss, with gilt ornaments.— Thorsbjerg find.

Fig. 342.—Silver helmet.—Thorsbjerg find.

Fig. 343.—Bronze serpent: probably ornament to helmet.—Thorsbjerg find.

and the skulls and skeletons of horses are cleft in many places.

These masses of objects seem to imply that they were either the spoils and remains of great fights between different chieftains, or offers to the gods thrown into sacred springs. In this latter case the finds must be the produce of a long series of years, and have been given to the gods at different times, the destruction, instead of taking place on the pyre, having taken place on the water.

This destruction was not apparently peculiar to the inhabitants of the North, for Cæsar relates of the Gauls, that when they went into battle they made a vow to consecrate the booty to the god of war. After the victory the captured animals were sacrificed, and the rest of the booty was brought together into one spot.

The narrative of Orosius offers the most striking similarity between this custom and that of the Cimbrians and Teutons,

Fig. 344.—Bronze buckle inlaid with gold and silver, for ring armour; the back shows how the rings were attached. ⅔ real size.—Thorsbjerg Bog-find.

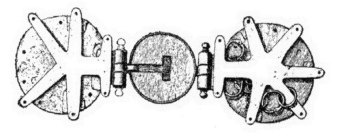

Reverse

who, when coming from the North after their victory over the Romans at Arausia (near the river Rhone), in the year 105 before Christ, sacrificed the whole of the booty. He relates :—

" When the enemies had taken possession of two camps and an immense booty, they destroyed under new and strange imprecations all that had fallen into their hands. The clothes were torn and thrown away, gold and silver thrown into the river, the ring armour of the men cut to pieces, the accoutrements of the horses destroyed, the horses themselves thrown into the water, and the men with ropes around their necks

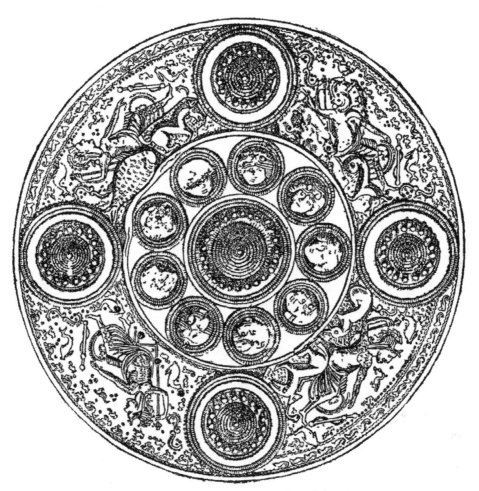

Fig. 345.—Bronze plate, covered with gold and silver, belonging to ring armour.—
Thorsbjerg find.

Fig. 346.   Fig. 347.

Fig. 348.   Fig. 349.
Figures, made of thin silver plates,
belonging to bronze plate.

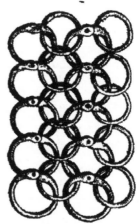

Fig. 350.—Fragment of ring armour.
Real size.

suspended to the trees, so that there was no more booty for the victors than there was mercy for the conquered."

One might suppose that Orosius has here described the feast of victory at Nydam or Thorsbjerg.

If any proofs were needed to show that the objects were intentionally placed in the water, we have them in the fact that several clay vessels have been sunk by heavy stones being put in them, and that other objects were fastened to the bottom by means of large wooden hooks. Finally, we ought to add, the space within which the antiquities were found was in several places marked off by fence-like wicker hurdles of twigs, or by poles, spears or swords, stuck into the mud.

The *Thorsbjerg*[1] *Bog-find.*—The researches in this find cover a period of six years, from 1856 to 1862, and is one of the most remarkable, for here were brought to light objects unknown in other similar finds. From the coins[2] enumerated below, we

---

[1] Thorsbjerg is situated south of Flensborg, in Southern Jutland. Among the objects found were fragments of swords, all double-edged, the hilts of all, with one exception, of wood, inlaid with bronze and silver, with scabbards of wood with metal mountings (on the metal bottom-piece of one scabbard is a very clear runic inscription); a sword-belt of thick leather, 41½ inches long and 3½ inches wide; buckles for sword-belts, all of bronze, with broken pieces of iron buckles; bows and arrows in a more or less complete state, the most perfect bow being about 60 inches long, but both ends are somewhat damaged, and the original length seems to have been a couple of inches more; a great number of arrow-shafts, all of similar shape, between 26–35 inches long and ½ inch thick, but the arrow-points are all destroyed, the iron having rusted; remnants of shields, flat and circular, composed of several smoothly-planed and pretty thin wooden boards, which are not equally broad all over, but become narrower towards the border:—the largest cross-measure is 42½ inches, the smallest 21 inches, the thickness of the middle boards, which as a rule are somewhat heavier than the rest, is about ½ to ¼ inch (the shield-buckles are of bronze, but broken pieces of iron ones have been found also; their cross-measure is between 6–7 inches); axes, whose blades are much decomposed by rust, with thirty good handles of ash and beechwood, which measured between 23 and 33½ inches in length; a few well-preserved spear-points, and others more or less destroyed by rust: four spear-handles, 32, 98½, 107½, and 116 inches in length; several riding and driving accoutrements; more than sixty fibulæ of many different styles; many broken pieces of gold rings, only two of which have been fitted together so as to form one complete ring; two spiral rings of bronze; a round pendant of gold; a hollow ornament of silver-mixed gold; a mass of beads; a piece of unworked amber, pincers; dice of amber; a variety of utensils and tools for domestic use, such as bowls of wood and clay, spoons, jugs, knives, &c; two pairs of coarse woollen trousers, &c; and several objects, the use of which is unknown.

[2] Thirty-seven *Roman coins* were found altogether. The earliest is of the year 60 A D; the latest, 194 A.D.—1 of *Nero*, 1 of *Vitellius*, 4 of *Vespasianus*, 1 of *Domitianus*, 7 of *Trajan* is, 6 of *Hadrianus*, 1 of *Aelius*, 6 of *Antoninus Pius*, 1 of *Faustina* the elder, 3 of *Marcus Aurelius*, 2 of *Faustina the younger*, 3 of *Commodus*, and 1 of *Septimius Severus*, the last-named being struck in the year 194 of our era.

must come to the conclusion that many of the objects found belong to the second century of our era. Among the most remarkable antiquities of warfare are the superb coats of mail found in the North, and the skill displayed in making war accoutrements at such an early period shows an advanced state of civilisation. These coats of mail (which are also found in graves) are a network of rings each of which is run through four others. In their workmanship they vary:— in some the rings are clinched; in others only every other ring is riveted, the alternate ones being welded together, so that each clinched ring grasps four welded ones, and each welded ring grasps four riveted.

THORSBJERG FIND.

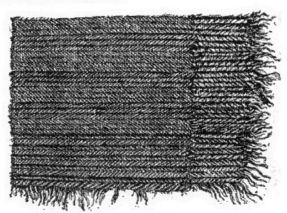

Fig. 352.

Fig. 351.—Trousers of woven woollen cloth.[1] Length 45 inches. Width round waist 38½ inches. On the waistband were several small loops which probably held the waistbelt. The socks which are sewn to the trousers are of the same pattern as that of the sleeves of the shirt, but the squares are smaller. ⅟₁₈ real size.

Fig. 353.

Fig. 354.

Fragments of woollen cloak, with border.

---

[1] On a superb silver vase at the Hermitage, St. Petersburg, found in Southern Russia, is a representation of a man wearing similar trousers

THORSBJERG FIND.

Fig. 356.—Woven border at bottom of the shirt.

Fig. 355.—Woollen shirt or blouse 33½ inches long, 20 inches wide, with wristbands of a stronger cloth and a lighter colour than the shirt, which is brownish red. Both sleeves are of a stronger cloth than that of the body of the shirt. $\frac{1}{20}$ real size.

Fig. 357.—Pattern of the body of the shirt.

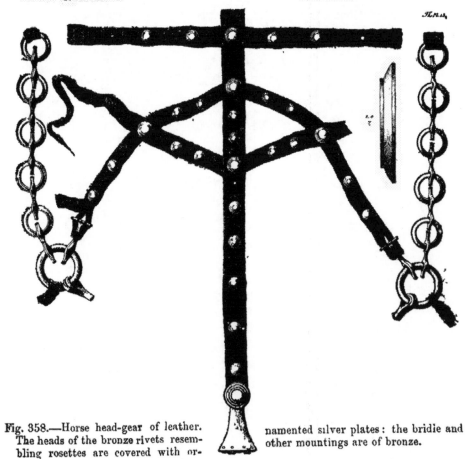

Fig. 358.—Horse head-gear of leather. The heads of the bronze rivets resembling rosettes are covered with or- namented silver plates: the bridle and other mountings are of bronze.

THORSBJERG FIND.

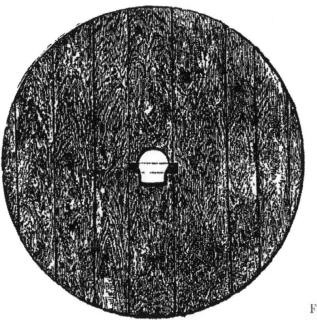

Fig. 359.—Flat round wooden shield, made of planed boards of different widths.

Fig. 360.—Wooden sword-hilt with bronze nails, the middle surrounded with braided bronze thread.

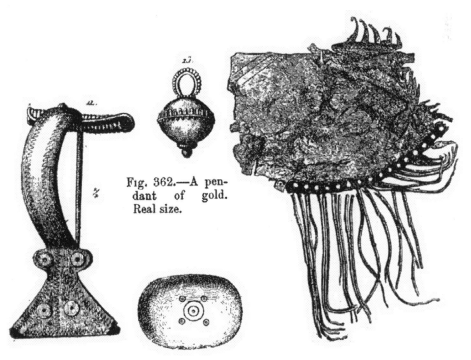

Fig. 362.—A pendant of gold. Real size.

Fig. 361.—Fibula of bronze with engraved ornament.

Fig. 363.—Amber die, rounded so as not to stand on the number. Real size.

Fig. 364.—Remains of leather shoe. ¼ real size.

THORSBJERG FIND.

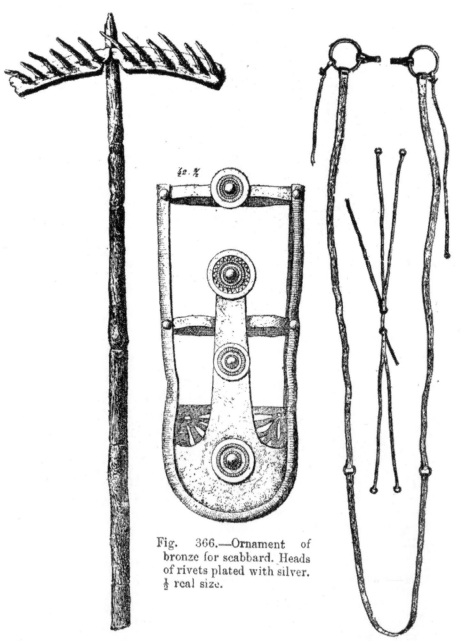

Fig. 366.—Ornament of bronze for scabbard. Heads of rivets plated with silver. ½ real size.

Fig. 365.—Rake of wood with teeth, about nine inches long.

Fig. 367.—Rein, made of three pieces of leather, with bronze ring.

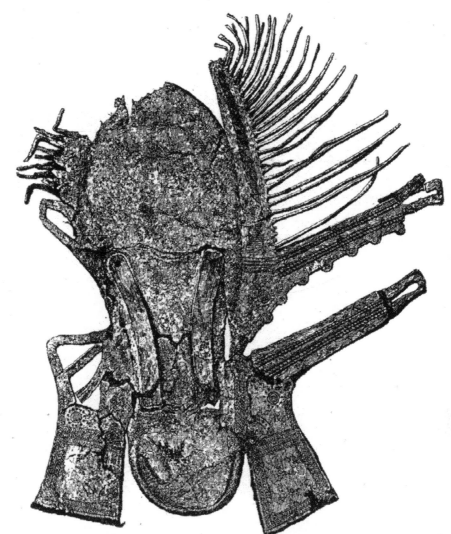

Fig. 368.—Leather sandal in one piece, for left foot.   ⅓ real size.   Fastened
over the foot with narrow straps and buttons.

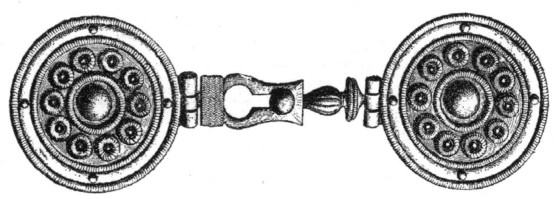

Fig. 369.—Shoulder clasp of bronze for ring armour, inlaid with gold and silver.

Fig. 370.—Fragment of a sandal with silver-plated rivets. ⅓ real size.

Fig. 371.—Ornament of bronze for wooden scabbard, with inscription in earlier runes. Real size.

Fig. 372.—Bronze ornamentation for scabbard, plated with silver and gold. ½ real size.

THORSBJERG FIND.

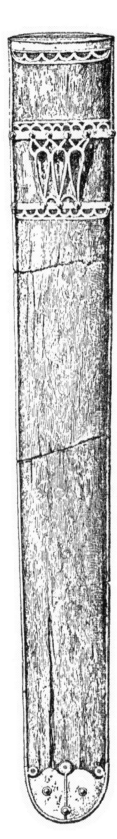

Fig. 375.—A bridle of bronze, the end-piece plated with silver and gold. ½ real size.

Fig. 373.—Scabbard of wood, with bronze mounting.

Fig. 374.—Embossed mounting of a scabbard strap, silver-plated, the whole centre inlaid with a thin gold plate.

Fig. 376.—Silver-plated bronze buckle.

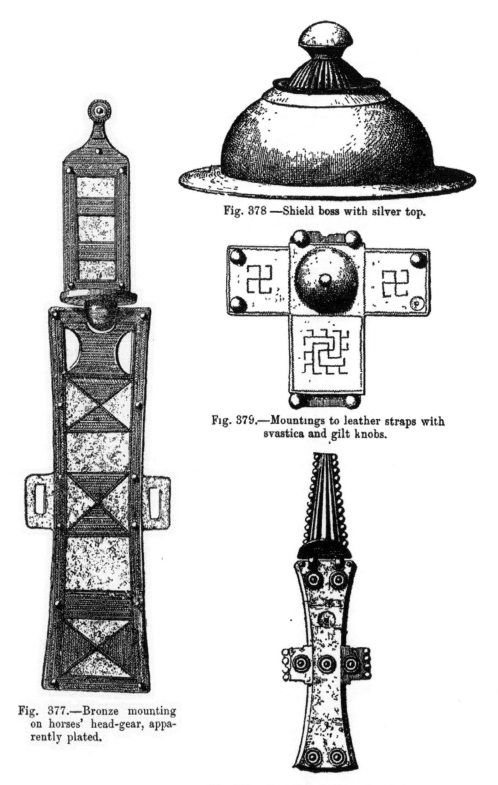

Fig. 378 —Shield boss with silver top.

Fig. 379.—Mountings to leather straps with svastica and gilt knobs.

Fig. 377.—Bronze mounting on horses' head-gear, apparently plated.

Fig. 380.—Bronze and silver-plated mounting for leather used on horses' head-gear.

THORSBJERG FIND.

Vimose Bog Find.—The explorations in the Vimose bog,[1] situated about five miles from Odense, Fyen, commenced in 1848, and since that time 3,600 objects have been gathered together, all of which were found in a space of 9,000 square feet. Sometimes there seemed to be a certain order in the way in which the articles had been sunk, for all the ring armour was together, and a number of small articles had been placed inside a shield-boss, while other articles were surrounded with broad bands of cloth. Many of the objects here were also badly damaged. Only one coin has been found, *i.e.* a silver denarius of the time of the Empress Faustina Junior (d. 175),

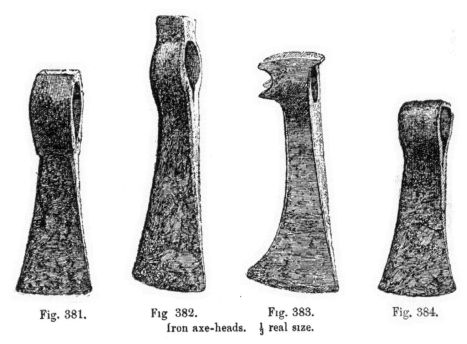

Fig. 381.   Fig 382.   Fig. 383.   Fig. 384.
Iron axe-heads. ⅓ real size.

with " Pudicitia " on its reverse. The number of single and double-edged swords, many of which are in tolerably good

[1] The principal objects in this find included a very great number of arrow shafts (most of them thoroughly decayed), with arrow-points of bone or iron; a remnant of a quiver of wood about 25 inches long; a mass of wooden scabbards, mostly for edged swords: 390 pieces of metal and bone mountings for the scabbards, some of silver. and one of bronze covered with silver and thin gold plates, with runes lightly traced; shield-boards, handles and buckles (180 of the latter of iron); about 150 knives, all of iron and different shapes; several remnants of belts, as well as about 40 buttons of bronze, some covered with gold, and about 60 double buttons of bronze; about 250 different pieces of buckles and other mountings of iron and bronze; about 150 different pieces of riding harness; a few horses' bones; bronze bowls, needles, keys; scissors; scythe-blades; 1 millstone; 1 small anvil; 6 hammers; 25 iron chisels; 3 iron files; 2 iron pincers; 57 bone combs, some with *svastica*, and one with runes on; 4 square, 2 oblong dice; amber, glass, and mosaic beads; fibulæ of bronze, iron, silver, &c, &c.

preservation, is 67. The single-edged swords, between 15¾

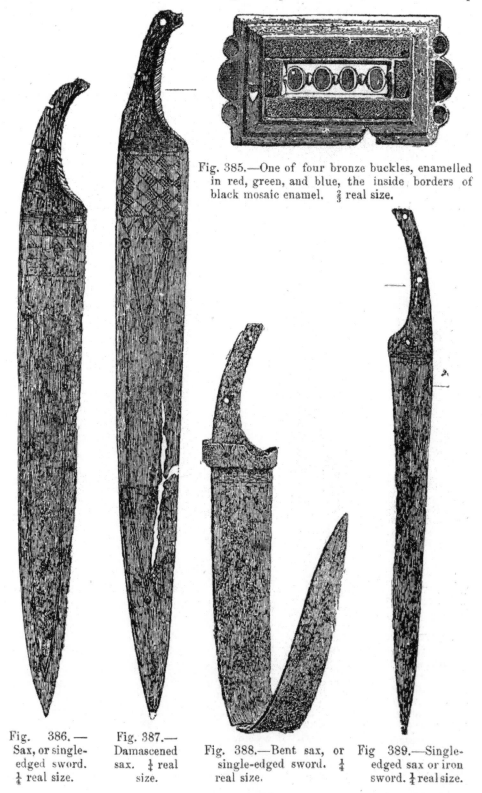

Fig. 385.—One of four bronze buckles, enamelled in red, green, and blue, the inside borders of black mosaic enamel. ⅔ real size.

Fig. 386.— Sax, or single-edged sword. ¼ real size.

Fig. 387.— Damascened sax. ¼ real size.

Fig. 388.—Bent sax, or single-edged sword. ¼ real size.

Fig 389.—Single-edged sax or iron sword. ¼ real size.

VIMOSE FIND.

and 24 inches long, are simply welded, sometimes having

ornaments traced on the blade, and several of these were still in their wooden scabbards when found. The double-edged swords vary in size from about 19 or 20 inches, to 35 or 36 inches. On several are factory stamps—a star-shaped sign on one side of the blade near the tongue or hilt point, and a ring-shaped figure on the sides of the hilt points, a mark which looks rather like a scorpion; in one stamp are Latin letters, which are somewhat difficult to decipher. Many are welded or forged from two united blades, while others are made of a single blade and have no factory mark. Four-teen are damascened in different patterns.

In this remarkable find several enamelled objects have been dis-covered. This art appears to have been unknown to the nations of classical antiquity. There is no word for it in Greek or Latin. Philostratus,[1] when describing a wild boar hunt, mentions the beauty

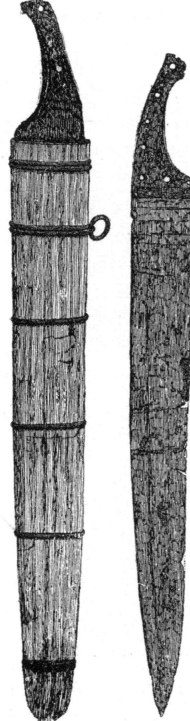

Fig. 390.   Fig. 391.

Sax, or single-edged swords, one in wooden scabbard.   ¼ real size.

---

[1] This Greek writer, who lived at the beginning of the 3rd century, was called to the Roman Court by Faustina, wife of Septimius Severus, whose numerous coins are found, and if this art was known by the Romans he would certainly have described it.

"Around this youth is a group of young men of fine appearance, and engaged in fine pursuits, as beseems men of noble birth. One of them seems to bear on his countenance traces of the palæstra, another gives evidence of gentleness, a third of geniality: here is one who you would say had just looked up from his book; and of the horses on which they ride no two are alike, one is white, another chestnut, another black, another bay, and they have silver bridles, and their trappings are adorned with golden and decorated bosses (φάλαρα). And it is said that the barbarians by the ocean pour these colours

and fine colour of the harness of the horses, and, when stating how these colours were produced, mentions that they were made by the barbarians living on the shores of the ocean.

Fig. 392.—Griffon's head, ornament belonging to helmet of bronze.   Real size.

This description may very well refer to the people of the North, the great splendour of whose riding gear and chariots we see from the finds and sagas.

---

on red-hot copper, and that the designs become hard, like stone, and are durable."— Philostratus, Imagines.   Chapter on Boar-hunting.

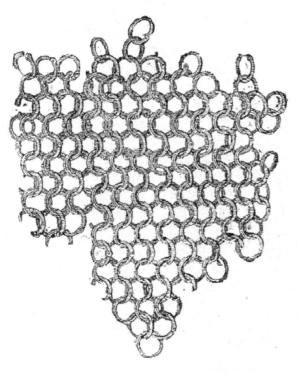

Fig. 393.—Fragments of ring-armour of hammered iron. Real size.

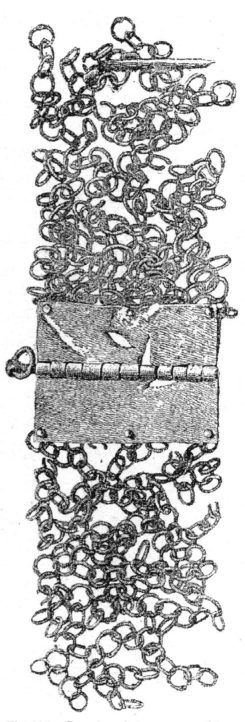

Fig. 394.—Bronze mounting, plated with gold silver, and belonging to ring-armour. Real size.

Fig. 395.—Remains of ring-armour of iron, with traces of gold plating. $\frac{1}{2}$ real size.

P 2

Fig 396.   Fig. 397.   Fig. 398.

Spurs, one of bronze, with iron point; the others of iron.

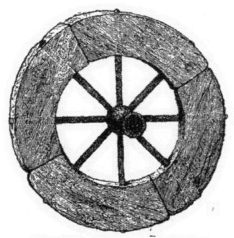

Fig. 399.—Wheel. $\frac{1}{20}$ real size.

Fig. 400.—Man's head on a piece of bronze   Fig. 401.—Ferrule of silver for
covered with a thin gold plate. Real size.   hilt plated with gold.   Real size

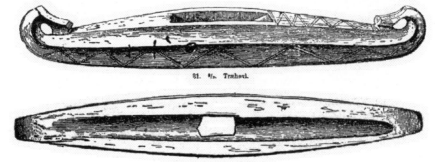

81. ⁴/₅. Træhøvl.

Fig. 402.—Parts of a wooden plane. $\frac{1}{3}$ real size.

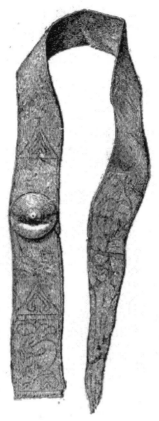

Fig. 403.—Shoulder-strap of leather, with bronze button and design of dolphin.   About ½ real size.

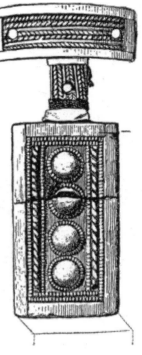

Fig. 404. — Silver ornament plated with gold.   Real size.

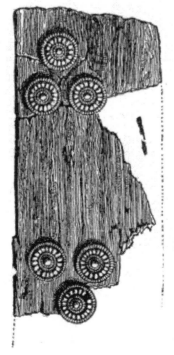

Fig. 405.—Fragment of wooden shield with gilt-headed nails.

Fig. 406.—Silver-plated bronze ornament.

Over 1,000 spears were found; the handles of most of them were broken off, but five have been preserved complete; these are 8 feet 7⅔ inches long, 9 feet 2 inches long

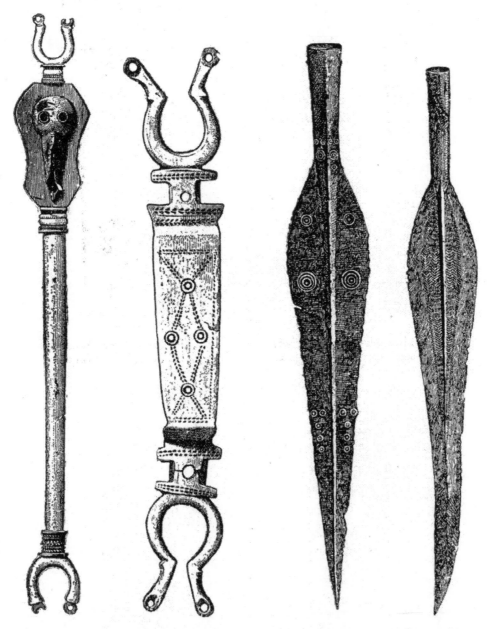

Fig. 407.—Silver mounting to scabbard. real size.

Fig. 408. — Silver mounting for scabbard. ½ real size.

Fig. 409.—One of 1,000 spears, inlaid with concentric circles. ⅓ real size.

Fig. 410.— One of 1,000 spears. ¼ real size.

9 feet long, 11 feet long, and 6½ feet long. The handles are made of ash, and some spears are ornamented with threads of gold, silver or bronze inlaid in concentric circles; sometimes

ornaments are traced up the middle of the blade, and originally these also were filled with some kind of metal.

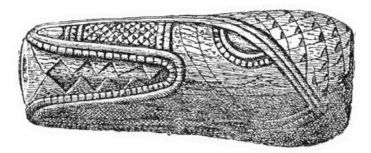

Fig. 411.—Crocodile's head carved in wood.   Real size

Fig. 412.—Brynja, or coat of mail, 3 feet long.

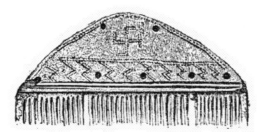

Fig. 413.—Bone comb with *svastica*.   ½ real size.

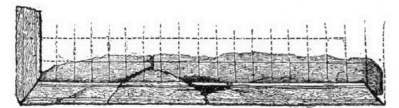

Fig. 414.—Fragments of checker-board.   ⅙ real size.

VIMOSE FIND.

Fig. 415 —Bronze enamelled bowl (1867), 2¾ in. high, 4¾ in. wide, in bog at
Maltbœk, Jutland.   The enamel in the serpentine line is red.

Kragehul Find.—In a small bog called Kragehul, situated
near the city of Assens on Fyen, objects have been found
which seem to belong to the 4th or 5th century.   The first
mention of the Kragehul bog is in 1751, when some articles

with rune inscriptions were found, which, unfortunately, have been lost, but it was not until 1864 that a regular exploration took place.[1]

Fig. 416.—Bundle of bent weapons.

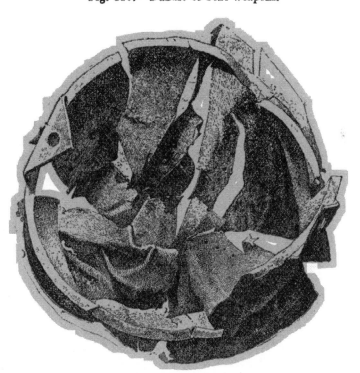

Fig. 417.—Bronze vessel destroyed by sword cuts. $\frac{1}{3}$ real size.

[1] The articles found include glass, mosaic, and porcelain beads; fragments of four bone combs; four tweezers of bronze, of which two hang on bronze rings; remains of wooden shields with metal mountings; bronze mountings; 10 iron swords, damascened in several patterns, the length of the blades being from 31 to 35 inches, their width $1\frac{3}{4}$ to 2 inches; and fragments of several others; fragments of wooden scabbards, of which one has remains of leather on it; several metal mountings for scabbards; a buckle of bronze; about 80 points of iron spears, all of different shapes; 30 spear-handles, ornamented with engraved lines, some straight, and others with snake lines; remains of a wooden bow, length $47\frac{1}{2}$ inches, and fragments of another; arrows; four

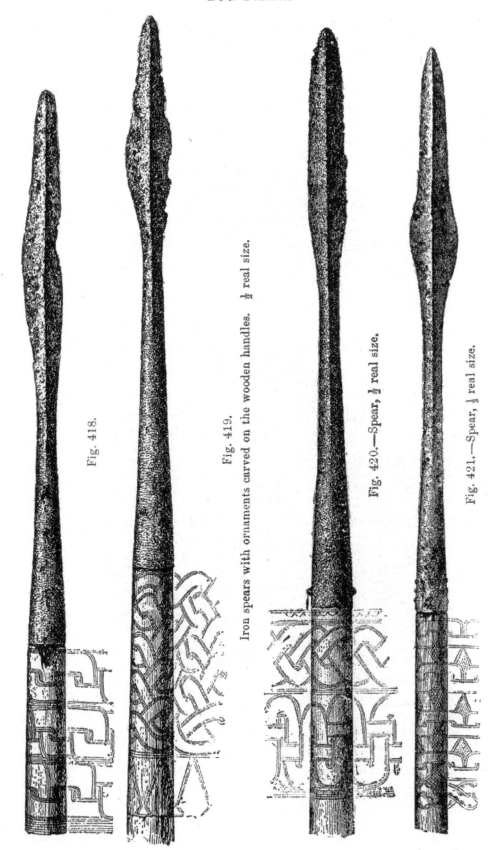

Fig. 418.

Fig. 419.

Iron spears with ornaments carved on the wooden handles. ½ real size.

Fig. 420.—Spear, ½ real size.

Fig. 421.—Spear, ½ real size.

KRAGEHUL FIND.

The antiquities, none of which are of Roman origin, seem to have been thrown in without any order, but spears with thin iron points on the end formed the boundary of the find.

In this as in the other bog finds, weapons are twisted together in extraordinary knots and many objects destroyed.

The Nydam Bog Find.—The remarkable bog find at Nydam [1] is extremely valuable on account of the boat, and the discovery of Roman coins enables us to approximate the date of the objects,[2] which is probably about the years 250 and 300 of our era.

The Nydam oak boat was discovered in 1863 near Slesvig, in Southern Jutland. Its length is about 75 feet; its widest part, about 10½ feet. It held 14 benches, and was rowed with 28 oars, the average length of which was 12 feet. By its side was the rudder, about 10 feet long.

The bottom plank, which is not a keel proper, is 45 feet 3 inches long, and of a single piece. The oar-tholes are fastened to the gunwales with bast ropes, and, though they have all one general shape, there are no two alike.

The boat is clinch-built; that is, the planks are held together by large iron bolts with round heads outside, and clinch plates

---

whole iron knives, between 7 and 10 inches long, and several handles and fragments; four oval-shaped whetstones and fragments of a square one; five small balance-weights; fragments of a heavy wooden post and of a small twig; some mountings of silver which probably belonged to riding harness; bones of three animals; &c., &c.

[1] Among the objects found in the bog were 106 iron swords, all double edged, with handles of wood sometimes covered with silver, or of bone or massive bronze; 93 damascened in different patterns, two wrought from two different pieces, and only eleven simply wrought. On several there are Latin inscriptions, and on one blade runes inlaid in gold. The condition in which the swords were when buried is peculiar. Generally they were without hilts and bent, on many were found deep cuts on both edges, one having 23 cuts on one, and 11 cuts on the other edge. Wooden scabbards, with mountings of bronze; mountings to sword-belts; buckles of iron and bronze; rings with loose end-mountings; 70 iron shield buckles; iron axes; iron bridles, three of which were still in the mouths of (skeleton) horses; 552 iron spear-points, several ornamented with gold; several hundred spear-handles; numerous household utensils of wood; several hundred arrow-shafts with traces of marks of ownership on them, and some with runes, &c

[2] Thirty-four Roman coins, struck between the years 69 and 217 A.D., are so-called denarii of silver, and date from the time of *Vitellius* (1), *Hadrian* (1), *Antoninus Pius* (10), two of which have the mark of DIVVS; *Faustina the elder* (4), *Marcus Aurelius* (7) (partly as Cæsar, between the years 140–143, and partly as Imperator), *Faustina the younger* (1), *Lucius Verus* (2), *Lucilla* (2), *Commodus* (5), and *Macrinus* (1), the latter a very rare coin, struck in 217 A.D

on the inside, at a distance of 5½ inches from each other. The

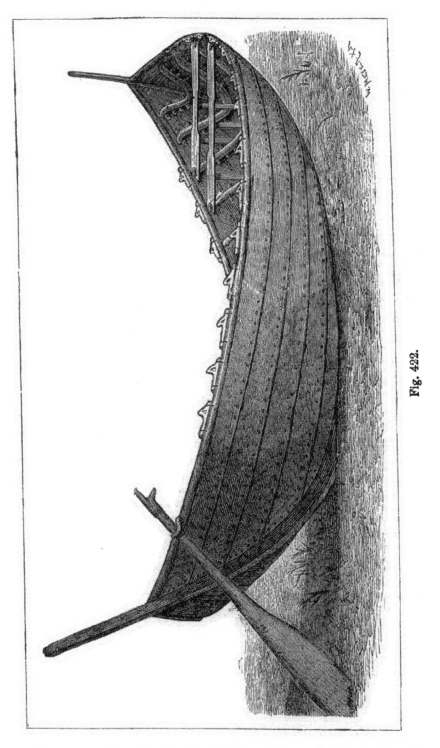

Fig. 422.

space between the planks is filled with woollen stuff and a
pitchy sticky mass. The boards are joined in a very common

manner to the frame with bast ropes. In the frame are holes, which correspond to elevated pieces on the boards which are also bored through; these pieces had not been nailed to the planks, but were hewn out of the latter, which thereby

Fig 423.—Oar-thole of red pine. $\frac{1}{10}$ real size.

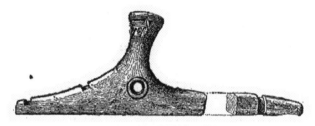

Fig. 424.—Oar-thole of the Nydam Boat. $\frac{1}{4}$ real size.

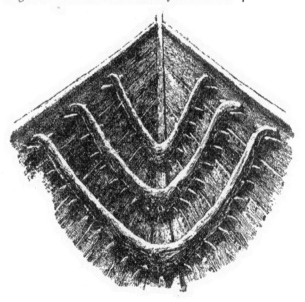

Fig. 425.—Inside view of one of the stems of the Nydam boat.

had lost more than half their thickness. Vessels by this peculiar manner of joining frame and boards acquired great elasticity, which must have been of good service in the surf and in a heavy sea.

The boat was shaped alike both fore and aft, so that it could

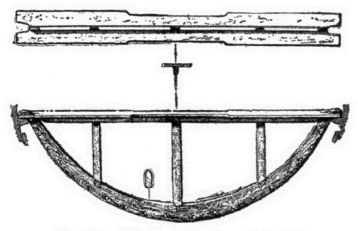

Fig. 426.— Rib of boat, showing seat attached

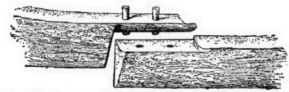

Fig. 427.—Wooden pegs fastening stem to bottom plank. $\frac{1}{17}$ real size.

Fig. 428.—Showing how the boards joined the ribs.

Fig. 429.—End face view of oar-thole. $\frac{1}{10}$ real size.

Fig. 430.—Rudder, 10 feet long, found alongside Nydam boat.

be rowed in either direction; and in both stems, which are fastened to the bottom plank, are two holes through which, judging from the manner in which they are worn, ropes were probably drawn, by which to drag the boat ashore at the beginning of winter. In the bottom there is a hole, which probably after the ship had been drawn up served to give outlet to the water collected in the boat.

The boat had undoubtedly been intentionally sunk, for in the planks under the water-line had been cut large holes to let in the water. Rust had destroyed the ends of the iron bolts which had held the planks together, and also the ropes with which the boards and the frame had been held together. The planks fell apart, therefore, and took their original straight shape; the oar-tholes were loosened from the

Fig. 431.—Wooden scoop for baling water.   ⅓ real size.

gunwale; the frame fell on different sides, and the two high stems fell down. As the joints loosened, the separate pieces sank to the bottom, and remained lying at about an equal depth, while the turf grew up above them and preserved them from destruction. After all the parts of the boat had been carefully collected and dried, it was possible to restore it to its original shape.

Another boat of red pine wood was discovered alongside it. This one was laid on the field and covered with bog mould, until the work connected with the other boat was finished. Unfortunately the war of 1864 put an end to the examination of the Nydam bog, so that the boat was left lying on the field, and strangers have carried off many pieces of it. The bottom plank was about 50 feet long, 13 inches broad, and ends in two spurs or rams. How high the prows were raised above the plank cannot be stated. Since this date the diggings have been done by inexperienced men, and consequently have given but little results. This sacred part of the land of the Danes had passed into the hands of its German conquerors, for the *Nornir*[1] are fickle, and what is fated to one generation to accomplish is often, in the course of time, undone by another.

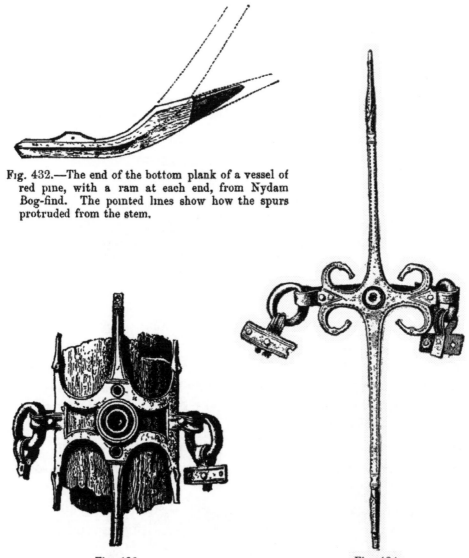

Fig. 432.—The end of the bottom plank of a vessel of red pine, with a ram at each end, from Nydam Bog-find. The pointed lines show how the spurs protruded from the stem.

Fig. 433.
Fragments wooden scabbard with bronze mountings.

Fig. 434. ½ real size.

NYDAM BOG FIND.

[1] See p. 385.

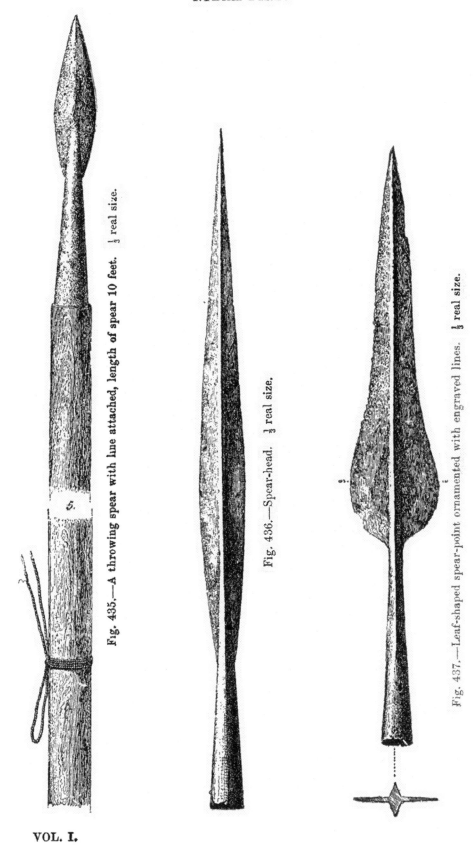

Fig. 435.—A throwing spear with line attached, length of spear 10 feet. ⅓ real size.

Fig. 436.—Spear-head. ⅓ real size.

Fig. 437.—Leaf-shaped spear-point ornamented with engraved lines. ⅓ real size.

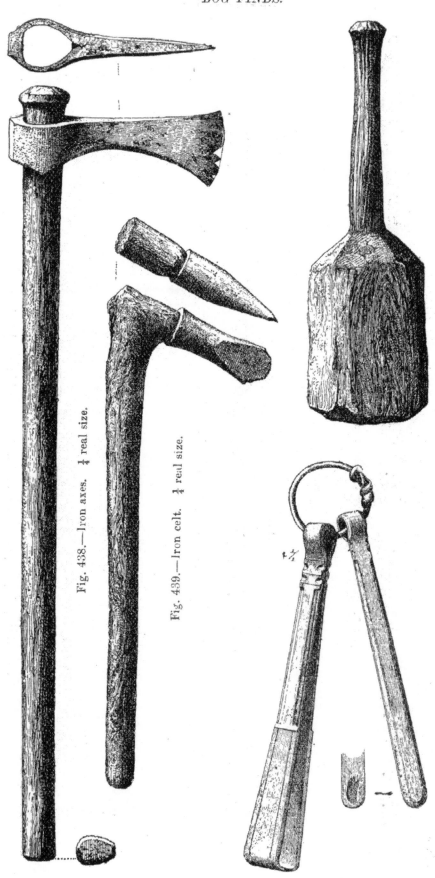

Fig. 438.—Iron axes. ¼ real size.

Fig. 439.—Iron celt. ¼ real size.

Fig. 440.—Tweezer and earpick of bronze hanging on a bronze ring. Real size.

Fig. 441.—Wooden club. ⅛ real size.

Fig. 442. — Black glass bead. Real size.

Fig. 443. — Light-green glass bead, with yellow points on a dark-red ground. Real size.

Fig. 444.—Green glass bead with red stripes. Real size.

Fig. 445.—½ real size.

Fig. 446.—½ real size.

Buckles.

   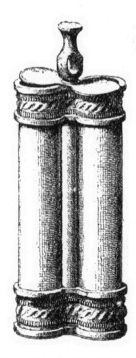

Fig. 447.—Silver tweezers. Real size.

Fig. 448.— Silver ear spoon. ½ real size

Fig. 449. — Iron knife with wooden handle. ¼ real size.

Fig. 450.—Double-barrelled tube of silver found with ear pick. Real size.

Q 2

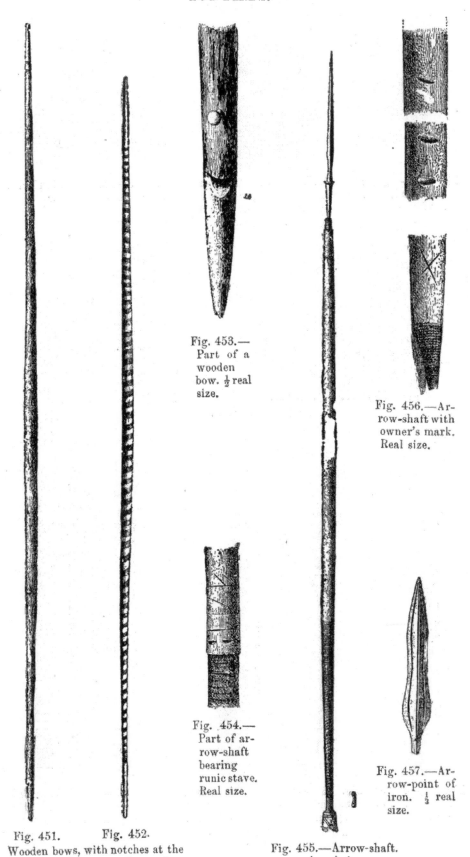

Fig. 453.—Part of a wooden bow. ½ real size.

Fig. 456.—Arrow-shaft with owner's mark. Real size.

Fig. 454.—Part of arrow-shaft bearing runic stave. Real size.

Fig. 457.—Arrow-point of iron. ⅓ real size.

Fig. 451. Fig. 452.
Wooden bows, with notches at the end for fastening the string. ¹⁄₁₁ real size.

Fig. 455.—Arrow-shaft. ⅓ real size.

NYDAM BOG FIND.

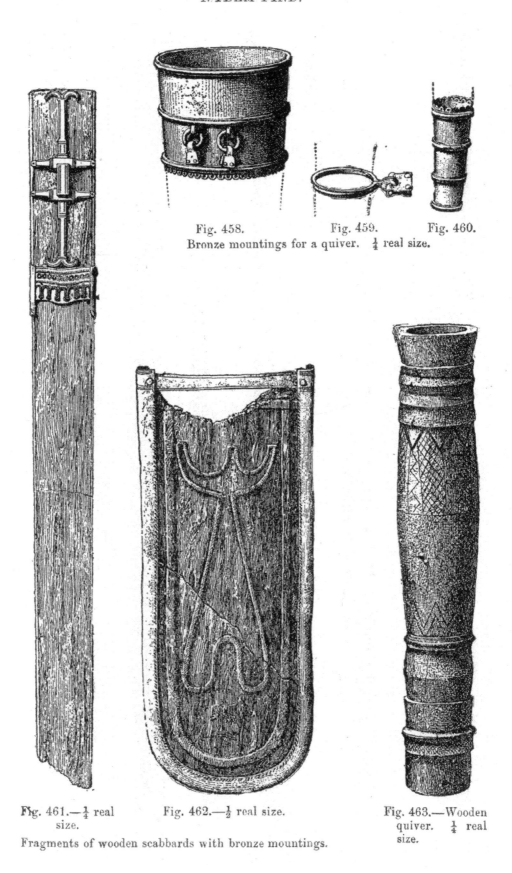

Fig. 458.

Bronze mountings for a quiver. ¼ real size.

Fig. 459.

Fig. 460.

Fig. 461.—¼ real
size.

Fig. 462.—½ real size.

Fig. 463.—Wooden
quiver. ¼ real
size.

Fragments of wooden scabbards with bronze mountings.

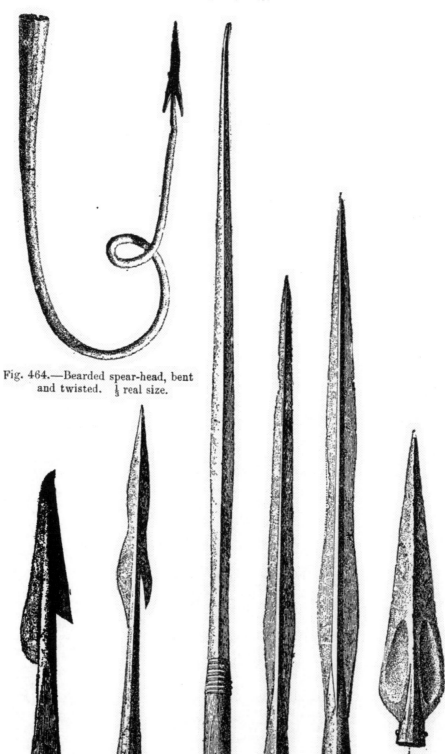

Fig. 464.—Bearded spear-head, bent and twisted. ⅓ real size.

Fig 465.
Bearded spear-points of iron. ⅓ real size.

Fig. 466.

Fig. 467.—Iron spear - point, bayonet shaped. ⅓ real size.

Fig 468. Iron spear-points. ⅓ real size.

Fig. 469.

Fig. 470.—Leaf shaped iron spear-point. real size.

254

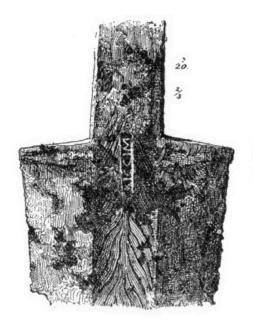

Fig. 471.—Iron sword, damascened, bearing Latin inscription. ⅔ real size.

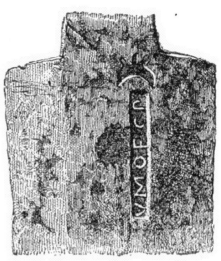

Fig. 472.—Iron sword bearing Latin inscription. ⅔ real size.

Fig. 473. — Iron sword bearing Latin inscription.

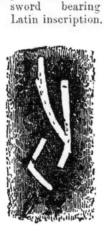

Fig. 474. — Part of sword blade with runes inlaid with gold.

Fig. 475. Fig. 476.
Damascened blades. ⅔ real size.

Fig. 477.—Wooden bowl. ⅙ real size.

Fig. 478.   Fig. 479.

Iron ferrules to scabbard, inlaid with flat hammered gold wire. ½ real size.

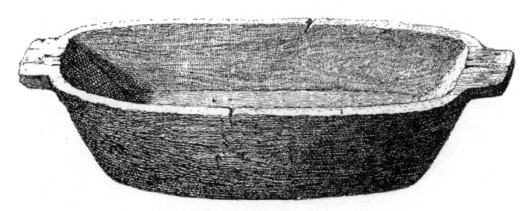

Fig. 480.—Wooden trough   ⅙ real size.

NYDAM BOG FIND

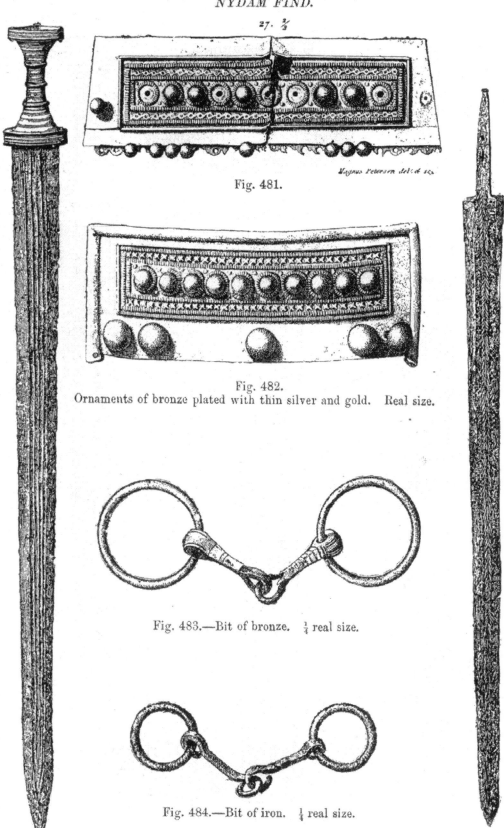

27. ⅔

Fig. 481.

Fig. 482.
Ornaments of bronze plated with thin silver and gold.   Real size.

Fig. 483.—Bit of bronze.   ¼ real size.

Fig. 484.—Bit of iron.   ¼ real size.

Fig. 485.—Double-edged damascened sword with silver handle.
½ real size.

Fig. 486.—Double-edged dama
scened sword.   ⅓ real size.

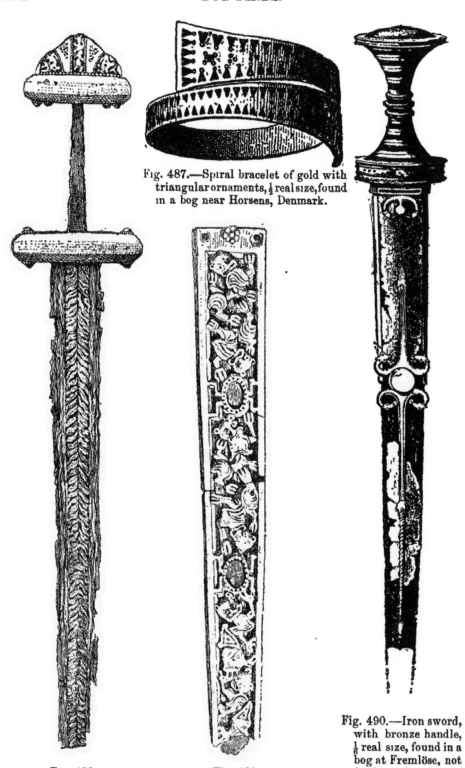

Fig. 487.—Spiral bracelet of gold with triangular ornaments, ½ real size, found in a bog near Horsens, Denmark.

Fig. 488.
Damascened iron sword, ¼ real size, of the later iron age, with mounting for scabbard, made of silver, in relief work and gilt. Found in a bog near Slagelse on Zealand, Denmark.

Fig. 489.

Fig. 490.—Iron sword, with bronze handle, ⅙ real size, found in a bog at Fremlöse, not far from the town of Odense, on Fyen, with fragments of two other iron swords, &c. Earlier iron age.

CHAPTER XIII.

NORTHERN RELICS—GROUND FINDS.

The custom of hiding objects—Discovery of numerous golden objects near
the surface—Necklaces of gold—Golden horns discovered at Mögletönder
—The Bangstrup find.

THE objects found in the earth, and classified under the name
of *ground finds,* are often not only very valuable but also very
beautiful; in many instances they are of the same type and
period as those of the bogs and graves. The custom of intentionally hiding objects which existed in the stone and bronze
age lasted until the end of the Viking age. and one of the
finest archæological fields in the whole of Scandinavia is that
of Broholm, situated on the island of Fyen. These finds are
divided into three principal groups, viz. :—Lundeborg, Gudme,,
and Elsehoved. Almost all the objects were so near the
surface of the soil that they were discovered either when
ploughing, or digging with a spade.

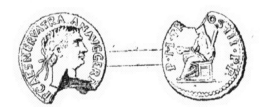

Fig. 491.—Denarius ; Trajan (98–117). Broholm. Real size.

Fig. 492.—Fibula of bronze. Broholm. Real size.

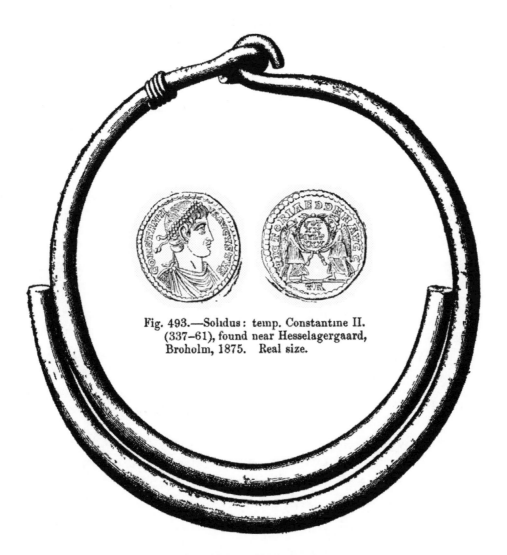

Fig. 493.—Solidus: temp. Constantine II.
(337–61), found near Hesselagergaard,
Broholm, 1875. Real size.

Fig. 494.—Largest Neck-ring, Broholm. Heaviest rings, weight 3 lbs., 1 lb. 14½ oz.,
1 lb. 2½ oz.; ½ real size. Among other objects discovered with this neck-ring
were three other neck-rings, one weighing about 2 lbs. 2 ozs., another 1½ lb.;
six pieces of massive gold belonging to neck-rings; six spiral gold rings;
a spiral finger-ring of gold; bent gold bars probably used as money; and
bracteates.

Fig. 495.—Roll of flat· Fig. 496.—Gold bead. Fig. 497.—Gold
gold band.   Real size. Broholm.   band.

Fig. 498.—Solidus: temp. Constantine II. Broholm.
Real size.

Fig. 499.—Gold Neck-ring, from Hesselagergaard, Broholm. ⅔ real size.

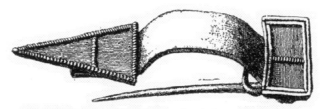

Fig. 500.—Fibula of gold. Broholm. Real size.

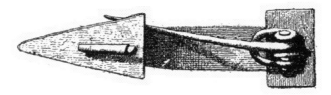

Reverse of Fig. 500.

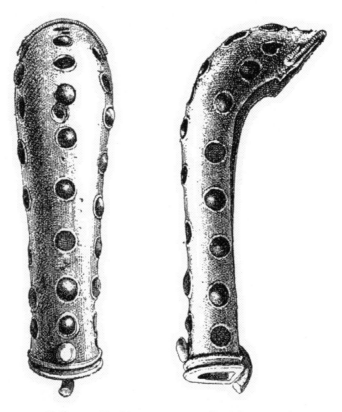

Fig. 501.—Hollow gold object, ornamented with cornelians, found at Lundeberg, Broholm. Real size.

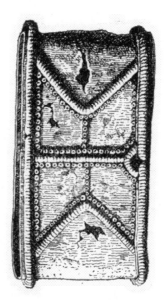

Reverse of Fig. 502.

Fig. 502.—Gold Mounting for sword scabbard. Real size. Broholm.

Fig. 503.

Fig 504.

Gold bracteates.   Real size.

Fig. 505.—Mosaic bead.
Real size.

Fig. 506.—Gold bracteate, showing
fibula on the neck.   Real size.

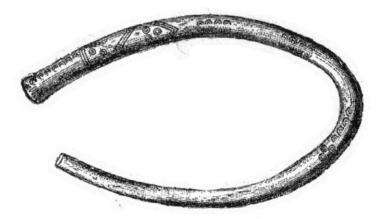

Fig. 507.—Gold ring used as money.   Real size.

Fig. 508.— Gold spiral ring. Elsehoved, Broholm. Real size.

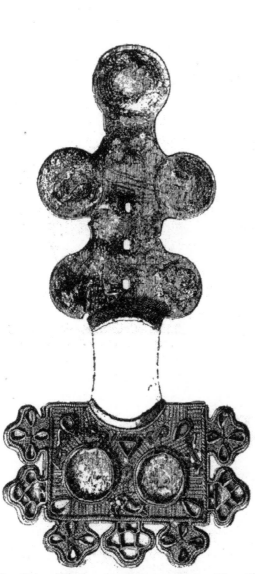

Fig. 509.—Fibula of copper covered with gold, and ornamented with garnets, one of which remains intact; a bird will be seen at the bottom. ½ real size.

Fig. 510.—Roman coins of the 5th century, forming part of a necklace, with a string of gold beads (Valentinianus, 425–455; Julius Majorianus, 457–461; two Leo I., 457–474; Zeno, 474–491; two Anastasius, 491–515).

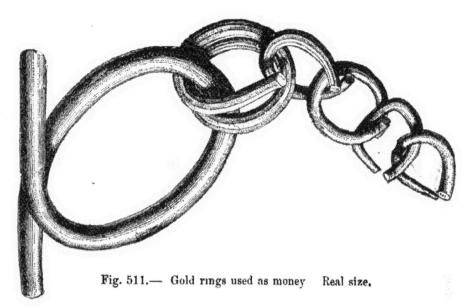

Fig. 511.— Gold rings used as money   Real size.

Among the finest and most valuable objects found in the North were the two superb golden horns discovered at Mögeltonder on the peninsula of Jutland, which were once the pride of the great Museum of Northern Antiquities in Copenhagen.

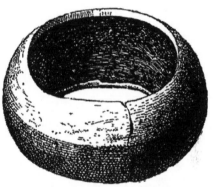

Fig. 512.—Ring of gold.   Real size.

They were without equals in any part of the world; their exterior was made of different bands of gold, with figures in repoussé work, fastened to the harder gold of the body of the horn. Both were stolen from the old Danish Museum on the 4th of May, 1802, and the ignorant thief melted them; thus those two superb specimens were for ever lost to science, and with an unfortunate fatality the cast of each has also been lost; but luckily the drawings made can be relied on. The thief was captured a year after, and his punishment was not adequate to the crime he had committed.

The representations given upon them must have had a meaning; these were symbolical, and were probably very significant and not used for mere ornamentation; what the figures and symbolical signs meant is impossible for us to tell. Among the most remarkable of the former is the

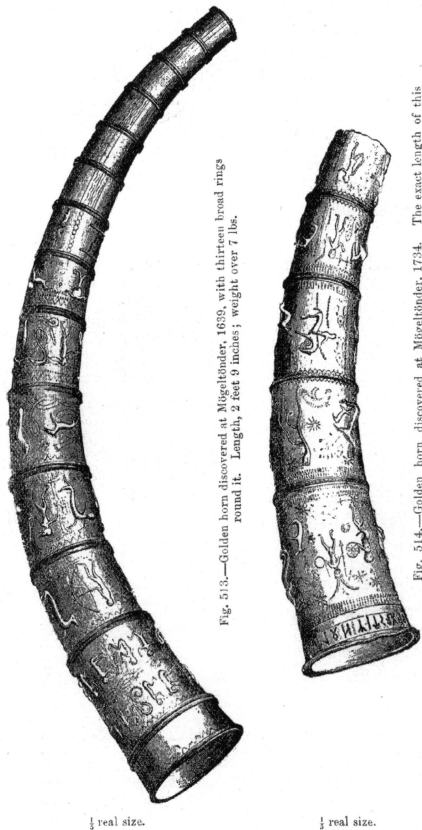

Fig. 513.—Golden horn discovered at Mögeltönder, 1639, with thirteen broad rings round it. Length, 2 feet 9 inches; weight over 7 lbs.

⅓ real size.

Fig. 514.—Golden horn discovered at Mögeltönder, 1734. The exact length of this horn, which had round its broadest end an inscription in earlier runes, has not been stated, but, judging from a *facsimile* in silver gilt made by command of Frederick VII. from the old drawing, and presented by him to the old Northern Museum, it must have been over 20 inches long. Though the lower part was broken off and lost, it still weighed more than 8 lbs.

⅓ real size.

Fig. 515.—Inscription in earlier runes on horn.

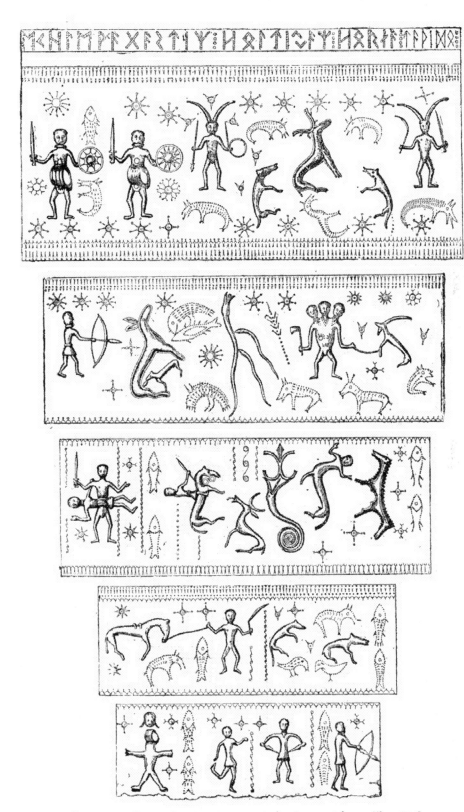

Fig. 516.—Facsimile of each ring of the damaged horn (Fig. 514).

R 2

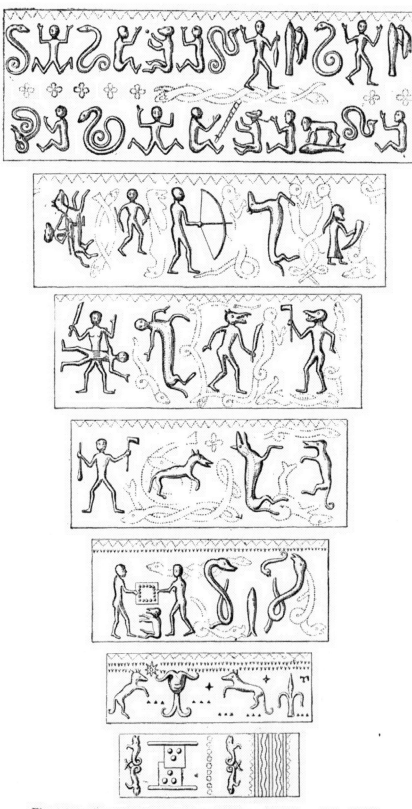

Fig. 517.—Facsimile of the rings of the perfect horn (Fig. 513).

three-headed man, holding in one hand what appears to be an axe, while with the other he leads some kind of horned animal.

Bangstrup Find (Fyen).—Conspicuous among many remarkable finds is the Bangstrup find (Fyen, 1865), in which rings of gold used as money, ornaments of peculiar shape, and 46 gold Roman coins, which were pierced or had a loop attached to the top, were discovered. The coins, ranging from the time of Trajanus Decius (249–251) to that of Constantine II. (337–351), give an approximate idea of the time of the deposit of the find; for, while most of the earlier coins are well worn, the later ones are very well preserved and the coinage is very sharp and clear, thus indicating that they cannot have been long in circulation. As the dates of these later coins are about 340–350, the find cannot have been buried much later than that time.

307–323.
Fig. 518.
IMP. LICINIVS. P. F. AVG.
ORIENS AVGVSTORVM.

306–337.
Fig. 519.
CONSTANTINVS PFAVG.
VICTORIA . CONSTANTINI. AVG.

Fig. 520.—Gold coin.

Fig. 521.—Crescent-shaped pendant of gold.

The crescent-shaped ornaments have, so far as is known, never been found elsewhere in the North; but in the Ukraine similar ones have been discovered, and are described in the work "Account of the Mounds, &c., of the Government of Kiew," by Privy Councillor J. Foundouklei, Kief, 1848.

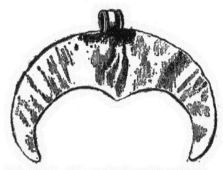

Fig. 522.—Crescent-shaped pendant
of gold.

Fig. 523.—Crescent of gold pendant-
shaped : representing two lions drinking out of a cup.

Fig. 524.—Leaf-shaped pendant
of thin sheet gold.

Fig. 525.—Leaf-shaped pendant,
sheet gold.

Fig. 526.—Rectangular pendant
of sheet gold, with embossed
human figure.

Fig. 527.—Semi-spherical gold ornamentation
of unknown use.

BANGSTRUP FIND.

CHAPTER XIV.

DESCRIPTION OF SOME REMARKABLE GRAVES AND THEIR CONTENTS.

Sepulchral chambers containing skeletons—The objects in these graves not destroyed—Numerous Roman and Greek objects—The Vallöby grave—The Bavenhöi grave—The Varpelev graveyard.

To return to the subject of graves, we will now speak of the sepulchral chambers containing skeletons. They generally vary in size, from the length of a man upwards, being about four feet wide and two or three feet high. Sometimes the

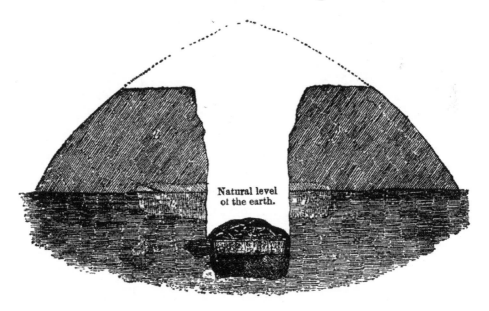

Fig. 528.—Mound, about 13 feet above the ground, showing sepulchral chamber five feet below the surface. The body had been placed upon woollen pillows filled with down. Six oak logs supported the side planks forming the sepulchral chamber, which had an oak floor. The space between the timbers had been filled with tresses of wool and other hair of animals. The chamber had been carefully covered with clay.—Bjerring, near Viborg, Northern Jutland.

corpse had been laid upon woollen stuff, cattle-hair, or birch-bark, the head turned southwards, and the feet towards the north. The inside lining is often of planks, between which and the outer stone wall bark has been placed, the seams between the timber being filled with pitch. Above the burial-chamber, which was sometimes below the level of the ground, a mound or cairn was often raised.

The objects found in these graves have not been destroyed, and the weapons, which are few, have not been made useless.

In the graves containing skeletons are found costly silver

Fig. 529.—Burial Chamber, Nörrevingstrup, near Hjörring, Jutland.
Inside measurement—height, 4 feet ; length, 5½ feet ; breadth, 3½ feet.

and glass cups, pottery, wooden pails with metal mountings, drinking-horns or their fragments; gold, silver, bronze, or silver-gilt jewelry; great masses of glass, amber, gold and mosaic beads; metal mirrors (these are scarce), bone combs, riding and driving harness, &c. The damaged weapons are often richly ornamented, and of exquisite workmanship.

A remarkable fact is the number of unmistakable Roman

and Greek objects, and sometimes coins, which occur in the finds. In the graves of women the objects chiefly found are pins, needles, buttons, jewels, ornaments, combs, knives, &c.

Vallöby Grave.—The antiquities in this grave plainly show two civilisations: the Roman or Greek, as represented by the

Fig. 530.—Vallöby Grave; showing the natural eminence, with arrangement of stones, cist, and mound.

Fig. 531.—Horizontal view; showing how the objects were placed. Coffin proper, 9 feet long, 2 feet deep.

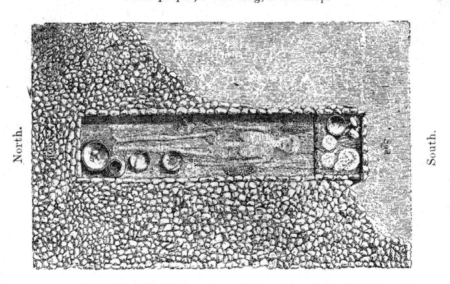

Fig. 532.—Bird's-eye view of grave, seen from above. Length of outer inclosure between 11 and 12 feet; height about 2 feet; width about 2½ feet.

bronze vessels; and the Northern, by the silver cups and black clay vessels, &c., &c.

The grave was made with especial care, and was sunk about six feet below the natural surface of the bank; the stone inclosure was built of rounded stones, of the size of a man's fist, placed together with great regularity.[1]

Fig. 533.—Samian Clay Bowl. Hunting scenes in bas-relief. Inscription ("Cos. L. Viri—") partially defaced. ⅔ real size.

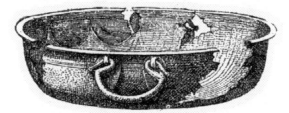

Fig. 534.—One of two flat bronze bowls. In the earth above were two small silver knobs, one covering the other, the use of which is unknown ⅓ real size

Fig. 535.—Fluted bowl of bronze. ⅓ real size.

[1] In the coffin itself, on the right side of the skeleton, were found, among other objects, forty-six checker pieces of glass, sixteen dark red, the others of whitish colour, ¾ to 1½ inch; three finger-rings of gold, and a spiral bracelet, similar to the one from Öland (vol. ii., p. 311); two fibulæ of silver, one gilt. On the left, sixty checker pieces, thirty-one of which were black, the others whitish; with these was a small amethyst stone with rough, unworked surface. At the feet, bronze vessels, one placed on the other, two small bosses of silver of unknown use.

Fig. 536.—⅓ real size.   Fig. 537.—⅔ real size.

Fragments of bronze kettle.

Fig. 538.—Kettle handle.   ½ **real size.**

Fig. 541.—Bottom of bronze
kettle.   ¼ real size.

Fig. 539.—Side view.   Fig. 540.—Front view.   Fig. 542.—Side view of bottom
Handle of kettle.   ⅔ real size.   of kettle.   ¼ real size.

Bavenhöi Grave Find.—At Bavenhöi, in Himlingoi, Zeeland, is a large bank of gravel, of slight elevation, only about 200 to 230 feet in length.   This had evidently been used as a common cemetery, as the bodies were found deposited in the earth without a coffin, though partly surrounded by stone settings. The antiquities found at various times with the skeletons seem to belong to the latter part, or perhaps the middle, of the early iron age.

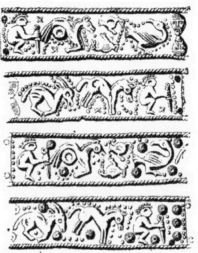

Fig. 543.—Bronze vase. ¼ real size.

Fig. 544.—Border of silver goblet; plaqué with gold and ornamented with figures in relief—viz , a double head with moustaches and helmets; a helmeted man crouching, with a dagger in his hand; two quadrupeds with manes; a horned animal; and three birds. Between the figures are dots, circles, and crosses.

Fig. 545.—Silver cup. ½ real size.

Fig. 546.—Silver goblet, with repoussé work of silver plated with gold; similar to the Vallöby one. ⅓ real size.

BAVENHÖI GRAVE FIND.

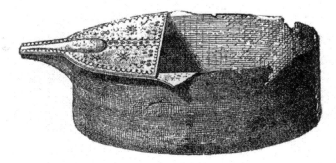

Fig. 547.—Flat basin or stewpan of bronze, containing two goblets of silver, &c. ⅙ real size.

Fig. 548.—Bronze pail. ⅙ real size.

Fig. 549.—Bronze vase, ¼ real size, with border upon which are engraved hunting scenes, a lion, two horses, a tiger or leopard, and two bucks, a dog and two deer; these animals are separated by trees and plants, the leaves of which, to judge from some traces, must have been silvered over.

Fig. 550.—Part of the design round the border of vase, representing hunting scene.
½ real size.

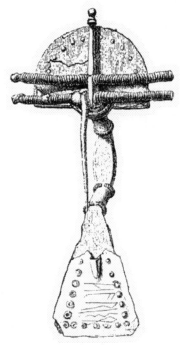

Fig. 551.—Bronze fibula covered with gold, with an inscription scratched in earlier runes. ⅔ real size.

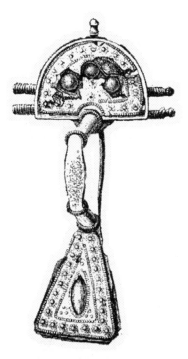

Fig. 552.—Bronze fibula plated with embossed gold ornamented with 3 blue glass knobs and an oval piece of glass of the same colour. ⅔ real size.

Fig. 553.—Fibula from Storeheddinge, Zeeland, showing the part missing in the one above. ⅔ real size.

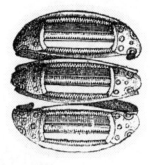

Fig. 554.—Gold ring of three spirals flattened and ornamented with heads of animals, found still adhering to the bone of the hand. Real size.

BAVENHÖI GRAVE FIND.

At Varpelev, Zeeland, a grave was found covered by several slabs; it is nearly 4 yards long, 1¾ yard broad, the bottom being about 3 yards under the surface of the earth. Within lay the skeleton of a full-grown man, with its head to the S.S.W., and its feet to the N.N.E.; alongside of it were numerous objects, the most interesting of which are those of glass.[1]

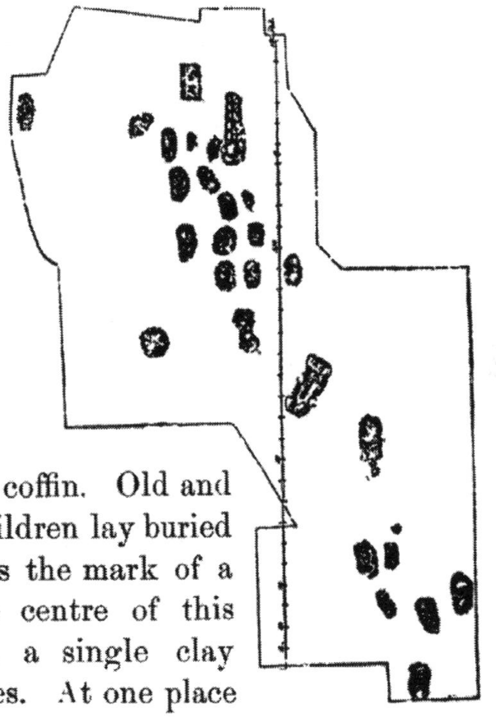

The grave-yard at Varpelev is a low bank 200 feet long, 125 feet wide. The bodies were laid down, generally, in a bent position in the sand or gravel, in their clothes or grave-dress, but without a coffin. Old and young men, women and children lay buried here, and one corpse bears the mark of a heavy sword-cut. In the centre of this skeleton graveyard stood a single clay urn, containing burnt bones. At one place there was a bed made of paved stones burnt and smoked, which had evidently been used as a pyre.

Fig. 555.—Ground plan of the Graveyard at Varpelev.

The richest grave was situated under the highest point of the bank, at a depth of 9 feet under the surface; it was

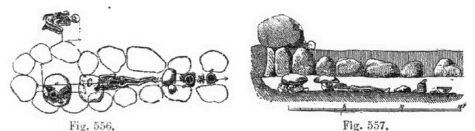

Fig. 556.   Fig. 557.

Grave at Varpelev.

made in the gravel, and was surrounded by sixteen rough stones of different size and shape. The majority were 2 feet

---

[1] See also pages 280, 282, 284.

in diameter; the large stone at the head measured 3 feet in length and width, and was 2 feet thick. The interstices were filled up with blue clay. A large slab, 2 feet long, 1½ feet broad, and 8 inches thick, was laid on the head, which like the rest of the bones was much decomposed, and proved to be that of a heavy-built man. The corpse lay on its back, nearly straight, with its head to the south-west; it had originally had over it some kind of covering, as there are remains of clothes or a grave-dress.

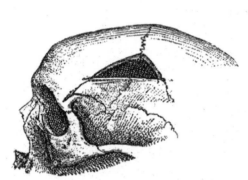

Fig. 558.—Skull (with sword-cut?), Varpelev Grave. ⅔ real size.

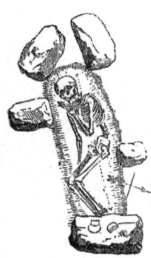

Fig. 559.—Skeleton of man; above the head two large stones. Varpelev. 1877.

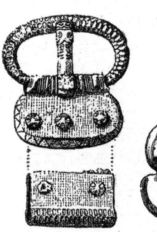

Fig. 560.—½ real size.

Fig. 561.—Real size.

Fig. 562.—Real size. Fig. 563.—Real size.

Gold rings found on finger bones.

Two silver buckles: one found near the middle of the corpse, one near the head.

VARPELEV GRAVE FIND.

Fig. 564.   Fig. 565.

Roman Coin of Probus, 276–82 ; found lying by right ear of corpse.
Real size.

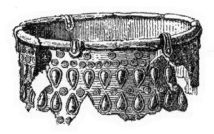

Fig. 566.—Fragment of thin ornamented silver plating, probably the
mounting of a drinking-horn.   ½ real size.

Fig. 567.—Fibula of silver, *svastica* shape, plated with
gold, with amber knob in the centre ; beautiful small
birds may be noticed on each arm ; found in a woman's
grave.   ½ real size

Fig. 568.—Hair-pin
of gold, top orna-
mented with gar-
net ; found in a
woman's grave.
⅔ real size.

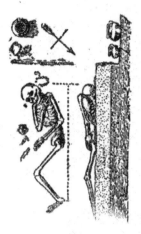

Fig. 569.—Skeleton of woman.

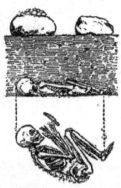

Fig. 570.—Skeleton lying on its left side, with an iron knife near the hands.

Fig. 571.

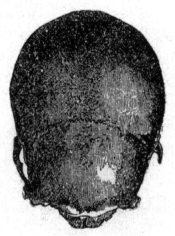

Fig. 572.

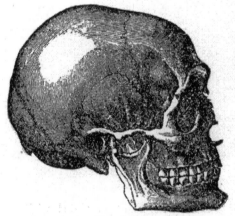

Fig. 573.
Skull, seen from three sides.

VARPELEV GRAVE FIND.

CHAPTER XV.

GREEK AND ROMAN ANTIQUITIES IN THE NORTH.

Similar antiquities in the North and in Southern Russia—Roman coins—
The trade of Gotland in earlier times—Ornaments and other objects of
bronze.

AMONG the archæological wealth of the North still belonging
to the earlier, but not earliest, iron age, we find a class of
graves and antiquities which are of special importance, for
they help us to fix very closely a date for the period to
which they belong, and for this light we are indebted to Roman
coins and other objects, both Roman and Greek, which these
graves contain.

Many of the finds of this period are most interesting, as
showing the taste of the people in the North, and a wealth
and civilisation of which we were not aware. They are the
more valuable because we see from them the wide extent of
the maritime expeditions and overland trading journeys of the
people towards the beginning of the Christian era. They show,
as has already been pointed out, the intercourse which the
people of the North had with those of the Black Sea and the
Mediterranean, and also with the newly-acquired north-western
provinces of the Roman empire (Gaul, Britain, and Frisia).
But, what is still more important, they help to prove the
general truthfulness of the earlier Edda and Sagas, for they
show that the Asar, or whoever the emigrants were, who came
north, and who were said to have brought their civilisation
with them and to have given it to the people there, were
either related to or on intimate relations with the people who
inhabited the shores of the Black Sea; for many of the
antiquities which were claimed to be of a peculiar northern
origin are identical with those found there; while similar

s 2

ornaments of unmistakable Greek origin are found in both regions. To complete the chain of proof, many of the antiquities, both in the Museums of Kief and Smolensk, are similar to those of the North.

Many of the forms of the antiquities, such as neck-rings and gold snake-shaped bracelets, fibulæ, &c., which were thought to belong exclusively to the North, are found in great number in the graves of Kertch, in Southern Russia, where they lie almost side by side with the exquisite Grecian antiquities—the pride of the Hermitage Museum in St. Petersburg—mementoes of the colonies established by Greece on the shores of the Black Sea. They show that at that period there were two distinct civilisations and peoples living near each other—one Greek, the other native. The natives were probably of the same stock as a great number of the people of the North.

Western and Eastern, Roman and Byzantine, coins have been found; the gold solidi were for the most part used by the people in the North as ornaments, for loops have been attached to or holes made through them. The two largest discoveries hitherto made of Roman coins are those of Hagestaborg, in Scania, southern Sweden (550 denarii), found in 1871, and of Sindarfe (Hemse parish), Gotland, at which latter spot about 1,500 Roman coins were found, in 1870, in a clay urn.[1] Few coins dating before the Christian era have been found.

---

[1] The earliest coins (Gotland) are those of Augustus (29 B C. A D. 14) Then follow those of Nero, and coins of all the different emperors to Alexander Severus (222–235); the greatest numbers are those of Trajan (98–117); Hadrian (117–138); Antoninus Pius (138–161); Faustina, wife of Antoninus Pius, Marcus Aurelius (161–180); Faustina junior, wife of Marcus Aurelius, and Commodus (180–192). At Hagestaborg the most numerous were those of Antoninus Pius, Marcus Aurelius, Faustina the younger, and Commodus. The earliest are of the time of Nero (54–68), the latest of that of Septimius Severus (193–'211.. In Öland the earliest are those of Trajan, the latest those of Alexander Severus. In Zeeland the earliest are of Vespasian, the latest of Macrinus (217, 218). In Fyen the earliest are of Tiberius (14–37), the latest of Geta (211, 212) In Bornholm the earliest are of Nero, the latest of Septimius Severus. In Jutland the earliest are also of Nero, the latest of Macrinus (217, 218). In southern Sweden the earliest are of Claudius (41–54), the latest of Alexander Severus, but only one or two of the latter have been found; after the time of Commodus the silver denarii became rarer and rarer On the island of Fyen a complete series of gold coins from Decius (249–251) to Licinius the elder (307–323) have been found. The Byzantine coins are of gold, and chiefly used as ornaments, date from Constantinus Magnus (306–337) to Anastasius (491–518); one also of Justinius I. (518–527) has been found. In Norway the gold coins of the above period

The people had to learn that these coins had an intrinsic value, and that with them they could buy goods. In every country where barter takes place it has taken a certain, sometimes a great, number of years for the people to learn this value.[1] The fact that the earlier coins are rare does not conclusively prove that intercourse between the North and the Western parts of Europe had not taken place before that time.

Judging from the extensive hoards of coins discovered, it is not improbable that they were kept for some opportune time when their need would be required, such as for purchases when travelling back to the Western or Eastern Roman provinces. That the people were well acquainted with the value of these coins is beyond dispute, for otherwise they would not have kept them.

We must remember that human nature is and always has been the same; there were misers in those early days as there are now. The Sagas give us some examples of the practice of hoarding, and the probability is that some of the hoards found may have been collected during the lifetime of one or more persons. But the numbers found, in hoards or otherwise, even without those which remain undiscovered, show the existence of commercial intercourse.

One of the countries of whose earlier history we know nothing, except that it is mentioned here and there in the Sagas, is the island of Gotland; but from the finds, which are especially rich in coins, we are led to the conclusion that it was a great emporium of trade at least from the beginning of the Christian era to the twelfth century. Roman, Byzantine, Arabic, and earlier English coins are found in far greater num-

---

are exceedingly rare, only one of Valens (364–378) and one of Gratuanus (367–375) having been discovered; also one of Tiberius Constantius (578–582), one of Mauricius Tiberius (582–602), one of Constantius V Copronymus (741–775), one of Michæl III. (842–867) all of gold. Some of the earlier Arabic coins had already made their appearance in Scandinavia The Roman coins from the Bangstrup find date from between A D. 249 and 361. See also Appendix.

[1] I have myself seen an illustration of this on the African coast, where natives could not understand that coins represent the value of goods, though traders had come to their country for a long time, and in some places they were loth to take money as payment, while a few miles inland it was refused.

bers than in all the Scandinavian lands together. Of the latter, those of Ethelred are even more numerous than in England itself. Situated in a sea whose shores at that period seem to have been inhabited by a dense population, Gotland appears to have occupied the position of commercial supremacy which England holds in Europe to-day.

We have historical evidence of its being a great emporium of trade as late as the fourteenth century, until Wisby, its chief town, was destroyed by the Danes. Its magnificent towers, walls, and ruined churches still bear witness to its past greatness.[1]

From the time of Alexander Severus (A.D. 235) to Theodosius (A.D. 395), which comprises a period of 160 years. the coins become very scarce, and Roman gold coins take the place of

---

[1] See "Land o the Midnight Sun." The islands of Zeeland and Fyen are especially rich in Roman objects and show the existence of great intercourse with the Roman provinces; while Gotland is particularly rich in coins. In the hamlet of Ryk (Tanum parish), Bohuslän, a Roman coin struck A.D 179 for the Emperor Marcus Aurelius was found in the ground. From the inscription on the coin the date can be accurately fixed, for it was said that it was coined in the year when Marcus Aurelius was Tribune for the thirty-third time, Imperator for the tenth time, and Consul for the third time.

A gold coin of Tiberius (14–37) was found in a stone-set coffin at Rorbœk; a silver denarius of Nerva (96–98) in the find of Fraugdegard, Fyen; and a silver denarius of Antoninus Pius (138–161), with a skeleton, in a natural hill at Bennebo, near Holbœk; a silver denarius of Lucius Verus (161–169), with a skeleton, in a hill at Gunnerugs, near Presto; a barbaric imitation in gold of a Roman imperial coin, with a loop soldered to it, found with a skeleton at Aareslen in Odense amt, Fyen One limit of time obtained by means of the coins is certain enough, for the graves cannot have been closed before the year of their coinage.

Pyteas mentions Guttanæ. The Gotlanders in the Sagas are called Gutar; they may have met him on some of their trading journeys. The two names seem to be sufficiently similar to make this a probable supposition. In the island of Gotland a Greek coin of copper was found, but it seems to have been struck at Panormus in Sicily. On the obverse is a female head looking to the right, on the reverse a horse galloping to the left; it has no Punic letters. (In the collection of Capt. C. T. von Braun, of Ystad.) Two Macedonian coins of silver were also found; one of them is a diabole of Philip II., similar to the coins described in Müller, "Der Macedoniske Konge Philipp II.'s Mynter," p. 3, Nos. 14–16, and engraved Plate 1. (Both were in the collection of Capt. v. Braun, of Ystad; now only one remains there.)

Also Roman coins anterior to Augustus, found together about 100 years ago. A silver coin of the family of Lucretia: a silver coin of the family of Nævia; a coin of the family of Sulpicia. They are all unusually well preserved, but shorn on the border. (In the collection of Capt. von Braun Ystad.) A silver coin of the family Funa; a silver coin of the family Poblicia; one subærate coin of the family Postumia; one silver coin of the family Procilia; a silver coin of the family Tituria; a silver coin of the family Veturia. (In the collection of Capt. von Braun.) A silver coin of the family Nævia, given by Capt. Braun to the Museum at Uddevala; and a silver coin of the family Sicinia, both well preserved (In the Wisby Museum; formerly in the collection of Mr. P. A. Save.)

silver.[1] From the finds we see that this period in the North becomes exceedingly rich in gold jewels, and it seems probable that the people preferred gold coins to those of silver.

The North is particularly rich in finds of bronze vessels, which appear to be more specially of Greek, or some perhaps of Roman manufacture; the scarcity of them in Britain and Gaul would imply that they are chiefly of Greek origin; they seem to have been highly prized by the people.

Near the fishing village of Abekås, Southern Scania,

Fig. 574.—Bronze vessel, ½ real size, containing burnt bones, ring armour, coat or mail, dipper of bronze with a sieve belonging to it, two glass tumblers, &c, under a stone slab buried in the ground.

in Jutland, a dipper has been found with the name of the Roman manufacturer on it, and the words " P. CIPI POLIBI." Another, with a name on it, was also found in Helsingland, Sweden.

---

[1] Three hundred and forty-four silver denarii, coined by the emperors between Nero and Marcus Aurelius, among them many of Trajan, Hadrian, and Antoninus Pius, have been found at the mouth of the Elbe.

Under a large stone on a bank at Sengerich, in Hanover, 1,100 silver denarii were dug up, coined between the years 96 and 211.

In Mecklenburg the finds of imperial coins embrace the period from Augustus to Valentinian.

Finds of Roman coins from the first two centuries after Christ have also been made at the mouth of the Vistula and in its lower course, near the Oder.

An especially interesting discovery was that of a Greek denarius coined in Lycia by Trajan; the only Greek coin discovered in Hanover.

Fig 575.—Piece of the coat of mail. Real size. Oremölla.

Fig. 576.—Vessel of glass. ⅓ real size. Oremölla.

Fig. 577.—Dipper of bronze, with sieve. ⅓ real size. Oremölla.

Fig. 578.—Urn. ⅔ real size. Oremölla.

Fig. 579.—Bronze vessel of Roman workmanship, containing burnt bones, and a few pieces of melted glass. Height, 18 inches. Inscribed on it are the following words in silver:[1] "Apollini Granno donvm Ammillivs Constans præfectvs templi ipsivs votvm solvit libentissimo merito." Mound, Fycklinge, Vestmanland, Sweden. ⅓ real size.

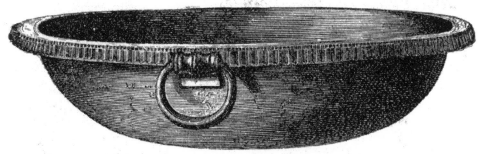

Fig. 580.—Roman bowl of bronze, found, with several antiquities, under a slab at Sojvide, Gotland.

---

[1] Apollo Grannus, to whose temple the vase once belonged, was worshipped by the tribes of Gaul and Belgium. The Roman historian Dio Cassius relates that he was one of the gods worshipped by the Emperor Caracalla, who was murdered in A.D. 217. The name has also been discovered in Transylvania on a stone which Quintus Axius Ælianus, Governor of Dacia at the beginning of the second century, had cut. It, however, happens that this Ælianus had before this resided in Belgium, whither he had probably brought with him the worship of the god.

Fig. 581.—Ornament of a large bronze
vase, with hole for the handle; found
when ploughing. ⅔ real size. Öland.

Fig. 582.—Handle of a Roman bronze
vase. ⅔ real size. Öland.

Fig. 583.—Bronze vessel, ½ real size, with burnt bones,
in a tumulus, with two bronze spurs exactly alike,
a bent double-edged sword, a spear-head damaged
purposely, lying over the kettle, another larger
spear-head well preserved, &c. Norway.

Fig. 584.—Restored bronze vase,
containing ashes and bones,
length 8½ inches, encircled by
glittering stones and inlaid with
silver. Angvaldnœs, Karmoen,
Norway.

Fig. 586—Silver vase. ⅓ real size. Byrsted, Aalborg amt, North Jutland.

Fig. 585.—Bronze statuette,[1] representing Juno. ⅓ real size. Ösby, Gräsgard parish, Öland.

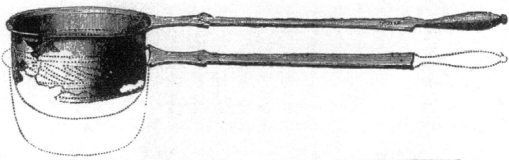

Fig. 587.—Sieve of bronze, ⅓ real size, found with ornaments of bronze and a drinking horn, a gold charm, two gold rings, and a small gold button found in a sepulchral chamber of little over 4 yards in length, and about 2 feet 3 inches wide. Norway.

Fig. 588.—Handle of the sieve. Real size.

---

[1] More than forty different statuettes have been found.

Fig. 589.—Ornament of a bronze vase, ⅔ real size, found in a tumulus. Norway.

Fig. 590.—Ornament of bronze. ½ real size. Norway.

Fig. 591.—Bronze vessel from Mosbœk bog. Jutland.

Fig. 592.—Fragments of a bronze chain, probably part of riding gear. ⅓ real size. Bog, Karby on Mors.

Fig. 593.—Head at fastening of the handle of the bronze vessel.

Fig. 594.—Bronze basin, over a kettle containing burnt bones, ¼ real size, in round tumulus, inside a little stone cist built of slabs; with it also were a bronze kettle and a glass cup. Norway.

Fig. 595.—Bronze vase containing burnt bones, wrapped in a dark green woollen cloth with greenish and yellow stripes, fastened with a fibula of silver. In the chamber were a pair of shears and other objects. Ringkjobing amt, Jutland.

Fig. 596.—Vase, ¼ real size, found in a round mound, Vang. Hdm., Norway, with fragments of another bronze vessel of the same size, but of a somewhat different form. It has on it the inscription " LIBERTINVS. ET. APRVS. CVRATOR [ES. POS] VERVNT." Originally it must have belonged to a Roman temple of one of the northern provinces of the empire, and was offered to this temple by two of the administrators (curatores) named above. The shape of the letters leads to the conclusion that the vase belongs to the first century of our era.

Fig. 597.—Bronze bucket of Roman make, ½ real size, found in a round mound, Norway, together with a spear of iron and other objects of the same metal, but these were so decayed as to be undistinguishable.

Fig. 599.—Flat finger-ring of silver and alloyed gold, real size, found together with fragments of Roman or Greek bronze vessels, four small beads of greenish glass, and two bronze fibulæ, in a mound, Hjorring, Jutland

Fig. 598.—Bronze vessel about 10 inches high. Angvaldnœs mound, Norway.

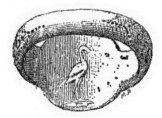

Fig. 600.—Bronze ring, real size, with Latin inscription, "Divo Trajano Parth. Avg. Patri." Holbæk, Denmark.

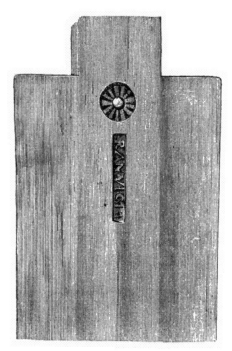

Fig. 601.—Part of bent sword, real size, showing inscription in Latin "RANVICI," probably a name, and above it a stamp, probably constituting the trade-mark of its maker.—Similar swords have been found at other places in the North, in the Nydam and Vimose bogs.

Fig. 602. — Bent sword, ¼ real size, found in a mound at Einang, Kristians Amt, Norway, on a layer of charcoal and burnt bones.

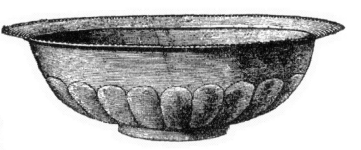

Fig. 603.—Bronze vessel, of Roman manufacture, mound 48 to 50 feet diameter, 6 feet high, found in a mound at Harf, Meldelpad Sweden, above a slab, filled with burnt bones, an iron spear-point, fibula of bronze, fragments of clay urns, &c. ¼ real size.

Fig. 604.—Bronze kettle, ⅛ real size, Brokær, Ribe, Jutland; found with fragments
of Roman bronze vessels; and of two massive coats of mail; fragments of
artistically woven cloth; double-edged sword with scabbard; comb, fragments
of checkers, oblong dice of bone, and fragments of a silver drinking-horn, &c.

Fig. 605.—Ornaments of silver for drinking-horn, Brokær, Ribe, Jutland. ½ real size.

On the farm of Brottby, Ösby, Upland, a grave-mound
of about 150 feet in circumference and 13 feet in height was
found. The mound, the exterior of which was of earth,
covered a cairn, in which was found a stone burial chamber
enclosing a clay urn. The upper part contained bones, which
were entirely unburnt, below which were pieces of the skull,
also unburnt.[1]

---

[1] Among the bones outside the urn were found various fragments of bronze, six clinch-nails of iron, remains of glass, a burnt oblong loaf of bread, two pieces of a head ornament of bronze with rivets of iron, a ring of bronze, twelve beads of glass of different size and appearance, a damaged hanging ornament of bronze, a square plate of bronze with iron rivets, a denarius of the Emperor Marcus Aurelius coined in A.D. 162.

Fig. 606.—Grave-chamber found at Bröttby, Upland.

Fig. 608.   Fig. 609.   Fig. 610.

Fig. 607.—A buckle of bronze found with an iron needle. Brottby.

Glass beads, of pale red colour, with white flowers with light and dark-green leaves; one is fastened to a silver wire. Of the twelve beads, three are represented here. Bröttby.

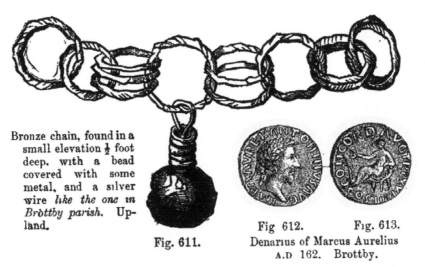

Bronze chain, found in a small elevation ½ foot deep. with a bead covered with some metal, and a silver wire *like the one in Bröttby parish.* Upland.

Fig. 611.

Fig 612.   Fig. 613.
Denarius of Marcus Aurelius
A.D 162. Brottby.

Fig. 614.—Fibula of gold, ornamented with eight garnets. Aareslev, Fyen. Real size.

Fig. 615.—Fibula with hanging ornament of gold, real size, representing a lion's head; the filagree work is ornamented with garnets, found with another large silver fibula, a crystal ball, a vase of bronze, an imitation of a Roman coin, &c. Aareslev, Fyen.

Fig. 616.—The crystal ball with Greek inscription found near a skeleton with hanging ornaments, &c. Aareslev, Fyen. Real size.

Fig. 617.—Part of a belt buckle, silver gilt. ⅓ real size.

AARESLEV FIND.

Fig. 619.—Bronze or-
nament, real size,
found with kettle.
Möllegaard, Bro-
holm.

Fig. 618.—Bronze vessel, ⅕ real size, so brittle, that only by covering it all around
with clay could it be moved away. It is made of two parts joined together
in the middle with small flat rivets of bronze, and contained six quarts of burnt
bones, among which were seventeen human teeth, different articles of iron and
bronze, which had been packed in apparently coarse linen, small fragments of
which only remained; a bronze mounting for a drinking-horn, and different
kinds of iron knives; iron mounting for a knife-handle, remains of two iron
awls, an iron key, two small melted lumps of silver, remains of about thirty-two
bone needles, a glass bead with green ground and yellow stripes, remains of four
earthen vessels, &c. Mollegaard, Broholm.

Fig. 620.   Fig. 621.

Fig. 622.   Fig. 623.

Byzantine gold coins, fifth century, Libius
Severus and Leo. found in Bjorn-
hofda, Oland, with thirty-three other
coins of the same century. Real size.

Barbaric imitation of Byzantine coin of
the fifth century. Real size. Mall-
gards, Gotland.

Fig. 624.   Fig. 625.

Antonini Pii

Fig. 626.   Fig 627.

Faustina the younger.

CHAPTER XVI.

GLASS.

Vessels with painted figures—Vessels with Greek letters—Drinking-horns of glass—Cut glass.

NOTHING perhaps can give us a better idea of the refined taste of some of the Northmen than the beautiful glass objects which have been found in different parts of the country. Many of these are evidently of Greek, some perhaps of Roman,

Fig. 628.—2½ inches high; diameter across top, 3 inches; across bottom, 1⁷⁄₁₀ths of an inch. A blue panther, with grey or brown contours and dots, attacks a brown stag; on the other side of which is a brown lioness. Between the animals are circles of dots, brown and yellow by turns, with a brown spot in their middle.

Fig. 629.—3½ inches high; 3⁹⁄₁₀th inches diameter. A brown bull, with a blue band with brown dots, attacks a brown bear. To the left a man in yellow coat and green breeches, holding a whip in one hand, in the other a blue shield; to the right a stag, being torn by a lion, both brown.

These two vessels were found in a field, Nordrup, Zeeland, in a grave 3 feet 4 inches under the ground. It contained a skeleton, and, besides the two vessels, a Roman bronze vessel and bronze sieve, a gold finger-ring, a silver fibula, forty-one beads of glass and glass mosaic, a clay vessel, and fragments of two clay vessels.

origin. In the museums of Italy, Greece, or Russia no such exquisite bowls are found, which after having been painted they seem to have been baked or subjected to heat in order that they might retain their colour.

Glass, as we have seen, has been found in the later bronze

Fig. 630.—4 inches high, 3¾ inches in diameter across top.   In a mound, Viborg amt, Jutland.

ΠΙΕΖΗCΑΙCΚΑΛΩC

Fig. 631.—Fragment of glass vessel, with gladiator and shield of blue tint, the gloves and shoulders are brown.   Arm and legs of the other gladiator flesh colour. Thorslunde.

Fig. 632.—Fragments of glass bowl found in a grave by Thorslunde, Fyen.   ¾ real size. The wolf is greyish upon light yellow ground.   The arm and legs are of a brown tint, the dots yellow and brown.   These lay alongside remains of skeletons which seem to have been buried in sitting posture; some of the designs are raised.

age : the ancient name for *amber* in the North was *gler*,[1] which was well known by the stone age people ; but we are aware that glass was unknown to them.

Fig. 633.—Fragment of a glass bowl of a green tint, ⅔ real size, found in a grave mound by Thorslunde.

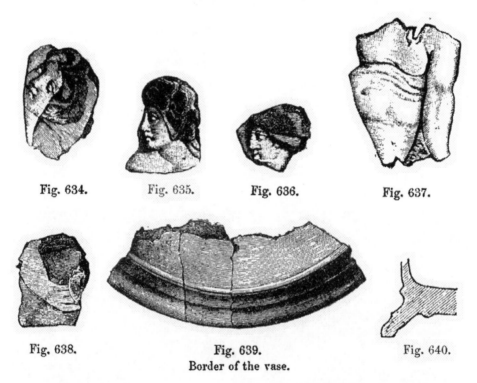

Fig. 634.   Fig. 635.   Fig. 636.   Fig. 637.

Fig. 638.   Fig. 639.   Fig. 640.
Border of the vase.

Besides the glass vessels of Roman or Greek workmanship

---

[1] The word amber occurs in three earlier poems. Magical runes were written on gler.—Sigidrifumal. Pliny in his 'Natural History,' Book xxxv. 3, 42, speaks of amber as being "formed in the islands of the Northern Ocean."

others of inferior quality, as is the case in every country, have been found; some of these, which are generally of a bluish green, yellow or white tint, are cut, some ornamented with thread patterns in relief.

Fig. 641.   Fig. 642.

Fragments of what must have been a magnificent glass vase of a dark blue colour; the figures in relief are of an opaque white and represented most probably some mythological subject. Sólberg, Lower Eker, Norway.

Fig. 643.—Glass drinking-horn. **Norway.**

Fig 644.—Thin greenish glass vessel, open at both ends. ¼ real size. **Varpelev.**

Fig. 645.—Amethyst-coloured glass bowl. ¼ real size. Varpelev.

Fig. 646.—Glass drinking-horn, length 8 inches, diameter of mouth 2½ inches; very rare in the North. ¼ real size. Bavenhoi.

Fig. 648.—Glass vessel. ⅓ real
size. With white and blue
ornamented threads, found
with beads, and bronze pans
and sieves, in a woman's
skeleton grave. Ringsted,
Zeeland.

Fig. 647.—Vessel or goblet of
greenish glass, ornamented
with fillets. ¼ real size.
Bavenhöi.

Glass with thread-like lines have been found in a stone coffin, Roman, near Dusseldorf.

Fig. 649.—Dark blue glass bowl mounted with silver, on which was inscription in Greek
letters, ΕΥΤΥΧѠC (with good luck). ½ real size. Above the head of the
skeleton in the grave, but more or less damaged by the large stone, were at least
six glass vessels and fragments of clay urns. Varpelev.

Fig. 650.—Vessel of greenish white glass with representations of various animals, found broken in many pieces. ² real size. Bavenhöi.

Fig. 651.—Animals represented on this glass vessel. Lion, yellow and brown; bear, dark brown with light yellow outlines; animal with fore part of body missing, probably an ox. ⅓ real size. Bavenhöi.

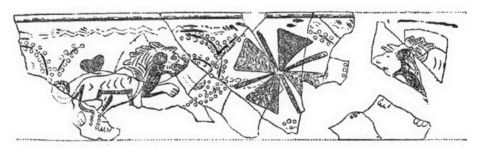

Fig. 652.—Portion of glass vessel, much damaged. ½ real size. Two lions, light yellow, blue outlines, a double cross in the middle. Bavenhöi.[1]

---

[1] For other objects in Bavenhöi find, see p. 252–254

Fig. 653.—Vessel of whitish green glass, ornamented in various colours which have been burnt on the vessel itself. The colour of the four letters D.V.B.P. represented on the cup has been destroyed by the effects of time, as has also that of the beak, wings and legs of the bird. This, however, perfectly resembles the bird on the opposite side of the cup, which is better preserved, and on which the wing is light yellow with dark brownish outlines, the beak and legs red. $\frac{2}{3}$ real size. Varpelev.[1]

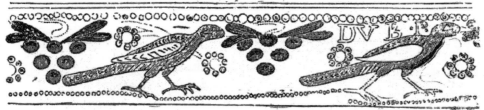

Fig. 654.—General design of vase. $\frac{2}{3}$ real size.

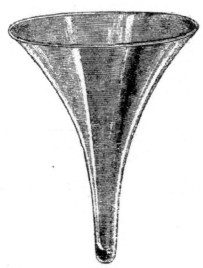

Fig. 655.—Glass cup, funnel shape. Bjorko, Södermanland.

Fig. 656.—Glass cup, $\frac{1}{4}$ real size, found in a round tumulus, with a large bronze vase with two arms, the bronze ornamentation of a wooden bucket, &c., &c. Norway.

---

[1] For other objects found at Varpelev, see p. 256–258.

Fig. 657.—Glass vessel. ¼ real size. Norway.

Fig. 658.—Glass vessel. ¼ real size. Norway.

Fig. 659.—Found deep in a stone circle. The cup or glass covered an urn of clay with burnt bones and some glass beads, etc. ½ real size. Upland.

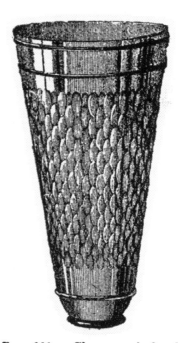

Fig. 661.—Glass vessel found in a stone cist containing a skeleton, with a clay vessel, an iron knife, and bronze mounting for two drinking-horns. ⅓ real size. Gotland.

Fig. 660.—In a stone cist, with a skeleton, some arrow-heads of bone, and a clay urn, etc., etc. ¼ real size. Oland.

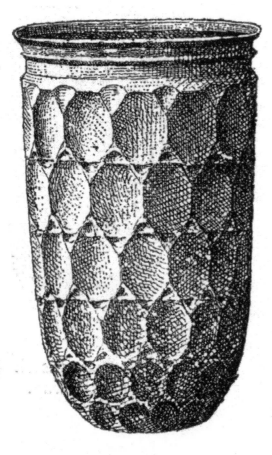

Fig. 662.—Tumbler of thick green glass ½ real size, Varpelev.

Fig. 663. — Glass vessel found in a mound with unburnt skeleton. Norway.

CHAPTER XVII.

HORSES—WAGGONS.

Favourite colours of horses—Splendour of the harness—Iron and bronze bits—Spurs—Bridles.

WE have ample proof from the Sagas that the people of the North were great breeders of horses, and took pride in their adornment. We are told of the favourite colours of horses, and the finds bear witness to the gorgeousness of their harness and trappings.

"Stein was for a while with King Knút, and was conspicuous for his weapons and clothes, and was called Stein the Proud. Old and wise men have told how Stein was so haughty that he had his horse shod with gold, and the hoof above adorned. King Knut thought Stein vied with him in magnificence, and therefore Stein left him" (Fms. v. 181).

"King Adils liked good horses very much, he had the best horses at that time. One of his horses was called *Slöngvir* (the flinging one), and another *Hrafn* (Raven); the latter he took from Ali when he was dead, and another horse also called *Hrafn* was bred by him; he sent it to King Godgest in Hálogaland. Godgest rode on it and could not stop it and fell down, and was killed"[1] (Ynglinga Saga, ch. 33).

The chief Thorstein Kuggason had to seek shelter during bad weather at the farm of Björn Hitdælakappi while going to help his foes. When Thorstein took leave:

"Björn sent for the stud-horses which were near the hay-house, for fodder was given to them while the bad weather lasted. The stallion was a son of *Hvíting* (some famous stallion) and was white, but the mares were chestnut. Another

---

[1] Cf. also Flateyjarbók, i. 401; Hrólf Kraki, c. 44; Heidarviga Saga, c. 20; Eyrbyggja Saga, c. 13.

son of Hvíting, also white, was in Thórarinsdal; but the mares (with him) were black. Bjorn had the stud-horses led to Thorstein, and said he wished to give them to him. Thorstein said he would not take them; "for I am not yet worthy of gifts from thee, and if I reward thee not for this entertainment which I have now received from thee then I shall probably not reward thee for further benefits, but, if I reward the entertainment as well as thou deservest, then I will receive the horse, and see that thou gettest something in return" (Bjorn Hitdæla kappi's Saga, p. 55).

An Icelander, Odd Úfeigsson, had traded with the Finns, which no man was allowed to do without the king's leave Thorstein, one of Harald Hardrádi's hirdmen, saved him from Harald, who wanted to slay him, and Odd escaped to Iceland. On one occasion, when Hárek, Thorstein's kinsman came to Iceland.

. "Odd sent with him to Norway a good stud of horses as a gift to Thorstein, and said, as was true, that Thorstein had saved the lives of him and his crew. Hárek came to Norway to his kinsman Thorstein, who was still with the king. He brought him the horses and said they were sent to him by Odd. Thorstein said: 'This is very unfortunate for me as but for this the help that I gave Odd and his men would not have been known; now I cannot hide it, and it is somewhat difficult to escape.' Thorstein showed the horses to the king, and said, 'they were a gift sent by Odd.' The king answered: 'I was not worthy of gifts from Odd; he has sent them to thee and not to me'"[1] (Fornmanna Sögur, vi. 383–384).

The magnificence with which the harness used by these people was ornamented is shown by their horse-collars, several of which, made of wood and richly decorated, are now in the Museum of Northern Antiquities in Copenhagen. The fact that such collars have always been found in pairs shows that two horses were generally harnessed to the waggons used; the pair is always similar, and the ornamentation at the ends, often of bronze gilt, or silver, or gold, generally consists of animals' heads such as are so commonly represented on fibulæ. At the top of the collars is a hole, through which the

---

[1] Cf. also Finnboga Saga, c 23; Gunnlaug Ormstunga's Saga, c. 5.

rein passed, and the wood is decorated with representations of human heads of metal, the triskele, and birds, &c., riveted on.

Fig. 664.—Collar for driving of gilt bronze, grave mound, Jutland. ¼ real size.

A remarkable horse-collar was found at Sollested, Assens, Fýen, in a sepulchral chamber, 30 feet long, 9 feet broad, with its entrance facing the north-east; the representations of heads

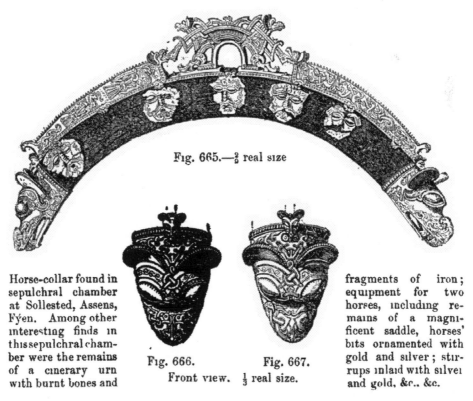

Fig. 665.—⅔ real size

Horse-collar found in sepulchral chamber at Sollested, Assens, Fýen. Among other interesting finds in this sepulchral chamber were the remains of a cinerary urn with burnt bones and

Fig. 666.
Front view. ⅓ real size.

Fig. 667.

fragments of iron; equipment for two horses, including remains of a magnificent saddle, horses' bits ornamented with gold and silver; stirrups inlaid with silver and gold, &c., &c.

riveted to the collar are similar to numerous ones found in Southern Russia, of which many examples are to be seen in the Hermitage, St. Petersburg.

Fig. 668.—Fragments of harness with nails and other ornaments of iron covered with silver, sewn on leather. Real size. Denmark.

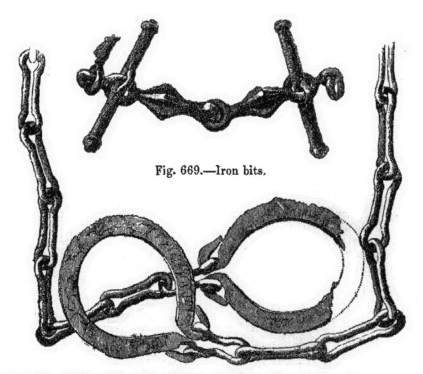

Fig. 669.—Iron bits.

Fig. 670.—Chains of iron, ¼ real size, with large rings at the end. Sollested

Fig. 671.—End of waggon-pole. Real size. Sollested.

Fig. 672.   Fig. 673.

Parts of a bit of bronze gilt, ⅔ real size, found in a round tumulus explored in 1852, containing the remains of a ship and a waggon, pieces of a wooden saddle riveted with gilt bronze ornaments, several stirrups, bones of several animals, &c.   Vold Borre, Norway.

Fig. 674.—Iron spur found in a tumulus.
⅓ real size.   Norway.

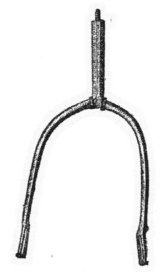

Fig. 675.—Ornament to horse collar of
bronze gilt.   ½ real size.

Fig. 676.—Iron spur, found in
a tumulus with a stone vase,
a single-edged sword, an axe,
two spear-heads, a shield-boss,
a pair of stirrups, &c.   ⅓ real
size.   Norway.

Fig. 678.—Bronze bridle, little less than ⅓ real size, found in a tumulus.   Norway.

Fig. 677.—Part of horse collar of bronze.   ½ real size.

Fig. 679.—Iron bit, $\frac{2}{5}$ real size, found in a tumulus with a two-edged sword, two spear-heads, an axe, three knife-blades, fragments of a shield-boss, &c., all of iron.   Norway.

Fig. 680.—Iron bit, $\frac{2}{5}$ real size, found in a tumulus with a large axe, a spear-head, thirteen arrow-heads, six shield bosses, two knife-blades, clinch nails, &c. Norway.

Fig. 681.—Iron bit found in a tumulus. $\frac{2}{5}$ real size.   Norway

Fig. 682.—Iron bit. $\frac{2}{5}$ real size.   Norway.

Fig. 683.—Iron bit, $\frac{2}{5}$ real size, found in a tumulus, with burnt bones.   Norway.

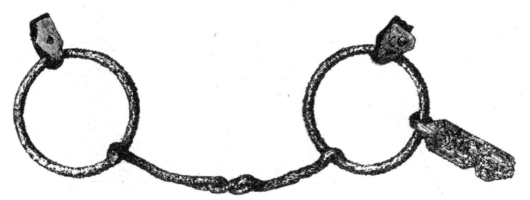

Fig. 684.—Iron bit for horses.   ⅓ real size.   Ultuna.

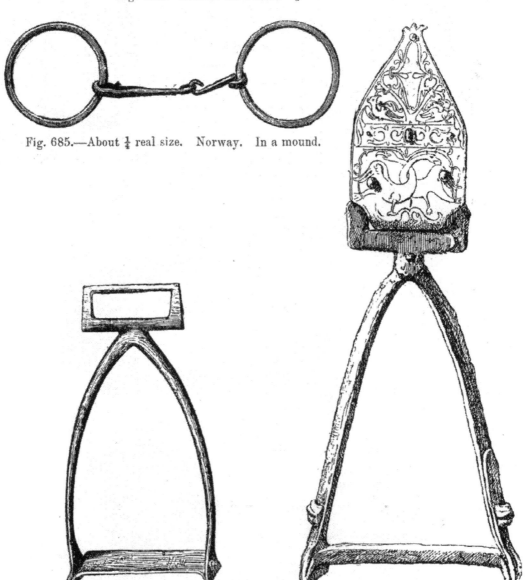

Fig. 685.—About ¼ real size.   Norway.   In a mound.

Fig. 686.—Stirrup, ⅓ real size, found in a mound upon the island of Bjorko.

Fig. 687.—Stirrup of iron inlaid with silver. ⅓ real size. Viborg, Jutland. In a grave with other riding gear.

U 2

Fig. 688.—Iron stirrup. ⅔ real size. Norway.

Fig. 689. — Iron stirrup, found in the upper part of a large round mound, with two double-edged swords bent in two, three spear-heads, five horses' bits, a pair of shears, pincers, two bronze fibulæ, horses' teeth, burnt bones, &c. ⅔ real size. Norway.

Fig. 690.—Iron stirrup ⅔ real size. Norway.

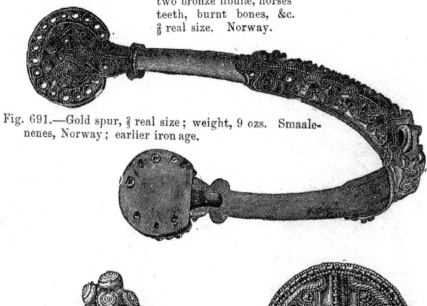

Fig. 691.—Gold spur, ⅔ real size; weight, 9 ozs. Smaale-nenes, Norway; earlier iron age.

Full   view.

Fig. 692.   Fig. 693.

Ornaments of above spurs, real size; weight, 1⅙ ozs.; the point of iron missing; traces of the rust still seen. Smaalenenes, Norway.

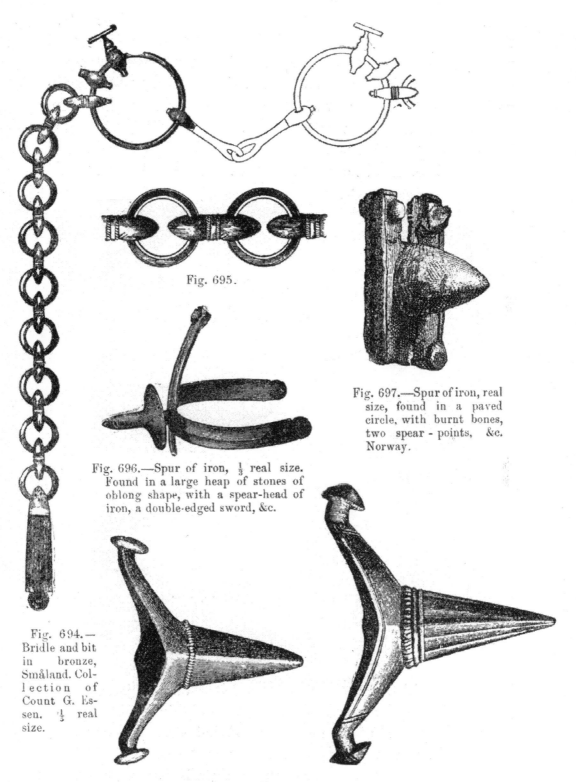

Fig. 695.

Fig. 697.—Spur of iron, real size, found in a paved circle, with burnt bones, two spear - points, &c. Norway.

Fig. 696.—Spur of iron, ⅓ real size. Found in a large heap of stones of oblong shape, with a spear-head of iron, a double-edged sword, &c.

Fig. 694.— Bridle and bit in bronze, Småland. Collection of Count G. Essen. ⅓ real size.

Fig. 698. — Spur of bronze. Öland. Real size.

Fig. 699.—Spur of bronze, real size, found in mound, with another spur quite similar, a bronze kettle, a bent double-edged sword, a spear-head spoiled intentionally, &c. Norway.

Waggons are seldom mentioned in the Sagas, and no description of their appearance is given; but we learn that dead warriors were sometimes put in them and burned on the pyre, and the correctness of this statement is proved by the finds in various graves, among others in one at Broholm, Fyén, where fragments of a waggon have been found together with burnt bones, a large kettle, several iron swords, shield bosses, gold jewels, &c.,&c. But though remains of waggons have been found,

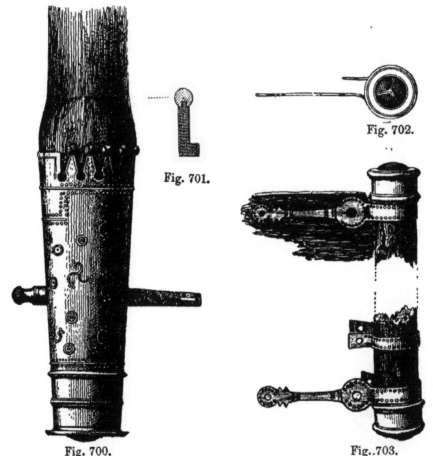

Fig. 701.

Fig. 702.

Fig. 700.

Fig..703.

Parts of perch of waggon with symbolic signs, Denmark

it was not till the discovery in the bog of Deibjerg, Ringkjöbing in the North of Jutland, that we obtained a knowledge of their shape and of the splendour of their ornamentation.

In this bog two waggons of a similar pattern, one of which in an almost complete state of preservation is represented here, were discovered. The spokes of the wheels had evidently been bent by heat, and the iron tires round them had apparently been bent by force; the pole, which was also richly ornamented with bronze, and the bottom and sides were well preserved, but the waggon of which a representation is given was more copiously ornamented with mystic signs than its companion. The following extracts from Sagas refer to the use of these

Fig. 704.

Fig. 705.

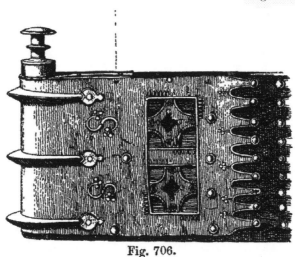

Fig. 706.

Parts of sides of different waggons with symbolic signs. Denmark. ¼ real size.

waggons by the people. It is interesting to note that these waggons are almost identical in shape with the modern *Kàrra*, used in Sweden. (See 'Land of the Midnight Sun,' Vol. i., p. 51).

Gunnar said he was ready   To redress claims,
    To offer gold,   And also Högni;

She (Grimhild) [1] asked	And into waggons
Who would go	Welsh (foreign) wives were lifted.
To saddle the horse,	We rode seven days
To horse the waggon,	Over the cold land,
To ride the steed,	And other seven
To fly the hawk,	We pressed the waves,
To shoot arrows	And the third seven
Of the yew-bow. [2]	We stepped on dry land.
Then on a horse	
Was every warrior seen,	(Gudrúnar Kvida, ii. 18, 35.)

"King Sigurd of Hringariki had two children, a daughter Ragnhild, and a son Guthorm. Haki the Berserk slew him and took his son and daughter home with him. Hálfdán the black sent one hundred men for them, who fetched them and burned the hall of Haki. They tented a very fine waggon, and put Ragnhild and Guthorm in it" (Hálfdán the black's Saga, ch. 5).

"One summer King Eirek had a feast made at Uppsalir. Then he had two waggons driven to the place where he sacrificed to the god called Lýtir. It was customary for the waggon to stand there during the night and for the god to come in the morning. Now Lýtir did not come as he usually did, and the king was told that he disliked to do so. The waggon stood for two nights and he did not come. Then the king began to offer much greater sacrifices than before, and the third morning they became aware that Lýtir had come. Then the waggon was so heavy that the horses fell dead from exhaustion before they could pull it to the hall. The waggon was then put on the middle of the floor of the hall, and the king walked to it with a horn, and welcomed Lýtir, and said, he wanted to drink to him and was very anxious that he should undertake the journey, and that he would give him large gifts as before" (Flateyjarbók, i. 579–580).

"When he was ready to ride away two white horses with black ears were led forward, they belonged to Thord Breidavad and had disappeared that summer at the Thing" (Heidarviga Saga, c. 20).

"The queen 'Yrsa' had twelve horses led forward, they were all brown except one which was white as snow, and on this one Hrolf was to ride They were the best horses of King

---

[1] Grimhild had asked her sons Gunnar and Hôgni to pay *weregild* to Gudrún because they had slain her husband, Sigurd Fafnisbani.

[2] This shows that bows of yew as well as of elm were used.

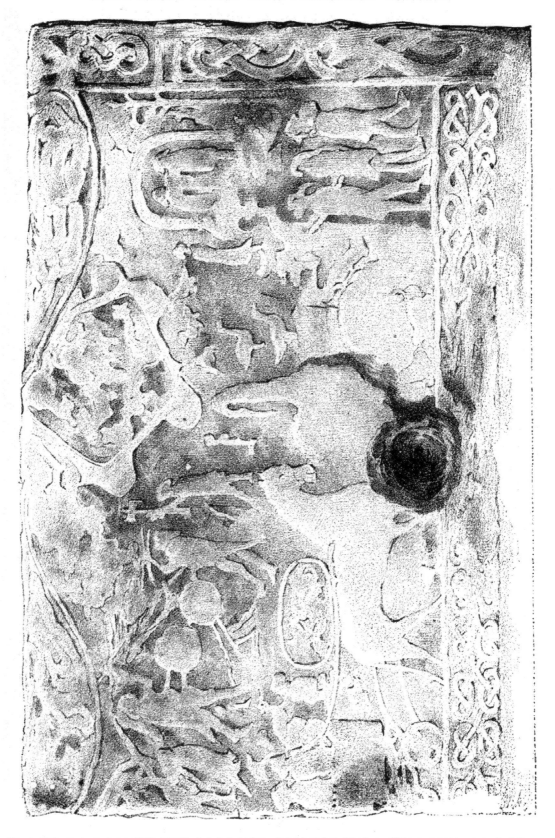

Fig. 707.—Scene with waggon ; bas-relief ; length, 5 feet 9 inches ; height, 4 feet 6 inches. This remarkable stone had been a good deal cut in order to range with other stones forming the flooring of the church of Alskog, Gotland. It was preserved from entire destruction by Prof. P. A. Save. Unfortunately, from the softness of the sandstone and the tramping of feet, it has become very indistinct. What the scene was intended to represent it is difficult to say.

Adils and covered all over with armour" (Hrolf Kraki Saga, c. 44).

"There were four stud horses of Thorstein's of red colour. They looked well but not fully broken. Thorstein offered to give him the horses, but Gunnlaug said he needed no horses as he was to leave Iceland. Thereupon they rode towards the stud horses, there was a gray stallion with four mares. It was the best stallion in Borgarfjord" (Gunnlaug Ormstunga, c. 5).

Fig. 708.—Runic stone, with waggon and horse.—Near Levede, in Gotland.[1]

We find that the laws contained regulations in regard to the making of the roads, and the shutting of gates.

"The highroad shall be so broad that a man can sit on a saddled horse and put his spear-handle on the ground and put his thumb as high up as he can and the spear shall be one span longer. It shall be laid down across the road. It shall not be broader" (Gulath).

"If a man walks through the gate of a fence he who opens it shall be answerable as to shutting it. If cattle or horses go inside and spoil a field or meadow, then the opener of the gate shall pay back according to valuation all the damage made" (Gulath).

---

[1] Another stone in relief has been found by Prof. Save, nearly 12 feet high, at Larbró, in the northern part of the island of Gotland; of the same horse-shoe shape as shown here and on p. 58, with representations of ships, horses, and the eight-footed horse Sleipnir.

CHAPTER XVIII.

VARIOUS FORMS OF GRAVES.

Different forms of graves—Picturesque situation—Various shapes of mounds—Bautastones—The Hjortehammar burial-ground—Stone-set graves—Ship-form graves—Triangular graves—Anund's mound.

MOULDERING bones and ashes of mighty heroes and noble women now forgotten under the mounds, or in the graves made hoary by the centuries that shroud you by their oblivion, I salute you! We also shall be forgotten.

The thousands of mounds, cairns, *bautasteinar* (memorial stones) and graves found to this day all over the North show the high veneration the earlier English-speaking tribes had for their dead; these mounds or cairns are always situated on some conspicuous place by the coast, from which a magnificent view can often be had

We have already treated of graves at some length with special reference to the age—stone, bronze, or iron—to which they belonged, and also with relation to the objects found in them. Before, however, proceeding to speak of the burial customs of the Norsemen it may be well to give some further idea of the various classes of graves.

Sweden is particularly rich in these mementoes of the past, in the midst of which the high roads not unfrequently pass, forming a most impressive scene. What emotion have I felt when standing upon many of these graves, deeply impressed by the beauty or loneliness of the site chosen and of its surroundings; perhaps never more so than on the coast of Bohuslän—the Viken of yore.[1] There the cairns have been

[1] In Tanum parish, Bohuslan, alone there are more than 2,000 mounds, the largest being about 300 feet in circumference; near Upsala nearly 600; at Ultuna, 700.

The greatest number of mounds found in any one spot is east of the ancient Birka Bjorko, where there are over 1,000 of them; while seven graves, as will be seen in the course of the narrative, are found close together.

erected on the summit of the bare solid rocky hills of primary formation, several hundred feet above the level of the water, and overlooking a panorama of fjords, sounds, barren islands and desolate coast, with the open seas beyond, and with the sun sinking below the horizon. The waves strike at their base, and with the wind sing mournfully a requiem over the forgotten dead; their work is done, the glorious mission they had to accomplish in the history of the world is ended, the mighty drama of the sword is closed.

It is towards evening, before the twilight fades gradually

Fig. 709. —Cairn, Bohuslän, Sweden.

into darkness, that the scene of this weird landscape is most impressive, and no one can really imagine its effects until he stands upon the spot and sees the view spread before him.

In some parts of Norway the contrast is often great in the extreme; the mounds there have huge mountains in the background with their summits clad in snow, and in the foreground the grand open sea. One of the bleakest spots in the country, where these have been erected, is on the flat gravelly coast of Lyster, which lies between the mountain and the sea;—there, over the last resting-places of those warriors, the wind blows most fearfully in winter-time, and the sea dashes on the shore in huge foamy white waves.

In Denmark and parts of Sweden there are places on the elevated points of the coast full of charms, looking over the Sound, the Cattegat, the Baltic, or the waters of some of the great lakes. Many of these resting-places of man are now covered by forests, and upon some of the mounds huge oaks sprung from the acorn of their sires tell forcibly of the centuries that have passed over them.

We can vividly realise why the people laid their dead to

Fig. 710.—Grave, Einang, Norway; diameter, 50 feet; earlier iron age.

rest by that sea they loved so much during their lifetime, and upon which they had sailed so often. The mariner as he passed by could behold the graves of the dead and victorious champions, whose memory was always kept fresh by the *scalds* [1] who sang his exploits generation after generation, thus filling the youth of the country with pride, and making them wish to emulate the deeds of these men, often their kinsmen of old, who had gone to Valhalla.

The mounds and cairns are not always round, they are sometimes square, oblong, rectangular or triangular. The

---

[1] Poets, see vol. ii. p. 389.

round mounds and cairns exist in different parts of the world, and in Scandinavia as far back as the stone and bronze ages; the vast number of bautastones seen all over the country shows also how well the injunctions of Odin were carried out by his followers in that respect. Some of these are very imposing, and their dark forms look weird enough against the landscape or the clear or gloomy sky. One of the finest stood

Fig. 711.—Bautastone (from grave shown on p. 301) with nineteen runes; $\frac{1}{15}$ real size; 5 feet 8 inches in height; width, 3 feet 2 inches; 9 inches thick; length of rune, 2 feet 1½ inches.

in Brastod parish, Bohuslän, now lying prostrate and broken, its height being 26 feet; and its place was on one corner of a stone set of rectangular graves 40 feet in length and 28 feet in width.

Fig. 712.—Bautastone on a mound 200 feet in circumference and 7 feet high, Runesten Grimeton (Bohuslän), Halland ; 19½ feet high, 4½ feet wide. Surrounding it are mounds and graves of various shapes.

Fig. 713.—Oblong mound, Yttersala, Södermanland ; 33 feet in diameter. In the vicinity are numerous other graves of various shapes.

Fig. 714.—Square stone-set grave. Södermanland.

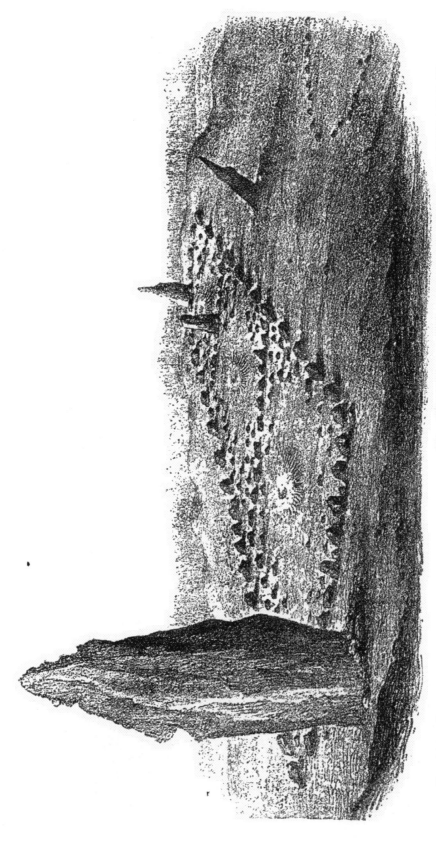

Fig. 715.—Rectangular stone-set graves with bautastones   Length, 70 feet ; width, 24 feet.—Färentuna parish, Upland, Sweden.

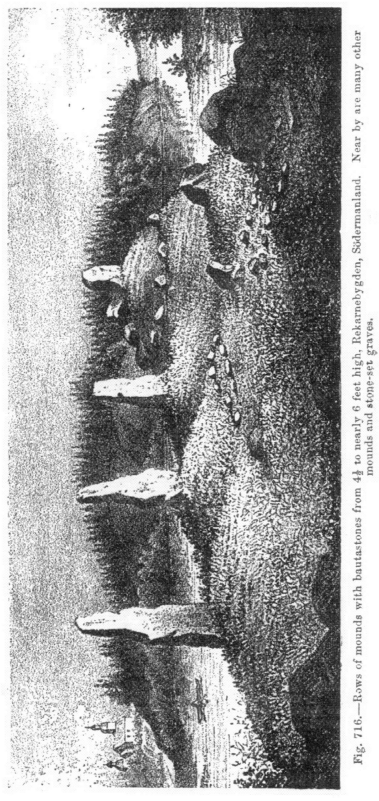

Fig. 716.—Rows of mounds with bautastones from 4½ to nearly 6 feet high, Rekarnebygden, Södermanland. Near by are many other mounds and stone-set graves.

The most interesting of the graveyards which I have seen is that of Hjortehammar, situated in the province of Blekinge on a narrow promontory lost in the maze of islands which dot the

Fig. 717.—Square stone-set graves with large boulders at the corners and centre.

Fig. 718.—Triangular grave; sides of triangle about 50 feet; corner stones about 3 feet high. In the middle of the south-west side are two stones, 5 feet apart, with a slab between them, one 3 feet, the other 4 feet high. Thorsbacken, Nerike, Sweden.

coast of Sweden on this part of the Baltic. It is joined now to an island situated near its further end by a causeway and a small bridge. This is not only remarkable from its position and size, but on account of the numerous forms of graves of various sizes it contains. The length of the cape is about 1,200 feet, and its greatest breadth about 200 feet. The engraving gives an idea of the shape and size of the different graves, some of which are shown in large scale. This cape is but a continuation of a ridge full of graves ; heather and juniper cover many of them; and well chosen was this secluded and quiet spot for the last resting-place of their departed kinsmen or friends.[1]

In the *Háleygjaṭal*, a poem on the genealogy of the famous Hákon jarl, tracing his pedigree to Odin, there is a passage which recalls the burial-place Hjortehammar.

> Straumeyjar-nes which is
> Stone-marked
> Round the Fylkir's[2] body
> Is widely known.

[1] I was sorry to see the place being gradually destroyed, the gravel taken away, and the embankments, made by the digging, falling down with the grave.

[2] Gudlaug, Hakon's ancestor.

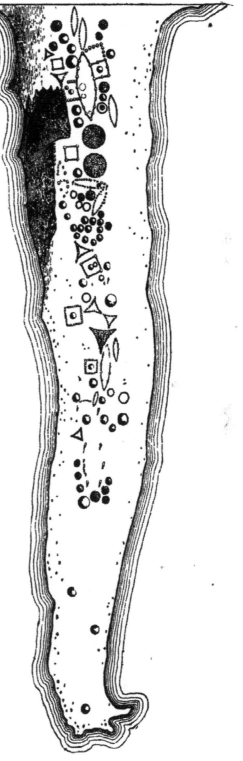

Fig. 719.—Hjortehammar burial-ground, with various shaped graves.

x 2

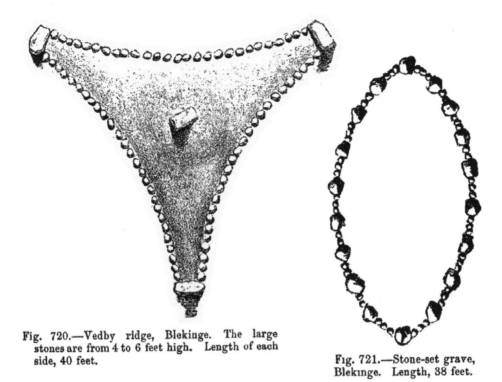

Fig. 720.—Vedby ridge, Blekinge. The large stones are from 4 to 6 feet high. Length of each side, 40 feet.

Fig. 721.—Stone-set grave, Blekinge. Length, 38 feet.

Fig. 722.—Triangular grave. Sides 60 to 65 feet long, with a small elevation in the middle, and a bautastone nearly 5 feet high and 2 feet 6 inches broad. Lyngstad, Södermanland.

Among the most remarkable and not uncommon stone-set graves are those of the so-called "*ship-form*" setting; they belong both to the earlier and later iron age. This peculiar form of grave is found on the peninsula of Scandinavia and on

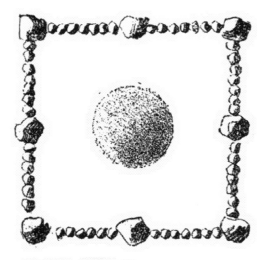

Fig. 723.—Blekinge. Diameter, 30 feet.

Stone-set graves.

Fig. 724.—Listerby ridge, Blekinge.
Diameter, 18 feet.

Fig. 725.—Graveyard with mounds and stone-set graves at Åsby, Södermanland.

the islands of Gotland, Öland, and other islands of the Baltic, in Courland and Livonia, and was also erected in England and Scotland by the people of the North.

One of the most interesting is that where the rowers' seats

are marked, and even a stone placed in the position of the mast.

The longest ship-form grave which I think is known is one near Kåsberga, a fishing village in the southern part of Sweden, with a length of 212 feet and a width of 60 feet. It is made by thirty-eight stones, the two forming the prow being 12 and 18 feet in height above the ground—the latter being the northern one.

But the finest of all, though less in size, is the famous one

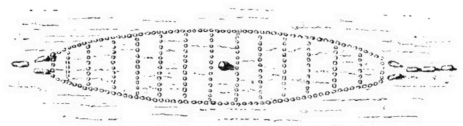

Fig. 726.—Ship-form grave, Karums parish, Öland.

of Blomsholm, near Strömstad, the whole neighbourhood of which is surrounded with mementoes of the past—graves, dom-rings, mounds, bautastones, and rock-tracings.[1]

[1] At Eds, Upland, there is a very fine ship-form grave of twenty-eight stones, 182 feet long and 50 feet wide. The largest stone at one end is 9 feet in height, and is evidently a bautastone; the rest, although large, each measuring several feet in circumference, are common boulders. At the centre of the ship there lies a similar stone, where, as well as at the ends, there is a small mound-like elevation.

In the woods at Braidfloar, between Levide and Sproge in Gotland, there is a ship-form grave 144 feet long, but only 16 feet at its widest part; the stones, however, are small, none being higher than 3 feet.

At Lungersas, Gotland, Nerike, there is a ship-form grave in which stands a stone with an inscription in later runes.

There is also a bautastone with runes, in one end of a ship-form at Lilla Lundley in Lids, Sodermanland, upon which are the words " *Spjute and Halfdan* raised this stone after *Skarde* their brother. He went eastward with Roar In Serkland lies the son " (See p 356 Yellow Book, Den yngre jernalder.)

A ship-form grave between the post-stations of Ljungby and Hamneda province of Kronobergs is 92 feet long and 32 feet broad; the neighbourhood is full of grave-mounds and bautastones.

Another near the shore of the Baltic, in Eista parish, Gotland, is 50 feet by 16 feet. A third, on the island of Faró, near Gotland, is 50 feet by 8 feet.

We see by this that their breadth does not always bear the same proportion to their length.

In two ship forms at Hjortehammar, in Blekinge, there were found burned bones, ashes, two of the bowl-shaped fibulæ of bronze so common during the later iron age, a round fibula of silver, some glass beads, &c

In one at Raftotangen, in Tanum parish, was an urn filled with ashes, on the top of which lay a finely ornamented damascened sword of the later iron age.

Fig. 727.—Ship-form graves, Blomsholm, Bohuslän, made of forty-nine upright stones (formerly there were fifty-one). Length, 141 feet; greatest breadth, 31½ feet; prows north and south, the northern headstone 11 feet high, the southern 14½, the stones gradually diminishing in size towards the centre, where the largest is about 3 feet. Built on a small mound or elevation which was higher in former times.

Fig. 728.—Sjusta mound, Skog parish, Upland; 204 feet in circumference; 28 feet high; with a row of stones at its base. At the south end is another stone-set mound.

Fig. 729.—Type of Mound with bautastone at the top and circle of stones at the base.

Fig. 730.—Mound, 3 feet high, with bautastone, Balunda parish, Westmanland.

Fig. 731.—Triangular graves; stone forming the apex, with runes, is about 25 feet from the two others, which are 14 feet apart.—Björktorp, Blekinge.

Fig. 732.—Incomplete mound; 50 feet in circumference; 10 feet high; largest stone over 6 feet high; in Thortuna parish, Westmanland.

Fig. 733.—Mounds on Kjula-ridge. Södermanland.

Fig. 734.—Mound set with boulder-stones, Dalsland; circumference of boulders,
100 feet; height of mound, 4 feet, on the top of which are two flat stones
standing on edges. Near it is a boulder stone-setting, probably a dom-ring.

Many of the cairns, which are often beautifully arranged, are small, being 4 or 5 feet in height, or sometimes almost even with the ground, their diameter varying from 20 to 80 feet. Numbers of them have stone-settings, sometimes close, sometimes not.

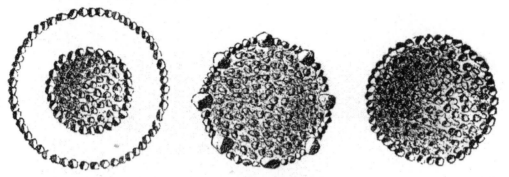

Fig. 735.—Diameter, 20 feet. Fig. 736.—Diameter, 16 feet. Fig. 737.—Diameter, 16 feet.

Cairns—Blekinge.

Fig. 738.—Round cairn at Björkeby, Foresund, Södermanland.

Fig. 739.—Square cairn, island of Öland.

342

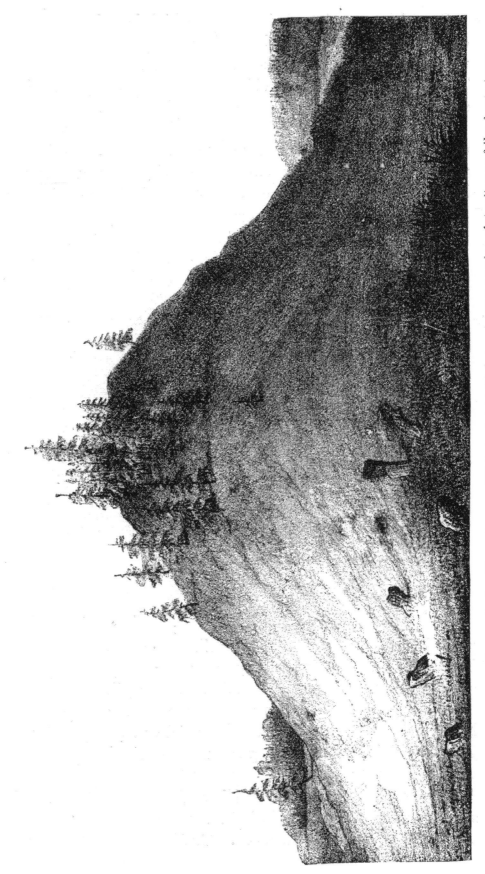

Fig. 740.—Anund's mound, Vestmanland. Circumference, 652 feet; height 84 feet. A great number of standing or fallen bautastones are found near the mound.

One of the most interesting graves which have been recently opened in England is one belonging to the manor of Taplow, near Maidenhead, about fifty miles by river above London. The mound, 240 feet in circumference, and 15 feet high, overlooks the Thames and the surrounding lands.

Among the objects were two shield bones, one sword, fragments of others, fragments of a spear head, one bronze vessel, one wooden bucket so common in the graves of the North, with bronze hoops, &c., two pairs of glass vessels (one

Fig. 741.—Gold fibula ornamented with garnets and red glass. ⅔ real size. Taplow, England.

Fig. 742.—Fibula of bronze, ½ real size, the edge of the triangle and nail heads of bronze, the middle a thin silver plate. Found in a mound with 14 urns and burned bones, a spear point of iron, &c. Zeeland, Denmark.

of which is here represented) similar to one found with a burial ship in Vold in Norway, forty checkers, two pairs of ornaments for drinking horns (all of silver gilt), one green glass bead, &c. &c.; a fibula of the same form as those of the North. But the most remarkable article was a quantity of gold thread belonging to a garment, the triangular form of the pattern still remaining.

This grave, like the one of King Gorm of Denmark and several others of the North, is in the old churchyard where the ancient parish church stood. On the slope of the mound

itself several Christian graves are seen. The viking, like some
of the chiefs of the North, was probably buried on his estate,
on the land that had descended to him through his ancestors

Fig. 743.—Vessel of green glass.
⅔ real size. Taplow, England.
11⅛ inches in height.

Fig. 744.—Ornament of silver gilt,
showing end of drinking horn. ½ real
size.

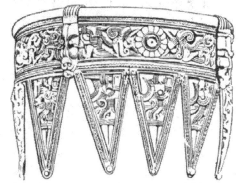

Fig. 745.—Silver gilt ornamentation for
mouth of drinking horn. ½ real size.
The horn itself, found in a mass of small
fragments. Taplow, England.

or which possibly he might have conquered from some of his
foes. These antiquities by their form seem to belong to the
later iron age.

CHAPTER XIX.

BURIALS.

The two modes of burial—Burning of the dead on the pyre—The law of
Odin—Ceremonies after death—Laws and superstitions connected with
the dead—The journey to *Hel*—The burial of Sigurd and Brynhild—
Burial on waggons—Burial of weapons with the dead—Burials in ships
—The Gokstad ship's sepulchral chamber—The Moklebust mound.

THE Eddas and Sagas abound with descriptions of funeral
rites and burials, the accuracy of which is most fully vindicated
by the finds.

Two modes of burial were prevalent among the people, one
that of burning the dead, the other of burying them unburned.[1]

It was the belief of the people that the dead burned on the
pyre would go to Valhalla with all the weapons and wealth
burned with them, and that these would afterwards resume
their original shapes. Horses, dogs, falcons, or other animals
which the deceased had liked, were often added, and sometimes some of his thralls were killed and burned on the pyre
with him.

"Odin enacted the same laws in his land as had formerly
prevailed with the Asar. Thus he ordered that all dead men
should be burned, and on their pyre should be placed their
property. He said thus: that with the same amount of
wealth should they come to Valhalla as they had on the pyre;
that they should also enjoy what they had themselves buried
in the ground. But the ashes should be thrown into the sea
or buried in the earth; that over great men mounds should
be raised, as memorials; and over men who had some manful-
ness *bautasteinar* should be erected, and this custom was
observed for a long time" (Ynglinga Saga, c. 8).

"It was the custom of powerful men, whether kings or jarls,

---

[1] Such expressions occur as "i haug lagdr," mound laid; "heygdr," mounded.

at that time to learn warfare and win wealth and fame; that property should not be counted with the inheritance, nor should sons get it after fathers, but it should be placed in the mound with themselves " (Vatnsdæla, 21).

" The first age is called the age of burning; then all dead men were burned and bautastones raised after them. But after Frey had been mound-laid at Uppsalir many chiefs raised mounds as well as bautastones to the memory of their kinsmen. Afterwards King Dan the Proud had his own

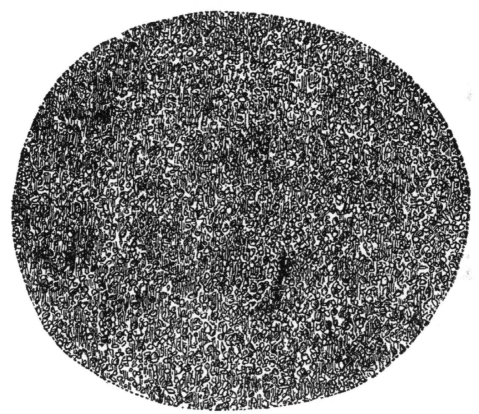

Fig. 746.—Largest pavement of pyre, 33 feet in diameter.—Broholm, Fyen, Denmark.

mound made, and bade that he and also his horse with the saddle on and much property should be carried to it when dead in king's state and in war-dress. Many of his kinsmen did the same afterwards, and the mound-age began in Denmark. But the burning age lasted a long time after that with the Northmen and the Swedes " (Prologue of Heimskringla).

" The first age was the one when all dead men were to be burnt. Then the mound-age began when all powerful men were laid in mounds and all common people buried in the ground " (St. Olaf's Saga. Prologue).

Y

As we read the Sagas we get a vivid and impressive idea of the grand and solemn pageant that must have taken place when the body of a great warrior was put on the funeral pile, and his companions in arms, relatives or former foes bid him happy speed to Valhalla, as the flames ascended high up towards the sky, or the ship sailed from the land in a lurid blaze, while the purifying fire was consuming the corpse. Then followed the ceremony of carefully gathering the charred bones, which were sacredly preserved in an urn or valuable vessel.[1]

The first duty to the dead was to close the eyes and mouth and pinch together the nostrils, which ceremony was called *nabjargir.*

Ninthly I advise thee	Let a bath be made[3]
To take care of corpses[2]	For those who are dead;
Wherever on earth thou findest them;	Wash their hands and head,
Whether they die from disease,	Comb and dry them
Or are drowned,	Ere they are laid in the coffin,
Or killed in battle,	And bid them sleep happily.
	(Sigrdrifumál.)

It appears to have been a case of outlawry not to cover a body with mould, and if a slayer maimed the body of his enemy when dead he was fined. The body seems to have been left on a cover until they could lay it in the mound.

"No man shall have a dead man longer than five days in his house except in a necessity, such as if there is impassable ice or a snowstorm. Then it shall be taken to an outhouse and covered with timbers or straw, and removed as soon as the weather is good" (Eidsivathing law II. 41).

If the deceased had during life been a wild and unruly man, fierce in temper, who it was feared might after death, as a

---

[1] There seem to have been special places built for the burning of the dead. On the island of Fyen, not far from Broholm, and about 1,200 yards from the numerous graves, are two sites of pyres, round in shape, about 120 yards distant from each other. The pavement, about 7 inches in thickness, is made of cobble stones of the size of a man's fist set very close together, and broken into sharp angles. The stones, especially those in the middle, have been exposed to the action of fire, but have been preserved by being covered with earth that had gathered over them brought by wind and rain in the course of centuries.

[2] Nabjargir.

[3] In Sigrdrifumál the texts have in stanza 34 *laug* = bath, and *haug* = mound. The letters *h* and *l* being very like in the manuscripts, we can choose whichever we like best of the two.

ghost, cause trouble in the house where he had lived, some very peculiar ceremonies were observed. The person who was to perform the *nabjargir* did not approach the body from the front, but from behind, and closed the eyes, and not till then did any one else venture to approach to prepare it for funeral. Such a corpse was not carried out of the house through one of the usual entrances, but a hole was broken in the wall behind it, through which it was carried backward.

"Snorri godi (temple priest), the great chief, had received a forest from Thorólf Bœgifot (lame-foot), who wanted to get it back.

"Thorólf Bœgifot (after visiting his son to get his help in this matter) came home in the evening, and spoke to no one. He sat down in his high-seat, but did not eat that evening. He sat there when the people went to sleep, and in the morning when they rose Thorólf still sat there, and was dead. The housewife sent a man to his son Arnkel to tell him the death of Thorólf. Arnkel rode to Hvamm with some of his servants, and saw that his father sat dead in the high-seat. All the people were full of fear, for all thought there was something frightful in his death. Arnkel went into the hall and in along the seats to the back of Thorólf; he bid every man to beware of walking in front of him while the *nabjargir* had not been performed. Arnkel then took hold of the shoulders of Thorólf, and he had to use his strength ere he could lay him down. Then he wrapped a cloth around his head, and prepared his corpse for burial according to custom. Thereupon he had the wall broken behind him, and got him out there. Then oxen were yoked to a sledge, on which Thorólf was placed, and driven up to the valley of Thorsa; but he was not easily brought to the place where he should be. There they buried him carefully. After the death of Thorólf many thought it bad to be out of doors after the sun had set; and as the summer was about to close, they became aware that Thorólf did not rest quiet, for then men could never be at peace outside after sunset. In the spring, Arnkel took Thorólf's body out on a ness, and there buried it anew. He had a fence made across the cape above the grave, so high that nothing but a flying bird could get over it There Thorólf lay as long as Arnkel lived, but when he afterwards again became troublesome his body was burned, and the ashes thrown into the sea " (Eyrbyggja, c. 33).[1]

---

[1] Cf. also Egil's Saga, c 61.

The ceremony was sometimes considered as an incitement for the performer to avenge the dead.

Hoskuld, an illegitimate son of Njal and Hródný, was attacked by six men on his way home and slain. Hródný's shepherd found the corpse and told her. They went during the night to Njal's farm, Bergthórshvál.

"Then they both walked to the house and knocked at the door. A húskarl opened the door. She . . . went to Njal's bed. She asked if Njal was awake. He answered: 'I have slept till now, but now I am awake, and why art thou here so early?' She said: 'Rise from the bed of my rival and walk out with me, with her, and with thy sons.' They rose and went out. Skarphédin (Njal's son) said: 'Let us take our weapons with us.' Njal said nothing; they ran in and came out armed with their weapons. Hródný walked in front till they came to the sheephouse. She went in and told them to follow her. She took a creeping light (lantern) and said: 'Here, Njal, is thy son Hoskuld. He has got many wounds and now needs to be healed.' Njal said: 'I see marks of death on him but no marks of life. Why hast thou not given him nabjargir as his nostrils are open?' She answered: 'I intended that for Skarphédin.' Skarphédin walked to the corpse and performed the nabjargir. Then he said to his father: 'Who, sayest thou, has slain him?' Njal answered 'Lýting of Sámsstadir with his brothers has probably slain him.' Hródný said: 'I intrust it to thy hands, Skarphédin, to avenge thy brother. I expect thou wilt do thyself honour though he is not legitimate, and that thou wilt take the revenge into thy hands'" (Njala, c. 98).

Before putting a body in the mound *hel* shoes were put on for the journey to Hell.

"Thereafter Gisli and all his household made ready for the mounding of Vestein, his brother-in-law. He intended to mound him in the sand plain . . . . below Sæból. When they were on their way with the corpse Thorgrím with many men joined him. When they had made the mound Thorgrím godi walked to Gisli and said: It is now the custom, brother-in-law, to tie Hel-shoes on the feet of men before they are mound-laid. For it was said that they (the shoes) should go to Hel when the man was dead, and therefore a man who dresses much when he goes out, or is long in dressing, is said to prepare for Hel. Thorgrím said: I will do this with Vestein and tie the Hel-shoes on his feet When he had done it, he said: I know

not how to tie Hel-shoes if these are unfastened " (Gis
Súrsson's Saga).

In the weird description of the burial of Sigurd and Brynhild[1] we see that the mound was reddened with blood, and
that human beings were burned with them on the pyre.

I will ask of thee
Only one boon;
It will in the world
My last one be;
Let so wide a burgh
Be raised on the plain
That under us all
It be equally roomy,
Beneath us all who shall die
With Sigurd.

Surround that burgh
With tents and shields,
With welsh linen, finely painted,
And Welsh people (thralls);
Burn the Hunnish one[2]
At my one side.

Burn at the other side
Of the Hunnish one
My servants,
With good necklaces,
Two at his head
And two hawks;
Then all is
Equally shared.

Let there yet lie between us
A ring-wound weapon,[3]
A sharp-edged iron
As it before was laid,

When we both
Stepped into one bed
And were called
Husband and wife.

The shining hall-door,
The ring-ornamented [4]
Will not then
Strike him on the heel[5]
If my retinue
Follows him hence;
Then our journey
Will not be poor.

For there follow him
Five bond-maids,
Eight servants,
Of good kin,
My bond-nurse,
And the inheritance [6]
Which Budli gave
To his child.

Much have I told,
More would I tell,
If fate
Gave more time for speaking;
My voice decreases,
My wounds swell,
I told only truth,[7]
Now I will cease.

(Third Song of Sigurd.)

---

[1] In Brynhild's ride to Hel we have a
different account:—

"After the death of Brynhild two
pyres were made, one for Sigurd. which
was first set on fire, but Brynhild was
burned on the other and was in a carriage tented with *god-web* (a kind of
fine cloth). It is told that Brynhild
drove in the carriage on the road of Hel,
and went through the tun where the
jötun-woman dwelt." (Hel-reid Bryn-
hildar).

[2] Sigurd.

[3] See Volsunga, ch. 20 and 31.

[4] Probably on account of the ring on
the door, as fine doors were ornamented
with them.

[5] We will follow on his heels, so that
the door will not be shut after he enters,
but be open while we enter.

[6] The inheritance—wealth, treasure,
dowry, &c., &c.

[7] In the preceding stanzas she has
foretold the fate of Gudrun, Gunnar and
Högni, as is told in Volsunga.

Another custom no less imposing was to bury the chiefs with their carriages and horses, so that they might make their entries driving into Valhalla, or riding on horseback; and it was considered honourable to go to Odin with many slain.

"The second day after the battle (of Bravoll), in the morning, King Hring caused a search to be made among the slain for the body of King Harald, his kinsman, and a great part of the slain host lay on the top of it. It was mid-day before the search was completed and it was found. King Hring took the body of his kinsman, and washed the blood from it, prepared it magnificently, according to old custom. and laid it in the waggon which King Harald had in the battle. He then raised a large mound, and caused the body to be carried in the same waggon with the horse which King Harald had in the battle, and thus he had him driven to the mound. There the horse was killed. Then King Hring took the saddle he himself had ridden on and gave it to King Harald his kinsman, and bade him do as he liked, either ride to Valhalla or drive. He held a great feast to celebrate the going away of his kinsman. Before the mound was closed, King Hring bade all his high-born men and champions who were present to throw into the mound large rings (gold and silver) and good weapons, to honour King Harald Hilditónn, and the mound was carefully closed" (Sögubrot of Fornkonungum).[1]

If circumstances allowed, the deceased seems to have been placed on a bed prepared for the purpose, until the burial could take place.

"Glúm also went home with his men, and had the dead carried into an outhouse, where Thorvald's body was prepared more honourably than the others, for clothes were laid under him, and he was sewed up in a skin" (Viga Glúm's Saga, c. 23).

In a large burial chamber at Lower Aure, Norway, were found the remains of a chair, thus confirming the accounts of the Sagas about men being placed on their chair in the grave. Some of these chambers were occasionally built of wood.

"Aran, a foster-brother of Asmund, died suddenly. Asmund had a mound raised over him, and placed at his side his horse

---

For battle, see Vol. ii., p. 436.

with saddle and bridle, his standards, and all war-dress, his hawk and dog. Aran sat on a chair in all his armour. Asmund let his chair be put into the mound and sat down upon it, and then the mound was closed. The first night Aran rose from the chair, killed the hawk and the dog, and ate them both. The second night he rose, killed the horse and cut it to pieces, tearing it much with his teeth; he ate the horse, the blood streaming down from his mouth; he invited Asmund to eat with him. The third night Asmund began to feel sleepy; and suddenly Aran seized his ears and tore them off. Then Asmund drew his sword, and cut Aran's head off; and afterwards burned him to ashes. He thereupon went to the rope and was drawn up, and the mound was closed; Asmund took with him the property which had been placed in the mound" (Egil and Asmund's Saga, c. 7).

"Angantyr had a large mound raised below the Havada-mountains, at the place where the king had been slain. It was built with timber, and was very strong" (Hervarar Saga, c. 16).

Sometimes the body of a man was divided into several portions, and each of these buried in different parts of the country.

"While he (Hálfdán) was king there were very good years. The people made so much of him that when they heard he was dead, and that his body had been taken to Hringariki to be buried there, powerful men from Raumariki, Vestfold and Heidmörk came, and all asked for leave to take his body and mound it in their *fylki*;[1] they thought that those who got it were likely to have good seasons. They agreed to divide the body in four pieces, and the head was mounded at Stein in Hringariki; the others took their pieces home and mounded them, and they are all of them called the mounds of Hálfdán (in Snorri's time)" (Hálfdán the Black's Saga, ch. 9 (Heimskringla)).

Friends often wished to be buried near each other, for they believed that their spirits could talk to each other or look over their household before important events occurred.

"Then Thorstein fell sick. He said to Fridthjof: 'My son, I beg of thee that thou wilt yield to the king's sons with regard to thy temper, for that befits thee on account of their dignity, and I have good hope of thee. I want to be laid in a

---

[1] A division of land.

mound opposite to King Beli, on this side of the fjord, near the sea, for then it will be easy for us to call to each other before great events.' The foster-brothers of Fridthjof were Björn and Asmund; they were tall and strong men. A short time after Thorstein died; he was mounded as he had prescribed, and Fridthjof got his land and personal property " (Fridthjof's Saga, c. 1).

Several persons were often buried in the same mound; and after a battle many of the slain were buried together.

"After this Hjálmar died. Odd then placed the Berserks in a heap, and piled upon them boughs. This was near the sea. He put with them their weapons and clothing, divesting them of nothing. He covered this with turf and cast sand over it. He then took Hjálmar on his back, carried him to the sea, and laid him down on the shore. He went out on the ships, took ashore every one who had fallen, and there threw up another mound over his men. It is said by those who have gone thither, that to this day are seen those mounds which Odd there made " (Orvar Odd's Saga, c. 14).[1]

"On the following morning Hrolf had the field cleared, and divided the booty among his men. There were raised three very large mounds. In one Hrolf placed his father Sturlaug and Krák, Hrafn's brother and all the best champions of their host who had fallen. In that mound were put gold and silver and good weapons, and all was well performed. In the second was placed King Eirik, Brynjólf and Thórd and their picked men. In the third was Grim Ægir, near the shore, where it was thought least likely that ships would approach. The warriors were buried where they had fallen " (Gongu Hrolf's Saga, ch. 34).

From many descriptions we see with what awe the ancient Vikings regarded the mounds under which renowned chiefs were buried. Over the mounds of great warriors flames were seen at night, and the ghost of the departed was believed to remain there.

When the burning did not take place, the warrior was buried with his weapons and entire equipment. Sometimes he slept with his sword under his head. Angantyr's shoulders rested upon the famous sword *Tyrfing*, and Angrim's sons were buried there in that manner. Many of the weapons placed

---

[1] Cf. also Gongu Hrolf's Saga, c. 3.

with them were very famous and supposed to possess special or supernatural qualities, and mounds were sometimes broken for the sake of getting

" A little after she (the Amazon Hervor) left by herself in a man's dress and weapons and went to Vikings, and was with them for awhile, and was called Hervard. A little after the chief of the Vikings died, and Hervard got the command of them. Once they came to Sámsey. Hervard went up on land, and none of his men wanted to follow him, for, they said, it would not do for any man to stay out there at night. Hervard said that much property was likely to be in the mounds, and went up on the island near sunset. They lay in Munarvag. She met a herd-boy there, and asked him about news. He said, 'Dost thou not know the island? Come home with me, for it will not do for any man to stay out here after sunset; I am going home at once.' Hervard·replied : 'Tell me ; where are the mounds of Hjorvard?' The boy said : 'Thou art unwise, as thou wantest to search for that at night which few dare search for at mid-day ; burning fire plays on the mounds after sunset.' Hervard replied he would certainly go to the mounds. The shepherd said : 'I see that thou art a bold man, though thou art unwise. I will give thee my necklace if thou wilt come home with me.' Hervard answered: 'Though thou wouldst give me all thou ownest thou couldst not hinder me from going.' When the sun set they heard hollow noises in the island, and the mound fires appeared. The shepherd got frightened and took to his feet, and ran into the forest as quickly as he could, and never looked back."

As she comes by the mound she sings :—

Awake, Angantyr !
Hervor thee rouses,
The only daughter
Of thee and Svafa ;
Yield to me from the mound
The sharp sword
Which the Dvergar
For Svafrlami forged.

Hjorvaid ! Hervaid !
Hrani ! Angantyr !
I awaken you all
Beneath the tree-roots,
Who are clad in
Helmet and coat of mail

With shield and sharp sword,
And reddened spear.

Sons of Arngrim !
Much harm doing,
Much have you
The mould increased,
As no one
Of the sons of Eyfura
Will speak to me
At Munarvag.

Hjörvard ! Hervard !
Hrani ! Angantyr !
So be the mind
Of you all

As if you were rotting
In an ant-hill
Unless ye yield
The sword forged by Dvalin;
It is not fit for ghosts
Costly weapons to hide.

Angantyr.

Hervor, my daughter!
Why callest thou thus
Full of baneful words;
Thou art going to fare badly;
Mad hast thou become
And out of thy senses,
Mind-bewildered,
As thou awakenest the dead.

Neither father buried me
Nor other kinsmen;
The two who lived
Kept *Tyrfing*;
Although at last
One became its owner.

Hervör.

Thou dost not tell me truth;
The As shall leave thee
Unharmed in the grave-mound
If thou hast not *Tyrfing*;
Thou art unwilling
To give the heritage
To thy only child.

Then the mound opened and looked
    as if it were all on fire and flame.
Angantyr sang:

Ajar is the gate of Hel;
The mounds are opening,
All the island-coast
Looks as if on fire;
Outside all
Is awful to behold;
Hasten thee, maiden, if thou canst,
To thy ships.

Hervor.

Ye can not light
Such a flame at night

That I would
Fear your fires;
The *mind-town* of thought[1]
Of the maid does not quail
Though she sees a ghost
Standing in the door.

Angantyr.

I will tell thee, Hervór,
Listen the while,
Wise daughter,
What will happen;
This *Tyrfing* will,
If thou canst believe it,
All thy kin,
Maiden, destroy.

Thou shalt beget a son
Who afterwards will
Tyrfing carry
And trust to his own strength;
This one will the people
Heidrek call,
He will be the mightiest born
Under the tent of the sun.

Hervor.

I thus spellbind
The dead champions
That you shall
All lie
Dead with the ghosts,
Rotting in the mound,
Unless thou yieldest me, Angantyr,
The slayer of Hjalmar,[2]
The one to armours dangerous,
Out of the mound.

Angantyr.

Young maiden, I say,
Thou art not like man
As thou art strolling about
Among mounds in the night
With inlaid spear
And the Goth's metal,
With helmet and mail-coat
Before the hall-door.

---

[1] Breast.

[2] Tyrfing.

Hervor.

I thought hitherto I was
A human being
Ere I called
At your halls;
Hand me from the mound
The hater of mail-coats,[1]
It will not do for thee
To hide the Dvergar's smithying.

Angantyr.

The slayer of Hjalmar
Lies under my shoulders;
All around it is
Wrapped in fire;
No maiden I know
Above the mould
That dares this sword
Take in her hand.

Hervor.

I will hold
And take in my hands
The sharp *mœkir*
If I may have it;
I do not fear
The burning fire;
At once the flame lessens
When I look at it.

Angantyr.

Foolish art thou, Hervór,
Though courage owning,
As thou with open eyes
Into the fire rushest;
I will rather yield thee
The sword from the mound,
Young maiden!
I cannot refuse it to thee.

Then the sword was flung out into
the hands of Hervör.

Hervór.

Thou didst well,

Kinsman of vikings,
When thou gavest me
The sword from the mound;
I think, king!
I have a better gift
Than if I got
The whole of Norway.

Angantyr.

Thou knowest not,
Thou art wretched in speech,
Imprudent woman,
At what thou art glad.
This *Tyrfing* will,
If thou canst believe it,[2]
All thy kin,
Maiden, destroy.

Hervor.

I will go down
To the steeds of the sea;[3]
Now is the king's daughter
In a good mind;
I fear little,
Kinsman of chiefs,
How my sons
May hereafter quarrel.

Angantyr.

Thou shalt own it
And enjoy it long,
But hidden keep
The slayer of Hjalmar;
Touch thou not its edges,
Poison is in both,
This doomer of men
Is worse than disease.
Farewell, daughter,
I would quickly give thee
The vigour of twelve men
If thou would'st believe it;[4]
The strength and endurance,
All the good
That the sons of Arngrim
Left after themselves.

---

[1] Tyrfing.
[2] I would wish thee to believe it.
[3] Ships.
[4] That Tyrfing was dangerous

"Then she went down to the sea, and when it dawned she saw that the ships had left. The vikings had been afraid of the thunderings and the fires in the island"[1] (Hervarar Saga, c. 10).

Burial in ships.—The mode of burial in ships would appear to have belonged exclusively to the North, where it seems to have been in much favour, and shows in a remarkable manner the seafaring character of the people.

Until recently few descriptions have been more ridiculed by persons who did not believe in the Saga literature, than those which gave accounts of burials of chiefs, warriors, and others in ships. Here again archæology has come to our aid to prove the truthfulness of the Sagas, and in such a perfect manner as to settle the question beyond controversy; for we find ships in which the body of the dead warrior was not burned, and other ships which have been used as a pyre. The earliest account of such burial is in Voluspa, amplified in the later Edda, which gives us a vivid description of the funeral of Baldr, the son of Odin.

"The Asar took the body of Baldr and carried it down to the sea. Hringhorni was the name of Baldr's ship; it was larger than any other ship. The gods wanted to launch it for the *burning-voyage* of Baldr, but it did not move. Then the *gyg* (Jotun-woman)[2] in Jotunheim, named Hyrrokkin, was sent for. She came riding on a wolf, with snakes for reins. She leapt from the steed, and Odin called to four Berserks to take care of it, but they could not hold it except by throwing it down. She went to the stem of the ship and pushed it forward at the first attempt, so that fire issued from the rollers and the ground trembled. Then Thor grew angry, seized his hammer, and would have broken her head if the gods had not asked him to spare her. The body of Baldr was carried out on the ship, and his wife Nanna, Nep's daughter, on seeing this died

---

[1] I visited the island of Samsö in order to see if I could discover any indication of the mound of Angantyr. This island stands in the middle of the great belt; it is only in clear weather that part of the coast of the peninsula of Jutland can be seen; its shores are in many parts lined with huge boulders. In some parts mounds, passage graves, dolmens, &c., are to be seen; everything tends to show that in olden times it was a great burial place. Many of the mounds are either hidden by woods, or stand solitary amidst cultivated fields. The scene described in Hervara came forcibly upon my mind, and I wondered not that Hervor knew not where the mound of her father was. This island was well chosen for the resting-place of these men of the sea.

[2] The gyg (ogress, witch) seem to have been women of Jotun race, possessing supernatural strength.

from grief. She was laid on the pyre and it was set on fire. Thor went to it and consecrated it with *Mjolnir*. At his feet there ran a Dverg named Lit. Thor pushed him with his foot into the fire, and he was burned. To this burning came many kinds of people. First went Odin and his ravens and Frigg, as well as the Valkyrias. Frey drove in a carriage drawn by the boar called *Gullinbursti* (gold bristle) or *Sliðrugtanni* (the awful-tusked). Heimdal rode the horse *Gulltopp* (gold tuft), and Freyja with her cats. There came also many Hrim Thursar and Bergrisar. Odin laid on the pyre the gold ring *Draupnir*; afterwards every ninth night there dropped from it eight equally heavy gold rings. The horse of Baldr was led on the pyre in full harness" (Gylfaginning, ch. 49).

"They carried him in the snow-storm to Naustanes, where a tent was put over him at night. In the morning, at high water, Skallagrim was laid in a ship, and they rowed to Digranes. Egil had a mound made near the end of the ness (cape), and in this he was laid, with his horse, his weapons, and smithying tools. It is not mentioned that loose property was put in the mound with him. Egil took the inheritance, lands, and loose property; he took care of the farm" (Egil's Saga, c. 61).

Gudrun after having slain her husband Atli said:

I will buy a ship (knörr),[1]
And a painted coffin,
Wax well the sheets[2]

To wrap thy corpse with;
Think of every need,
As if we were friends.

"Geirmund died at Geirmundsstadir, and was laid in a ship in the woods near the farm (gard)."

Of this Geirmund much is told of in Sturlunga as a great chief.

"Thórir, An's brother, fell in a battle against king Lugjaldi of Naumdœlafylki.

"An had a mound made and put a ship in it and placed Thórir in its lypting, but the king's men he placed along both sides of the ship that it might look as if all served him" (An Bogsveigi's Saga, ch. 6).

"The brothers Eirik and Jorund became very famous by this deed (slaying King Gudlaug of Hálogaland), and they thought themselves far greater men than before. When they heard

---

[1] Volsunga Saga. ch. 38; instead of a ship he is buried in a stone coffin, but the poetry must be more trusted.
[2] Smear well with wax the sheets.

that King Haki had allowed his champions to go away, they
sailed to Sweden and collected a host, and when it was known
that the two Ynglings had returned the Swedes flocked to them
in great numbers. They sailed up into the Log (Lake Malar)
and went to Uppsalir against King Haki, who met them on
Fyrisvellir. A great battle ensued; King Haki rushed forward
with such valour that he slew all that were near him, he finally
killed Eirik and cut down the standard bearers of the brothers,
whereupon Jorund fled to his ship with his men. Haki received such severe wounds that he saw his days would not be
long. He then had a *skeid* which he owned loaded with dead
men and weapons, he had it launched on the sea, and the
rudder adjusted and the sea sail hoisted. He had tarred wood
kindled and a pyre made on the ship, the wind blew towards
the sea. Haki was almost dead when he was laid on the pyre.
Then the burning ship sailed out to sea. This was very famous
for a long time after " (Ynglinga Saga, c. 27).

"King Hakon then took the ships belonging to Eirik's sons,
which lay on the dry beach, and had them dragged ashore.
He placed Egil Ullserk, together with all who had fallen on
his side, in a ship, which was covered with earth and stones.
He also had dragged ashore several more ships, and into these
were laid the dead. The mounds are still to be seen south of
Frædarberg. High bautastones stand at the mound of Egil
Ullserk " (Hakon the Good's Saga, ch. 27).

Women were sometimes buried in ships.

"After this Unn, who was now quite old, as was her custom,
went into her sleeping-house to rest, but bade her guests enjoy
themselves, and ordered that they be entertained as splendidly
as possible. When she retired the feast continued until it was
time to go to bed. The next day, as Unn remained longer
than usual in her sleeping-room, Olaf went in and found her
dead. He returned to the guests and announced this to them,
who all said that Unn had well kept up her dignity to the last.
"At the same time Olaf's wedding and Unn's *arvel* were held.
On the last day of the feast her body was carried to the mound
which had been prepared for it. She was placed in a ship
therein, and with her a great deal of property, and then the
mound was closed." Olaf then took possession of his grand-
mother's property, and, after the feast was over, gave fine
presents to the foremost of those present, and all departed
(Laxdæla, ch 8).[1]

---

[1] Cf. Landnama, ii. An Bogsveigi's | Laxdæla Saga, ch. 7.
Saga, c. 6. Atlamál. Gisli Súrsson. |

Men were sometimes buried in a ship's boat.

" Ingimund was laid in the boat of the ship Stigandi, and his body prepared honourably as was the custom with high-born men. Thorstein said to his brothers : ' It seems to me right that we shall not sit in our father's seat at home, or at feasts, while his slaying is unavenged.' This they did, and neither went to games nor other gatherings " (Vatnsdæla Saga, 22).

One of the most valuable discoveries, showing the burial of a warrior in a ship without his body being burned, is that of the Gokstad ship.

Very few things in the North have impressed me more than the sight of this weird[1] mausoleum, the last resting-place of a warrior, and as I gazed on its dark timber I could almost imagine that I could still see the gory traces of the struggle and the closing scene of burial when he was put in the mortuary chamber that had been made for him on board the craft he commanded.

The warrior had been buried according to his position in life ; remains at least of twelve skeletons of horses were found in different parts of the mound on each side of the ship ; there

---

[1] Other ship-graves, such as that of Tune, Borre, &c., have been found with skeletons of horses.

Among other ships found is the Gunnar-haug ship, discovered in Bergen Stift in 1887. The large mound in which it was found had a diameter of over 125 feet, and stood about 500 feet from the shore.

The ship was only partly preserved owing to the action of the soil. Its planks were of oak, thicker and less broad than those of the Gokstad ship, fastened by clinch-nails. In the upper-most planks, considerably thinner than the rest, there are holes at distances of a little over 3 feet. Its keel is about the same length as that of the Gokstad ship.

It stood *north to south*, and has been supported by six stones, each about 6 feet high. Its inside has been clothed with a layer of moss, evidently to hinder decay by the soil, and on one side of it was a heap of shavings, chips and bark, left by the carpenters. There are reasons for thinking that a wooden roof had been erected over the ship, and afterwards broken down.

Of the Viking's body no trace is left, but the remains found indicate his place in the middle of the ship ; these are two swords, forging-tools, five long whetting-stones, a tinder-box and pieces of a wooden box. Farther north : several large beads of mosaic glass and fine chesspieces of amber and coloured glass, part of a waxen tablet, a bracelet of gold, &c.

Near the weapons lay an iron kettle and both the stones of a hand-mill, which shows that the Vikings ground their grain at sea. The stem was filled with rust.

Oars and carved tools were also found, and planks of an exceedingly well-built boat of oak, over which there lay a fir plank, several feet long, with steps cut in it, evidently a landing-board (cf. Gokstad ship).

This is the first burial-place found in Bergen Stift where the body was unburnt, but they are common further south.

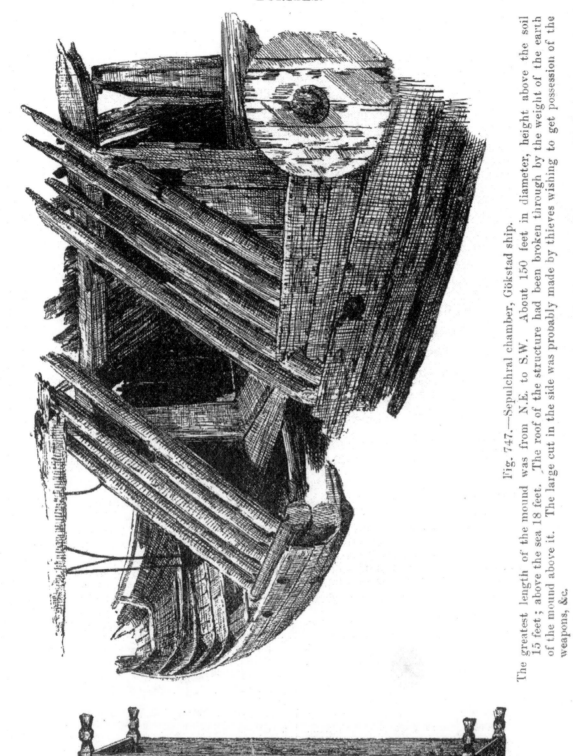

Fig. 747.—Sepulchral chamber, Gökstad ship.

The greatest length of the mound was from N.E. to S.W. About 150 feet in diameter, height above the soil 15 feet; above the sea 18 feet. The roof of the structure had been broken through by the weight of the earth of the mound above it. The large cut in the side was probably made by thieves wishing to get possession of the weapons, &c.

Fig. 748.—Bedstead, upon which the dead warrior had been placed, found in the sepulchral chamber, Gökstad ship.

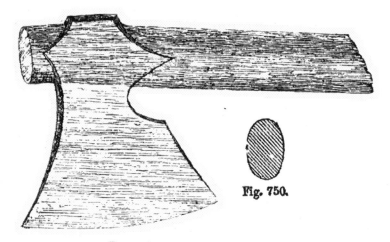

Fig. 749.
Axe, ¼ real size, found in mound

Fig. 750.

Fig. 751.   Fig. 752.   Fig 753   Fig. 754.

Fig. 755   Fig. 756.   Fig. 757.   Fig. 758

Fig. 759.

Fig. 760.

Some objects of bronze or iron.—Gókstad ship.

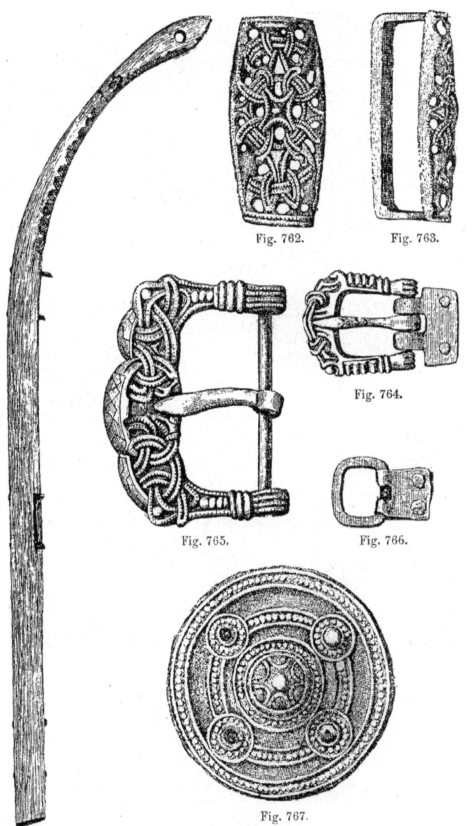

Fig. 762.

Fig. 763.

Fig. 764.

Fig. 765.

Fig. 766.

Fig. 767.

Fig. 761.—Part of a sledge.

Some objects of bronze or iron. Gökstad ship. See Vol. ii., Frontispiece and pages 162 to 168.

were also remains of skeletons of several dogs. The bones and feathers of a peacock were inside the ship, the prow of which, like that of the Tune boat, looked towards the sea as if ready for a voyage.

One of the finest discoveries, illustrating the use of a ship as a pyre for the burial of the dead warrior, was in a mound 12 feet high and 92 feet in diameter, opened in 1874 in Moklebust Eids parish, Bergen Stift, Norway.

Among the objects were a vast number of rivets or clinch-nails, and a great number of shield-bosses belonging to shields which adorned the sides of the ship ; perhaps several warriors had been burned together. On the bottom of the mound, on the level of the ground, was a layer of charcoal and burned soil intermingled with small pieces of bone, which extended nearly to the sides, but was heaviest in the middle. Separated from this by a layer of light shore-sand was another similar layer.

Inside an oval about 28 feet in length and 14 feet in width these two layers were interspersed with burned bone-splints, clinch-nails, and spikes.[1] In the eastern half of the charcoal layer were found six shield-buckles ; and in the western half, shield-buckles scattered about in various ways, sometimes singly, sometimes close to one another. In nearly every one of them lay a clinch-nail, evidently placed there intentionally,

---

[1] In a large mound at Vold, Borre parish, Norway, was a small vessel about 54 feet long, but in such an imperfect state of preservation that only the clinch-nails with pieces of the planks were left. On the right side lay a horse's skeleton, near which were found remains of a fine bridle and saddle of leather and wood, the mountings of bronze and silver ; also fragments of a glass bowl similar to the one found in a mound at Taplon (see p. 319). On the left side lay the skeletons of another horse and of a dog. Above the ship, over the entire mound, was spread a layer of charcoal. Among the objects found were a wrought-iron chain, an iron axe, fragments, and an iron kettle containing ashes, &c. This grave was made in a group of large mounds.

In Tune, Norway, about five miles from the river Glommen were found in 1867, in a mound, the remains of a viking ship, now in Christiana. This mound lay on a hill not far from the Visterflo, one of the branches of the river Glommen. It was about 24 feet in height, and 500 feet in circumference. Behind the mast lay the unburned corpse of a man, with part of the skeleton of a horse at his side. At the stern were the remains of ring armour.

At Lackalanga, near Lund, there are several earth-mounds. In one of these were found—fragments of a ship, the wood being incrusted with iron rust ; an urn of clay, with burned bones and coal ; fragments of weapons, &c. ; at least 100 clinch-nails of iron, and some other pieces of the same metal, probably originally belonging to a vessel buried in the mound ; two larger buckles of iron, like those used on saddles ; two stirrups bits for a bridle, &c.

z 2

just as some of the shield-buckles were filled with bone fragments and charcoal.

A little to the west of the centre of the mound was found a large bundle of strongly-bound and intentionally bent weapons and other implements. Right under this bundle was a bridle-bit of iron, and under this, in a hole dug below the natural level of the ground, a whole collection of shield-bosses, which all lay with their convex sides downward, and formed a

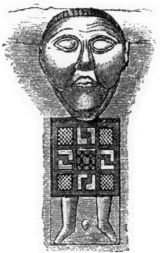

Fig. 768.—Bronze kettle filled with burnt bones mixed with ashes, charcoal, &c., and covered with twelve shield-bosses; nearly ⅕ real size. Moklebust.

Fig. 769.—Handle of kettle; real size. Moklebust.

covering for a large bronze kettle, represented above, without any other protection but the above-mentioned bosses.

In the middle of the bones lay an arrow-point 6 inches long; also six draughtsmen and three dice of bone. The draughtsmen were ball-shaped; on one side a small part was cut off, so as to give a flat surface, in the middle of which there was a small hole (fitting the pegs in the board itself, as seen from other finds of boards with pegs which were undoubtedly made thus for use at sea, so as to keep the pieces in position).

It seems as if the men of this warrior had dragged his ship ashore, placed the corpse therein with all his weapons and one or more horses, and had adorned it and hung their shields on its sides, hoisted the sails, and then let the flame consume the whole. The bones were then gathered and placed in the urn,

Fig. 770.—Enamelled bottom of kettle on p. 340 (inside), ⅔ real size ; found in a mound, Moklebust.

Fig. 771.—Enamelled bottom (outside), of most brilliant colours, real size. Moklebust.

and the twelve shield-bosses placed over it, provisions placed at its side, and the whole covered with a mound. But right over the urn the bridle had been placed, so as to be near at hand; then his weapons and the remains of the ship's chest, and then the two layers of other remains from the pyre.

Fig. 772.

Fig. 773.

Bronze figure representing a man; with inscription. Found with a bronze kettle containing burnt bones, a double-edged sword bent, several spear-heads, a shield boss, melted pieces of glass, &c.; earlier iron age. Norway.

CHAPTER XX.

RELIGION.—WORSHIP, SACRIFICES, ETC.

Odin's religion—Sun worship—The Three Annual Sacrifices—The Atone-
ment Boar and Bragi Toast—The Victory Sacrifice—Temple Priests—
Animals for Sacrifices—Sacrificial ceremonies—Divination—Chips—
Drawing of lots—Consecration of land and property—Worship of Thor
—Sign of the Hammer—The Svastica—Story of Framar.

THE earlier Edda or Sagas which relate to us the traditions
about Odin and the Asar do not give any description of the
sacred ceremonies or rites they performed.

From the Ynglinga Saga we learn that the hero Odin of the
North sacrificed after the manner of the Asar, and that the
sacrifices made by him, Njord, Frey, and Freyja, were to a
power worshipped by them, but we are not told who the god
or power was. It probably was in some instances the sun,
represented perhaps by the eye of the earlier and mythical
Odin of the Voluspa—who, as we have seen, pledged his eye
for a drink from the well of Urd; we know that the worship
of the sun was widely spread at one period in the history of
the world.[1] How the change from the worship of this unknown
power to the worship of Odin and the other gods took place
we are not told; but it may, we think, be taken for granted
that many of the ceremonies and beliefs mentioned in the
Sagas were of very ancient origin.

It is only by a study of all the Sagas that we gain a knowledge of the beliefs, religious ceremonies, mode of worship
and superstitions of the people of the North, which are often
minutely described. It is somewhat difficult for the present

---

[1] According to Herodotus, i. 212,
Tomyres, queen of the Massagetæ, whose
son had been taken prisoner by Cyrus,
sends to him the following message:—
"Restore my son; depart out of the
country, unpunished. . . . . But if you
do not do this, *I swear by the sun, the
Lord of the Massagetæ,* that insatiable as
you are, I will glut you with blood."

generation of English people, living in Great Britain and other countries, to realise that no more than eight centuries ago many of their forefathers believed and practised the rites we are going to describe, and that so slow was the march of Christianity, that six or seven hundred years ago the provinces of North-Eastern Prussia, Vindland, Pomerania, &c., whose inhabitants are among the finest in Europe, were still heathen.

It is certain that Odin and some of the Asars were deified and worshipped in all the countries of the North, and with the lapse of time their fame is found to increase. The attributes of Odin were believed to be many

There were three principal sacrifices a year, at which the people assembled in the chief temples :—*Vetrarblót, Midsvetrarblót*, and *Sigrblót*.

" It is their custom to have a sacrifice in the autumn and welcome the winter, another at mid-winter, the third at the beginning of summer ; then they welcome the summer. The *Eynir, Sparbyggjar, Verdælir* and *Skeynir* take part in this. There are twelve men [1] who are the foremost in managing the sacrifice-feasts : this spring Ölvir is to hold the feast ; he is now very busy in Mæri, and all provisions needed for the feast are brought thither." (St. Olaf, 115 ; cf. id. 123).

The first of these, called *Vetrarblót* [2] (Winter sacrifice), which took place on winter nights [3] in the month of Gói, was a sacrifice for a good winter. The 14th of October, which was the ancient month of Gói, is still called winter-night, or the first night of winter.

" That autumn the news was told King Olaf from Thrándheim that the Thrands had had great feasts during the winter nights : there had been great drinking. The King was told that all cups were hallowed to the Asar according to ancient custom.

---

[1] " East of Tanakvisl (Tanais, Don) in Asia was Asaland, or Asaheim, and the head-burgh (chief town) in the land was called Asgard. In the burgh was a chief called Odin ; it was a great sacrificing-place (blótstad). It was customary there that twelve temple-priests (hofgodar) were the foremost, and had charge of the sacrifices and judged between men. They were called *diar* or *drottnar* ; all the people were bound to give them service and reverence " (Ynglinga Saga, c. 2).

[2] *Vetrarblót* = winter-sacrifice ; from *vetr* = winter, and *blót* = sacrifice. The milky way is called *vetrarbraut* = winter way, because people thought that the appearance of the milky way predicted the course of the winter.

[3] The people counted by nights instead of days.

It was also said that cattle and horses were slaughtered there, the altars reddened with blood, and sacrifices made for the bettering of the year. Also it was said that they all thought it evident that the gods were angry because the men of Hálogaland had become Christians " (St. Olaf, 113. Heimskringla).

The second *Midsvetrarblót* (Mid-winter sacrifice), also called *Jólablót*[1] (Yule sacrifice), was held at mid-winter, or in the beginning of the month of Thór (middle of January), to ensure a good year and peace, and lasted three days; at this feast it was customary to make vows to some of the gods, especially Frey, at Yule-eve. It seems to have been the greatest and most important of all, and many animals were slaughtered at it.[2] The 12th of January is still called mid-winter in Norway.[3] This sacrifice plainly shows that the blessings of peace were appreciated by this warlike race. The Swedes, as we have read, wept over the death of Njörd, for during his time there were good years and peace.

"King Fornjót ruled Jötland (Jötunland) which is called Finnland and Kvenland, that is east of the arm of the sea which goes on the opposite side of Gandvik and which we call Helsingjabotn (Bothnian Gulf). Fornjót had three sons: Hler, whom we call Aegir, Logi, and Kári, who was father of Frosti, the father of Gnár the old; his son was Thorri, who had two sons, Nor and Gor; his daughter was Gói. Thorri was a great sacrificer; he had a great sacrifice every year at mid-winter which was called Thorra blót; from this the month was named (Thorri). One winter Gói disappeared at the Thorri sacrifice; she was searched for and not found. When the month had passed Thorri had a sacrifice in order to find out where Gói was; this they called *Góiblót*, but they learnt nothing about her" (Fornaldar Sögur ii., p. 17).

On the Yule-eve it was the custom to lead in procession a boar, consecrated to Frey, called *Sónar golt* (atonement-boar), and on this those present placed their hands, made solemn vows, and drank the *Bragi* toast.

"King Heidrek had a boar fed; it was as large as the largest bull, but so fine that it seemed as if every hair on it was of

---

[1] This was also sometimes called Thor's sacrifice.

[2] It seems that at this season other sacrifices than those to Frey were some-

times offered. Cf. Hálfdán the Old. Skaldskaparmal, c. 13.

[3] Cf. Ynglinga Saga, 8; St. Olaf, 115.

gold. He placed one hand on its head and one on its bristles, and made a vow that never should a man transgress so much that he should not have the lawful judgment of his wise men, and these men should take care of the boar, or else he should come with riddles which the king could not guess" (Hervarar Saga, c. 14).

In the evening vows were made, and the atonement-boar (*sónar golt*) was led forward; the men laid their hands on it, and made vows at the *Bragi* toast" (Helga Kvida Hjörvardssonar).[1]

"In the winter the foster-brothers (Ingólf and Leif) made a feast for the sons of the Jarl (Herstein, Hástein and Hólmstein, the sons of Atli-jarl). At this feast Hólmstein made a vow that he would marry Helga, the daughter of Örn, or no other woman. Men disliked this vow, but Leif was seen to become red (in his face), and he and Hólmstein were no friends when they parted at the feast" (Landnáma i., c. 3.)

"Thórodd was with another man at Thórar's. There was a great Yule-feast, the ale being provided by each one himself. There were many besides in the hamlet, who all drank together during Yule. A short way off there was another hamlet. There the brother-in-law of Thórar, a powerful and wealthy man, lived; he had a grown-up son. They were to drink during the half of the Yule at each other's farm, and first at Thórar's" (St. Olaf, c. 151).

"One winter at Yuletide, when the people were assembled to drink, Finn said: 'Vows will be made in many places this evening, where it is not better to be than here; now I vow that I will serve the king who is the highest and in all things surpasses others'" (Fornmanna Sögur ii., ch. 201.)

The third, called *Sigrblót* (Victory sacrifice), for luck and victory, occurred in the beginning of spring, about the middle of April, being fixed at that time of the year because warfare and most Viking expeditions took place in the summer. It was in honour of Odin, to whom alone, as we see from the Sagas, sacrifices were made for victory.[2]

In those warlike days sacrifices relating to war were the most important, for the life of the nation depended upon victory, and they were consequently foremost among the people.

---

[1] Cf. also Hörd's Saga and Hervarar Saga, c. 14. The boar was consecrated to Frey.

[2] Cf. also Hakon Adalsteinsfostri's Saga, c. 15; Olaf Tryggvason (Hkr.), c. 28.

"Dag, son of Högni, made a sacrifice to Odin, to avenge his father (who was slain by Helgi); Odin lent his spear to him. Dag met his brother-in-law Helgi at the place called Fjoturlund, he pierced him with the spear, and Helgi fell there" (Helga kvida Hundingsbana II).[1]

"In Sweden it was an old custom, from heathen times, that the chief sacrifice (höfudblót) should be at Uppsalir in the month of Goi, and that the sacrifice should be for peace and victory for the King, and men should come thither from all over the Swedish realm" (St. Olaf, c. 76, Heimskringla).

When Hakon jarl returned from Denmark, he ravaged both shores.

"When he had sailed eastward as far as the Gauta Skerries (rocky islets), he went ashore and made a great sacrifice. Two ravens, which croaked loudly, flew towards him, and the jarl thought that Odin must have accepted the sacrifice and that he would have a good chance of victory. He thereupon set fire to his ships and burned them all, and went into the country with his men with warlike intentions" (Fornmanna Sogur, vol. i.).

Sacrifices.—The superintendents of the sacrifices as we have seen were in the earliest times in the North the *Hofgodi* (*temple priests*), who were called Diar and Drotnar, and were held in great esteem and veneration by the people; but in later times temporal rulers were also priests, and had charge of the sacrifices.[2]

"All over Sweden men paid taxes to Odin; one penning (piece of money) for every nose; and he had to defend their land against war; and sacrifice for a good year" (Ynglinga Saga, c. 8).

The animals for sacrifice, which were generally oxen, horses, sheep, boars, and falcons, fattened in order to be of large size and fine appearance, were slaughtered by the temple priest, and in later times, as a rule, in front of the idols.[3] Sometimes the superintendence of the sacrificing feast alternated between a certain number of the foremost bœndr [4] of the fylki.[5]

"It happened in Sweden that the bull which was to be sacrificed was old and so well fed that it was vicious; when

---

[1] Cf. Hakon Adalsteinsfostri's Saga, c 15. Snorri's Olaf Tryggvason, c. 28.
[2] See chapter on Godis, p. 525.
[3] Olaf Tryggvason in Fms. ii. 173.
[4] See p. 496, a landowner.
[5] St. Olaf 115, Heimskringla.

men wanted to capture it it ran into the woods and became furious " (Ynglinga, ch. 30).

The people believed that good or bad years were often caused by faith, or want of faith, in the Asa creed ; a year was good when their chiefs sacrificed much, bad when they were not zealous sacrificers.[1]

The ceremony was divided into two parts : first the slaughtering of animals, and reddening of the temple and altars with blood—probably on the first night ; then the sacrificial feast.

In some places the expenses[2] of these feasts were defrayed by the godi, who in return had the care of the temple possessions and of the temple tolls :[3] in the earliest times people had to pay taxes—a custom said to have been instituted by Odin.

It was the custom to cook the flesh of the slaughtered animals in large kettles hanging over these fires along the floor of the temple. The people then assembled to eat it seated along the walls, and the filled horns were carried between or round the fires, which were probably regarded as holy, the person having charge of the feast consecrating the horns and the meat (*i.e.*, making the sign of the hammer of Thor over them). First was drunk the horn of Odin, for victory and power ; then Thor's horn by those who trusted in their own strength and power ; Njord's and Frey's horn for good years and peace ; Bragi's when solemn vows were made ; and the memorial toast for dead kinsmen which was proposed by the sacrificing priest.[4]

Of the solemn ceremonies which took place at the slaying of the living animals we have no description, but the blood from the sacrifices of either animals or human beings was collected into a bowl (*Hlaut-bolli*), generally of copper, which had its place in the temple at the principal altar. The altars and walls of the temple, and the people and idols, were spattered with blood with a kind of broom called *Hlaut-tein* (blood-twigs).

---

[1] Ynglinga, 47. Snorri's Olaf Tryggvason, 16.

[2] Sometimes the expenses devolved on the king, at others the feasts were provided for by the food and ale brought by those in attendance (Hakon Adalsteinsfostri, 16, 18). How far people went for sacrifices is seen in Landnáma v , 8.

[3] Eyrbyggja, 4, 10.

[4] In Herraud's Saga, ch. 12, the toasts are given in different order. The first toast is dedicated to Thor; then one to all the Asar; then one to Odin; and lastly, one to Frey.

"Sigurd Hlada-jarl was a very great sacrificer, as his father Hakon had been; he kept up all the sacrificing-feasts in Thrandheim on the king's behalf. It was an old custom when a sacrifice was to take place that all the bœndr should come to the temple, and take with them the provisions needed while the feast lasted. Every man·was to bring ale; there were also slaughtered all kinds of small cattle, as well as horses. All the blood which came therefrom was called *hlaut* (sacrifice blood), the vessels for holding it *hlaut-bowls*, and the twigs, *hlaut-twigs.* With them the altars had to be reddened all over, and also the walls of the temple inside and outside; then the men were to be sprinkled with them, but the flesh had to be boiled for people to eat.

"Fires were to burn on the middle of the temple floor, and kettles to be put on them; the drinking-horns had to be carried around the fire. The chief who made the feast had to consecrate the horns, and all the sacrifice-food. The horn (toast) of Odin must be drunk first, for the victory and power of their king; and then the horn of Njord and Frey, for a good year and peace. Many ussd to drink Bragi's horn next to these. Men also drank horns for those of their kinsmen who had been great men; these were called *minni* (memorial horns). Sigurd jarl was a most open-handed man; he did a very famous deed, as he held a great sacrificing feast at Hladir, and himself alone paid all the costs" (Hakon Adalstein-fostri (Hkr.), ch. 16).

It was customary to try and find out the decrees of fate or the will of the gods by a kind of divination or casting of lots with chips dipped in the blood of sacrifices; the most common way of making inquiry was by *Blótspán* (sacrifice chip) and by lots (*hlut*)—both methods of casting lots, but differently performed—the former of which apparently meant the throwing these sacred chips of wood.

Mention is made of the use of scales with lots in them, on one side favourable, on the other side unfavourable; if the favourable one went higher up than the other, it was a good omen.

Einar, an Icelander, and one of Hakon jarl's scalds, wanted to leave him and join Sigvaldi his foe at the battle of the Jomsviking, for he thought he had not as much honour with the jarl as formerly.

"When Hakon saw that he was going, he shouted for him to come and speak with him, and so he did; the jarl took two scales of burnished silver, gilt all over; with them were two weights, one of gold, the other of silver, on each of which a likeness was made; they were called *lots* and were of the kind customary with men. Strong qualities were in them, and the jarl used them for all things of importance to him. He used to put them on the scales and tell what each of them should signify to him. When it went well, and the one he wanted came up, the lot in the scale which signified what he wanted never kept quiet, but moved on the scale and made a tinkling sound. These costly things he gave to Einar, who became merry and glad, and desisted from going to Sigvald. From this he got a name and was afterwards called Skálaglam = 'scale tinkle'" (Jomsviking Saga).

"Ingjald gathered men and went against Granmar and his son-in-law, Hjörvard; he had a far larger host than the two others. The battle was hard, and after a short time the chiefs of Fjadrundaland, Vestr-Gautland, Nœriki, and Attundaland (they were with Ingjald), and all the host from these lands, fled. Ingjald received many wounds, and with difficulty escaped to his ships; his foster-father Svipdag the Blind fell there, with both his sons, Gautvid and Hulvid. Ingjald went back to Uppsalir dissatisfied with the expedition; he saw that the hosts from the kingdoms he had conquered were unfaithful. After this there was a great war between the kings; but when it had lasted some time the friends of both brought about a reconciliation. The kings appointed a meeting, met, and all three made peace, which was to stand while they lived; this was bound with oaths and pledges. The next spring Granmar went to Uppsalir to sacrifice for peace, as was the custom towards summer. The sacrifice-chip fell so as to show that he would not live long" (Ynglinga Saga, c. 42).

Marks were cut on pieces of wood or other material, and each person had his mark. Sometimes the places at feasts were assigned by lot, and lots were also drawn for human sacrifice. The images of some of the gods were sometimes marked on the lots.[1]

"At the advice of powerful men it was agreed that the kings should draw lots as to which of them should hereafter rule, and the *lots were to be cut* and put in the folds of a cloak. Then Eystein asked his brother King Olaf with whom he sided in this matter. He answered: 'We have long kept our love for each other and agreed well; thy will in regard to the

---

[1] Hallfredar Saga.

rule of the land and the laws, King Eystein, is also mine. Eystein said : ' I advise thee, King Sigurd, to cut the third lot for the cloak, for King Olaf, like ourselves, is the son of Magnús.' Sigurd answered : ' Men can see that every expedient has now been tried, for thou wantest to have two lots where I have one, but I will not deprive King Olaf of any honour.' Then the lots were put into the cloak, and the lot of King Sigurd came up, and he was to rule " (Sigurd Jorsalafari's Saga, c. 21).

It seems to have been the custom among zealous sacrificers to consecrate their lands and property to the gods, without however denying themselves the use and enjoyment thereof. That this was customary all over the North we may conclude from the mass of names of farms, villages, &c., named after the gods Odin, Frey, and Thor.

In their colonies the people followed the same custom of dedicating their settlements or lands to the gods, and we find ample proof of this in England, Normandy, Iceland, the Orkneys and Faroe Islands.

Among the gods most worshipped besides Odin were Frey, Thor and Njord.

We find from the Sagas that Frey was worshipped equally in Norway, Iceland, and Sweden, and no doubt also in Denmark.

One summer when Hallfred and his followers came from Iceland to Norway, and asked for tidings, they were told that there had been a change of chiefs in Norway ; that Hakon Jarl was dead, and Olaf Tryggvason had come instead with a new creed and commandments.

" Then the men on the ship agreed to make a vow ; they vowed to give much property to Frey if they got a fair wind to Sweden, but to Thor or Odin if they got to Iceland ; if they should not get a fair wind to sail, the King should have his way." They never got a fair wind, and had to sail to Thrándheim (Hallfredar Saga, c. 5).

" When Hrafnkel had settled at Adalbol (Iceland) he had a great sacrifice. He had a large temple made   He loved Frey more than other gods, and gave him one-half of all his most precious things. He settled in the whole valley and gave lands to the people, but wanted to rule them and became *godi*

(=temple-priest and judge) over them. After this his name was lengthened and he was called Frey's godi."

"Hrafnkel owned one valuable thing which he loved more than any other. This was a horse with a dark stripe along its back which he called Freyfaxi; he devoted to his friend Frey one-half of this horse, and loved it so much that he made a vow to slay any man who rode it against his will" (Hrafnkel Freysgodi's Saga).

Thorkel had been forced to sell his land to Glum. Before he departed from Thverá he went to the temple of Frey, leading thither an ox, and said:

"Frey, who long hast been my patron, and hast accepted many gifts from me and rewarded me well, now I give this ox to thee, so that Glum may leave Thveráland as much against his will as I do now; let me see some token whether thou acceptest it from me or not. At this the ox bellowed loud and fell dead, which Thorkel liked well, and he was less sad because he thought his prayer was heard" (Vigaglum's Saga, c. 9).

Fig. 774.—Runic stone, with hammer, at Stenqvista Södermanland, Sweden). Stones with a similar-shaped hammer have been found in several places in Denmark and Sweden.

Thor[1] like Frey was invoked. The poetical and figurative names given to him are far from being as numerous and beautiful as those given to Odin. It was customary, at least in the earliest times,

---

[1] In the earliest times Thor was the great enemy of the Jötnar. He was called upon by wrestlers also (Gunnlaug Ormstunga, 10), and showed his anger by causing loss of property (Flóamanna Saga, c. 20).

to make the sign of the hammer at burials and marriages.[1] This hammer was called Mjollnir, and (Lokasenna) when Thor is taunted by Loki, he answers each time by these lines—

" Be thou silent, coward,	Mjollnir[2]
My Thrudhamar (mighty hammer)	Shall take thy talk from thee."

But that the svastica was emblematic of the sign of Thor, and had been adopted as such by the people of the North, is only an hypothesis, for it is also found in Greece and other countries; there is nothing in the Sagas to prove the assertion.

" Asbjorn Reyrketilsson and his brother Steinfinn took up land above Krossá, and east of Fljot. Steinfinn lived at Steinfinnstadir, and no man has descended from him. Asbjörn consecrated his land to Thor, and called it Thorsmörk " (Landnama v., 2 ch.).

The hammer as an ornament is not uncommon, and may have been used as an amulet, as is seen on several runic stones (see p. 352).

Even Christians called upon Thor for help in sea voyages and difficulties.

" Eyvind, from Sweden, went on expeditions westward, and in Ireland married Raförta, daughter of the Irish king Kjarval. She bore him a son, Helgi, and they sent him to the Hebrides to be fostered. Two winters later they came back to the Hebrides, and did not recognise him, as he had been starved. They therefore called him Helgi the Lean, and took him away. He was after this fostered in Ireland, and when grown up became a highly honoured man, and was married to Thórun Hyrna, daughter of Ketil Flatnose. They had many children; Hrólf and Ingjald were their sons. Helgi the Lean went to Iceland with his wife and children. He had a very mixed creed; he believed in Christ, but nevertheless invoked Thor for help in sea voyages and in difficulties. When he saw Iceland, he inquired from Thor where he should take up land. The answer told him to go to the north coast of Iceland " (Landnama iii., 12).[3]

---

[1] Thrymskvida. The bridegroom and bride were to be marked with the holy sign. (Vol. II., p 12.)

[2] St. Olaf's Saga, 44. " He was marked after Thor and hammer in the hand."

[3] In the account of Fornmanna Sogur about the battle of Svold, Eirik jarl is said to have had Thor in the prow of his ship. "He took it away and put the cross instead, which he did on the advice of Olaf Tryggvason," otherwise he would not get the victory.

Worship of Njord.—Njörd [1] was also worshipped, though we have no account of sacrifices made to him; but the formulary of the oath, "So help me Frey, Njord, and the Almighty As (Odin)!" shows the existence of his worship. Egil calls upon him and the two other gods to drive Eirik Blood-axe from the land.[2]

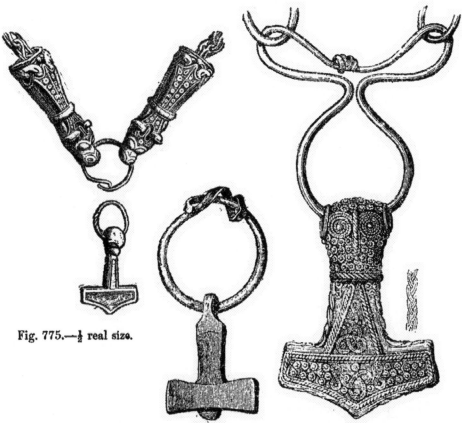

Fig. 775.—½ real size.

Fig. 776.—Thor's hammer. In a field. Läby, Uppland. Real size.

Fig. 777.—Thor's hammer and chain of silver.—Bredsätra, Öland. Real size.

There were men who did not believe in and did not worship Odin, as may be seen from the following example:—

"Then came to Hrafnista, Framar, a viking king; he was a sacrificer and iron did not wound him. He demanded in marriage Hrafnhild, the daughter of Ketil Hæng. Ketil answered that she should choose a husband herself. She refused Framar. Therefore Framar challenged Ketil to *holmganga* at Arhaug, on the first day of Yule, and said he should

---

[1] In Vafthrudnismál, Njörd is said to have ruled over many temples by the old Asgard.

[2] Cf. Egil's Saga, c 58.

be every man's nithing if he did not come. On Yule-eve he came to Arhaug. Framar and the men of the land sacrificed for good years.

"Bödmód, the son of Framar, after inviting Ketil to his hall, mentioned Odin. When he named Odin, Ketil got angry, for he did not believe in him; and sung a song:—

Odin worship	I know that Framar
Did I never,	Will fall sooner than
Though long I have lived;	This high head.

Twice the sword of Ketil did not bite; the third time it cut Framar from the shoulder down to the loins. Then Framar sung:—

There is courage in Hæng,	Now the father of Baldr proved false
Dravendil is sharp,	It is unsafe to trust him;
It bit the word of Odin	Enjoy well thy hands,
As if it were nothing;	Here we shall part.

Framar thereupon died, and Ketil went home" (Ketil Hæng's Saga, c. 5).

CHAPTER XXI.

RELIGION.—ALTARS, TEMPLES, HIGH-SEAT PILLARS, ETC.

The most primitive form of altar—The earliest Asa temple in the North—
    The temples in Norway and Denmark—Size and materials of temples—
    Their magnificence—Temple priests—Support of temple—Holiness and
    sacredness of temples—High-seat pillars—Sacred pegs.

THE *horg* was a sacred altar, built of stones, often mentioned
in the Eddas and Sagas, but never described, and was quite
distinct from the *stalli*, or altar. Perhaps it was an enclosed
structure, or was built over a sacrificing mound or upon some
elevation.   Its primitive form makes it undoubtedly of far
greater antiquity than the temple, though both were retained
as we see in later times by the people in their worship.
It seems to have been especially used for sacrifices to the
Alfar and Asar;[1] and from the words of Freyja to Hyndla,
who was her friend, when speaking of Ottar, we find that
a hörg had been raised to her by the latter, and sacrifices
made to her.

He made me a hörg   He reddened it in
Reared of stones;   Fresh ox blood.
Now have these stones   Ottar believed
Become *gler*.[2]   Always in Asynjur.

[Hyndluljód, st. 10.]

The first temple belonging to the Asa creed which Odin
is fabled to have established was at Sigtuna; afterwards the
most celebrated of all the temples in the North was that of
Upsala, but unfortunately we have no description of it in the

---

[1] From Vafthrúdnir's answer to Odin
about Njord's origin we find that he
ruled over temples and horg. (Vafthrúd-
nismál, 38.)

[2] Shining like glass. Amber is called
gler; and in Sigrdrifumál, st 17, we
find that runes were written on gler or

amber.

The hörg is also mentioned in Voluspa, 7; Helgakvida Hjorvardssonar, 4;
Landnáma ii. 16; Elder Gulathing's Law,
ch. 29; Orvar Odd, p. 29; Hervarar
Saga, 1.

Sagas; its fame was so great that on special occasions people from all over the North came to it.

The two principal temples in Norway were in Hladir in Thrandheim, and in Gudbrandsdal.

"Gudbrand of Dalir was a great friend of Hakon Jarl. They owned a temple which was the second for size in Norway, the largest being at Hladir (in Thrandheim). The former was never unlocked except when the Jarl came thither" (Njala, 87).

The largest one in Denmark was in Hleidra (Zeeland), but unfortunately in this case also the Sagas give no description. Other temples of less repute were also built.

The *Hof* or temple was often of large size, and the Sagas give us examples of their appearance, some of them being of great splendour; they were generally if not always rectangular buildings,[1] with a rounded addition at one end like the apse of a church. Some had two parts: an inner or more sacred one, where the images of the gods were placed; and an outer one, where the sacrificial feasts were held. At the *blotveitsla* or sacrificial feast the people seem to have remained standing, high seats existing only for the *blotgodi* (sacrificing priest). At the farther end the *God* (god-idols) stood on their *stall* (altar).

"Olaf sailed to Hladir, and had the temple broken down, and all the property and ornaments taken out of it and off the gods. He took a large gold ring from the temple door, which Hakon Jarl had made, and then had the temple burnt.

"Olaf sent the large gold ring which he had taken from the temple door to Queen Sigrid, Storrada (the Proud) in Sweden (he wanted to marry her). She had it broken, and brass was found inside. She got angry, and said that Olaf was likely to be false in more things than this" (Olaf Tryggvason, 65, 66).

Sometimes these buildings were magnificently furnished and adorned with costly and precious metals; their walls were hung with tapestries, and otherwise ornamented,[2] and on the door was a golden ring.[3] Many of them must have been the

---

[1] See Landnama v, 2; Hrafnkel Freysgodis Saga, pp. 4–6.
[2] Olaf Tryggvason Heimskringla, ch. 65, 66.
[3] Kjalnesinga, 2; Droplaugarsona, Saga about Bessi temple, Landnáma v. 12.

property of powerful and wealthy bœndr,[1] as may be inferred from the fact that some chiefs when they left the country tore them down and took them away, together with the temple mould on which they stood, which was holy.

" Ketilbjörn, a famous man in Norway, went to Iceland, and dwelt at Mosfell. He was so rich in personal property that he told his sons to make a cross-beam of silver in the temple which they were building. As they would not, he with his thrall Haki and his bondmaid Bót drove the silver up on the mountain with two oxen; they hid it so that it has never been found since; then he killed Haki in Hakaskárd, and Bót in Bótarskard " (Landnama v. 12).

" Thorhad the old was temple-priest in Thrandheim, in Mœri. He wished to go to Iceland, but first took down the temple, and carried with him the temple mould and the altars. He came into Stodvar-fjord and made the whole fiord as holy as the temple place in Mœri, and allowed nothing to be slain there except homestead cattle. He lived there all his life afterwards; the Stodfirdings are descended from him "[2] (Landnama).

The *hof-godi* or temple-priest was occasionally a woman.

" Steinvor was a priestess, and took care of the head temple; to this all bœndr had to pay temple tax. Steinvor went to the chief Broddhelgi, for she was related to him, and told him her trouble, that Thorleir, the Christian, did not pay temple tax like other men. Broddhelgi said he would take up this case for her against Thorleif."[3]

---

[1] Landowner (see p. 496)

[2] Adam of Biemen about 1070 writes that not far from *Sictona* (Sigtuna) is the temple *Ubsola*, where were the three gods, *Thor*, *Wodan* and *Fricco* (Fiey). What he says about this temple makes it evident that not only its roof but also the whole inside of the structure was covered with gold plates. Further he says that close to it there was a large tree, which no one knew, and which stretched its branches far out, and was always green, as well as a spring, near which the heathen made their sacrifices, and wherein a live man was thrown; the people believed that his wishes would be fulfilled, in case he sank; also a golden chain went around the temple, and hung from the roof.

[3] Saxo writes that the Danish king Halfdan journeyed to Upsala in order to find out the cause of his daughter's sterility, and was answered that he must first satisfy the spirit of his brother, whom he had unwittingly slain; this he did, and then she, in accordance with the promise of the oracle, bore Harald Hilditonn.

At the present old Upsala church there were discovered the foundations of an old building, a mass of coals, molten copper and silver pieces, with small traces of pure gold, as well as a rusty nail with a little gold on it, and finally skulls of pigs and hawks, and cheek-bones and teeth of horses, all of which tend to show that the old heathen temple of Upsala, so famous during pagan times, stood there (Verelius Notæ in epist def. Shefferi, p. 16.)

A tax, as we have seen, was said to have been imposed in Odin's time for the support of the temple; in the time of Frey a change took place, according to the sagas, and certain lands and properties in the several districts called *Uppsala-Aud* (Uppsala wealth) were set apart for this purpose; but in later times again, in Norway at least, and probably in other parts of the North, the bœndr had to pay taxes for the support of the temples. some of which seem to have been the private property of the godi.

The temples were considered so holy that any one damaging them or entering them armed was declared an outlaw, and no one who had committed an offence punishable by law was allowed to enter; such person was called *Varg i Veum* (wolf in the sanctuary). The grove or fields surrounding the temples were often regarded as inviolate, so that no act of violence would be permissible within their precincts. This was expressed by the ancient name of *Ve* (sanctuary, sacred place), which was extended so as to embrace the *Thing*-place, which was also regarded as sacred, while the *Thing* was going on.

"Ingimund went into the temple, and before he was aware of it Rafn ran in with a sword. Ingimund turned towards him and said, ' It is not the custom to bring weapons into the temple, and thou wilt turn the wrath of the gods against thee; such a thing is impossible unless it is atoned for ' " (Vatns-dœla, c. 17).

"Búi went to the temple, and when he arrived there, saw that the enclosure as well as the temple was unlocked. He entered and perceived that Thorstein lay on his face in front of Thor. Búi walked silently until he came to Thorstein, and grasped his knees with one hand and his shoulders with the other in such a manner that he lifted him and struck his head so hard against a stone that his brains were scattered over the floor; he died immediately. Búi carried him out and threw him near the fence of the enclosure, and entered the temple again. He took the sacred fire, and, kindling lights, carried them around the temple and set the hangings on fire. The fire quickly caught one thing after the other, and in a short time the temple was in flames. He went out and locked both the temple and the enclosure, and threw the keys into the fire and departed. Thorgrim Godi awoke in the morning and saw the temple burning; he called on his people, men and women, to run with water vessels and save it; he also called upon his son, Thorstein, but he was nowhere to be found. When they reached the gate of the enclosure it was not easy to pass, for it was locked, and the keys were nowhere to be found; they were obliged to break open the door, for the fence was so high that they could not get over it. Entering the enclosure, they saw Thorstein there dead; the temple was also locked. and nothing in it could be saved. Hooks were brought and the temple was pulled down, and thus part of the temple was saved " (Kjalnesinga Saga, c. 4).

For this Búi was outlawed by Harald Fairhair, but was subsequently forgiven.

"King Beli ruled over Sygna-fylki (in Norway); he had three children; Helgi and Hálfdán were his sons, and Ingibjörg his daughter. Ingibjörg was fair-looking and wise; she was the foremost of the king's children. On the shore west of the fjord there was a large bœr,[1] called Baldr's hagi (Baldr's field or enclosure), which was a place of peace,[2] where a large temple stood, surrounded by a high wooden fence; there were many gods, though Baldr was most worshipped. The heathen[3] men were so careful about the temple that neither man nor beast was to be hurt there; men were not allowed to stay with women there " (Fridthjóf's Saga, 1).[4]

" When Fridthjóf had left Norway the kings held a *Thing*, and outlawed him from all their lands, and took to themselves all his possessions. King Hálfdán settled at Framnes, and rebuilt the burned part of the farm; and they repaired the whole of Baldr's hagi, but it was a long time before the fire was extinguished. King Helgi disliked most of all that the gods had been burned. It was very costly to build Baldr's hagi again as good as it was. King Helgi then resided at Syrstrond " (Fridthjóf's Saga, c. 10).

The fact that some of the old temples were a subject of pilgrimage to those who had emigrated from the land is further proof of the veneration paid to them.

" Lopt Ormsson went from Gaulardal in Norway to Iceland when young, and took up land along the Thjórsá river. Lopt

---

[1] This implies that in the sacred precincts there were several buildings.
[2] Gridastad means place of truce.
[3] The writer or copyist seems to have

been a Christian.
[4] Fridthjóf means the thief of peace, the one who steals or destroys peace.

went to Norway every third summer for himself and for his mother's brother Flosi, to sacrifice in the temple which his grandfather Thorbjórn had guarded" (Landnama v., ch. 8).

Inside the principal door of the temple stood the high-seat pillars, which were highly venerated, and in which were placed the so-called *reginnaglar* (sacred pegs). It was the custom for families to take these pillars when they left their old home for Iceland, and when at sea to throw them overboard, and settle where they came ashore : they, the timbers of the temple, and the mould under the altars of the gods, were considered sacred.

" The summer that Ingólf and Hjörleif went to settle in Iceland, Harald Fairhair had been king in Norway for twelve years. There had passed from the beginning of this world six thousand and seventy-three winters; but from the birth of our Lord, eight hundred and seventy-four winters.

"They sailed together till they saw Iceland, and then separated. When Ingólf saw Iceland, he threw overboard his high-seat pillars for luck, saying that he would settle where the pillars went ashore.

"Ingólf took up his abode where his high-seat pillars had come to land ; this was at Reykjarvik, and there the high-seat pillars still remain in a hall "[1] (Landnama).

"Thórólf Mostrarskegg made a great sacrifice, and inquired from his beloved friend Thor whether he should reconcile himself to the King (Harald Fairhair), or go away from the country and seek other fate. The answer pointed out to him Iceland. Thereupon he got a large seagoing ship, and made it ready for the Iceland journey, and took with him his household and live stock. Many of his friends went on the journey with him. He took down the temple and carried with him most of the timbers which had been in it, and also the earth and mould from under the altar on which Thor had sat. Thereupon he sailed out to sea with fair winds, reached the land, and went along the south coast westward past Reykjanes. Then the fair wind ceased, and they saw that large fjords went into the land. Thórólf threw overboard his high-seat pillars, which had been standing in the temple ; the image of Thor was carved on one of them. He declared that he would live in Iceland, at the place where Thor landed them As soon as they left the ship they drifted to the western fjord. Then

---

[1] Cf. also Landnama, iv. 5 ; Kormak's Saga, 11.

there came a breeze; they sailed westward past Snjófellsnes and into the fjord; they saw it was very broad and long, with very high mountains on both sides. Thórólf named it Breidifjord (broad fjord). He landed on the southern side, nearly at its middle, and laid the ship in the bay, which they afterwards called Hofs-vag. They searched the shore, and found on the point of a ness north of the bay that Thor had there landed the pillars. The ness was called Thórsness. After this Thórólf went with fire around the land which he took up from Stafá (river) to the river which he called Thórsá, and there settled his ship's crew. He raised a large house at Hofs-vag which he called Hofstadir. There he had a large temple built; there was a door on the side wall, near the one end; inside stood the high-seat pillars, and pegs were in them; they were called *regin naglar*. Inside this there was a great *peace-place;* in the innermost part of the temple was a room like the choirs in churches now, and a platform was raised on the middle of the floor like an altar, on which there lay a jointless ring weighing two ounces, and on this all oaths had to be sworn. The temple priest had to wear that ring on his arm at all meetings" (Eyrbyggja, c. 4).

After Ingimund had departed from Norway for Iceland he landed at Borgarfjord. He was met by Grim and Hámund, the former of whom invited him to remain with him, and take whatever he wanted, whether real or portable property. For the offer Ingimund thanked him, but said he would only remain over winter, and in the spring would go to look for the place he intended to settle on. The following summer he wandered about, and in the autumn took winter quarters in a valley called Vididal, at a place which was afterwards named Ingimundarhöll.

"When spring came and the snow began to melt on the mountain sides Ingimund said, 'I should like some men to go up on a high mountain to look if there is less snow in other places, for I do not think we will settle in this valley, for it is not an equal bargain.' They went up on a high mountain and saw far away. They returned and told him that the mountains on the north-west were very snowless, and soon they were all on their way thither. As they approached the Vatnsdal valley Ingimund recognised it from the description given by the Fins; and when they came to the Vatnsdal river Vigdis said 'I must rest a little while, for I feel sick.' She gave birth to a girl who was named Thordis, after Ingimund's mother. He then said that the place should be called Thordisarholt. He chose a site for his residence in a very beautiful grove, raised a large temple, one hundred feet in length; and when he was digging holes for his high-seat pillars he found the image of Frey of silver, as he had been foretold. Then he said, 'It is indeed true that you cannot go against fate, but nevertheless I like this. This farm shall be called Hof (temple)'" (Vatnsdæla, 15).[1]

Lodmund the old, a Norwegian from Voss, went to Iceland:

" He threw his high-seat pillars overboard at sea, and said he would settle where they were driven ashore. They landed in the eastern fjords, and he settled in Lodmundarfjord, where he lived that winter. When he heard that his high-seat pillars were on the south coast he carried on board the ship all his property, hoisted the sail, laid himself down, and bade no one be so bold as to utter his name. After he had been lying down for a short time a loud crash was heard, and it was seen that a large land-slip had come down upon the farm where Lodmund had dwelt. He rose and said, 'It is my imprecation that the ship which hereafter sails out from here shall never come undamaged back from the sea.' He took up land where the high-seat pillars had come ashore" (Landnama iv. 5).[2]

---

[1] Cf. Landnama, iii., c. 2, 7.
[2] Cf. also Vatnsdæla, 12. Landnama, i., c. 10. Ondvegissula = high-seat pillar.

CHAPTER XXII.

RELIGION.—HUMAN SACRIFICES.

Sacrifices to Odin—Human sacrifices resorted to on momentous occasions—
Kings sacrificed—Children sacrificed by their fathers—Sacrifice to pro-
long life—Warriors given to Odin after battle—Sacrificing springs—
Sacrifices on Thor's stone—Sacrificing place at Blomsholm—Sacrificing
mound—The blood-eagle sacrifice—Giving oneself to Odin on a sick-
bed—The earliest account of human sacrifice in the North—The
abandonment of human sacrifices.

BESIDES the sacrifices already mentioned others were held
when the aid of the gods was required; the most important
of them were human sacrifices, which were offered in times
of great calamity, such as famine, or in order to avoid some
great evils, or to obtain victory, or for some other weighty
reasons.

"At this time occurred a very bad year in Reidgotaland, and
it looked as if the land would become a waste. Lots were
then thrown by the wise men, and they threw the sacrificing-
chip; the answer came that there never would be a good year
in Reidgotaland until the highest-born boy in the land should
be sacrificed. A *Thing* was summoned, and all agreed that
Angantýr, son of Heidrek, was the foremost there, because of
his kin, but nobody dared to mention it. Then they resolved
to submit this question to the decision of King Hofund in
Glœsisvoll (Heidrek's father); the most high born were to be
chosen for the journey, but everybody declined. King Harald
and many others asked King Heidrek to assist in deciding this
question, and he consented. He at once had a ship made ready,
on which he went with many renowned men, and sailed to
Risaland. When King Hofund heard of his arrival he at once
wanted to have him slain, but Queen Hervör remonstrated, and
so managed that they were quite reconciled. Then Heidrek
told his errand and asked for his decision, and Hofund said
that his son was the foremost in the land. At this King
Heidrek changed colour and thought the case became difficult;
he asked his father to give him advice how to save the life of the
boy. Hofund said: 'When thou goest home to Reidgotaland,
thou must summon the men to a Thing from thy possessions

and those of King Harald, and there pronounce thy decision about thy son.   Then thou shalt ask how they will reward thee if thou allowest him to be sacrificed.   Say that thou art a foreigner, and that thou wilt lose thy land and people if this is to take place.   Then thou shalt make it a condition that one-half of the men of King Harald present at the Thing shall become thy men or else thou wilt not give up thy son, and this shall be confirmed by oaths.   If thou dost get this. I need not give thee advice as to what thou shalt do thereafter.' Heidrek thereupon took leave of his father and mother, and sailed away from Risaland.   When Heidrek returned to Reidgotaland he summoned a Thing, to which he spoke thus : ' It is the decision of my father, King Hofund, that my son is the foremost here in the land, and is to be chosen for sacrifice ; but in return for this, I want to have power over one-half of those of King Harald's men who have come to this Thing, and you must pledge me this.'   That was done, and they came into his host ; then the bœndr asked that he should deliver his son to them, and thus improve their season.   But after the hosts had been divided, Heidrek asked his men to take oaths of allegiance. This they did, and swore that they would follow him out of the land and in the land to wherever he wanted.   Then he said : ' I think that Odin gets the value of a boy if, instead of him, he gets King Harald and his son and his entire host.'   He bid them raise his standard to attack King Harald and slay him and all his men.   The war horns were sounded and the attack made. The battle soon turned against King Harald and his men, for they had far fewer men and were unprepared.   But when they saw there was no escape they fought with great valour, and cut down the men of King Heidrek so fiercely that it seemed uncertain which would be defeated.   When Heidrek saw his men fall thus in heaps, he rushed forth with the sword *Tyrfing* and killed one after the other ; at last King Harald and his son and a great part of their men fell there, and Heidrek became the slayer of his father and brother-in-law.   This was reckoned to be the second *nithings-deed* committed with Tyrfing according to the spell of the Dvergar.   King Heidrek reddened the temple-altars with the blood of King Harald and Halfdan, and gave Odin all the dead men who had fallen there, in the place of his son Angantýr, in order to improve the season.   When Queen Helga heard of the death of her father she was so affected that she hanged herself in the *disar-hall*[1] of the temple " (Hervarar Saga, c. 11 & 12).

---

[1] Disar = genii.

Several instances are mentioned in which powerful kings were sacrificed or offered their children on the altars of the gods.

"There was a great crowd of men who left Sweden because of King Ivar's rule. They heard that Olaf Tretelgja[1] had good lands in Vermaland, and so many went thither that the country could not support them. There then came a very bad season and a great famine. They attributed this to their king, as the Swedes are wont to hold him accountable for both good and bad seasons. King Olaf was not a zealous sacrificer, and this the Swedes did not like, thinking that therefore arose the bad years. They then gathered a host, went against the king, surrounded his house, and burned him, giving him to Odin as a sacrifice for good years. This was at Vœnir (Venern)" (Ynglinga Saga, c. 47).

The custom of sacrificing a beloved child of a chief was considered, as it well might be, the highest atonement that could be offered, and is one of such antiquity that its birth is lost in the dim light of past ages. We have remarkable instances of this custom mentioned in the Bible; the story of Abraham and Isaac, and of Jephthah's vow show the existence of the practice in very early times. In Lev. xx. 2-4, the practice is mentioned as taking place among the heathen; and we see that, as in the North, the father had absolute power over the life of his child, otherwise he could not sacrifice him.

The most thrilling accounts of sacrifice of children are those of the sacrifice by Hakon Jarl of his own son, and by King Aun of nine sons.[2]

---

[1] Olaf, son of Ingjald Illrádi . . . fled to a forest district of Vermaland, where he cleared the land of its woods; therefore he was called Tretelgja (tree-cutter).

[2] "The scene of most interest, and at the same time of most horrors, taken from the mythical or poetical history of Greece is one which represents the sacrifice of Trojan captives to the *manes* of Patroclus. Achilles himself is the priest or butcher, for he occupies the centre of the scene, clad in brazen cuirass and greaves, his long yellow locks uncovered by a helmet, and seizing by the hair the wretched Trojan captive who is seated naked at his feet imploring mercy, he thrusts his sword into his neck, just as the 'swift-footed son of Peleus' is repre-sented to have treated Lycaon, the first victim he sacrificed to his friend Patroclus. Above the Trojan stands Charon, in red jacket and blue chiton, wearing a cap or helmet, and bearing his mallet on his shoulder ready to strike. The right half of the scene is occupied by the two Ajaces, each bringing forward a victim, naked and wounded, whose hands are bound behind their backs. Ajax Telamonius, the more prominent of the two, is fully armed; and Ajax Oïleus is similarly armed, but without a helmet. The funeral pyre on which the corpse of Patroclus was already laid before the sacrifices of captives, horses, and dogs were made to his manes is not shown. This episode forms the subject of the first wall paintings found in Etruria

In the beginning of the battle of the Jomsvikings against Hakon Jarl and his sons luck was against him, and the Jarl called his sons ashore, where he and they met and took counsel.

"Hakon Jarl said: 'I think I see that the battle begins to turn against us; and I dislike to fight against these men; for I believe that none are their equals, and I see that it will fare ill, unless we hit upon some plan; you must stay here with the host, for it is imprudent for all the chiefs to leave it, if the Jomsvikings attack, as we may at any moment expect. I will go ashore with some men and see what can be done.' The Jarl went ashore north to the island. He entered a glade in the forest, sank down on both his knees and prayed; he looked northwards and spoke what he thought was most to the purpose; and in his prayers he called upon his fully trusted Thorgerd Hórdatróll; but she turned a deaf ear to his prayer, and he thought that she must have become angry with him. He offered to sacrifice several things, but she would not accept them, and it seemed to him the case was hopeless. At last he offered human sacrifices, but she would not accept them. The Jarl considered his case most hopeless if he could not please her; he began to increase the offer, and at last included all his men except himself and his sons Eirik and Svein. He had a son Erling, who was seven winters old, and a very promising youth. Thorgerd accepted his offer, and chose Erling, his son. When the Jarl found that his prayers and vows were heard, he thought matters were better, and thereupon gave the boy to Skopti Kark, his thrall, who put him to death in Hakon's usual way as taught by him"[1] (Fornmanna Sögur, xi. 134).

Human sacrifices were resorted to by kings in order to lengthen their own life.

"When King Aun was sixty he made a great sacrifice in order to secure long life; he sacrificed his son to Odin. King Aun got answer from Odin that he should live another sixty winters. Thereupon he was king for twenty-five winters at Uppsalir. Then Áli the Bold, son of King Fridleif (in Den-

which were illustrative of Hellenic myths, but since their discovery that of the Grotta del Orco at Corneto has afforded us additional proof that the Etruscans did not always confine the pictorial adornments of their sepulchres to the illustration of the peculiar cus- toms, funeral observances, or religious creed of their native land" (Dennis's 'Etruria')

[1] From this passage we see that it was the custom of Hakon Jarl to make sacrifices, but unfortunately the manner in which he made them is not told.

mark), came with his host to Sweden against King Aun; they fought, and Áli always gained the victory. King Aun left his realm a second time and went to the western Gautland. Áli was king at Uppsalir for twenty-five winters, till Starkad the Old slew him. After his death Aun came back to Uppsalir and ruled the realm for twenty-five winters. He again made a great sacrifice for long life and offered up another son. Odin told him that he should live for ever if he gave him a son every tenth year, and would call a *herad*[1] (district) in the land after the number of every son whom he thus sacrificed. During ten winters after he had sacrificed seven of his sons he was unable to walk, and was carried on a stool. He sacrificed his eighth son and lived ten winters more in bed. He sacrificed his ninth son and lived ten winters more, and drank from a horn like a young child. He had one son left and wanted to sacrifice him, and thereupon to give Uppsalir with the *herads* belonging to it to Odin, and call it Tíundaland.[2] The Swedes stopped him; then he died and was mound-laid at Uppsalir" (Ynglinga, c. 29).

Men, particularly the slain after a battle, were sometimes given to Odin for victory, the largest number ever given being those who fell at the famous battle of Bravalla. It seems to have been customary to redden the altars with the blood of the fallen chiefs.[3]

Prisoners of war, no matter what their rank, were called thralls, and were sacrificed; sometimes they were slaughtered like animals, their blood put into bowls, and their bodies thrown into bogs or a spring outside the door of the temple called *blót-kelda* (sacrificing spring), or their backs broken on sharp stones; sometimes they were thrown from high cliffs.[4]

"Thorgrim Godi was a great sacrificer; he had a large temple raised in his grass-plot,[5] one hundred feet in length and sixty in breadth, and every man was to pay temple-tax to it. Thor was most worshipped there; the inmost part of it was made round as if it were a dome; it was all covered with hangings, and had windows; Thor stood in the middle, and other gods on both sides. There was an altar in front made with great skill and covered above with iron; on it there was to be a fire which should never die out, which they called holy

---

[1] See p 478.
[2] Tíundaland = land of the tenth.
[3] Hervarar Saga, 9, 10, 11, 12.

[4] Kristnisaga, Fornmanna Sogur ii, 228.
[5] I.e. Tun or open space.

fire. On the altar was to lie a large ring of silver, which the temple priest was to wear on his arm at all meetings. Upon it all oaths were to be taken in cases of circumstantial evidence. On the altar was to stand a large bowl of copper, in which was to be put the blood which came from the cattle or men given to Thor; these they called *hlaut* (sacrifice-blood), and *hlaut-bolli* (sacrifice-bowl). The *hlaut* was to be sprinkled on men and cattle, and the cattle were to be used for the people (to eat) when the sacrificing feasts were held. The men whom they sacrificed were to be thrown down into the spring which was outside near the doors, which they called *blót-kelda*. The cross-beams which had been in the temple were in the hall at Hof, when Olaf Jónsson had it built; he had them all split asunder, and yet they were still very thick" (Kjalnesinga, c. 2).

"On Thorsness, where Thórólf Mostrarskegg landed, there was a very holy place (helgi-stad); and there still stands Thor's stone, on which they broke [1] those men whom they sacrificed, and near by is that *dom-ring* where they were sentenced to be sacrificed" (Landnama ii., c. 12).

This passage shows that the dom-ring where men were sacrificed was different from the dom-ring where the people met to judge; the former seems to have been always made with stones, while the latter, as we have seen from Egil's Saga, were made with hazel poles. It is probable that many of the *dom-rings* which are now seen were used as sacrificing places.

Not far from the large ship-form grave of Blomsholm, in a silent pine forest, stands a magnificent *Dom-ring* (see next page), a witness of the great past. What unwritten records are stamped upon its stones! what unrevealed histories lie for ever buried from our sight! how much they would tell if they could speak! The ring is about 100 feet in diameter, and is composed of ten standing stones. Near by is the eleventh. In the centre is a huge boulder, overlooking the rest; its uncovered part stands about 5 feet above the ground; it is 9 feet long by 7 feet wide.

"When Thórd gellir established the fjordungathing (quarter Things) he let the Thing of the Vestfirdingar be there (on Thorsness); thither men from all the Vestfjords were to come. There may still be seen the *dom-ring* within which

---

[1] Meaning. broke the backs of.

men were doomed to be sacrificed. Within the ring stands
Thor's stone, on which those were broken who were used for

Fig. 778.—Dom-ring, or sacrificing ring, Blomsholm, Bohuslän.

sacrifice, and the blood-stains can still be seen on the stone "
(Eyrbyggja, c. 10).

Many dom-rings [1] are seen in the country without the sacrificing stone in the centre; these may have been used as enclosures for duelling, while others similar to the above engraving may have been horg or sacred altars.

Sacrificing mounds, and apparently mounds in which offerings were deposited, are mentioned, but unfortunately we have no description of them.

"King Olaf [2] had there (Karlsá) broken the sacrificial mound of the heathens; it was so called because usually, when they had great sacrifices for a good season, or for peace, all were to go to this mound, and there sacrifice prescribed animals; they carried thither much property, and put it into the mound before they went away. King Olaf got very much property there" (Fornmanna Sögur v. 164.)

Fig. 779. —Probably a sacrificing slab, on a rocky ridge at Viala, Vingåkers parish, Södermanland, overlooking Lake Kolsnaren; 7 feet 10 inches in length, 5 feet 10 inches in width, and 10 inches thick.

"A mound composed of earth and pure pfennings; for thither must be carried a handful of silver and a handful of mould for every one who dies, and also for every one who is born. Odd said: 'Then kinsman Gudmund you shall go ashore with your men to the mound this night, according to this man's direction; and I will take care of the ships with my men.' They did this, and went to the mound, where they collected as much money as they could carry, and with their burden returned to the ships. Odd was well satisfied with the results, and delivered the man into their keeping. 'Keep good watch over him,' he said, 'for his eyes are all the time turned towards the shore, so that he could not have found it as disagreeable there as he says.' Odd with his men then

---

[1] Not far from nearly every one of the (twenty) dom-rings of Nerike there is a spring tending to confirm the Icelandic tradition of their use.

[2] King Olaf was on an expedition into France.

2 B 2

went ashore, and up to the mound. Gudmund and Sigurd, meanwhile watching the ships, put the man between them, and began to sift away the mould from the silver; but when they least expected it he jumped up and overboard, and swam towards the land. Gudmund snatched a harpoon and shot after him; it pierced the calf of his leg, but he reached the shore and disappeared in the forest. When Odd with his companions arrived at the mound, they each decided to take burdens according to their strength, but on no account heavier than could be easily carried "[1] (Orvar Odd's Saga, c. 9 & 10).

Among the human sacrifices were those called *blódorn* (blood eagle), so called on account of the skin or flesh being cut down the whole back to the ribs, from both sides of the spine, in the shape of an eagle, and of the lungs being drawn through the wound. This special mode of sacrifice seems to have been practised on the slayer of a man's father.[2]

"After King Harald Fairhair's sons had grown up they became very unruly, and fought within the country. The sons of Snœfrid, Halfdan Háleg (high leg) and Gudröd Ljómi, slew Rögnvalld Mœra Jarl. This made Harald very angry, and Halfdan fled westward over the sea, but Gudröd got reconciled to his father. Halfdan went to the Orkneys, and Einar Jarl fled from the isles to Scotland, while Halfdan made himself king of the Orkneys. Einar Jarl returned the same year, and when they met a great battle took place, in which Einar was victorious, and Halfdan jumped overboard. The following morning they found Halfdan on Rinar's hill. The Jarl had a blood eagle (blodörn) cut on his back with a sword, and gave him to Odin for victory. After that he had a mound thrown up over Halfdan. When the news of this reached Norway his brothers were very angry, and threatened to go to the islands and avenge him; but this Harald prevented. Somewhat later Harald went westward across the sea to the isles; Einar went away from the islands, and over to Caithness (Katanes). After this men intervened and they became reconciled. Harald laid a tribute on the islands, and ordered them to pay sixty marks of gold. Einar Jarl offered to pay the tribute, and in return possess all the *odals* (allodial rights) This the bœndr agreed to, for the rich thought

---

[1] Odd evidently, like some other of his countrymen, as seen in this narrative, was not orthodox in the religion of his fathers, for he robbed the graves.

[2] Cf. also Ragnar Lodbrók, 18; Norna Gest. 6; Olaf Tryggvason. 179; Sigurdar Kvida Fafnisbana ii., 26; Orkneyinga Saga, ch. 8

they would buy them back, and the poor had not property enough to pay the tribute. Einar paid it, and for long after the jarls possessed all the odals, until Sigurd Jarl gave them up to the men of the Orkneys. Einar Jarl ruled long over the Orkneys, and died on a sick bed " (Flateyjarbók, p. 224, vol. i.).

The custom of a man giving himself to Odin on a sick bed by marking himself or being marked with the point of a spear, probably arose from the disgrace which was supposed to attach to a man who died unwounded in his bed, and not in battle. Odin himself[1] followed this practice, which enabled a man to come to Valhalla. When tired of life, or of old age, men gave themselves to Odin by throwing themselves from the rocks.

Eirik the victorious, who fought against Styrbjörn, gave himself to Odin in order to get the victory; and Harald Hilditonn was killed by Odin himself, because he had become so old.

The earliest account given of a human sacrifice in the North is that of Domaldi, which, if we may trust the genealogies, took place about the beginning of the Christian era.

"Domaldi inherited and ruled the land after his father Visbur. In his days there was in Sweden great hunger and famine; then the Swedes made large sacrifices at Uppsalir. The first autumn they sacrificed oxen, but the season did not improve; the second autumn they sacrificed men, but the season was the same or worse; the third autumn the Swedes came in crowds to Uppsalir when the sacrifice was to take place. The chiefs held their consultations, and agreed that the hard years were owing to their king, and that they must sacrifice him for good years, and should attack and slay him, and redden the altars with his blood. And thus they did" (Ynglinga Saga, ch. 18).

"Before the holding of the Althing (in the year 1000) in Iceland the heathens held a meeting, and resolved to sacrifice two men from every district of the land (Iceland was divided into four quarters), and to invoke their gods that they should not let Christianity spread over the country. Hjalti and Gizur had another meeting with the Christians, and said they would have human sacrifices as many as the

---

[1] Ynglinga Saga, 10.

heathens, adding : 'They sacrifice the worst men and cast them down from rocks and cliffs, but we will choose them for their virtues, and call it a victory-gift to our Lord Jesus Christ; we shall live the better, and more warily against sin than before. Gizur and I will give ourselves as a victory-gift on the behalf of our district ' " (Biskupa Sögur i.).

From the following passage it will be seen that when Christianity gained a footing in Iceland, human sacrifices were abandoned :—

" Thorólf Heljarskegg (Hel-beard) settled in Forsœludal (Iceland) ; he was a very overbearing man and unpopular, and caused many a quarrel and uproar in the district. He made himself a stronghold (virki) south at Fridmundará, a short way from Vatnsdalsá, in a ravine; a ness was between the ravine and the river, and a large rock in front of it. He was suspected of sacrificing men, and there was not one in the whole valley that was more hated than he" (Vatnsdœla, ch. 16).

Hallstein, an Icelandic chief, son of the Norwegian chief, Thorólf Mostrarskegg,

" Dwelt at Hallsteinsnes. There Hallstein sacrificed his son, in order that Thor might send him high-seat-pillars (126 feet); thereafter a tree came on his land, sixty-three ells in length and two fathoms (6 ells = 12 feet) thick; this was used for his high-seat-pillars, and of it are made the high-seat-pillars of nearly every farm in the Thverfjords " (Landnama ii., c. 23).[1]

---

[1] Gisla Suisson mentions the same.

CHAPTER XXIII.

RELIGION.—IDOLS AND WORSHIP OF MEN AND ANIMALS, ETC.

The introduction of idol worship—The gods magnificently dressed—Besmearing the gods—Descriptions of the gods in temples—Amulets representing the gods—Worship of men after death—Animal worship—Worship of groves and natural objects—Fire regarded as holy.

IT is impossible to tell at what time idols or representations of the gods came to be introduced; it is however certain from the Sagas, that they were already very common in the temple before Christian missionaries came to preach a new religion. At some period, and we know not how the change took place, we see that likenesses were made to represent some of the gods, which were often adorned with fine clothes and ornaments of silver and gold, and as a rule stood on an elevation or pedestal, which also seems to have served as an altar.[1] Occasionally they were besmeared with fat, possibly to give them a bright appearance.

There must have been many idols representing different persons who were worshipped besides the Asar, as we find that Thorgerd Hordabrud was also represented.

In the great temple in Mœri, in Norway, all the gods were seated on chairs, and the idol of Thor was magnificently adorned with precious metal. This god was also in the temple belonging to Hakon and Gudbrand in Gudbrandsdal.

"Then they (Fridthjof and Björn) heard that Beli's sons were in Baldr's hagi at the *disablót*;[2] they went up there, and asked Hallvard·and Ásmund to damage all ships small and large which were near; and so they did. They went to the door in Baldr's hagi; Fridthjof wanted to go in; Björn told him to be wary, but he wanted to go alone. Fridthjof asked

---

[1] Olaf Tryggvason, Hkr., c. 76; Halfredar Saga, 6; Vatnsdæla, c. 10, 16.

[2] See p. 411, sacrifice to the Disir

him to stay outside and keep watch. Then Fridthjof went in, and saw that few people were in the *disar-hall*. The kings were at the *disablót* and sat drinking; there was fire on the floor, and their wives sat at the fireside and warmed the gods, and some besmeared them with grease and wiped them with a cloth " (Fridthjof's Saga, 9).

When Sigmund was ready to start for an expedition to avenge his father—

" The Jarl (Hakon) went out with him and asked, ' What belief hast thou ? ' Sigmund answered, ' I believe in my might and strength.' The Jarl replied, ' It must not be so; thou must seek for help where I put all my trust, which is in Thorgerd Hördabrud. Let us go to her, and try to get luck for thee from her.' Sigmund told him to do as he liked; they went to the woods, and then, by a little by-path, to an open space in the forest where there was a house with a fence around it; this house was very fine, and the carvings were ornamented with gold and silver. Hakon and Sigmund entered with a few men; there were many gods, and so many glass-windows, that there was no shadow anywhere. A splendidly dressed woman was in the inner part of the house opposite the entrance. The Jarl threw himself down, and lay long before her feet; then he rose and told Sigmund that they must make her some sacrifice, and put silver on the stool before her. ' But as a mark that she will accept, I want her to let loose the ring she wears on her arm; thou, Sigmund, wilt get luck from that ring.' The Jarl took hold of the ring, but it seemed to Sigmund that she clenched her fist and he did not get it. He threw himself down a second time before her, and Sigmund saw that he wept; he rose, and took hold of the ring, which then was loose, and gave it to Sigmund, who promised not to part with the ring " (Færeyinga Saga, ch. 23).

When Hakon Jarl, after having been baptized in Denmark, had again adopted the practice of the pagan religion,

" He heard of a temple which was the largest in Gautland, while it was heathen. In that temple were one hundred gods. Hakon took all the property which was in it. The men who guarded the temple and the sacrificing-place fled, while some of them were slain; Hakon went back to his ships with the property and burnt and destroyed all that he met with on the way, and had very much property when he came down. While he was making this ravage in Gautland, Ottar Jarl, who ruled over a great part of Gautland, heard of it; he quickly started and gathered all the land host against Hakon Jarl, and attacked him. They at once began the battle; Hakon was overpowered, and at last fled with his men, and went to Norway. Thereafter Ottar Jarl summoned a *Thing*, and declared at it that Hakon should be called *varg-i-veum* (wolf in the holy place), because, said he, no man had done worse deeds, for he had destroyed the highest temple in Gautland, and wrought many other evil deeds; that no one knew any example of such things, and that wherever he went he should have that name" (Jómsvikinga Saga, ch. 12).

" King Olaf Tryggvason (995–1000) went to Thrandheim to christianize the bœndr; they agreed that he should go into their temple and observe their customs. He went into the temple, with a few of his men and some of the bœndr. They were all unarmed except the king, who had a staff ornamented with gold in his hand. As they entered there was no lack of carved idols; Thor sat in the middle, for he was most worshipped; he was large and ornamented all over with gold and silver; he sat in a splendid chariot, to which were harnessed two very well-made wooden he-goats. Both the chariot and the he-goats rested on wheels, and the rope around their horns was of twisted silver. All was made with wonderful skill" (Flateyjarbók i., p. 319).

Votive offerings of jewels and other valuable objects have been made in temples and churches in all lands and ages, and to this day the practice holds in some Roman and Greek Catholic countries.

The use of small images as amulets by the Northmen is shown by Kálf's answer when asked by the King (Olaf Tryggvason) where Halfred was.

"'He probably still adheres to his custom of sacrificing secretly; he has the image of Thor made of a tooth in his purse, and too little is told to thee, lord, about him, and thou canst not see how he really is.' The King asked them to call Halfred that he might answer for himself. Halfred came. The King said, 'Is it true of thee, that thou sacrificest?' 'It is not true, lord,' answered Halfred; 'now search my purse; here no trick is possible, even if I had wanted to use one.' Nothing of the kind was found with him" (Olaf Tryggvason's Saga).

" When King Olaf (Tryggvason) had been a short while in Thrandheim he heard a rumour that some men in Thrandheim still kept up heathendom, and that the idol of Frey stood there unbroken, and that those men who were there sacrificed to the idol. When he heard this he was displeased, and at the time he got these evil tidings he was at a feast. There were also some men from Thrandheim with him. He accused them of sacrificing to Frey as some witnesses had told him, and as they knew that they were not guiltless they did not deny it boldly, but would not acknowledge it. He said: 'It will be seen how much of your words is true, and I will try it in this way—I command you to break the idol of Frey, to which I am told you sacrifice, and if you will not do that I believe that the accusation I bring against you is true.' They answered: 'We will not break the idol of Frey, for we have served him long, and it has helped us well.' He said: 'I and my men will break it though you forbid it.' They answered: 'Certainly we will forbid and hinder the destruction of Frey, though we expect that he will valiantly defend himself and help us if we follow him boldly, for he has more power than thou thinkest.' He said: 'This shall be tried. You shall defend Frey and I will attack him with God's grace and the help of good men. Let him then defend himself if he is able. To-morrow we shall hold a *Thing* where I appoint. I will take Frey there and judge him boldly, and slay him, and do the good for you which God teaches me, if you will leave your false belief.' They did not think this very advisable, but saw it had to be as the king wished. They went to their ships and rowed in the fjord and strove with both sails and oars. The luck of the king was stronger than the witchcraft of Frey and the evil belief of those who followed him, and therefore it happened as the best one (God) wished, and the king's ship went much faster and he got first to the temple. When he came ashore his men saw some stud horses near the road which they said belonged to Frey. The king mounted a stallion and let others take the geldings, and they rode to the temple. He alighted from the stallion, went into the temple, and struck down the gods from their altars. Then he took Frey under his arm and carried him out to the horse, and shut up the temple. He rode with Frey to the meeting and came before those summoned. His land-tent was pitched, and he waited there. Now the men of Thrandheim came to the temple and opened it and went in. They saw that Frey had disappeared and the other gods were maimed, and they knew for certain that the king had caused this. They went to the meeting. When they had come there the king spoke mostly of things connected with the rule of the land and the laws. He then sent men to his tent and bad them carry Frey out, and when he was brought to the king the king took him and set him up and said: 'Do you know this man?' They answered: 'We know him.' 'Who is he then?' said the king. 'One whom thou dost not know; he is Frey, our god.' He said: 'What good can Frey do, that you think it needful or a great necessity to believe in him?' They answered: 'We thought him very powerful until within a few years.' 'Why is he less powerful now?' said the king. They answered: 'Because he is now angry with us, which thou causest, for since thou didst tell us to believe in another god, and we partly followed thy persuasions, he thinks we have forsaken him, and therefore will not take any care of us.' He then said, as if in mockery or jest: 'It is unfortunate that Frey is angry with you, but in what way did he before show the power which you now miss?' They answered: 'He often spoke with us and foretold future things, and gave us good years and peace.' He said: 'I maintain that Frey has not spoken with you, but the devil himself.' . . . He took a large axe and went to Frey, and said: 'Now I will try, Frey, if thou canst talk and answer me.' Frey was silent. 'If thou,' said the king, 'canst not or wilt not, then may the one who is in thee, and has long strengthened thee, answer.' . . . Frey was silent. The king said: 'Still I speak to thee, Frey; if thou canst give to men strength or power, then spare it not, and do what thou art able to do, and if thou sleepest, awake and defend thee, for now I will attack thee.' He raised his hand and cut off Frey's hand, but he did not move. Then he struck one blow after the other until he had cut asunder the whole idol. . . . (Flateyjarbók, I. Olaf Tryggvason).

The gods were not the only beings worshipped, for we have some examples of men being worshipped after their death.

"Olaf Geirstada-alf had a dream, at which he was much surprised, and which he would not tell when asked. He then summoned a *Thing* from all his realm, which was held at Geirstadir. The king asked the people to finish their cases, and afterwards he would make known why he had summoned them, as many might think that there was little reason for it. 'I will tell my dream here,' said he. 'It seemed to me that a large black and fierce-looking bull entered the land from the east; it went about the whole realm. It seemed that so many men fell before its breath, that only half were left. Finally it killed my hird.' He asked them to explain it, for he knew it must signify something. They answered that he himself could guess best what it meant. He added: ' There have long·been peace and good seasons in this kingdom, but many more people than it could sustain. The bull of which I dreamt is probably a foreboding of a sickness which will begin in the eastern part of this land, and cause many deaths. My hird will be attacked last, and it is most probable that I shall follow, for I cannot, more than others, survive my destined death-day. Now this dream is explained, and it will prove to be true. I advise the multitude here assembled to throw up a large mound out on the cape, and make a fence across it higher up, so that no cattle can go thither. Into the mound let every man of prominence put half a mark of silver to be buried with him. Before the disease ceases, I shall be placed in the mound. I warn all not to behave like some who worship by sacrifice, after their death, those in whom they trusted while alive, for I think dead men can do nothing useful. It may also happen that those who are worshipped will be suddenly bewitched. I think the same evil spirits (*vœttir*) sometimes do useful, sometimes harmful things. I fear much that a famine will come in the land after I have been *mounded,* and nevertheless we shall be worshipped and afterwards, bewitched in spite of ourselves.' It happened as King Olaf said, and according to his explanation of the dream. The disease came before it was expected, many died, and all men of any prominence were laid in the mound; for King Olaf immediately sent men to make an exceedingly large mound, and the people made the fence according to his advice. It also happened that the hird died last and was *mound laid.* At last Olaf died, and was quickly laid among his men with much property and the mound was closed. Then fewer people died. Bad seasons and famine followed. It was then resolved to offer sacrifice to King Olaf for good seasons, and they called him Geirstada-alf" (Flateyjarbók ii. c. 6).

"There was a king named Godmund in Jotunheim; his farm was called Grund, and the *herad* (district) in which it was situated Glæsisvellir. He was a powerful man and old, as well as all his men, and lived for so many generations that people believed Odains Akr (the land of the undying) to be in his realm. The place is so healthy that sickness and old age vanish from every man who comes there, and nobody can die there. It is said that after the death of Godmund, men worshipped him and called him their god. King Godmund had a son, Hofund, a seer and a wise man; he was made judge over all the adjoining lands; he never gave a wrong judgment;

nobody dared or needed to doubt his judgment" (Hervara Saga, c. 1).

"Thórólf Smjör (butter, because he said Iceland was so fertile that butter dripped from every blade of grass) was the son of Thorstein Skrofa, son of Grim, who was worshipped after his death on account of his popularity and called Kamban" (Landnama i., ch. 14).

Animal Worship.—The worship of animals and birds seems to have sometimes taken place.

Once some men went to Eystein and told him that a large host had come into his realm so hard to deal with that it had devastated all the land, and left no house standing.

"When Eystein heard these tidings he thought he knew who these vikings were. He sent an *arrow-message* all over his realm and summoned all who were willing to help him and could wield a shield. 'Let us take with us the cow Sibilja, our god, and let her run in front, and I believe that, as before, they will not be able to stand her bellowing. I urge you all to valiantly drive away this large and evil host.' This was done, and Sibilja let loose; Ivar saw her coming, and heard her fierce bellowing; he bade all the host make a great noise both with weapons and war-cries, lest they should hear the voice of the evil beast which went against them. Ivar told his hearers to carry him forward as far as they could, and when the cow came at them to throw him on her, and then either he or she should die; and to take a large tree and cut it into the form of a bow, and also bring him arrows; this strong bow was now brought, and the large arrows he had ordered, which were not manageable by any other. Ivar then urged every one to do his best. Their host went onward with great rushing and tumult, and Ivar was carried in front of their ranks. The bellowing of Sibilja sounded so loud that they heard it as well as if they had been silent and stood still; they were so startled that all, except the brothers. wanted to fight among themselves. When this wonder was going on, those who carried Ivar saw that he drew his bow as if it were a weak elm twig, and they thought he was going to draw his arrows beyond the point.[1] They heard his bowstring sound louder than they had ever heard before; they saw that his arrows flew as swiftly as if he had shot with the strongest cross-bow, and so

---

[1] I.e , draw the string so hard that the point of the arrow is inside the curve.

straight that one arrow went into each eye of Sibilja ; and she stumbled and fell down on her head, and her bellowing was much more than before. When she came at them he bid them to throw him on her, and he was as light to them as a little child, for they were not very near to the cow when they threw him ; he came down on the back of Sibilja, and became as heavy as if a rock fell on her, and every bone in her was broken and she was killed.

" Although the sons of Ragnar were valiant, they could not stand both an overwhelming force of men and witchcraft ; nevertheless they made a stout resistance, and fought like warriors with great renown. Eirik and Agnar were in the front that day, and often went through the ranks of King Eystein, but Agnar fell " (Ragnar Lodbrok's Saga).

" King Olaf was at a feast in Ögvaldsnes. One evening there came to the farm an old man, very wise in talk, one-eyed, with a hood low down over his face ; he could tell of every country. He began to talk with the king, who liked it very much and asked about many things, but he was able to answer any question, and the king did not go to bed for a long time that night. Then the king asked if he knew who Ögvald was, after whom the bœr and the ness (cape) were named. The guest said he had been a king and a great warrior, and had worshipped a cow more than anything else, and taken it with him wherever he went, as he thought it wholesome to drink its milk. Ögvald fought against a king called Varin, and fell in the battle ; he was *mounded* there a short way from the bœr and the bauta-stones raised, which stand there still. In another place near to this bœr the cow was *mounded* (Olaf Tryggvason's Saga, c. 71).

" Floki Vilgerdarson, a great Viking, made himself ready in Rogaland to search for Snow-land (Iceland). He made a large sacrifice to the three ravens, which were to show him the way. They sailed to the Faroes, and then put to sea with the three ravens, to which sacrifice had been made in Norway ; when the first was let loose it flew in the direction of the stern ; the second rose into the air, and came back to the ship ; the third flew in front of the prow in the direction in which they found the land.

" They landed at the place called Vatnsfjord, in Breidifjord. The fjord was so full of fish that they neglected to gather hay on account of the fishing, and during the winter therefore all their cattle died. The spring was rather cold there, and Floki went up on a mountain on the north side of the fjord, and on the other side saw a fjord filled with ice. Therefore they called the land Iceland " (Landnama i., c. 2).

Natural objects, such as groves and the sacrificing stone,

were worshipped, and no one was allowed to look at Helgafell (a holy mountain) before he had washed himself in the morning, and no cattle were to be killed there.

"Eyvind, the son of Lodin, settled in the valley of Flatey (his land extending) as far as Gunnsteinar (Gunn-rocks), which he worshipped."

"Thorir Snepil took up the whole of Fnjóskadal to Odeila, and dwelt at Lund (grove); he worshipped the grove" (Landnama iii., ch. 17).

"Hord's brother-in-law Indridi wished to slay the bondi Thorstein Gullknapr (gold-button), and waited for him on the way to his sacrificing house, whither he was wont to go. When Thorstein came, he entered the sacrificing house and fell on his face before the stone he worshipped, which stood there, and then he spoke to it. Indridi stood outside the house; he heard this sung in the stone:—

Thou hast hither | Before the sun shines,
For the last time | The bard Indridi
With death-fated feet | Will justly reward thee
Trodden the ground; | For thy evil doings.

"Thorstein went out and home; Indridi distinctly saw him going, and told him not to run so fast. He went in front of him, and at once struck him with the sword of Soti under the chin so that his head flew off" (Hord's Saga, c. 37).

"On the ness stands a mountain, which he (Thórólf Mostrarskegg) held in such reverence that no one was allowed to look on it unwashed, and nothing was to be killed on it, neither men nor cattle. He called it Helgafell (holy mountain), and he believed he would go thither when he died, as well as all his kinsmen on the ness. On the point at which Thor had landed he made the place for all judgments, and there established a *herad-thing* (a *Thing* for the district). This place was so holy that he would not allow the field to be defiled in any manner" (Eyrbyggja, c. 4).

Fire seems to have been looked upon as holy; and it was sometimes the practice to ride round the land with fire, or to throw a burning arrow, so as to signify ownership.

"Jorund godi (temple-priest), son of Hrafn Heimski, settled west of Fljót, where it is now called Svertingsstadir; there he raised a large temple. A small piece of land lay unsettled east of Fljót, between Krossá (river) and Joldustein; Jorund went

with fire around this, and made it the property of the temple "
(Landnama v., c. 3).

"Onund the wise took up land in the valley east of Merki-
gil. When Eirik (from Goddalir) wanted to settle in the
valley west of it, Onund threw sacrificing-rods to ascertain
when Eirik would come and take up the land. Onund then
forestalled him, and shot with a burning arrow across the river,
and thus took possession of the land west of it and dwelt on it "
(Landnama iii., c. 8).

The chief Blundketil was burnt in his house by his foes.
When the chief Tungu-Odd heard of it he rode to the place
with the son of the burnt chief.

"Odd rode to a house which was not quite burnt down.
He stretched out his hand and pulled a rafter of birch-wood
out of the house, and then rode against the sun (from west to
east) round the houses with the burning brand and said:
'Here I settle on this land, for I do not see any homestead;
may the witnesses present hear it. He then whipped his
horse and rode away" (Hœnsa Thori's Saga, c. 9).

CHAPTER XXIV.

RELIGION.—THE NORNIR AND VALKYRIAS.

The shaping of man's future at his birth—The three Nornir—Their dwelling-place—Their kin—Good and Evil Nornir—They water the ash Yggdrasil—The maids of Odin—They determine the issue of battle—Choose the warriors for Valhalla—Figurative names—They ride through the air—Their appearance—They help warriors in battle—Their sojourn among men—The first and second songs of Helgi.

IT was believed by the Northmen that the future life of all men was shaped at their birth by genii called *Nornir*, who preordained the fates of men and all that happened in the world. The gods themselves seem to have been under their control.

There were three Nornir, called *Urd*, the past; *Verdandi*, the present; and *Skuld*, the future, they dwelt by Urd's well, situated at the foot of the ash Yggdrasil, whose roots they watered with their wisdom and the experience of the past:[1] they spun the threads of fate at the birth of every child, and measured the boundaries of his doings, and the days of his life.[2]

The names of these three Nornir were to those men of old the embodiment and philosophy of life. They could not have existed without their fathers before them, hence Urd was the symbol of the great past.

Verdandi, the present, symbolised the present life itself, consequently was closely connected with Urd.

---

[1] Cf. also Sigrdrifumál, 17; Helgi Hundingsbani; Norna Gest; Flateyjarbók; Fornaldar Sögur, i. Later Edda; Orkneyinga; Egil's Saga; Hávamál; Atlakvida.

[2] Helgakvida Hundingsbana.

Skuld, the future, represented the growth, the shooting forward, and was an inseparable part of the triad.

"There stands a fine hall under the ash, near the well, and from that hall come three maidens, who are named Urd, Verdandi, and Skuld. These forecast the lives of men, and are called Nornir.

In Vafthrúdnismal, Odin asks Vafthrúdnir—

Much have I travelled,	Who are the maidens
Much have I tried,	That soar over the sea;
Many powers have I known;	The wise-minded ones travel.

In Voluspa, Heid the sybil, in her vision—

Thence come three maidens,[1]	Who raised on the Idavöll[2]
Knowing many things,	Altars and high temples;
Out of the hall	They laid hearths,
Which stands under the tree;	They wrought wealth,
One was called Urd,	They shaped tongs,
Another Verdandi,	And made tools.
The third Skuld;	
They carved on wood tablets,	They played chess on the grass-plot;
They chose lives,	They were cheerful;
They laid down laws	They did not lack
For the children of men,	Anything of gold
They chose the fates of men.	Until three
They disturbed the peace of the	Very mighty
golden age of the gods.	Thurs maidens came
The Asar met,	From Jótunheim.

"But there are other Nornir who come to every one that is born, to shape his life. Some are of the kindred of the gods, others of Alfar kin, and some of Dvergar kin" (Gylfaginning, c. 15).

Vafthrúdnir.	Of the maidens of *Mögthrasir.*
	They are the only destinies
Three great rivers	That are in the world,
Fall over the field	Though they dwell with Jötnar.

In time the number of Nornir seems to have increased.

---

[1] These three maidens came from Jotunheim, the home of the Jotnar; here they are no doubt meant to designate the three Nornir, who came and disturbed the peace of the golden age by establishing past, present, and future, i e., change, fluctuation, development, and growth.

[2] Idavoll, *ida,* movement; *voll,* plain. This stanza tells of the golden age when the Asars were happy and lacked nothing.

In Fafnismál, **Sigurd** asks the following question of Fafnir :—

Sigurd.	*Fafnir.*
Tell me, Fafnir,	Very different born
As thou art said to be wise	I think the Nornir are;
And know many things well,	They own not kin together,
Who are the maidens	Some are Asar-born,
That are helping in need	Others are Alfar-born,
And deliver mothers of children?	Others are daughters of Dvalin.[1]
	(Fafnismál.)

Atli says to his wife Gudrún :—

	Gudrún.
The Nornir have just	It forebodes fire
Roused me	When one dreams of iron;
With forebodings of evil;	The anger of woman
I want thee to read them.	Means pride and sorrow;
Methought that thou,	I shall have to burn thee[2]
Gudrún, Gjúki's daughter,	Against sickness,
Didst thrust me through	Heal thee and help thee,
With a poisoned sword.	Though I hate thee.
	(Gudrúnarkvida, 11.)

" Gangleri said : ' If the Nornir rule the fates of men, they deal them out very unevenly, for some have a happy and rich life, while others have little property or praise—some a long life, some a short one.' Hár replied : ' Good Nornir, and of good kindred, forecast a happy life; but when men have evil fates, the evil Nornir cause it ' ' (Gylfaginning, c. 15).

The water with which the Nornir watered the ash Yggdrasil was considered holy.

" Further it is told that the Nornir who live at Urd's well take water out of it every day, and also the clay which lies round it, and pour it over the ash-tree that the branches may not dry up or grow rotten. This water is so holy that everything which comes into the well grows white like the film called *skjall* which lies next to the eggshell. The dew which falls thence on the earth is called honey-dew, and the bees feed on it. Two birds live in Urd's well, called swans, and from them has sprung the kin of birds with this name " (Gylfaginning, c. 16).

The Valkyrias were the maids of Odin, and were sent by him to determine the issue of battle, and choose those who were to

---

[1] Grimnismál, gives a somewhat similar account.

[2] Burn a spot on the skin as a cure.

2 c 2

fall and dwell with him in Valhalla. The belief in Valkyrias appears to have been of very great antiquity, and is one of the most striking, poetical, and grand features of the Asa faith. In no record of the religions that have come down to us do we find anything that would make us suppose that such belief ever existed in other parts of the world, and it was well adapted to the creed of a people among whom war and the conquest of other lands were leading features.

Heid in Voluspa gives the names of the Valkyrias and in her version we learn that

She saw Valkyrias	Gunn, Hild, Göndul,
Come from far off,	And Geirskögul;
Ready to ride	Now are numbered
To Goth-thjód.[1]	The maidens of Herjan,[2]
Skuld held a shield,	The Valkyrias ready
Skögul was next,	To ride over the ground.

So we see that originally the number of Valkyrias belonging to Odin was only six, afterwards their number increased. Sometimes they appear nine together, at others treble that number.

Others are mentioned in Grimnismal. Odin, speaking to Geirrod, says—

I want Hrist and Mist	Göll and Geirahöd,
To carry the horn to me;	Randgrid and Rádgrid,
Skeggjöld and Skögul,	And Reginleif,
Hild and Thrúd,	They carry ale to the Einherjar."[3]
Hlökk and Herfjötur,	

"Hjorvard and Sigrlin had a large and handsome son. He was silent, and no name had been fastened to him.[4] He sat on a mound, and saw nine Valkyrjas riding, and one of them seemed the foremost—she sang :—

Late wilt thou, Helgi,	On the Rodulsvellir,[6]
Rule over rings[5]	If thou art ever silent."

"The daughter of King Eylimi was Svava; she was a Valkyrja and rode over air and sea; she gave this name to Helgi, and often afterwards sheltered him in battles " (Helga Kvida Hjörvardssonar).

The following among other poetical and figurative names

---

[1] Thjód nation, nation of the Goths.
[2] Odin.
[3] Warriors.

[4] See pp. 31, 32.
[5] Wealth.
[6] Sun plains.

are given to the Valkyrias:—The maidens of victory, the goddesses of the fight, the graspers of spears, the witches of the shield, the maidens of the slain, the exultant ones, the strong one, the entangling one, the silent one, the storm-raisers. They are mentioned as riding through the air, over the sea, and amid the lightning, helmet-clad, with bloody brynjas, and glittering spears; the spear which carried death and victory being the emblem of Odin. When their horses shake their manes, the froth which comes from their bitted mouths drops as dew into the valleys, and hail falls from their nostrils into the woods.

The slain were called *Val* (chosen), and belonged to Odin. From the word *Val* are derived the names of Valkyrias, Valfödr (the father of the slain), Valhalla (the hall of the slain), Valól (field of battle, field of the slain), and probably also of those birds of prey which after the battle visited the field of action.

Skuld, the youngest of the three Nornir, who personified the future, followed the Valkyrias, probably in order to witness the decrees of fate given to men at their birth.

" There are others that have to serve in Valhöll, carry drink and take care of the table-dressing and the beer cups. These are called Valkyrias; Odin sends them to every battle; they choose death for men and rule victory. Gunn and Róta and the youngest Norn, Skuld, always ride to choose the slain and rule *man-slayings* " (Gylfaginning, ch. 36).

It was believed that during a battle warriors sometimes saw Valkyrias coming to their help: how grand and beautiful must have been the vision created in their mind by their faith in them, as they thought they saw them riding on their fiery steeds, and sweeping over the battle-field, by land or by sea. It is hard to realise a grander picture for a warrior to behold.

Helgi saw :—

Three times nine maidens,
But one rode foremost
A white maiden under helmet;
Their horses trembled,
From their manes fell

Dew into the deep dales,
Hail on the lofty woods;
Thence come good seasons among men,
All that I saw was loathsome to me.
[Helga Kvida Hjórvardssonar.]

Sometimes the Valkyrias came to earth and remained among men.

" Nidud was a king in Sweden. He had two sons and one daughter, whose name was Bodvild. There were three brothers, sons of the Finna-king, one Slagfinn, the other Egil, and the third Völund; they ran on snow-shoes, and hunted wild beasts. They came to the Ulfdal, where there is a lake called Ulfsjár (Wolf's lake), and there made themselves a house. Early one morning they found at the shore of the lake three women who were spinning flax, near them lay their swan-skins; they were Valkyrias. Two of them were daughters of King Hlòdver (Louis), Hladgunn Svanhvit (Svan-white), and Hervor Alvitr (All-wise); and the third Ölrún, daughter of Kjar of Valland. The brothers took them to their house. Egil got Ölrún; Slagfinn, Swan-white; and Volund, All-wise. There they dwelt for seven winters; after which the women went to visit battle-fields, and did not return. Then Egil went on snow-shoes to look for Ölrún, and Slagfinn for Svan-white, while Völund remained in Ulfdal. He was the most skilled smith that is spoken of in ancient Sagas. King Nidud had him captured, as is told in the song " (Volundar Kvida).

Helga Kvida gives an account of how Sigrun, a Valkyria, betrothed herself to Helgi, and of how she comes with other Valkyrias to protect him. Their appearance is thus described :—

Then gleams flashed	The southern disir[3]
From Logafjoll,[1]	If they would home
And from those gleams	With hildings[4]
Came lightning;	That night go;
The high ones[2] rode helmet-clad	There had been clang of bowstrings.
Down on the Himinvangar;	
Their brynjas were	But from the horse
Blood-bespattered,	The daughter of Högni (Sigrun)
And from their spears	Hushed the clatter of shields;
Sprang rays of light.	She said to the king,
	I think we have
Early (in the day) asked	Other work to do
From the wolf-lair	Than drink beer
The *doyling* (the king) about this	With the ring-breaker (Helgi)

---

[1] Fire-mountain. Here the text is corrupted, but I follow Bugge in the suggestion that this is a place-name, the battle taking place on the plain beneath the Logafjoll, from which the Valkyrias come down to take the slain.

[2] The Valkyrias.

[3] Valkyrias are here called disir, guardian spirits, and seem to come from the South, the ancient home of the Asar.

[4] Chiefs. Helgi invited them to come home with him and his chiefs that night, and they would not.

In the second song of this poem we learn the mode of thought, the religious ideas and customs of the people of the North, and glean some new facts; that men and women were sometimes thought to be born again; that Helgi derived his name from Helgi Hjorvardson, and that he was brought up by Hagal. His foes, and not the sons of Hunding, search for him, but he escapes by dressing himself in the garb of a bondwoman. This episode of his life and the following fights must have taken place after those of the first song. The connection between the two poems is somewhat obscure.

"Granmar was a powerful king who lived at Svarinshaug; he had many sons, among them Hodbrod, Gudmund, and Starkad. Hödbrod was at an appointed meeting[1] of kings; he betrothed himself to Sigrun,[2] daughter of Högni. When she heard this she rode with Valkyrias over the sea and air to search for Helgi. He was then at Logafjoll (Fire-mountains), and had fought against the sons of Hunding; there he slew Alf and Eyjolf, Hjorvard and Hervard; he was very weary of the fight, and sat down at Arastein (Eagle's stone); where Sigrun found him, threw her arms about his neck and kissed him, and told him of her errand, as is related in the old Volsunga-kvida:—[3]

Sigrun sought
The glad king,[4]
She took Helgi's
Hand in hers;

She kissed and greeted
The king under his helmet;
Then did his mind
Turn to the maiden.

She said she loved
With all her mind
The son of Sigmund
Ere she had seen him.

I was to Hodbrod
In the host betrothed,
But another chief
I wanted to have.

Yet I fear, chief,
The anger of my kinsmen;
I have broken
The *mind-marriage* of my father.[5]

The maiden of Högni
Spoke not against her mind;
She said she would
Have the love of Helgi.

Helgi.

Do not care for
The wrath of Högni,
Nor for the ill-will
Of thy kin;
Thou wilt, young maiden,
Live with me;
Thou, good maiden, hast kinsmen
Whom I do not fear.

---

[1] We find that kings sometimes had meetings among themselves.

[2] Probably she was betrothed by her father, not being present herself.

[3] From this we see that this beautiful story is derived from the lost Volsunga-kvida (a great loss), and from which Volsunga itself is probably mostly taken.

[4] Glad because of victory.

[5] The marriage which her father had set his mind upon.

"Helgi then gathered a large fleet, and sailed to Frekastein (Wolf's stone). At sea they met with a dangerous tempest, and lightning flashed down on the ships. They saw nine Valkyrias riding in the air, and recognised Sigrun; then the storm abated, and they came safely to the land. The sons of Granmar sat on a rock when the ships sailed towards the shore.

"Gudmund rode home with news of war; then the sons of Granmar gathered a host. Many kings came there. There were Högni, the father of Sigrun, and his sons Bragi and Dag. There was a great battle, and the sons of Granmar fell, with all their chiefs, except Dag, son of Högni, whose life was spared, and who promised on oath to follow the Völsungs. Sigrun went among the slain, and found Hodbrod near death's door. She sang:—

Sigrun of Sevafjöll[1]
Will not,
King Hödbrod,
Fall into thy arms;
Gone is the life
Of Granmar's sons;
The grey steeds[2] of jötun-women
Many corpses tear.

She met Helgi, who answered:—

All is not given to thee,
Mighty wight;[3]
For I say the Nornir
Wield some power.
This morning fell
At Frekastein
Bragi and Högni;
I was their slayer.

"Helgi married Sigrun, and they had sons; but Helgi did not live long. Högni's son Dag sacrificed to Odin for revenge on his father, and Odin lent him his spear. Dag met his brother-in-law Helgi at Fjoturlund; he thrust the spear through him, Helgi fell, and Dag rode to Sevafjoll and told Sigrun the tidings:—

Loth am I, sister,
To tell thee the sorrow,
For unwilling have I
Made my sister weep;
This morning fell
At Fjoturlund
The Budlung[4] who was
The best in the world,
And stood on
The neck of hildings.[5]

Sigrun.

Thee shall all
Oaths harm[6]
Which thou to Helgi
Hast sworn

---

[1] Sigrun speaks to the dying Hödbrod on the battle-field.

[2] Wolves.

[3] Meaning: "Everything is not in thy power, as the Nornir have great power also over the fates of men." The death of Helgi was against Sigrun's will.

[4] King.

[5] A custom found in the Old Testament (Joshua), of putting the foot on the subdued king's neck.

[6] Dag broke his oath, as we have seen before; and Sigrun cursed him for having done so.

At the bright
Waters of Leiptr [1]
And at the rain-cold
Rock of the sea.
The ship shall not move
Which should carry thee,
Though a fair wind to thy wish
Blows on it.
The horse shall not run
Which is to run with thee,
Though thou hast to
Escape from thy foes.

The sword shall not bite
Which thou drawest,
Except when it sings
About thy own head;
Then were the death
Of Helgi avenged,
If thou wert an outlaw
Out in the forest,
Lacking property
And all enjoyment,

And hadst not food
Unless thou tearest corpses.

Dag.

Mad art thou, sister,
And out of thy wits
As thou invokest curses
On thy brother;
Odin alone
Causes all the ills,
For between kinsmen
Runes of strife he bore.

Thy brother offers thee
Red rings, [2]
All Vandilsve [3]
And Vigdalir; [4]
Take half of my lands
As indemnity for sorrow,
Thou ring-adorned maiden
And thy sons.

"Sigrun was short-lived from grief and sorrow. It was the belief in olden times that men were reborn, but now it is called an old woman's story. It is said that Helgi and Sigrun were born again; he was then named Helgi Haddingjaskati, and she Kara, [5] Hálfdán's daughter, 'as is sung in the lay of Kara, [6] and she was a Valkyria.'" [Helgi Hundingsbani II.]

---

[1] Leiptr = flash of lightning. Probably this was a swift river, or waterfall.

[2] Here we see the custom of wergild, so often described in the Sagas.

[3] The temple of Vandil.

[4] Valleys of fight.

[5] Cf. also Helga Kvida Hjörvardsonar.

[6] The song of Kara is lost. Svafa in the first song, Sigrun in the second, is Svafa reborn; and Kara in the third and lost song is Sigrun reborn.

OTHER BOOKS FROM CGR PUBLISHING AT CGRPUBLISHING.COM

1939 New York World's Fair: The World of Tomorrow in Photographs

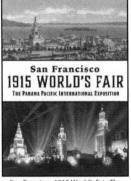

San Francisco 1915 World's Fair: The Panama-Pacific International Expo.

1904 St. Louis World's Fair: The Louisiana Purchase Exposition in Photographs

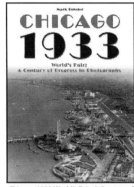

Chicago 1933 World's Fair: A Century of Progress in Photographs

19th Century New York: A Dramatic Collection of Images

The American Railway: The Trains, Railroads, and People Who Ran the Rails

The Aeroplane Speaks: Illustrated Historical Guide to Airplanes

The World's Fair of 1893 Ultra Massive Photographic Adventure Vol. 1

The World's Fair of 1893 Ultra Massive Photographic Adventure Vol. 2

The World's Fair of 1893 Ultra Massive Photographic Adventure Vol. 3

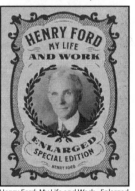

Henry Ford: My Life and Work - Enlarged Special Edition

Magnum Skywolf #1

Ethel the Cyborg Ninja Book 1

The Complete Ford Model T Guide: Enlarged Illustrated Special Edition

How To Draw Digital by Mark Bussler

Best of Gustave Doré Volume 1: Illustrations from History's Most Versatile...

OTHER BOOKS FROM CGR PUBLISHING AT CGRPUBLISHING.COM

Ultra Massive Video Game Console
Guide Volume 1

Ultra Massive Video Game Console
Guide Volume 2

Ultra Massive Video Game Console
Guide Volume 3

Ultra Massive Sega Genesis Guide

Antique Cars and Motor Vehicles:
Illustrated Guide to Operation...

Chicago's White City Cookbook

The Clock Book: A Detailed Illustrated
Collection of Classic Clocks

The Complete Book of Birds: Illustrated
Enlarged Special Edition

1901 Buffalo World's Fair: The Pan-
American Exposition in Photographs

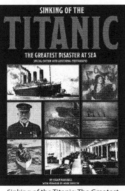

Sinking of the Titanic: The Greatest
Disaster at Sea

Gustave Doré's London: A Pilgrimage:
Retro Restored Special Edition

Milton's Paradise Lost: Gustave Doré
Retro Restored Edition

The Art of World War 1

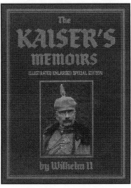

The Kaiser's Memoirs: Illustrated
Enlarged Special Edition

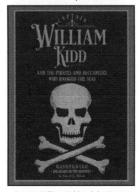

Captain William Kidd and the Pirates
and Buccaneers Who Ravaged the Seas

The Complete Butterfly Book: Enlarged
Illustrated Special Edition

Made in the USA
Monee, IL
30 June 2022

57c2821f-79fe-4130-8c31-cc39e298d0e4R01